Assessing Accomplished Teaching

Advanced-Level Certification Programs

Committee on Evaluation of Teacher Certification by the National Board for Professional Teaching Standards

Milton D. Hakel, Judith Anderson Koenig, and Stuart W. Elliott, *Editors*

Board on Testing and Assessment

Center for Education

Division of Behavioral and Social Sciences and Education

NATIONAL RESEARCH COUNCIL
OF THE NATIONAL ACADEMIES

THE NATIONAL ACADEMIES PRESS
Washington, D.C.
www.nap.edu

THE NATIONAL ACADEMIES PRESS   500 Fifth Street, N.W.   Washington, DC 20001

NOTICE: The project that is the subject of this report was approved by the Governing Board of the National Research Council, whose members are drawn from the councils of the National Academy of Sciences, the National Academy of Engineering, and the Institute of Medicine. The members of the committee responsible for the report were chosen for their special competences and with regard for appropriate balance.

This study was supported by Contract No. ED-04-CO-0139 between the National Academy of Sciences and the U.S. Department of Education. Any opinions, findings, conclusions, or recommendations expressed in this publication are those of the authors and do not necessarily reflect the views of the organizations or agencies that provided support for the project.

Library of Congress Cataloging-in-Publication Data

Assessing accomplished teaching : advanced-level certification programs : Committee on Evaluation of Teacher Certification by the National Board for Professional Teaching Standards / Milton D. Hakel, Judith Anderson Koenig, and Stuart W. Elliott, editors.
    p. cm.
    ISBN 978-0-309-12118-7 (pbk.) — ISBN 978-0-309-12119-4 (pdf) 1. Teachers—Certification—United States. I. Hakel, Milton D. II. Koenig, Judith A. III. Elliott, Stuart W. IV. National Board for Professional Teaching Standards (U.S.)
    LB1771.A77 2008
    371.120973—dc22
                                    2008026490

Additional copies of this report are available from the National Academies Press, 500 Fifth Street, N.W., Lockbox 285, Washington, DC 20055; (800) 624-6242 or (202) 334-3313 (in the Washington metropolitan area); Internet, http://www.nap.edu.

Suggested citation: National Research Council. (2008). *Assessing Accomplished Teaching: Advanced-Level Certification Programs*. Committee on Evaluation of Teacher Certification by the National Board for Professional Teaching Standards. Milton D. Hakel, Judith Anderson Koenig, and Stuart W. Elliott, editors. Board on Testing and Assessment, Center for Education, Division of Behavioral and Social Sciences and Education. Washington, DC: The National Academies Press.

THE NATIONAL ACADEMIES
Advisers to the Nation on Science, Engineering, and Medicine

The **National Academy of Sciences** is a private, nonprofit, self-perpetuating society of distinguished scholars engaged in scientific and engineering research, dedicated to the furtherance of science and technology and to their use for the general welfare. Upon the authority of the charter granted to it by the Congress in 1863, the Academy has a mandate that requires it to advise the federal government on scientific and technical matters. Dr. Ralph J. Cicerone is president of the National Academy of Sciences.

The **National Academy of Engineering** was established in 1964, under the charter of the National Academy of Sciences, as a parallel organization of outstanding engineers. It is autonomous in its administration and in the selection of its members, sharing with the National Academy of Sciences the responsibility for advising the federal government. The National Academy of Engineering also sponsors engineering programs aimed at meeting national needs, encourages education and research, and recognizes the superior achievements of engineers. Dr. Charles M. Vest is president of the National Academy of Engineering.

The **Institute of Medicine** was established in 1970 by the National Academy of Sciences to secure the services of eminent members of appropriate professions in the examination of policy matters pertaining to the health of the public. The Institute acts under the responsibility given to the National Academy of Sciences by its congressional charter to be an adviser to the federal government and, upon its own initiative, to identify issues of medical care, research, and education. Dr. Harvey V. Fineberg is president of the Institute of Medicine.

The **National Research Council** was organized by the National Academy of Sciences in 1916 to associate the broad community of science and technology with the Academy's purposes of furthering knowledge and advising the federal government. Functioning in accordance with general policies determined by the Academy, the Council has become the principal operating agency of both the National Academy of Sciences and the National Academy of Engineering in providing services to the government, the public, and the scientific and engineering communities. The Council is administered jointly by both Academies and the Institute of Medicine. Dr. Ralph J. Cicerone and Dr. Charles M. Vest are chair and vice chair, respectively, of the National Research Council.

www.national-academies.org

Acknowledgments

The Committee on Evaluation of Teacher Certification by the National Board for Professional Teaching Standards (NBPTS) was formed in response to legislation passed by the U.S. Congress asking the National Academies to develop a framework for evaluating programs that offer advanced-level certification to teachers and to apply that framework in an evaluation of the impacts of the NBPTS. The committee began its work in September 2005 and, over the course of the next 30 months, held six meetings, commissioned numerous papers and analyses, and collected a variety of information as part of its evaluation. The committee's work benefited tremendously from the contributions of many people, and the committee is grateful for their assistance and support.

The work was overseen by the U.S. Department of Education with management handled by Susan Sanchez. We thank Susan for her expert guidance and quick response to our many questions.

Over the course of the project, we made many requests of NBPTS staff, including numerous requests for information, documentation, research reports, and data files; visits to their office and meetings with their staff; and presentations at our committee meetings. We extend our heartfelt thanks to Mary Dilworth for her diligence and patience in responding to our extensive inquiries. Mary gave generously of her time, and we thank her for all the information she provided in response to the committee's questions. We also thank NBPTS president Joseph Aguerrebere and staff members Lillie Saunders and Joan Auchter for the valuable information they provided.

During the course of this evaluation, the Educational Testing Service (ETS) served as the test development contractor to NBPTS, and we wish to acknowledge the assistance of several ETS staff members. We are grateful to Mari Pearlman for recapturing for us the history of the development of the assessment program and to Drew Gitomer for providing his review of research on the NBPTS program. We especially thank Steve Schreiner for providing an overview of the assessment scoring process and for guiding us through a review of sample portfolio materials and videotapes submitted by teachers. This review contributed greatly to our understanding of the assessment and the requirements that teachers must meet to earn board certification.

Our evaluation drew on work conducted for us by several researchers. Our initial review of the research base revealed a large number of studies focused on the impact of board-certified teachers on their students' achievement. The findings from these studies presented a complex set of somewhat conflicting results. We thank Henry Braun and Paul Holland, both at ETS, for their insights about these studies, which helped us to sort out details of research methodologies and statistical analyses. We decided to conduct a full-scale review of these studies combined with work to identify and conduct additional analyses to help resolve the differing findings. The researchers who assisted us in this endeavor greatly contributed to our evaluation, and we are indebted to each of them, including Doug Harris at the University of Wisconsin–Madison, Helen Ladd at Duke University, Daniel McCaffrey at the RAND Corporation, Steven Rivkin at Amherst College, and Tim Sass at Florida State University. We are especially grateful to Tim Sass for the many additional analyses he conducted for us. We also thank Jon Fullerton and Tom Kane at Harvard University, Steve Raudenbush at the University of Chicago, and Bill Sanders at the SAS Institute, Inc., for their presentations at our third committee meeting and their insights about this body of work.

We also commissioned a psychometric review of the NBPTS assessments. This was an extensive task, given that NBPTS awards certification in 25 areas, each using different assessments. We are indebted to Teresa Russell at the Human Resources Research Organization (HumRRO), who led this work for us. Her thorough and painstaking efforts to review a multitude of documents and summarize the psychometric characteristics of the assessments were a tremendous resource to the committee.

In addition, we commissioned analyses of NBPTS participants and comparisons of their characteristics with those of nonparticipating teachers. David Perda, a doctoral student at the University of Pennsylvania, assisted us with these analyses. We sincerely appreciate his thorough and careful analyses and are particularly grateful for his responsiveness to our numerous follow-up requests for additional analyses.

To learn more about the history of the NBPTS program, we conducted interviews of a number of key people involved with its early development. We are very grateful for the time these individuals spent with us and the wealth of information they provided. We thank former NBPTS staff members Joan Baratz-Snowden at the American Federation of Teachers (former vice president of assessment and research); Chuck Cascio at ETS (former director of test development); Ann Harman at Harman and Associates (former director of research); Jim Kelly, retired, who served as the first president of NBPTS; and David Mandel at Carnegie-IAS Commission on Mathematics and Science Education (former vice president for policy development at NBPTS). We are also grateful for the information provided by Sally Mernissi (former vice president and corporate secretary), who died in January 2006. We also thank the following individuals who assisted the NBPTS staff with development of the program: Lloyd Bond at the Carnegie Foundation (former director of the NBPTS Technical Analysis Group); Emerson Elliott at the National Council for Accreditation of Teacher Education; Mary Futrell at George Washington University (former president of the National Education Association and member of the NBPTS board of directors); Lee Shulman at the Carnegie Foundation (former consultant to the NBPTS board of directors); Gary Sykes at Michigan State University (former consultant to the NBPTS board of directors); and Suzanne Wilson at Michigan State University (former consultant to the NBPTS board of directors). We also thank Joshua Boots at the American Board for Certification of Teacher Excellence (ABCTE) and Kathy Madigan, formerly at the ABCTE, for the information they provided about their assessment program.

We sought to gather information from teachers and teacher educators with regard to their experiences with and perceptions of the NBPTS program. Members of the Teacher Advisory Council of the National Research Council (NRC) spoke with us on numerous occasions. In addition four teachers and teacher educators attended our third meeting: Sara Eisenhardt with the Cincinnati school system, Maxine Freund and Mary Futrell at George Washington University, and Carol Matern with the Indianapolis public schools and Indiana University–Purdue University, Indianapolis. We thank these individuals for their insightful comments about the program.

During the course of this project, we spoke with and heard presentations from numerous individuals who conducted research on the NBPTS program. We are particularly grateful to the following researchers for their responsiveness to our questions and the time they took to help us better understand their findings: Linda Cavaluzzo at CNA Corporation, Carol Cohen at the Finance Project, Dan Goldhaber at the University of Washington, Michael Hansen at the University of Washington, Dan Humphrey at SRI International, Julia Koppich at J. Koppich Associates, David Lustick at Michigan State University, Jennifer King Rice at the University of Maryland, and Jannese Woodward Moore at East Tennessee State University.

Senior staff members of the NRC's Division of Behavioral and Social Sciences and Education helped the committee move this project forward. Michael Feuer, executive director, enthusiastically backed the project and lent his wisdom and advice at key stages. Patricia Morison, associate executive director and acting director of the Center for Education, provided sage advice throughout this project. Eugenia Grohman, associate executive director, lent her deep knowledge and experience with NRC procedures and the committee process. Christine McShane, senior editor, provided expert editing assistance. Kirsten Sampson Snyder, senior report review officer, ably guided the report through the NRC review process.

Special thanks are due to Teresia Wilmore, senior project assistant, for her masterful handling of the logistical aspects of this project. Teresia very capably managed all of the committee meetings and is now pursuing a graduate degree in nursing—we wish her great success. We also thank Viola Horek and Dorothy Majewski, who ably stepped in to assist at various stages of the project. We are grateful to Lisa Alston, who provided support throughout the project and to Monica Ulewicz for her assistance with the literature reviews during the early stage of this project.

On behalf of the committee and as its chair, I wish to recognize three members of the NRC staff who did everything needed to ensure the quality and timeliness of this project. First, we are grateful to senior program officer, Alix Beatty, for her expert research, writing, and critical thinking skills. Alix provided initial drafts for several portions of the report, a service that was invaluable because it immediately propelled the committee's deliberations. Second, Stuart Elliott, director of the Board on Testing and Assessment, provided calm and steady input at every stage of our deliberations. Stuart was particularly adept at helping us as individuals to understand ideas from others' disciplines and to establish shared interpretations of particular research findings.

Third, and deserving a solo bow, is Judith Koenig, our study director. Beginning with preparation of the committee proposal and then the vetting of nominees for membership on the committee through to the completion and publication of this report, Judy did it all. Although that is probably true for every NRC study director, what stands out about Judy are three attributes: she is very smart and learns quickly, she always listens and hears both what is said and what is not said, and she takes the initiative collaboratively. While the committee could have conducted the evaluation and issued its report without her, our tasks would not have been completed as rapidly nor as well. Thank you, Judy, for your graceful leadership at the center of our efforts.

Finally, I wish to thank the committee members for their dedication and outstanding contributions to this study. They drafted text, prepared background materials, reviewed numerous versions of this report, and gave generously of their time. In its first meeting, the committee adopted a pattern of collaborative inquiry and meticulous analysis that endured through the final signoff. Despite marked differences in our fields of expertise and differing viewpoints about what constitutes noteworthy evidence, the entire committee remained focused and engaged throughout. I am deeply grateful to each member.

This report has been reviewed in draft form by individuals chosen for their diverse perspectives and technical expertise, in accordance with procedures approved by the NRC's Report Review Committee. The purpose of this independent review is to provide candid and critical comments that will assist the institution in making its published report as sound as possible and to ensure that the report meets institutional standards for objectivity, evidence, and responsiveness to the study charge. The review comments and draft manuscript remain confidential to protect the integrity of the deliberative process.

We wish to thank the following individuals for their review of this report: Lisa Barrow, Economic Research, Federal Reserve Bank of Chicago; Stephen B. Dunbar, College of Education, University of Iowa; David N. Figlio, Department of Economics, University of Florida; Robert E. Floden, Institute for Research on Teaching and Learning, College of Education, Michigan State University; Robert M. Hauser, Center for Demography of Health and Aging, University of Wisconsin–Madison; David H. Monk, Dean's Office, College of Education, Penn State University; Gary J. Natriello, Teachers College, Columbia University; John J. Norcini, Office of the President, Foundation for Advancement of International Medical Education and Research, Philadelphia; Ruth J. Palmer, Educational Psychology, School of Education, College of New Jersey; and Mark R. Wilson, Graduate School of Education, University of California, Berkeley.

Although the reviewers listed above have provided many constructive comments and suggestions, they were not asked to endorse the conclusions or recommendations nor did they see the final draft of the report before its release. The review of this report was overseen by Lauress Wise, HumRRO, Monterey, California, and Charles E. Phelps, university professor and provost emeritus, University of Rochester. Appointed by the NRC, they were responsible for making certain that an independent examination of this report was carried out in accordance with institutional procedures and that all review comments were carefully considered. Responsibility for the final content of this report, however, rests entirely with the authoring committee and the institution.

Milton D. Hakel, *Chair*
Committee on Evaluation of Teacher
Certification by the National Board for
Professional Teaching Standards

Contents

Summary

The National Board for Professional Teaching Standards (NBPTS) was created in 1987 in response to recommendations made by the Carnegie Task Force on Teaching as a Profession. These recommendations, reported in *A Nation Prepared: Teachers for the 21st Century*, called for large-scale reforms to improve the quality of the U.S. teaching force, including the formation of a national board whose task was to establish standards for exemplary teaching practice and to develop a means to award advanced-level certification to teachers who meet these standards.

The NBPTS has been offering advanced-level certification for teachers since 1994. The mission of the national board is to establish "high and rigorous standards for what teachers should know and be able to do, to certify teachers who meet those standards, and to advance other education reforms for the purpose of improving student learning in American schools."

The Committee on Evaluation of Teacher Certification by the National Board for Professional Teaching Standards was established at the National Research Council (NRC), at the request of the U.S. Congress and with support from the U.S. Department of Education, to evaluate the impacts of the national board's efforts.

The U.S. Congress asked the NRC to develop a framework for evaluating programs that award advanced-level teacher certification and to apply that framework in an evaluation of the impacts of the NBPTS. Congress specified that the framework should be general enough to be applied to other programs[1] when data are available to permit such an evaluation and should address the following issues:

1. The impacts on teachers who obtain board certification, teachers who attempt to become board certified but are unsuccessful, and teachers who do not apply for board certification;
2. The extent to which board certification makes a difference in the academic achievement of students; and
3. The cost-effectiveness of advanced-level certification as a means for improving teacher quality.

This report presents the committee's framework for evaluating programs that award advanced-level teacher certification and applies it to an evaluation of the impacts of the national board. Our principal findings are summarized below, and our conclusions and recommendations appear in their entirety in Chapter 12. We note that these recommendations are directed at the NBPTS, as our charge specifies, but they also highlight issues that should apply to any program that offers advanced-level certification to teachers.

THE EVALUATION FRAMEWORK

The evaluation framework developed by the committee is structured around eight sets of questions based on hypotheses about the way a program for certifying accomplished teachers might improve teaching:

1. *Specification of the Content Standards and Development of the Assessments:* To what extent does the certification program for accomplished teachers clearly and accurately specify advanced teaching practices and the characteristics of teachers (the knowledge, skills, dispositions, and judgments) that enable them to carry out advanced practice? Does it do so in a manner that supports the development of a test that is well aligned with the content standards?
2. *Technical Characteristics of the Assessments:* To what extent do the assessments associated with the certification program for accomplished teachers reliably measure the specified knowledge, skills, dispositions, and judgments of candidates and support valid interpretations of the results? To what extent are the performance stan-

---

[1]The American Board for Certification of Teacher Excellence (ABCTE) currently has a program under development for awarding advanced-level certification to distinguished teachers[SM].

dards for the assessments and the process for setting them justified and reasonable?

3. *Participation:* To what extent do teachers participate in the program?

4. *Impact on Outcomes for Students:* To what extent does the advanced-level certification program identify teachers who are effective at producing positive student outcomes, such as learning, motivation, school engagement, breadth of achievement, educational attainment, attendance, and grade promotion?

5. *Impact on Participating Teachers' Professional Growth:* To what extent do teachers improve their practices and the outcomes of their students by virtue of going through the advanced-level certification process?

6. *Impact on Teachers' Career Paths:* To what extent and in what ways are the career paths of both successful and unsuccessful candidates affected by their participation in the program?

7. *Impact on the Education System:* Beyond its effects on candidates, to what extent and in what ways does the certification program have an impact on the field of teaching and the education system?

8. *Cost-effectiveness:* To what extent does the advanced-level certification program accomplish its objectives in a cost-effective manner, relative to other approaches intended to improve teacher quality?

The NBPTS has been the topic of much discourse in the measurement, teacher education, and education policy literature; nearly 200 articles discuss the board's work. However, the majority of these documents do not report on empirical research, and only a handful yield valid findings related to the questions in our charge. Thus, we relied on an evidence base that was neither broad nor deep, which we supplemented with additional investigations.

DEVELOPMENT OF THE STANDARDS AND ASSESSMENTS

Over a seven-year period, the board worked to identify the essential characteristics of accomplished teaching and to develop a method for identifying teachers who demonstrated these practices. Their product is a set of standards for 25 teaching specialty areas. The standards in each area describe the ways accomplished teachers demonstrate that they know their students, their subject matter, and how to teach it; think systematically about their practice; and learn from their experience. Assessments for each specialty were designed to allow teachers to demonstrate their proficiency in classroom settings. To earn NBPTS certification, teachers must respond to six computer-based constructed-response exercises that measure subject matter knowledge and must assemble a portfolio consisting of videotapes of their teaching, written reflections on their goals and the outcomes of the lesson submitted, and student work.

We reviewed the processes used by the NBPTS to develop content standards for each specialty area as well as exercises to assess them. The board convened a diverse group of experts to develop standards for high-quality teaching, and it solicited considerable feedback before adopting the standards. Its development of standards and assessments for a wide array of teaching specialty areas is a significant accomplishment. Overall, we conclude that the board's approach was reasonable and, for the most part, conforms to professional standards for certification tests (Conclusions 5-1 and 5-2).[2]

We highlight two concerns, however. First, we initially encountered difficulty in obtaining documentation that was sufficiently detailed, although we note that the board eventually provided the information we needed to conduct our review. The board did not have a technical manual readily available, and the version it eventually provided was incomplete and still in draft form. Professional standards call for a testing program to maintain documentation about the technical characteristics of its assessments, and we recommend that the board make improvement in this area (Recommendation 5-1). Ongoing evaluation of an assessment program is critical to maintaining its quality and credibility, and providing thorough documentation that is easily accessible to outside evaluators is a critical element of this process.

Our second concern relates to the translation of the standards statements into assessment exercises. While the content standards are written in a readable style, the language is imprecise. Translating the general statements of the standard to specific assessment exercises requires a significant amount of judgment on the part of the test developer. We recommend that the board develop more precise explanations of the standards to facilitate the work of the test developer and to ensure that the assessment exercises measure the intended skills (Recommendation 5-2).

TECHNICAL CHARACTERISTICS OF THE ASSESSMENTS

We evaluated the procedures for scoring the assessment exercises and setting the passing score, the reliability and validity of the scores, and the extent to which the assessments fairly appraise the skills of all teachers applying. Overall, we judge that the board has taken appropriate steps to ensure that the assessments meet professional standards and results from

---

[2]Recommendation and conclusion numbers refer to the report chapter in which they are made and the sequence in which they appear in the chapter.

validity studies document that the assessments are effective in identifying teachers who demonstrate accomplished teaching practices. Improvement may be possible in two areas, however.

First, the portfolios that the NBPTS uses have the advantage of providing an authentic representation of a teacher's skills. At the same time, the scoring process for portfolio responses is less reliable than that for more objective forms of assessment. The reliability of the scores from the NBPTS assessments is consistent with expectations for a largely portfolio-based process but lower than that desired for a high-stakes testing program. We recommend that the NBPTS explore ways to improve the reliability of the scores, possibly by increasing the number of exercises, but we caution that efforts to improve reliability should not compromise the authenticity of the assessment or substantially increase the costs associated with scoring the exercises (Recommendation 5-3).

Second, a key responsibility of a high-quality testing program is regular evaluation. Our review reveals that the board has not devoted the same energy that went into the original assessment design to ongoing evaluation of how that design has worked over time, nor has it found ways to improve on it. Regardless of the assessment methods used, we think that the board should devote more effort to continuously improving its assessments. With tests that rely on multiple-choice items, developers are able to use statistical data to evaluate and refine the items before they are used operationally. Although this is not usually feasible with tests that consist of performance assessment exercises, data can be collected after their initial operational use and analyzed to identify exercises that exhibit relatively low reliability or disparate impact. It is not clear how closely the board tracks such data and uses them to improve assessment exercises. We recommend that the NBPTS collect and use the available operational data about the individual assessment exercises to improve the validity and reliability of the assessments for each certificate, as well as to minimize adverse impact (Recommendation 5-4).

TEACHER PARTICIPATION

Carnegie task force members envisioned that national board certification would become a widely recognized credential, that districts and states would value board-certified teachers, and that the numbers of board-certified teachers would grow. They expected that board-certified teachers would become a significant presence, helping to spread the influence of teaching standards by serving as leaders and mentors. From 1993, when the program began operation, through 2007, roughly 99,300 teachers applied for board certification, and 63,800 teachers earned the credential. While these numbers represent less than 3 percent of the country's current force of 3.7 million teachers, it is noteworthy that participation has increased over the life of the program, from about 540 applicants in the first year to about 12,200 in the 2006-2007 school year. Overall, the number of board-certified teachers translates to about three for every five schools.

Participation rates are not even across the country, however. There are higher concentrations in some states and districts, and in a few districts participation rates are approaching levels likely to be sufficient for the program to have the intended effects. Not surprisingly, the popularity of board certification appears to be related to the degree to which states and districts encourage it. Some states offer financial incentives to teachers—covering the $2,500 test fee and offering sizable salary increases to those who are successful—and have higher participation rates than states that offer minimal or no incentives.

With regard to participation, we highlight several issues as concerns. First, existing data about teachers who have gone through the board certification process are scant. Little is known about what teachers have done after completing the certification process, what has happened to teachers who did not pass the assessment, how many board-certified teachers are currently employed, where board-certified teachers currently work, and what jobs they do. We recommend that the NBPTS implement and maintain a database of information about NBPTS applicants and their career paths (Recommendation 6-1).

In addition, there are significant disparities in applicant participation rates, with teachers from advantaged schools more likely to participate than others. Furthermore, the absolute numbers of racial/ethnic minority teacher participants are low. We think these are issues deserving of additional attention, especially considering that one of the board's goals is to place board-certified teachers in schools with high-needs students. The board has efforts under way to recruit minority teachers to pursue board certification, and we encourage it to continue its work in this area.

EFFECTS OF BOARD-CERTIFIED TEACHERS ON STUDENT OUTCOMES

The question of how the program is related to student outcomes can be considered in two ways. First, passing the certification process may act as a signal of preexisting teaching effectiveness. Second, the process of becoming board certified may *cause* a teacher's classroom effectiveness to improve. Questions related to student outcomes have generated the largest number of research studies, with most focusing on the question of whether board certification acted as signal of (preexisting) teaching effectiveness. Nearly all of these studies compare the achievement test scores of students taught by board-certified and nonboard-certified teachers; few compare other student outcomes, such as motivation, breadth of achievement, or promotion rates. We reviewed 11 studies that measured student outcomes in terms of their achievement test performance. They focus primarily on North Carolina and Florida, states that have substantial numbers of board-certified teachers and have maintained longitudinal databases of teachers and students.

Findings from these studies show that, in both states, students taught by board-certified teachers had higher achievement test gains than did those taught by nonboard-certified teachers, although the differences were small and varied by state. North Carolina, a state with a long history of encouraging teachers to pursue board certification, showed slightly larger differences between the students of board-certified and nonboard-certified teachers, while group differences in Florida were smaller. We see a relationship between board certification and student achievement, although the relationship is not strong and is not consistent across contexts.

We recommend that additional research be conducted in this area, but we do not think that all research resources should be devoted to studies focusing on student performance on achievement tests, in part because such tests measure limited aspects of student learning. To the extent that existing data sets allow, we recommend replication of studies that investigate the effects of board-certified teachers on student achievement in states besides North Carolina and Florida, in content areas beyond mathematics and reading, and in grades beyond the elementary levels (Recommendation 7-1). Researchers pursuing such studies should work with the national board to obtain the information needed to study the effects of teachers who successfully obtained board certification, in comparison with effects for those applicants who were unsuccessful. We also recommend that researchers conduct studies of the effects of board certification on outcomes beyond scores on standardized tests, such as student motivation, breadth of achievement, attendance, and promotion (Recommendation 7-2). The choice of outcome measures should reflect the skills that board-certified teachers are expected to demonstrate.

IMPACTS ON TEACHERS' PROFESSIONAL GROWTH

One potential benefit of the NBPTS program is that the process of becoming familiar with the board's standards and completing the assessment could have a positive effect on a teacher's classroom practice. Considering the time required by the assessment and the depth and complexity of the tasks involved, it seems reasonable to expect some impact on the practices of those who complete the process.

Two studies directly investigated what teachers learn during the certification process. While the results suggest that the process contributes to their professional growth, the studies were small in scale and need replication. Several other studies compared the effectiveness of teachers in North Carolina and Florida in terms of their students' reading and mathematics achievement before, during, and after their teachers earned board certification. The findings from these studies are mixed.

Thus, in our judgment, the existing research neither proves nor refutes hypotheses about the effects of the certification process on teachers' practice. We think that additional research should explore this issue, and we make recommendations for three kinds of research to pursue.

First, we recommend that the NBPTS and other researchers investigate the effects of the process on the candidates using pretest/posttest and longitudinal designs; these studies should be designed to permit comparisons of responses for successful and unsuccessful candidates (Recommendation 8-1). We also recommend research on the effects of board certification on teachers' practices; these studies should utilize both quantitative and qualitative methods to examine a variety of measures of teachers' practices and a variety of student outcomes (Recommendation 8-2). Finally, we recommend that researchers work with the NBPTS to obtain the information needed to study the relationships between board certification and student achievement across the various stages of board certification; these studies should examine the impacts of the certification process on teachers' effectiveness in increasing their students' test scores, and specifically should examine effects for the years subsequent to the receipt of board certification (Recommendation 8-3).

IMPACTS ON TEACHERS' CAREER PATHS

The goals of the NBPTS include helping to professionalize the field, motivating districts and states to raise salaries for accomplished teachers, motivating districts and states to expand opportunities for leadership in the field, and increasing accomplished teachers' satisfaction with their careers. Little information is available to evaluate progress toward these goals.

One study examined teachers' longevity in the field. The results suggest that board-certified teachers are more likely than other teachers to indicate that they plan to remain in teaching, but the findings were based on teachers' responses to only a few survey questions. This finding was corroborated by results from our own analyses, which indicate that board-certified teachers actually do stay in teaching at higher rates than other teachers. However, our findings were based on a small national sample of teachers and need further corroboration. Neither the existing study nor our analyses permit causal inferences; that is, they do not indicate whether the NBPTS process causes teachers to stay in the field longer or whether the teachers who choose to become board certified are already more likely to remain in the field, regardless of whether they earn certification.

Another study addressed the question of whether acquiring board certification affects the mobility of teachers in the field. Data from North Carolina show that those who obtain board certification tend to change teaching jobs at higher rates than do unsuccessful applicants. These data also indicate that when they move, board-certified teachers are likely to move to teaching assignments with more advantaged conditions, such as schools with higher student achievement levels or fewer students in poverty. However, it is not clear that this tendency is any more prevalent for board-certified teachers than for other teachers with excellent qualifications.

Additional research is needed on the career paths of board-certified teachers before any firm conclusions can be drawn. We recommend that the NBPTS and other researchers study the subsequent career choices of teachers who have applied for board certification. These studies should use methodologies that permit comparisons of teachers' career choices before and after becoming board certified, and they should compare the choices of unsuccessful applicants for board certification, teachers who successfully obtained the credential, and teachers who did not apply for it (Recommendations 9-1 and 9-3).

IMPACTS ON THE EDUCATION SYSTEM

The Carnegie task force envisioned that the board's influence would reach beyond any impact that individual board-certified teachers might have on their students. The task force hoped that the board's standards would be widely influential and the demand for board-certified teachers would lead to improvements in working conditions for all teachers. Board-certified teachers would influence the way their colleagues taught, schools and districts would use the board standards as a guide and work to provide teaching environments conducive to the board's approach, and teacher preparation and professional development would spread the influence of the board's standards to future generations of teachers.

Little research is available on these kinds of spillover effects. Two studies examined the impact of board certification on teachers' roles in their schools, focusing on the six states with the largest populations of board-certified teachers. The results suggest that school systems are not making the best uses of their board-certified teachers and that board-certified teachers often work in unsupportive environments. The studies reveal instances of administrators who discourage board-certified teachers from assuming responsibilities outside the classroom and who worry about showing favoritism toward board-certified teachers. In some cases, administrators downplay the significance of the credential, and some board-certified teachers conceal their credential so as not to seem to be showing off.

Despite these negative findings, the studies described a few school systems in which board-certified teachers are rewarded, used effectively, and offered new opportunities. In these instances, board-certified teachers are used as mentors, team leaders, and organizers of professional development activities; board certification is viewed as part of a broader commitment to improving professional development and meeting higher standards for teachers.

With regard to influences on teacher preparation, the National Council for Accreditation of Teacher Education has aligned its accreditation standards for teacher education programs with the NBPTS standards. The curriculum standards for programs that prepare beginning teachers offered by the Interstate New Teacher Assessment and Support Consortium are also aligned. These efforts lay the groundwork for the NBPTS standards to impact teacher preparation, but there is no research to document the extent of the board's influence on the content of teacher preparation programs or the standards of individual programs.

From the small research base, we found little evidence that the national board is having the intended spillover effects, but we highlight the fact that much of the needed research has not been conducted. We think that board-certified teachers are unlikely to have a significant impact without broader endorsements by states, districts, and schools of the NBPTS goals for improving professional development, setting high standards for teachers, and actively utilizing the board-certified teachers in leadership roles. Furthermore, we think that the certification program is unlikely to have broad systemic effects on the field of teaching unless greater numbers of teachers become board certified and the Carnegie task force's other recommendations—for creating a more effective environment for teaching and learning in schools, increasing the supply of high-quality entrants into the field, and improving career opportunities for teachers—are implemented. However, our review of the evidence led us to conclude that there is not yet sufficient research to evaluate the extent to which the NBPTS is having systemic impacts on the teaching field and the education system (Conclusion 10-1).

THE COST-EFFECTIVENESS OF CERTIFICATION AS A MEANS OF IMPROVING TEACHER QUALITY

Our review revealed that the research base needed to support a cost-effectiveness evaluation of the NBPTS is inadequate. Making a rough calculation of the costs of the program is relatively straightforward, but evaluating how these costs compare with those of other approaches for teacher professional development presented significant problems because of a lack of data.

Advanced-level certification of teachers has the potential to offer three kinds of benefits: (1) it can provide a systematic way of identifying high-quality teachers, that is, a signal of quality; (2) the process itself can provide a means for teachers to improve their practices; and (3) it can improve the quality of teachers throughout the education system, keeping accomplished teachers in the field and attracting stronger teacher candidates in the future. The available evidence suggests that NBPTS certification does provide a means of identifying highly skilled teachers; however, this evidence does not provide sufficient information about the other two benefits.

Simply identifying high-quality teachers provides no direct benefit unless this signal of quality is used. One of the most important benefits that might result from the program—keeping high-quality teachers in the field—could not be evaluated because the necessary data have not been collected. While there is some evidence that policy makers have used the signal provided by board certification to improve teaching quality (i.e., by offering salary bonuses to teachers who earn board certification as an incentive to remain in teaching), the policies were not implemented in a way that allows an examination of their impacts. Furthermore, except in isolated instances, there is no evidence that districts or schools are using the signal of quality provided by board certification to encourage board-certified teachers to work in difficult schools or to mentor other teachers.

We identified three interventions designed to improve the practices of experienced teachers that could serve as comparisons in an evaluation of the cost-effectiveness of the NBPTS: (1) the ABCTE's proposed program to certify distinguished teachers^{SM}, (2) encouraging teachers to pursue master's degrees, and (3) providing relevant in-service professional development. Very little information useful for a full cost-effectiveness analysis is available about these interventions. Our cost analysis suggested that the annual per-teacher costs associated with board certification are probably lower than the annual per-teacher costs of obtaining a master's degree. However, the evidence about the benefits of master's degrees is too mixed to be able to derive a cost-effectiveness estimate that could be compared with that for board certification. For the other two possible comparisons, even less is known.

Thus, we conclude that, at this time, it is not possible to conduct a thorough cost-effectiveness evaluation of the NBPTS certification because of the paucity of data on its benefits and on both the costs and benefits of other mechanisms intended to improve teacher quality (Conclusion 11-2). Such an evaluation should be undertaken if and when the necessary evidence becomes available.

OVERALL ASSESSMENT

The board set out to transform the teaching field, and it has been innovative in its approach. The standards captured a complex conception of advanced teaching and stimulated thinking about what accomplished teachers should know and be able to do. The portfolio-based assessment that it developed to measure teachers' practice according to these standards pushed the measurement field forward.

The NBPTS has the potential to make a valuable contribution to efforts to improve teacher quality, together with other reforms intended to create a more effective environment for teaching and learning in schools, increase the supply of high-quality entrants into the field, and improve career opportunities and working conditions for teachers. Our review suggests, however, that much of the research needed to evaluate these intended impacts has not been conducted. Moreover, we point out that revolutionary changes of the kind the board's founders envisioned would be expected to develop over decades, not years. This evaluation thus provides an opportunity to take stock of what has worked well and to suggest changes needed to respond to the current policy environment.

For the national board to realize its potential, several key changes in its operation and approach are needed. We think that, if the board is to build on its accomplishments and thrive as a means of improving teacher quality in the United States, it will need to attend to the following:

- The NBPTS should conduct its work according to the highest standards for credentialing programs, make its operations accessible to external scrutiny, and conduct regular evaluations of its assessments to ensure continuous improvement.
- The NBPTS should pursue an ongoing research agenda to evaluate progress toward its goals.
- The NBPTS should periodically review its assessment model, both to evaluate how it has worked in practice and to adapt to changes in the policy environment and advances in research. As part of such ongoing evaluation efforts, the board should consider whether adjustments are needed in the types of information used as the basis for certification, which might include classroom observations, objective tests of content knowledge, or measures of student performance.
- The NBPTS should continue to invest in its larger mission of influencing the teaching field in broad, comprehensive ways.

The NBPTS offered a thoughtful approach to serious problems with the way this country's education system selects and prepares its teachers and the conditions in which teachers work. Given the magnitude of the problems the board addressed, the fact that there is only limited evidence of its impact does not prove that this approach cannot be successful. For the program to have the intended impacts on the teaching field, improvements will be needed, both in the operational aspects of the program and in the evidence collected, as we have recommended in this report. The board cannot achieve these goals alone, however. Meeting these ambitious goals will also require a serious commitment by education policy makers to the other recommendations made by the Carnegie Task Force on Teaching as a Profession.

1

Introduction

Since the publication of *A Nation at Risk* in 1986, policy makers have implemented a number of reforms aimed at improving the education of students in this country. These reforms have taken a variety of forms, but all are intended to improve the quality of the instruction provided to students and thus improve their learning. One prominent effort has been to develop and disseminate standards that define accomplished teaching and formally recognize teachers who meet these standards by awarding them advanced-level certification, beyond the basics needed for initial licensure. The guiding idea behind this reform is that articulating the components of high-quality practice, making these descriptions widely available, and acknowledging teachers who demonstrate these practices will improve teaching throughout the education system, which should in turn improve student learning.

Currently two organizations in the United States are pursuing such reforms: the National Board for Professional Teaching Standards (NBPTS) and the American Board for Certification of Teacher Excellence (ABCTE). The NBPTS has been offering advanced-level certification for teachers since 1994. The ABCTE's program to certify distinguished teachers^{SM} is relatively new and still under development. As described in more detail later in this chapter, the two organizations present alternative approaches to the assessment of accomplished teaching.

The national board has received over $100 million from the federal government through the U.S. Department of Education and the National Science Foundation, in addition to an equivalent amount from private foundations and corporate sponsors (Hannaway and Bischoff, 2005). Much of this funding supported research and development during the board's early years as it undertook development of the standards for accomplished teaching and the assessments, and the board is now largely self-sufficient financially.

In an attempt to learn more about the effectiveness of offering advanced-level certification for teachers as an educational intervention and to evaluate whether this money has been well spent, the U.S. Congress asked the U.S. Department of Education to contract with the National Academies both to develop a framework for evaluating programs for certifying advanced-level teachers and to apply that framework in conducting an evaluation of the impact of the NBPTS certification program. Specifically, Congress asked the National Academies (Consolidated Appropriations Act, P.L. 108-99; see http://www7.nationalacademies.org/ocga/Laws/PL108_199.asp):

> [To] conduct an evaluation of the outcomes of teachers who achieved NBPTS certification versus teachers who did not complete certification and teachers who did not participate in or apply for the program. [The National Academies] is requested to perform an independent, scientific study using the strongest practical methodology to evaluate the impact of board certification, including an assessment of whether the NBPTS certification model is a cost effective method of improving teacher quality and the extent to which certification makes a difference in student academic achievement. In carrying out this study, the NAS should commission the collection of new data and conduct appropriate, rigorous analyses of such data. The conferees also expect that a similar scientific evaluation will be conducted on the outcomes of the work of the National Council on Teacher Quality (NCTQ) when available data will permit such an assessment and therefore urge NCTQ[1] to begin to incorporate evaluation elements into the program now.

The National Academies established the Committee on the Evaluation of the Impact of Teacher Certification by the National Board for Professional Teaching Standards to carry out this study. The committee is composed of 17 individuals with expertise in assessment (educational and credential testing), economics and evaluation of education policy, education administration, program evaluation, teacher education, teaching, sociology, and sociological methodology. The committee worked on this study over the course of three years.

---

[1]This program is the one under development by the ABCTE to recognize distinguished teachers[SM].

NATIONAL BOARD FOR PROFESSIONAL TEACHING STANDARDS

The NBPTS was created in 1987 in response to recommendations of the Carnegie Task Force on Teaching as a Profession. Its recommendations, reported in *A Nation Prepared* (Carnegie Task Force on Teaching as a Profession, 1986), called for large-scale reform efforts intended to improve the quality of the U.S. teaching force, including a national board whose task was to establish the standards that represent accomplished teaching practice and to develop a means to certify teachers who meet these standards. The NBPTS was expected to establish "high and rigorous standards for what teachers should know and be able to do, to certify teachers who meet those standards, and to advance other education reforms for the purpose of improving student learning in American schools" (National Board for Professional Teaching Standards, 1991).

The board devoted seven years to defining these standards and developing the assessment to measure them and in doing so brought together individuals representing a wide and varied set of perspectives, charged with coming to consensus on the practices that represent accomplished teaching and the methods for identifying teachers who demonstrate these practices. Their product is a set of standards for 25 teaching specialty areas. The assessments for each specialty area were designed to allow teachers to demonstrate their proficiency in real-life situations.

To earn advanced-level certification, teachers must respond to a set of six computer-based constructed-response tasks that measure subject matter knowledge and also assemble a portfolio consisting of videotapes of their teaching, written reflections on their goals and the outcomes of the lesson submitted, and student work associated with the lesson. The computerized portion is administered during the course of a day at a testing center. Preparation of the portfolio typically occurs over the course of a school year. To be eligible for advanced-level certification, the teacher must have completed a bachelor's degree, have completed at least three full years of teaching or counseling before beginning the application process, and have had a valid teaching or counseling license throughout that period.[2]

The board's assessment program became operational in 1994. Since that time, approximately 63,800 teachers have earned board certification. More than two-thirds of the states encourage board certification with monetary rewards or other incentives, although the incentives vary significantly across states, and there are board-certified teachers practicing in every state.

---

[2]A candidate who does not have a license may be eligible if he or she has been teaching in a school in which licensure is not required that is "recognized and approved to operate by the state" (http://www.nbpts.org).

AMERICAN BOARD FOR CERTIFICATION
OF TEACHER EXCELLENCE

The ABCTE plans to implement a somewhat different approach to measuring effective teaching (American Board for Certification of Teacher Excellence, 2007). It currently plans to base certification decisions on four components: (1) three one-hour structured classroom observations conducted by trained observers; (2) a structured evaluation of the teacher's professionalism and leadership qualities conducted by his or her supervisor; a computer-based assessment of subject-matter expertise; and (3) evidence from statistical value-added analyses quantifying the impact the teacher has made on students' score gains on standardized achievement tests. The ABCTE plan is still under development, and the organization is conducting research on the reliability, validity, and feasibility of each component. Additional information is available at http://www.abcte.org.

THE COMMITTEE'S APPROACH

The Carnegie task force envisioned that a program that certifies accomplished teachers might affect overall teacher quality in a variety of ways. For example, by identifying the most effective teachers, the program could enable schools and districts to recognize and reward them and thus more easily retain excellent teachers. Participation in the program might improve teachers' practice, and their practice might in turn influence that of their colleagues. The existence of the program might also influence teacher preparation programs more broadly, which could affect the practice of teachers who never even seek certification. Furthermore, by professionalizing teaching as a career, the board might influence the next generation of teachers and attract more effective applicants into education careers.

These potential impacts of a certification program for accomplished teachers differ in kind, and many are difficult to assess in a rigorous way. The committee was charged not only with evaluating the NBPTS, but also with developing a framework that could be used both for that purpose and for the evaluation of other advanced-level teacher certification programs. Thus, we began our work by considering in detail the ways a certification program for advanced-level teachers might improve the schooling of children and the field of teaching in general. To provide a framework for our evaluation, we developed a list of key questions to ask about a program designed to accomplish these goals. With this evaluation framework in place, we identified specific research questions associated with each of our primary evaluation questions and considered the nature of the evidence that would be needed to answer each of them. The committee then reviewed the available research literature and data, analyzed its application to the evaluation framework questions, sought out additional data and analyses, and used this body of information to evaluate the NBPTS.

GUIDE TO THE REPORT

This report describes the committee's evaluation framework and presents our evaluation of the national board's program. Chapter 2 describes both the evaluation framework and its rationale and the kinds of published research, other data, and other sources of information we examined. An overview of the context in which the national board was developed and the program's history is presented in Chapter 3, and Chapter 4 describes the board, its operations, and the structure and content of the current certification process.

The committee's evaluation of the NBPTS is presented in Chapters 5 through 11. In Chapter 5 the psychometric characteristics of the assessment and the available evidence of its psychometric quality are described. Chapter 6 discusses the available data regarding participation in the national board certification process across the states and some of the factors that may influence participation. Evidence regarding outcomes for students taught by national board–certified teachers is discussed in Chapter 7, together with the committee's thinking about the issues surrounding this line of research. The question of the impact that national board certification has on teachers is addressed in Chapter 8, in which we consider the extent to which participation in the assessment changes teachers' practices and has an impact on their effectiveness. Chapter 9 deals with research regarding the career paths of board-certified teachers. Chapter 10 discusses evidence of possible spillover effects the board certification program may have, such as indirect effects on teacher preparation, professional development, and the status of the teaching profession. Chapter 11 addresses the cost-effectiveness of the national board program as a means of improving teacher quality. Our recommendations are included in these chapters and also summarized in Chapter 12, together with the committee's overall conclusions about the national board program and its impacts.

2

The Evaluation Framework
and Collection of Data

The committee's charge from Congress was to develop a rigorous conceptual and methodological framework for evaluating programs that award advanced-level certification to teachers and to apply that framework to the National Board for Professional Teaching Standards (NBPTS). In particular, Congress asked the committee to use the strongest practical methodologies to consider (1) the impacts on teachers who obtain board certification, teachers who attempt to become certified but are unsuccessful, and teachers who do not apply for such certification; (2) the extent to which board certification makes a difference in the academic achievement of students; and (3) the cost-effectiveness of NBPTS certification as a means for improving teacher quality.

In developing the framework and conducting this evaluation, we relied extensively on the professional standards that guide program and psychometric evaluations. This chapter begins with a discussion of those standards and procedures, particularly as they apply to evaluations of certification assessments. We then turn to the evaluation framework and describe its components and our rationale for including them. The final section focuses on the evidence, discussing the evidence available from existing studies and the information we collected ourselves.

CONDUCTING PROGRAM EVALUATIONS

The committee's charge was to conduct an evaluation of the NBPTS program. Program evaluation is a formalized approach to studying the goals, processes, and impacts of projects, policies, and programs. Such "systematic investigations of the worth or merits" of a program (Joint Committee on Standards for Educational Evaluation, 1994) often pose questions like these (Rossi, Lipsey, and Freeman, 2004): What is the nature and scope of the problem? Is the particular intervention reaching its target population? Is the intervention being implemented well? Is the intervention effective in attaining the desired goals or benefits? Does the program have important unanticipated consequences? Are the program costs reasonable in relation to its effectiveness and benefits? The evaluation plan is typically organized around the questions posed by those who commissioned the evaluation, but it also should be responsive to the needs of other stakeholders (Standard U3). Program evaluations are expected to address the issues that matter, collect information that is relevant and meaningful for the goals of the evaluation, analyze the information using rigorous and fair methods, and communicate the results in a form that is usable and meaningful to decision makers.

There are two major types of evaluations: (1) those designed to distinguish worthwhile programs from ineffective ones, and (2) those designed to help improve existing ones in order to achieve certain desirable results. The former are often called formative evaluations, and they are conducted to provide information on how a program should be delivered or to furnish information for guiding program improvement (Scriven, 1991). The latter are called summative evaluations, and they are conducted to determine whether a program's expectations are being met and what its consequences are (Scriven, 1991). This is the kind of evaluation that our charge required.

Summative evaluations generally focus on whether a given program (e.g., a social program, an educational intervention) is effective. For example, summative evaluations might study such issues as the program's accomplishment of its intended objectives, impacts beyond those that were intended, how effectively resources have been used, the benefits of the program and what it costs to produce these benefits, and alternative interventions that might produce similar benefits. Summative program evaluations usually focus on the effects of a program on outcomes for a client population and consider the extent to which the program changes the outcomes for participants.

For example, the United States has a long history of commissioning evaluations of government-sponsored employment training programs designed to help unemployed workers or workers with relatively few skills find employment. Such evaluations attempt to infer the causal impact of enrolling in the program on the outcomes of interest for the participant, such as the probability of obtaining a job or the level of wages earned.

A particular challenge with this kind of an evaluation lies in trying to determine whether a change in outcomes for participants is in fact attributable to the program itself. Events or processes outside the program may be the real cause of the observed changes (in the case of employment training programs, outcomes may be due to changes in the broader economy). Another challenge with this type of evaluation is that the program has an incentive to select candidates with the strongest skills rather than candidates with the greatest need, so that it achieves the best outcomes. Often data are not available that allow the evaluator to clearly isolate the effects of the program on the participants versus the effects from extraneous factors or the effects on the broader population compared with its effects on a particular subpopulation. We return to these issues in subsequent chapters as we discuss the findings from our evaluation.

Generally, a program evaluation involves collecting a variety of kinds of data using both qualitative and quantitative methodologies. Amassing a wide collection of data helps the evaluator determine the areas of consensus in the results with regard to the effectiveness of a program and the areas in which additional research is needed. Guidelines for conducting program evaluations are documented in *The Program Evaluation Standards: How to Assess Evaluations of Educational Programs, 2nd edition* (Joint Committee on Standards for Educational Evaluation, 1994). These standards lay out guidelines for accepted practices that represent the consensus opinions endorsed by practitioners in the field of program evaluation.

Evaluating Credentialing Tests

The national board's program consists primarily of a certification assessment, and several sets of standards exist for guiding evaluations of assessment programs. The most well known are *Standards for Educational and Psychological Testing* (American Educational Research Association, American Psychological Association, and National Council on Measurement in Education, 1999), *Principles for the Validation and Use of Personnel Selection Procedures* (Society for Industrial and Organizational Psychologists, 2003), and the *Standards for the Accreditation of Certification Programs* (National Commission for Certifying Agencies, 2004). In addition to the program evaluation standards, we relied on these sets of standards to formulate our framework and to guide our evaluation.

A certification test, such as the national board's assessment, falls into a category of examinations known as credentialing tests. Credentialing tests include those used in the process of initial licensure of new professionals and the voluntary certification of professionals (see Box 2-1 for an explanation of these terms as they are used in this report). Evaluation of these kinds of assessments typically focuses on a review of the processes used to develop the assessment and its psychometric properties. The review includes the methods for determining the content to be assessed and the

---

BOX 2-1
Terminology: Licensure Versus Certification

This report focuses on credentialing tests, which include those used for licensure or certification. Within the general category of credentialing tests, however, the terms licensure, credentialing, and certification are used in overlapping ways, and for that reason they can be confusing. We focus on certification tests that are designed to identify teachers who have advanced skills, significantly beyond those of entry-level teachers obtaining initial licenses. For the purposes of this report:

- Licensure is the granting of permission to practice a particular occupation or profession by a recognized authority.
- Certification is a voluntary means of establishing that certain individuals have mastered specific sets of advanced skills that come with expertise developed over time.

Thus, for example, beginning teachers are licensed, usually by states; graduates of professional or academic programs, such as medical school or a vocational training program, earn credentials; and practitioners who have developed advanced expertise (often after earning academic credentials and being granted a license), through some combination of training and experience, may be certified as having advanced status in their profession.

---

appropriateness of this content, the methods for scoring the assessment and the reliability of the resulting scores, and the methods for setting the score required to pass the assessment and the appropriateness of the pass score, and more. Psychometric evaluations also include the collection of validity evidence—evidence examined to ascertain the extent to which the inferences to be made about the test results are reasonable. There are several issues with regard to evaluating the validity of credentialing tests that warrant additional discussion.

Credentialing Tests and Validity Evidence

Although sensitive to the common misunderstanding that there are different "types" of validity, psychometricians have defined several different kinds of validity evidence that can be used to contribute to the question of whether inferences based on the scores from a given test are valid. Content validity evidence examines the extent to which the test covers the intended domain of content and skills. It is usually established through systematic judgments by experts who compare the content of the test with an external set of standards, specifications, or other descriptions of the domain of coverage. Construct validity evidence addresses the extent to which the assessment is measuring the construct (knowledge or skill) it is intended to measure, rather than unrelated skills. For example, a test that is intended to measure only mathematical skills but that includes items that are written in complex language, thus requiring advanced reading skills, may provide poor support for inferences about mathematical skills. A third kind of information is referred to as criterion-related validity evidence, which evaluates the extent to which test performance agrees with some criterion of interest and thus either correlates with some well-established measure of the domain of interest or accurately predicts future performance.

The intended purpose of most licensure and certification tests is to provide assurance that successful candidates have the knowledge, skills, and judgment required in practice. A preliminary case for the validity of this interpretation is typically made on the basis of content-related evidence, showing that critical knowledge, skills, and judgments have been identified (e.g., using a practice analysis or systematic study of the behaviors, knowledge, and practices of professionals in the field being assessed) and that these content areas are adequately sampled by the test. This validity argument is buttressed by a process of first identifying and then refuting challenges to the validity of the proposed interpretation and finally ruling out various potential sources of systematic error (such as the effects of varying test formats or inappropriate scoring standards). Assuming that the proposed interpretation—that a certain score indicates mastery of a domain of critical knowledge and skills—survives attempts to falsify it, the proposed interpretation can be presumed reasonable. It is rarely possible to provide convincing criterion-related validity evidence for credentialing tests because of the difficulty in obtaining external measures that themselves satisfactorily assess performance across all practice settings.

This is reflected in the established standards for the measurement field (e.g., American Educational Research Association, American Psychological Association, and National Council on Measurement in Education, 1999, p. 157), which require credentialing assessments to demonstrate content validity evidence but not criterion-related validity evidence. The standards explicitly do not require the collection of criterion-related validity evidence, in part because obtaining valid and reliable criterion measures for credentialing tests, such as on-the-job performance, is generally not feasible. Job performance is difficult to measure reliably and validly, especially for the kinds of professions that require complex decision making, continued self-education, and other complex cognitive capacities. Many characteristics beyond those that can be measured in an assessment program are needed for success, and the circumstances in which the job is performed also have a strong influence on performance. Thus, isolating the effects of the mastery that was established by passing the certification test from other influences on job performance is very difficult.

Our charge asks that we consider the impact of board certification on student learning. Measures of outcomes for students, such as their academic achievement, do provide a means of evaluating teachers' job performance, but there are some drawbacks to the use of this kind of a criterion measure. It is enlightening to consider what this would mean if extrapolated to other fields. For example, this is similar to evaluating the validity of a medical certification test by collecting information about the outcomes for patients of a board-certified physician or evaluating the validity of the bar exam by considering the outcomes for clients of a lawyer who had passed the bar exam and been admitted to the bar. Outcomes for patients reflect many factors other than the skills and knowledge of the physician who provides services, such as the severity of the illness being treated and the degree to which the patient adheres to the professional advice given. Likewise in law, the outcome for the client depends on such factors as the nature of the legal problem, the record of prior legal problems, and the extent to which the client follows the advice. Furthermore, should the outcomes for a high-priced lawyer, who can select his or her clients, be compared to the outcomes for a public defender? While data are available that might be used in such evaluations (e.g., rates of death or guilty verdicts) and several such studies have been conducted (e.g., Norcini et al., 2002; Tamblyn et al., 1998, 2002), many factors can contribute to the outcomes, making interpretation of the relationships very tricky.

The same concerns are present in using students' academic achievement to evaluate the performance of their teachers. Many factors interact to influence students' achievement, and it is difficult to isolate the contributions of the teachers from those of other factors. As the reader will see, researchers have tried a variety of statistical strategies to make the findings interpretable, but it remains difficult to obtain solid criterion-related validity evidence for this credentialing program. Because impact evidence is key to the broader program evaluation process and it was explicitly part of our charge, we defined our framework broadly and to encompass the notion of criterion-related validity.

THE EVALUATION FRAMEWORK

We developed the evaluation framework by first theorizing about the ways that an advanced-level certification program for teachers might affect teaching practices and the teaching profession. In laying out our theories, we reviewed the NBPTS founding documents to gain insight into how the founders thought such a program might operate (Chapter 3 describes this in detail). At the same time, we tried to balance the board's broad goals with those that other programs might have, and we considered how other professions view advanced-level certification. We developed a set of assumptions that capture our thinking about the kinds of impacts an advanced-level certification program might have and, after considering their feasibility, turned them into questions that formed the evaluation framework. Below are the assumptions we laid out.

- A program for offering advanced-level certification is intended to be a means for identifying teachers who possess the knowledge, skills, dispositions, and professional judgment that characterize accomplished practice.
- A program for certifying accomplished teachers is expected to improve teachers' practice in a number of ways.
  - The existence and wide distribution of defined standards and assessments will influence teacher preservice training and professional development.
  - The process of preparing for assessments will improve the practice of teachers who participate.
  - Board-certified teachers will serve as mentors for other teachers and influence their practice.
- A program for offering advanced-level certification is expected to improve job conditions for experienced and highly qualified teachers in a number of ways.
  - The existence of certified teachers will help to professionalize the field of teaching.
  - Board-certified teachers will be rewarded with higher pay.
  - Board-certified teachers will be offered expanded leadership opportunities as teachers, not just as administrators.
  - The recognition offered by board certification will increase teachers' job satisfaction.
- A program for certifying accomplished teachers is expected to improve education systems in a number of ways.
  - The opportunity for advanced-level certification and professionalization of the field will decrease the teacher turnover rate and, in particular, help to keep the most qualified teachers in the profession.
  - The presence of certified teachers will lead to better teaching among other teachers.
- Ultimately, all of these changes to the teaching field will help to improve teacher quality and, in turn, improve student learning.

The committee grouped these assumptions into eight primary questions that form the basis for the evaluation framework. The first two questions address the technical quality of the assessment. As mentioned earlier, meeting high technical standards is a fundamental criterion for the evaluation of any testing program (and to some, the only relevant criterion). The remaining questions address the various impacts associated with the program and as specified in our charge. For each primary question, we also identified subsidiary questions that lay out the kinds of empirical evidence needed. Box 2-2 displays the full evaluation framework.

The theory on which our eight primary questions are based can be understood as a model for thinking about the potential impact of a certification program for accomplished teachers on teacher quality and student learning, as shown in Figure 2-1. In this figure, rectangular boxes indicate aspects of the model included in our evaluation framework, and the numbers in parentheses indicate the specific framework question. We refer to this figure throughout the report as we develop our evaluation in terms of the eight questions.

COLLECTING EVIDENCE

The second major component of the committee's charge is to apply the general framework in an evaluation of the effectiveness of the national board's approach to certifying accomplished teachers. We began this task by assessing the available evidence. We scanned the ERIC database for articles written about the NBPTS from 1994 onward. This search covered articles in peer-reviewed journals, research reports published by the organization that sponsored the particular study, conference presentations, articles published by the NBPTS itself, dissertations, and books. In total, we identified 135 articles, although the majority consisted of position statements about the advantages or disadvantages of the certification program, how the board can be of use in reforming teacher education or professionalizing teaching, and the like. The NBPTS maintains its own bibliography of relevant studies (see http://www.nbpts.org/resources/research). As of June 2007, the NBPTS bibliography contained 161 articles. The majority of these articles were technical reports, and the remainder were position papers, advocacy pieces, reports of empirical research conducted by the board and independent researchers, and a set of studies referred to as the "grant funded studies." The technical reports and the grant-funded studies deserve additional explanation.

NBPTS Technical Reports

NBPTS' bibliography of 161 articles includes 128 that are technical reports, 6 prepared by the current contractor (the Educational Testing Service [ETS]) and 122 in a group of articles referred to as the Technical

BOX 2-2
The Committee's Evaluation Framework

Question 1: To what extent does the certification program for accomplished teachers clearly and accurately specify advanced teaching practices and the characteristics of teachers (the knowledge, skills, dispositions, and judgments) that enable them to carry out advanced practice? Does it do so in a manner that supports the development of a well-aligned test?

    a. What processes were used to identify the knowledge, skills, dispositions, and judgments that characterize accomplished teachers? Was the process for establishing the descriptions of these characteristics thoughtful, thorough, and adequately justified? Who was involved in the process? To what extent do the participants represent different perspectives on teaching?

    b. Are the identified knowledge, skills, dispositions, and judgments presented in a way that is clear, accurate, reasonable, and complete? What evidence is there that they are relevant to performance?

    c. Do the knowledge, skills, dispositions, and judgments that were identified reflect current thinking in the specific field? What is the process for revisiting and refreshing the descriptions of expectations in each field?

    d. Are the knowledge, skills, dispositions, and judgments, as well as the teaching practices they imply, effective for all groups of students, regardless of their race and ethnicities, socioeconomic status, and native language status?

Question 2: To what extent do the assessments associated with the certification program for accomplished teachers reliably measure the specified knowledge, skills, dispositions, and judgments of certification candidates and support valid interpretations of the results? To what extent are the performance standards for the assessments and the process for setting them justifiable and reasonable?

    a. To what extent does the entire assessment process (including the tasks, scoring rubrics, and scoring mechanisms) yield results that reflect the specified knowledge, skills, dispositions, and judgments?

    b. Is the passing score reasonable? What process was used for establishing the passing score? How is the passing score justified? To what extent do pass rates differ for various groups of candidates, and are such differences reflective of bias in the test?

    c. To what extent do the scores reflect teacher quality? What evidence is available that board-certified teachers actually practice in ways that are consistent with the knowledge, skills, dispositions, and judgments they demonstrate through the assessment process? Do knowledgeable observers find them to be better teachers than individuals who failed when they attempted to earn board certification?

Question 3: To what extent do teachers participate in the program?

a. How many teachers apply each year for board certification? Have there been changes in application rates over time? How do application rates compare across states and districts? What are the characteristics of teachers who apply compared with those who do not? What are the characteristics of teachers who successfully earn board certification compared with those who do not?

b. Why do teachers choose to participate or not? What do various agencies (the board, states, school districts, teachers unions, etc.) do to encourage participation? How do these actions influence teachers' attitudes toward certification and participation in the process?

Question 4: To what extent does the advanced-level certification program identify teachers who are effective at producing positive student outcomes, such as learning, motivation, school engagement, breadth of achievement, educational attainment, attendance rates, and grade promotion?

a. How does achievement compare for students taught by board-certified and nonboard-certified teachers, after controlling for other factors? Are the differences substantively meaningful? Do students taught by board-certified teachers have higher achievement or achievement gains than those taught by nonboard-certified teachers? Do student gains persist into the future?

b. How do other student outcomes (such as motivation, breadth of achievement, school engagement, attendance rates, promotion rates) compare for students taught by board-certified and nonboard-certified teachers?

Question 5: To what extent do teachers improve their practices and the outcomes of their students by virtue of going through the advanced-level certification process?

a. To what extent do teachers who go through the certification process improve their teaching practices and classroom climate, regardless of whether they become board certified?

b. Do teachers who obtain board certification become more effective at increasing student achievement in ways that are evident in their students' achievement scores?

c. Do teachers have a greater impact on other student outcomes (e.g., higher student motivation, higher promotion rates) after they obtain board certification than they did before they were certified?

Question 6: To what extent and in what ways are the career paths of both successful and unsuccessful candidates affected by their participation in the program?

Continued

BOX 2-2 Continued

a. What are the typical career paths for teachers? Does the career path change for those who obtain advanced certification? What are the effects on the career paths of teachers who attempt to become certified but who are unsuccessful?

b. Do departure rates differ for board-certified and nonboard-certified teachers with regard to leaving teaching (attrition), including those who leave classroom teaching for other jobs in schools (transition)?

c. Does the program have any effects on teacher mobility within the teaching field? Does it encourage teacher mobility in ways that are beneficial for lower performing students or in ways that contribute to inequities—for example, do board-certified teachers move out of urban areas to wealthy suburban districts?

Question 7: Beyond its effects on candidates, to what extent and in what ways does the certification program have an impact on the field of teaching, the education system, or both?

a. What are the effects of having one or more board-certified teachers in a school or district?

b. Has the board-certification program had any effects on:
- the course content, methods of preparation, and assessments used in teacher education programs, or
- the content of and strategies used in inservice training and professional development for practicing teachers?

c. Has the board-certification program had any effects on the applicant pool for teacher education programs? Since the board came into existence, have there been changes in the numbers of individuals entering teacher education programs or the characteristics of the applicants?

d. Has the existence of board certification had an impact on the allocation of teachers across districts and schools? Has the program been a useful tool for increasing the numbers of accomplished teachers in high-needs schools?

Question 8: To what extent does the advanced-level certification program accomplish its objectives in a cost-effective manner, relative to other approaches intended to improve teacher quality?

a. What are the benefits of the certification program?

b. What are the costs associated with the certification program?

c. What other approaches have been shown to bring about improvement in teacher quality? What are their costs and benefits?

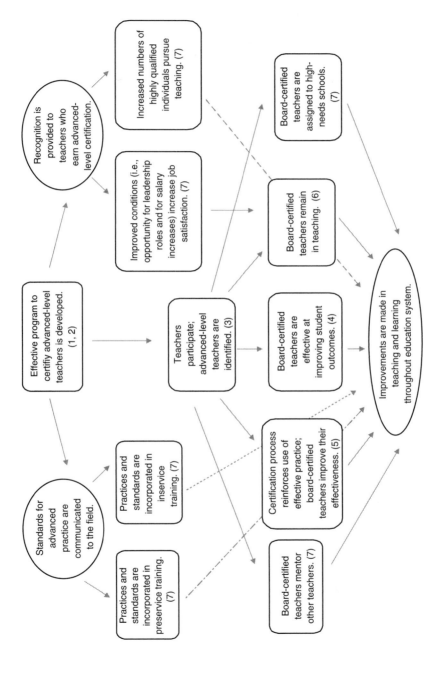

FIGURE 2-1 Hypothesized impacts of an advanced-level certification program for teachers.

Analysis Group (TAG) reports.[1] The TAG reports consist of articles that summarize studies conducted as the assessment program was being developed. They explore topics typically investigated during the development phase of a test, such as procedures for developing assessment tasks that evaluate the content standards, methods for scoring the assessment tasks and ways to increase the reliability of the scoring, determining the passing score for the assessment, and studies of adverse impact. Findings from these studies shaped the assessment, its scoring, and operational procedures. As such, these 128 studies were primarily useful for helping us to understand the history of the development of the assessment from a psychometric perspective and to address the first two questions in our framework regarding the psychometric soundness of the assessments and the processes used to produce the assessments.

NBPTS Grant-Funded Studies

The NBPTS bibliography included approximately 18 studies that are the result of a special board research endeavor supported through private grant funding. The board initiated this project in order to subject the program to external scrutiny and allow researchers to evaluate various claims that had been made about the program, both supportive and unsupportive (personal conversation, Ann Harman, former director of research with the NBPTS). In January 2002, the board launched this project by convening a special bidders' conference for prospective grant recipients. During the conference, NBPTS staff members identified the areas in which they sought investigation, including the impact of board-certified teachers on student achievement, the impact on low-performing schools, leadership activities of board-certified teachers, standards-based professional development, adverse impact associated with the assessment, the NBPTS digital edge program, and psychometric/technical issues. Subsequent to the conference, potential researchers submitted proposals. To ensure objectivity, the board arranged for researchers from the RAND Corporation to review and rate the proposals and make the funding decisions. The schedule called for completed reports to be submitted within a three-year period.

The peer review process established by the board for the completed reports is not documented, but we learned about it from NBPTS staff members. Accordingly, researchers were told that their reports would undergo a peer review process, but it was up to the researcher to decide on the nature of the review. The researcher could obtain a peer review prior to submitting

---

[1]The TAG was a group formed to advise the NBPTS on the development of the assessment. It was based at the University of North Carolina, Greensboro, and headed by Richard Jaeger, Lloyd Bond, and John Hattie (see Chapter 3 for additional details).

the final paper to the board and submit it as a reviewed product, or the researcher could submit the report as unreviewed, and NBPTS staff would handle the review. Our understanding of this process is that it was neither rigorous nor standardized. We raise this point because we were disappointed in the quality of many of the grant-funded studies. We think that a more rigorous peer review process, and perhaps additional oversight during the course of each study, may have led to a higher quality body of work.

Committee Criteria for Reviewing the Evidence

A comparison of the studies on the NBPTS bibliography and the list we generated identified approximately 44 articles that reported on empirical research related to our framework. The list includes studies that used a variety of quantitative and qualitative methods. To guide our review of the studies, we agreed on a set of standards for judging the quality and validity of the findings.

Numerous texts describe the characteristics of sound research and the factors that can jeopardize the integrity of research findings. We relied in particular on the guiding principles identified by the National Academies' Committee on Scientific Principles for Education Research (National Research Council, 2002, available at http://www.nap.edu/catalog.php?record_id=10236#toc) and in the *Standards for Reporting on Empirical Social Science Research in AERA Publications* (American Educational Research Association, 2006). While the committee did not attempt to develop its own comprehensive list, we did identify several criteria that were particularly relevant to the body of evidence available regarding the national board program:

- The design of the study—the framing of the question(s) to be investigated, the method of data collection, and the procedures for analyzing the data—is described clearly and in sufficient detail to allow the reader to form independent judgments about its adequacy.
- The methodology is a logical and defensible approach to answering the specified research question(s) and is carried out correctly.
- The approach to classifying the phenomena to be measured in quantifiable terms is adequately explained and justifiable.
- The identification of samples to be studied, as well as the sample selection procedures, are described in detail. They are appropriate to the research questions being addressed and adequately relate to the conclusions drawn.
- The effects of attrition or nonresponse of subjects are addressed in the findings and conclusions.

- The variables measured are appropriate for the specific research question(s) and are measured in a systematic and reliable manner.
- The findings are fully described and conclusions are justifiable, given the methodology and limitations of the study.

In general, we confined our attention to studies that follow the accepted practices and standards for the type of research attempted in the study. We expected studies to be conducted in a systematic fashion, regardless of whether the methods were qualitative or quantitative, and to be fully documented. In total, this body of research was of mixed utility because many of the studies had technical shortcomings that made the findings difficult to interpret. We made use of as many of them as we could and tried to balance our level of confidence in the findings with the methodological shortcomings and the extent of corroborating evidence. In all, we identified 25 studies that met our criteria and were relevant to our evaluation framework. Appendix A summarizes the studies we predominantly relied upon.

This evidence base was decidedly uneven with respect to the eight questions in our evaluation framework. Nearly half of the studies (10) addressed one aspect of Question 4 (comparisons of student achievement for board-certified and nonboard-certified teachers), and there was little or no evidence available for some of the other questions. To help fill in the gaps in the literature base and to help us fully understand the existing evidence, we arranged to collect our own data and conduct our own analyses.

Information Collected by the Committee

In all, the committee held six meetings, of which four included time for presentations intended to focus on specific aspects of the evaluation framework. We also arranged for a number of meetings outside committee meetings and additional analyses reported in four papers (Ladd, Sass, and Harris, 2007; McCaffrey and Rivkin, 2007; Perda, 2007; Russell, Putka, and Waters, 2007).

To understand the history of the program, its development, and its current operation, we arranged to meet with the following people who currently worked with the NBPTS or its contractor, ETS, or had previously been involved with the program. We obtained information from these individuals both by inviting them to make presentations at our meetings and by conducting structured interviews with them outside the meetings. The individuals we consulted are listed below.

Current NBPTS staff members:
- Joseph Aguerrebere, president and chief executive officer
- Joan Auchter, vice president, standards and assessment

- Mary E. Dilworth, vice president, higher education initiatives and research

ETS staff members:
- Drew Gitomer, distinguished research scientist
- Mari Pearlman, senior vice president; involved with NPBTS development from the outset
- Steve Schreiner, director of scoring for NBPTS assessments

Former NBPTS staff members:
- Chuck Cascio, ETS; former director of test development at NBPTS
- Ann Harman, Harman and Associates; former NBPTS director of research
- Jim Kelly, retired; first president and chief executive officer of NBPTS
- David Mandel, Carnegie-IAS Commission on Mathematics and Science Education; former vice president for policy development at NBPTS
- Sally Mernissi, deceased, January 2006; former vice president and corporate secretary at NBPTS

Representatives from stakeholder groups:
- Joan Baratz-Snowden, American Federation of Teachers; former vice president of assessment and research at NBPTS
- Joshua Boots, American Board for Certification of Teacher Excellence (ABCTE)
- Emerson Elliott, National Council for Accreditation of Teacher Education
- Mary Futrell, George Washington University; former president of the National Education Association and member of the original board of directors
- Kathy Madigan, formerly with ABCTE

NBPTS researchers and consultants:
- Lloyd Bond, Carnegie Foundation; former co-director of the Technical Analysis Group
- Lee Shulman, Carnegie Foundation; former director of the Teacher Assessment Project at Stanford
- Gary Sykes, Michigan State University; former doctoral student of Lee Shulman and consultant to the NBPTS board of directors
- Suzanne Wilson, Michigan State University; former doctoral student of Lee Shulman and consultant to the NBPTS board of directors

We also sought information and insights from teachers with a variety of experiences related to the NBPTS program. The National Research Council has a standing committee of teachers, called the Teacher Advisory Council (TAC). The council includes 11 high school, middle school, and elementary teachers of reading, mathematics, and science who have been recognized for their exceptional work.[2] This group serves as an advisory panel and resource for committees of the National Academies, to help make sure that the perspectives of teachers at the top of their field are taken into account in the conduct of education-related projects and to improve the usefulness, relevance, and communication of research-based findings. At the time, four of the TAC members were board certified. We attended their March 2006 meeting to learn more about their perceptions of the NBPTS and specifically to follow up on some of the findings reported in the research with regard to the influences of board-certified teachers in schools and school systems. In preparation for this discussion, we distributed a set of questions to the TAC members in advance of their meeting, which inquired about their reasons for deciding to pursue (or not pursue) board certification, their impressions of the program, and, for those who were board certified, any ways that it has impacted their practices or career. We then conducted a two-hour structured discussion to hear their responses to these questions.

A segment of our third committee meeting (June 2006) was also devoted to hearing firsthand accounts from teachers and teacher educators. The goal of this panel was to learn more about the ways in which the NBPTS has influenced teacher education and professional development. Mary Futrell, dean of education and former member of the NBPTS board of directors, and Maxine Freund, professor of special education, both with the George Washington University School of Education, discussed their perceptions of ways that the NBPTS has affected teacher training at their institutions. (Freund's work in developing mentoring programs for NBPTS applicants is documented in Freund, Russell, and Kavulic, 2005.) In addition, we invited two board-certified teachers with documented involvement in professional development activities in their school systems (see Cohen and Rice, 2005): Sara Eisenhardt, an elementary teacher in Cincinnati, Ohio, and Carol Ma-tern, employed with the Indianapolis public schools and an adjunct faculty member with Indiana University-Purdue University Indianapolis.

The committee focused considerable attention on the body of research related to student outcomes. We listened to presentations by authors of 6 of the 12 studies—Linda Cavaluzzo, Dan Goldhaber, Douglas Harris and Tim Sass, Thomas Kane and Jon Fullerton, Helen Ladd, and William Sanders. Together, the findings from these studies presented a complex set of results.

---

[2]More information about this group can be found at http://ww7.nationalacademies. org/tac/.

We asked five researchers (Henry Braun, Paul Holland, Daniel McCaffrey, Steve Raudenbush, and Steven Rivkin) to review these articles and assist the committee in synthesizing the results. McCaffrey and Rivkin assisted the committee by identifying additional analyses that would help clarify the results, and Harris, Sass, and Ladd conducted these studies.

We sought assistance in evaluating the psychometric qualities of the NBPTS assessment, and Teresa Russell helped with this aspect of our work. We also obtained a data set from the NBPTS and had David Perda conduct analyses that helped us understand who participates in the program and how they compare with other teachers on a national basis. Finally, we heard presentations by Carol Cohen and Jennifer King Rice, who discussed their work on estimating the costs of support programs for teachers going through the NBPTS process.

3

The Historical Context and Overview of the National Board

The National Board for Professional Teaching Standards (NBPTS) is a product of its time. It was developed in response to a combination of circumstances that include long-standing trends as well as immediate policy pressures. Its characteristics reflect developments in research on teaching and in educational measurement, and its progress has inevitably been affected by subsequent events and trends in the world of education policy. As we examined the board's goals, its history, and the context in which it was developed, we realized that a detailed understanding of these circumstances would be an important foundation for our evaluation. This chapter describes the context we think is necessary to understanding the board and what it has accomplished as well as the conclusions and recommendations we make.

We begin with a discussion of the education reform context in the United States that supported the board's creation in the late 1980s and its development during the 1990s. We then set the board's policy goals in the context of the way the field of teaching has developed and its status at the time the board was conceived. We describe the board's development and discuss some of the factors that have affected its progress. The chapter closes with some observations about the context in which the present evaluation has been undertaken. Chapter 4 provides an overview of the board's operations and the assessment process that certification candidates undergo.

THE CONTEXT FOR REFORM

The NBPTS was founded in 1987 as a central component in a comprehensive effort to reform the way public education was structured in the United States (Tucker, 1995). *A Nation at Risk*, a report issued in 1983 by the National Commission on Excellence in Education, had focused public attention on the need for a fundamental restructuring of the education system in this country. The charge to that commission, which was created by Secretary of Education T.H. Bell in 1981, was to examine the quality of education in the United States and make recommendations for its improvement. Citing a variety of indicators of poor student performance, including international comparisons of student achievement, the authors concluded that the United States was at risk of losing its economic edge in the world (National Commission on Excellence in Education, 1983). The report's grim prediction was accompanied by a forceful call to reform public education, and its recommendations included stronger graduation requirements, higher and measurable standards for students' academic performance, a longer school day, and steps to improve the preparation of teachers and to make the field of teaching more rewarding and better respected.

As a follow-up to *A Nation at Risk*, the Carnegie Forum on Education and the Economy decided in 1985 to form a task force, which included policy makers, educators, leaders of the teachers' unions, and business leaders, to study the quality of teaching in U.S. schools (see Box 3-1). In 1986, the Carnegie Task Force on Teaching as a Profession released its report, *A Nation Prepared: Teachers for the 21st Century*. The report represented a hard-won consensus among this diverse group of leaders, who became convinced that improving the quality of teachers and the status of the field would be essential to the education reforms the nation was demanding (Koppich, Humphrey, and Hough, 2006; Tucker, 1995).

The Carnegie task force argued that to meet the demands of the 21st century, schools had to help students reach levels of achievement previously thought possible only for a select few (Carnegie Task Force on Teaching as a Profession, 1986). Improving the quality of the nation's teachers would be the key to achieving this goal, and teachers, in turn, would require more and better preparation than was the norm. They would need a deeper understanding of the subject matter they would be teaching and of how knowledge is developed in the disciplines, improved understanding of how children learn and develop in different contexts, a wider repertoire of instructional strategies for reaching a diverse student population, and more varied skills for assessing students' understanding of the content and skills they had been taught. A certification program would identify those among the teaching force who had these attributes as accomplished teachers so they could be rewarded and mobilized to improve teaching and learning.

BOX 3-1
Members of the Carnegie Task Force on
Teaching as a Profession

Lewis M. Branscomb, chairman, International Business Machines Corporation
Alan M. Campbell, vice chairman of the board and executive vice president, ARA
   Services
Mary Hatwood Futrell, president, National Education Association
John W. Gardner, writer and consultant
Fred M. Hechinger, president, The New York Times Company Foundation
Bill Honig, superintendent of public instruction, State of California
James B. Hunt, attorney, Poyner & Spruill
Vera Katz, Speaker of the Oregon House of Representatives
Thomas H. Kean, Governor of New Jersey
Judith E. Lanier, dean, College of Education, Michigan State University
Arturo Madrid, president, The Tomas Rivera Center
Shirley Malcom, American Association for the Advancement of Science
Ruth E. Randall, commissioner of education, State of Minnesota
Albert Shanker, president, American Federation of Teachers

The Carnegie task force also argued that improving the status of the field and working conditions in the schools would be critical both for attracting and retaining capable teachers and for enabling them to do their jobs effectively. Schools would need to be transformed into learning communities designed to support both student achievement and teacher professionalism. Teachers would need more autonomy in exercising professional judgment and more influence over decisions that affect their work. They would also need support in developing truly collegial relationships with colleagues that would promote professional learning and development. Incentives for teachers would be tied to school-wide student performance. The task force insisted that without a comprehensive and integrated plan for restructuring the schools and redefining teaching as a profession, students were not likely to meet the more rigorous academic demands of the changing curriculum.

The members of the task force regarded the plan they proposed as radical, describing its elements as "sweeping changes in education policy," which were intended to work together to create "a profession of well-educated teachers prepared to assume new powers and responsibilities to redesign schools for the future" (Carnegie Task Force on Teaching as a Profession, 1986). The full set of recommendations follows (p. 3):

- Create a National Board for Professional Teaching Standards, organized with a regional and state membership structure, to establish high standards for what teachers need to know and be able to do, and to certify teachers who meet that standard.
- Restructure schools to provide a professional environment for teaching, freeing them to decide how best to meet state and local goals for children while holding them accountable for student progress.
- Restructure the teaching force, and introduce a new category of "Lead Teachers" with the proven ability to provide active leadership in the redesign of schools and in helping their colleagues to uphold high standards of teaching and learning.
- Require a bachelor's degree in the arts and sciences as a prerequisite for the professional study of teaching.
- Develop a new professional curriculum in graduate schools of education leading to a Master's in Teaching degree, based on systematic knowledge of teaching and including internships and residencies in the schools.
- Mobilize the nation's resources to prepare minority youngsters for teaching careers.
- Relate incentives for teachers to school-wide student performance, and provide schools with the technology, services, and staff essential to teacher productivity.
- Make teachers' salaries and career opportunities competitive with those in other professions.

We call attention to the full set of recommendations here and elsewhere in the report, because they are directly relevant to the task of evaluating the program. As we discussed in Chapter 2, the board was not expected to accomplish all of these goals on its own or solely through the advanced-level certification program. Several other organizations, including the Interstate New Teacher Assessment and Support Consortium and the National Council for Accreditation of Teacher Education (NCATE), for example, also adopted the goals of the task force and addressed other means of improving the quality of the teaching force.

Nevertheless, the board's charge was ambitious. As James B. Hunt, Jr., the first chair of the board, described it, NBPTS "was originally set up to try to help create a true profession of teaching because we didn't agree on standards, and we didn't assess teachers rigorously, and we didn't have ways to move them along in the profession" (Keller, 2006).

At the same time, performance assessment itself was a relatively new idea in the world of educational measurement, and the goal of administering a performance assessment for teachers on a large scale, as the national board set out to do, was unprecedented (Joan Baratz-Snowden, personal communication).[1] There had been other attempts to develop standardized performance assessments, such as a portfolio assessment of writing used in Vermont. However, by exploring ways to make a large-scale, standardized program of performance assessments for teachers operational, the national board was breaking new ground.

The national board attempted not only to redefine teaching as a profession in the public mind, but also to formally examine teaching practice in a new way that goes far beyond testing for knowledge—by exploring student work and interactions between teachers and their students in circumstances that would be genuine but could be standardized for scoring. By doing so, the national board sought both to expand understanding of what constitutes accomplished teaching and to pin down the elements that are critical to it. Board certification would identify teachers who have developed a body of expertise over time, and highlight the components of this expertise as distinct from the talent and skills that an excellent beginning teacher might have. Together with the other reforms enumerated in *A Nation Prepared*, the board certification program was intended to improve the overall quality of teaching.

THE GOAL OF PROFESSIONALIZING TEACHING

The NBPTS was viewed, in part, as a means of professionalizing the field of teaching. A brief look at the development of the teaching field in the United States, the distinction between professions and other occupational groups, the ways in which teachers have been trained and licensed, and other aspects of the field, provides background for understanding this goal.

Historical Context

Teaching is an ancient vocation, and from the earliest civilizations it has been recognized as a necessary and valuable activity—but its purposes have evolved. For much of recorded history, formal education was available to just a small percentage of the population. While families and occupational structures such as guilds have also educated young people, particularly in the skills and crafts necessary for self-sufficiency, until very recently, the

---

[1]Some of the details regarding the origins of the national board and its development were supplied through interviews conducted on behalf of the committee with a number of individuals who were closely associated with the program in its early days. See Chapter 2 for a list of people interviewed by the committee.

overwhelming majority of the world's people have been illiterate and have lacked numeracy skills.

The seeds of the modern commitment to education for all, that is now evident in much of the world, are found in the industrial and democratic revolutions of the eighteenth century. As the rights of citizenship were expanded, the many social benefits of an educated citizenry became more widely recognized. The development of schooling in the United States followed this trend. From the nation's founding, education (for white males) was regarded as essential to the success of a democracy. By the 1840s, the common schools, associated in particular with the name of Horace Mann, were beginning to provide a free elementary education to most of the children in a community in the same school, regardless of class; nonwhite children were still generally excluded. The 20th century saw both an expansion of educational opportunities for minority children and the expansion of required free public education to the secondary level.

The need for teachers to serve this expanding pool of public school students entailed a corresponding focus on how aspiring teachers might be prepared for the job.[2] The earliest U.S. schools for prospective teachers were not elite academic institutions. Most provided the equivalent of a high school education with some specialized training in pedagogy, although many later became well-respected four-year colleges and universities (Angus, 2001; Sedlak and Schlossman, 1986). In 1935 a bachelor's degree was comparatively rare for teachers as a group: just 10 percent of elementary school teachers, 56 percent of junior high school teachers, and 85 percent of high school teachers had them. However, by the early 1980s, virtually 100 percent of K-12 teachers had a bachelor's degree and nearly half had a master's degree (Sedlak and Schlossman, 1986).

Neither the training of teachers nor the study of pedagogy was widely regarded as an academic endeavor worthy of the nation's top postsecondary institutions until well into the twentieth century, and that bias generally mirrored the status of teachers in society (Labaree, 2000, 2004; National Research Council, 2001). Up to the present day, schools of education occupy a distinct and somewhat uncomfortable position—viewed as not genuinely rigorous by many colleagues in other academic fields, but also viewed as too theoretical by many observers focused on the practical realities of day-to-day life in schools (Labaree, 2004). This lack of status has weakened the influence of these programs and the status of teachers.

Academic programs that focused on the preparation of teachers, however, proliferated in the first half of the twentieth century, and states in-

---

[2]Here and throughout the report we focus on teachers in the K-12 public schools because they are the majority of teachers in the United States and because the national board program focuses on them.

creasingly looked to the credentials they offered as a means of establishing prospective teachers' qualifications. Today there are between 1,200 and 1,300 schools of education in the United States (1,206 such programs are university based) (Levine, 2006).

Characteristics of a Profession

The members of the Carnegie task force believed that teaching has not been viewed or treated as on par with professions, such as medicine or law. They and others have observed that the field has lacked an agreed-on base of knowledge, shared standards of excellence, and career pathways that formally reward the accumulation of skill and experience and allow teachers to progress professionally (Carnegie Task Force on Teaching as a Profession, 1986; Koppich, Humphrey, and Hough, 2006; Lucas, 1999; National Research Council, 2001a). But what is a profession? Teaching is not the only field in which the distinction between profession and other occupational categories has been an issue; social scientists have identified several features that characterize professions (Abbott, 1988; Carr-Saunders and Wilson, 1964).

One set of characteristics relates to the knowledge that practitioners hold. Professionals generally have command of a body of technical expertise that is not shared by those outside the profession. They obtain this knowledge through a long period of intensive training that is provided by experts in their field. Moreover, professionals develop expertise over time: skills and judgment that allow them to draw on and apply their theoretical knowledge in response to circumstances, to evaluate and make decisions about problems, and to develop strategies for addressing them.

In many cases, acquisition of this body of knowledge and expertise is marked by some form of licensure or certification, which also provides a public signal of the adequacy and validity of the training. Professional associations and the state are most often responsible for awarding the license or certificate and for overseeing the validity of the process. Often the licensure or certification system gives those who have the credential a monopoly, or near monopoly, in offering the services associated with the profession. For example, physicians who are not board-certified in cardiology are not generally granted privileges to practice cardiology in a hospital. These systems also contribute to the professions' latitude in policing themselves, both by defining and enforcing codes of ethics and by controlling entry into the profession.

Other factors relate to the way in which the members of a profession go about their work. In contrast to other kinds of workers, professionals are expected to have a strong personal commitment to their work, which some describe as a sacred calling and others as simply an ethic of service.

Members of a profession often define their calling or commitment in terms of service to a particular group—such as patients or students—but other considerations—such as respect for the law, journalistic integrity, or principles of design—might also play a part in the definition of the profession. A commitment to serve the group and other ideals of the profession is expected to override considerations of financial and personal gain. Professionals are also generally granted a high level of autonomy and discretion in carrying out their work and a large measure of control over the conditions in which they carry it out, by contrast with other workers.

In practice, occupational fields possess these characteristics in varying degrees. Medicine, for example, could be said to meet most of these criteria and is generally regarded as a profession. Others, such as engineering, accounting, or nursing, meet fewer of them. Many occupations, such as carpentry and other building trades, and many computer and other technical fields have periods of apprenticeship and require the development of expertise that may be acquired on the job or through schooling, but they are not normally recognized as professions. Furthermore, external circumstances may affect the practice of a profession. For example, some physicians have found that rising costs and changes in the financing and administration of health care have compromised their autonomy. Box 3-2 provides information about efforts to professionalize other occupations.

A review of these criteria suggests that teaching has some, but not all, of the characteristics that social scientists associate with professions, and that the task force was correct in its judgment that teaching is not a full profession. On one hand, public school teachers are required to accumulate a body of technical expertise and usually do so in a school of education. A state-granted license is a requirement for employment in the public schools, although the field itself has only limited influence on the individual states' requirements for licensure. Teaching is also perceived as a calling with an ethical or moral component, perhaps to an even greater degree than other professions, because it involves close relationships with children and youth. In fact, teaching has been imbued with a moral purpose in most contexts (Durkheim, 1956; Goodlad, 1994; Tom, 1984).

On the other hand, teachers have been widely viewed as not possessing the degree of knowledge and expertise required of other professionals, and they do not have control over entry into the field or standards of practice. As employees of school districts and schools, public school teachers have comparatively little professional autonomy or control over the conditions in which they work. It is generally the case that teachers unions, rather than professional associations, protect and advance the interests of teachers, a situation that tends to reinforce teachers' status as employees, not professionals.

It is also worth noting that although most teachers before the 19th

BOX 3-2
Professionalization in Other Occupations

Medicine was among the first fields in the United States to take up the challenges of both licensing its practitioners, by guaranteeing that particular standards have been met, and certifying that certain practitioners have met additional advanced and specialized requirements. The National Board of Medical Examiners was founded in 1915 to develop examinations that could be used to judge candidates for medical licensure (http://www.nbme.org/about/about.asp). To obtain a medical license, a candidate must satisfy a number of requirements, including passing three tests. States are responsible for licensing medical doctors and for specifying licensing requirements. State requirements vary somewhat, but all include several years of postgraduate study, passage of an examination, and a variety of additional steps (Federation of State Medical Boards, http://www.fsmb. org/index.html).

At the same time that general licensure for physicians was being established as a state requirement, the growing number of medical specialties led to calls for specialty boards. The purpose was not to add legal requirements to the practice of medicine, but to help the public identify physicians with specific qualifications. Today, the American Board of Medical Specialties recognizes the boards of 24 medical specialties as meeting its standards for education, training, and examination of candidates (http://www.abms.org/history.asp#Development).

Nursing is a field that has many parallels with teaching, both because its workforce has been predominantly female and because it has had a status somewhat below that of such professions as medicine and law.* Nurses are required to pass an exam created by the Council of State Nursing Boards, although each state has it own licensing requirements for nurses (http://www.nursingworld.org/ancc/cert/index.html; http://nursingcertification.org/index.html). Advanced certification for nurses is available in a number of areas, including acute care, family practice, gerontology, pediatrics, and psychiatry/mental health. Today more than 150,000 (of 2.4 million in the United States) registered nurses have obtained advanced certification through the American Nurses Credentialing Council, the American Board of Nursing Specialties, and the American Nurses Association.

Another field that has attracted large numbers of women is social work, a comparatively young profession that was first recognized as a field of study at Columbia University in 1898 (http://www.socialworkers.org/pressroom/features/general/history.asp, http://www.abecsw.org/info/bcd/i_faqs.shtml). Social workers who wish to be recognized for an advanced level of qualifications can seek certification from the American Board of Examiners in Clinical Social Work. The board issues the Board Certified Diplomate in Clinical Social Work to individuals who have met the requirements, which include clinical practice, a master's degree from an accredited institution, a license, and successful completion of a peer evaluation–based examination process.

---

*According to the U.S. Census Bureau, approximately 92 percent of registered nurses are female (http://www.census.gov/Press-Release/www/releases/archives/facts_for_features_special_editions/004491.html).

century were male, the field has been largely female for much of its history in the United States, and only since the 20th century has it edged toward greater gender balance (Sedlak and Schlossman, 1986). The perception of teaching as a women's field has not enhanced its status.

We note also that the goal of professionalizing teaching was articulated by the Carnegie task force and the national board at a time when professionalization was a topical concern in other fields as well. Other fields had been pushing to join the ranks of professions; a 1964 article identified social work, veterinary medicine, school teaching, nursing, and pharmacy, among others, as "in process" [of becoming professions] or "borderline" (Wilensky, 1964). Sociologists and others were also devoting attention to questions about the defining characteristics of professions, determining how professionals should be trained, and the intellectual relationship between research and professional practice (Schön, 1983; Wilensky, 1964). Thus, the proponents of professionalizing teachers were part of a trend, and they also faced some resistance from those who did not view the field as intellectually rigorous enough to join the ranks of the established professions.

Accreditation, Certification, and Licensure

The ways in which teachers are licensed[3] and schools/colleges of education are accredited have had a significant influence on the preparation of those who enter teaching. Teachers in the United States have been required to obtain licenses since the colonial period, although the standards for licensure have evolved (Lucas, 1999). At first the focus was on moral character and the capacity to maintain discipline, although some jurisdictions established written tests to assess basic competency in the subjects to be taught. Today, public school teachers in all 50 states and the District of Columbia are required to obtain teaching licenses, which are granted by the state department of education or licensure advisory committee (Bureau of Labor Statistics, http://www.bls.gov/oco/ocos069.htm#training).

The licensure requirements for teaching differ somewhat from state to state, however. Virtually all jurisdictions require the accumulation of a certain number of course credits or completion of a bachelor's degree. Many, but not all, jurisdictions use the same tests, and many also add or substitute additional requirements, with the result that both the nature of what is assessed and the standards that prospective teachers have to meet vary (National Research Council, 2001a). In addition, most states have allowed exemptions of various kinds from their licensure requirements, such

---

[3]The terms licensure and certification are sometimes used interchangeably. In this report, we use the term "licensure" to refer to the credential required for initial entry into the field. See Box 2-1.

as emergency credentials and alternate routes to certification for individuals who lack a teaching degree. According to a recent estimate, one out of five entering teachers currently comes through an alternate certification program in one of the 47 states that have them (Walsh and Jacobs, 2007).

Of the 50 states and the District of Columbia, 8 develop their own examinations for teacher licensure; 26 use some combination of the three components of the PRAXIS Series, offered by the Educational Testing Service (ETS); and 9 require some other combination of assessments (Baber, 2007). Of the states that do have a testing requirement, three also use a testing requirement to certify advanced teachers. Arkansas and Ohio use PRAXIS III for this purpose, and New York has its own assessment.[4] In general, entering teachers, who have met the entry-level requirements, receive a probationary certificate and then have a three-year period in which to complete additional requirements. Teachers who have satisfied these requirements receive a standard certificate, qualify for tenure, and are referred to as "advanced" teachers (some states identify as advanced only teachers who have earned a master's degree).

The majority of public school teachers are educated at a school of education. Fewer than 40 percent of these programs are nationally accredited, and, as a group, they are regarded as having comparatively low standards for admission and modest success in preparing excellent teachers (Levine, 2006; Murray, 2001). It is important to note that these programs vary in many respects, and that prospective teachers are not evenly distributed among them—as many as 50 percent of graduates come from teacher education programs in five states (California, Illinois, New York, Pennsylvania, and Texas), and more than one-fourth were in just two states: New York and California (U.S. Department of Education, 2006).[5]

As this brief overview suggests, the professional lives of teachers are subject to a wide variety of influences. In the 1980s, when the NBPTS was established, the circumstances in which teachers pursued their careers reflected the field's somewhat equivocal status. Then, as now, it was clear that much has been demanded of teachers, but that the circumstances in

---

[4]The three elements of the PRAXIS Series cover basic academic skills; general and subject-specific knowledge and teaching skills; and classroom performance (http://www.ets.org/).

[5]Most teacher education programs that do seek accreditation do so through NCATE, a national organization that accredits schools, colleges, and departments of education that prepare beginning teachers (Kraft, 2001). NCATE describes itself as "part of a continuum of teacher preparation and development that begins with pre-service preparation, and continues with stages of teacher licensure and advanced professional development, including National Board certification" (http://www.ncate.org/). As of June 2007, 632 institutions with teacher education programs were NCATE certified. An additional 59 are certified by the Teacher Education Accreditation Council, founded in 1997, which allows programs to identify the standards against which they wish to be judged (http://www.teac.org/quickfacts.asp).

which they do their work differ in important ways from what is customary in other fields, and the institutions that determine standards for their preparation and advancement vary significantly. With this profile as a backdrop, then, we turn to the development of the national board.

THE NATIONAL BOARD FOR PROFESSIONAL TEACHING STANDARDS

Development of the National Board

When the NBPTS was initially established in 1987, its board of directors included 63 members. As required in its bylaws, two-thirds of the members were teachers and the remaining third were administrators, policy makers, and members of the public. The board conducted its work by forming subgroups to handle specific tasks, such as defining performance and content standards by which teachers could be assessed, developing the structure for the certification assessment itself, determining what kinds of certificates would be awarded (i.e., in different subject areas and for students of different ages), and identifying the prerequisites that would be required.

The development of the program was significantly influenced by the work of the Institute for Research on Teaching (IRT), housed at Michigan State University and codirected by Judith Lanier and Lee Shulman, and later the Teacher Assessment Development Project (TAP), housed at Stanford University, led by Lee Shulman. The IRT researchers were exploring conceptions of teacher preparation and assessment that went beyond the skills acquisition model favored at the time. Shulman and his colleagues were influenced by observations of assessments used for other professions, particularly emergency medicine, which had recently incorporated simulations and performance assessments, though not on a large scale. Investigation of the methods used to assess and certify professionals in other fields inspired their thinking about possibilities for assessing teachers in more sophisticated ways. This thinking had been laid out in a 1986 paper that described a research plan for adapting this work to the field of teaching, and TAP was formed to carry out the work and to develop assessment prototypes that could assist the board in its work (Shulman and Sykes, 1986; Sykes and Wilson, 1988).

At the time, the multiple-choice National Teachers Examination (NTE) offered by the ETS was the principal instrument available for assessing teachers' competence, but it was widely viewed as too simplistic to effectively identify teachers of high quality. Moreover, the NTE was an assessment for teachers entering the profession and not intended to certify experienced teachers with advanced skills. TAP researchers sought to build an assessment of teaching around the challenges that teachers actually encounter in the classroom. They focused on ways teachers could present portfolios that could be scored in a standardized way but that would reflect collaboration with colleagues and other typical components of effective teaching.

The new portfolio assessment was designed to move past the ordinary conception that coaching or sharing ideas with others would undermine validity. Teachers were encouraged to consult with their peers and share ideas as they prepared their portfolios and to incorporate those activities into their written reflections. Thus, there was no need to control "cheating," although teachers did need to verify that all the written pieces were entirely their own work. This feature was particularly important because it reflected the assessment's focus on teachers' analytical skills, not simply their factual or technical knowledge.

Portfolio assessment was in its infancy at this time, and it had not yet been adopted for certification testing, so many challenges remained. Other kinds of performance assessments had been used effectively in other situations. For example, medical schools had been using Objective Structured Clinical Examinations (OSCE) to appraise medical students' clinical skills, such as communication, clinical examination, medical procedures, prescribing, and interpretation of results—often using actors as patients in simulated clinical situations. Efforts to use performance assessments to evaluate the skills of U.S. soldiers were also under way. Pilot work by the National Board of Medical Examiners investigated the value and feasibility of including an OSCE-like component in the medical licensure exam, although this component did not become operational until 2006 (http://www.nbme.org).

In the field of teaching, performance assessments were also being successfully used on a small scale to appraise the skills of teachers in training. For example, Alverno College had implemented a coherent program of performance assessments that took place during teachers' undergraduate preparation and culminated in the preparation of a portfolio. Thus, at the time, there was momentum to push forward the measurement field, particularly certification practices, and to move toward forms of assessment that were more authentic than the typical multiple-choice test.

The national board's Technical Analysis Group, chaired by Richard Jaeger at the University of North Carolina at Greensboro, was formed to bring additional psychometric expertise to bear on assessment design challenges that the board faced, such as developing tasks that would be comparable across assessment years; setting performance standards and cut scores for the assessments; designing ways to score the assessments that would yield valid and reliable scores; piloting the scoring and standard-setting procedures; evaluating issues of fairness, such as possible adverse impact on particular population subgroups; and conducting validation studies. The Technical Analysis Group, which was composed primarily of well-known experts in measurement and which frequently sought out additional expertise to address specific questions, existed from 1992 until 1996. Important questions about how such technology as videotaping could best be used, what kinds of impact the use of that technology might have on teachers from varying backgrounds, and many other issues were resolved in this period. A series of studies sponsored by the Spencer Foundation supported this effort.

In 1996, the national board issued a request for proposals and contracted with the ETS to assume operational development of the program of assessments. From 1997 to the writing of this report,[6] the ETS served as the test development contractor for the board. NBPTS also convenes various technical oversight panels to advise on technical issues related to the assessment.

Development of Content Standards

Among the national board's most important first tasks was to define its "vision of accomplished practice," which was issued in 1989 under the heading "What Teachers Should Know and Be Able to Do" and continues to guide the program's standards and assessments (National Board for Professional Teaching Standards, 1999). Two researchers, Suzanne Wilson and Gary Sykes, former students of TAP director Lee Shulman, served as consultants to the board of directors on this task. Previously, no substantial attempt had been made to pull the views of quality teaching that had been proposed into a unified conception.

Drawing on the work of the TAP, the group began with the assumption that accomplished teachers make use of a set of skills and knowledge (of students and pedagogy and of the content they teach) that are acquired through schooling, experience, the influence of colleagues, and other sources (Sykes and Wilson, 1988). Teachers' proficiency develops and improves over time, and their focus was on the attributes of experienced teachers. The board posited (National Board for Professional Teaching Standards, 1999, p. 4):

> The fundamental requirements for proficient teaching are relatively clear: a broad grounding in the liberal arts and sciences; knowledge of the subjects to be taught, of the skills to be developed, and of the curricular arrangements and materials that organize and embody that content; knowledge of general and subject-specific methods for teaching and for evaluating student learning; knowledge of students and human development; skills in effectively teaching students from racially, ethnically, and socio-economically diverse backgrounds; and the skills, capacities and dispositions to employ such knowledge wisely in the interest of students.

---

[6]The board has recently changed test development contractors.

From that foundation, the board of directors identified five core propositions, the characteristics that certification would "identify and recognize" in teachers:

1. Teachers are committed to students and their learning.
2. Teachers know the subjects they teach and how to teach those subjects to students.
3. Teachers are responsible for managing and monitoring student learning.
4. Teachers think systematically about their practice and learn from experience.
5. Teachers are members of learning communities.

In the view of James A. Kelly, the national board's first president, this document (the core propositions and their supporting text, shown in Box 3-3) was "a historic statement for what good teaching should be and represented a remarkable consensus" (Keller, 2006). The core propositions would guide the development of assessments in numerous areas, with a structure of certificates sorted by both the grade or age span of the students and the subject matter.

The vision developed by the board incorporates a number of contemporary ideas about professional practice, particularly theories proposed about the role that reflecting on one's practice can play in many professions (Schön, 1983). The term "reflection" was used to refer to the complex interplay of cognitive elements—including practical experience, theoretical knowledge, the capacity to improvise on the spot, and the capacity to learn effectively from experience—that constitute professional excellence. This concept became a cornerstone of the board's vision of accomplished teaching.

In 1993, the assessments for the first certificate were ready, and the first set of teachers earned board certification during the 1993-1994 school year. By the 2006-2007 school year, approximately 63,800 teachers had earned board certification.

Other Influences

Other developments that have taken place since the board's founding have had an impact on its progress. For example, the Interstate New Teacher Assessment and Support Consortium has worked to improve the preparation of new teachers, and the NCATE has focused on the educational quality of the programs that prepare teachers. Both of these groups have worked to align their standards with those developed by the national

BOX 3-3
The Five Core Propositions

1. Teachers are committed to students and their learning:
   • teachers recognize individual differences in their students and adjust their practice accordingly;
   • teachers have an understanding of how students develop and learn;
   • teachers treat students equitably; and
   • teachers' mission extends beyond developing the cognitive capacity of their students.

2. Teachers know the subjects they teach and how to teach those subjects to students:
   • teachers appreciate how knowledge in their subjects is created, organized, and linked to other disciplines;
   • teachers command specialized knowledge of how to convey a subject to students; and
   • teachers generate multiple paths to knowledge.

3. Teachers are responsible for managing and monitoring student learning:
   • teachers call on multiple methods to meet their goals;
   • teachers orchestrate learning in group settings;
   • teachers place a premium on student engagement;
   • teachers regularly assess student progress; and
   • teachers are mindful of their principal objectives.

4. Teachers think systematically about their practice and learn from experience:
   • teachers are continually making difficult choices that test their judgment; and
   • teachers seek the advice of others and draw on education research and scholarship to improve their practice.

5. Teachers are members of learning communities:
   • teachers contribute to school effectiveness by collaborating with other professionals;
   • teachers work collaboratively with parents; and
   • teachers take advantage of community resources.

SOURCE: Reprinted with permission from the National Board for Professional Teaching Standards (http://www.nbpts.org). All rights reserved.

board. Together with the NBPTS, these organizations are sometimes referred to as the "three-legged stool" of teacher quality (Bradley, 1997).

The nation's teachers unions have also played a part in the growth and
development of the board (Ballou and Podgursky, 2000; Hannaway and
Bischoff, 2005). Both the National Education Association (NEA) and the
American Federation of Teachers (AFT) were supportive of certification
for accomplished teachers from the beginning. Longtime AFT president
Al Shanker was a vocal supporter, although Mary Futrell, president of the
NEA at the time the board was founded and a member of the Carnegie task
force, was more hesitant. She was concerned that some of the task force's
conclusions and recommendations implied that existing teachers were not
performing adequately; however, in the end she endorsed the overall plan.
Union involvement was built into the bylaws of the organization, so that
the NBPTS board of directors would always include a number of teachers
who were union members. Both unions continue to be supportive of the
national board, despite their general resistance to differentiated compensation systems for teachers. A more recent influence on policy discussions
of teacher quality has been the federal No Child Left Behind Act of 2001.
Among the act's provisions is the requirement that all public school teachers
of core subjects (which includes reading, math, science, history, and geog-
raphy, among others) must be "highly qualified." The legislation specifies
that teachers should have a bachelor's degree, be fully licensed, and not
have been excused from any licensure requirements (U.S. Department of
Education, 2001). It also requires that they demonstrate competence in the
field in which they teach.

States have devised with a variety of ways to meet this requirement,
which focus primarily on the credentials of beginning teachers (Education
Commission of the States, 2004; National Council on Teacher Quality,
2004). The national board has proposed that its standards for accomplished
teaching provide an excellent blueprint for a more ambitious conception
of the attributes that highly qualified teachers should have (Dilworth et
al., 2006). Others have also suggested that board-certified teachers are
an important resource in this context and that linking board certification
with the legislative requirements would be an important way for states to
reap additional benefits from their investments in encouraging teachers to
become certified (Rotherham, 2004).

Obstacles to the National Board's Progress

A variety of circumstances have proved to be significant obstacles to
the board's achievement of its goals. The nation as well as individual states
have experienced shortages of teachers because of rapid population growth
in some regions, tough competition from other employment sectors, and

other factors. In times of shortage, states and districts have historically lowered requirements to allow people who might not otherwise have qualified to enter teaching. This pressure has worked against the push for raising standards for teachers. Shortages have been a particular problem for urban school districts, as well as in certain fields (particularly special education, mathematics, and science), and the problem has, in turn, exacerbated the unequal distribution of highly qualified teachers. The standard response to teacher shortages by policy makers has been to focus away from the development and recognition of teachers with advanced skills, in favor of measures to identify enough entry-level teachers to fill vacancies (Ingersoll, 2001).

Another factor that has impeded the board's progress has been a push to deregulate teacher education. The goal of privatizing public education, advanced primarily by politically conservative groups, has included an effort to expand responsibility for the preparation of teachers beyond the traditional providers, schools and colleges of education (see, e.g., Friedman, 1995; Zeichner, 2003), and has also created alternate routes to teaching, which some observers claim have watered down the standards for entering teachers (Walsh and Jacobs, 2007). Since the board's approach is premised on the value of building alignment among the entities that influence teacher quality, particularly between the goals for preparing new teachers and the goals that will guide experienced teachers toward certification, this development does not serve the board's interests.

Perhaps the most serious obstacle has been posed by some of the cultural traditions in the field of teaching in the United States. Researchers who have examined the culture of teaching from a sociological perspective have identified several characteristics that are to varying degrees antithetical to the approach advocated in the national board standards.

Teachers in the United States are not generally taught or encouraged to share their practice. Researchers who have studied teaching in other cultures have highlighted strong traditions in which teachers publicly share professional knowledge and actively collaborate to help one another improve and develop (Hiebert, Gallimore, and Stigler, 2002; Stigler and Hiebert, 1997; Wang and Paine, 2003). It is common in Japan, for example, for teachers to observe and critique one another's lessons and to meet regularly to discuss their practice and critique their own and others' work (Lewis and Tsuchida, 1998). This practice allows teachers to develop both a shared language with which to talk about their experiences and a shared base of professional knowledge. Similar practices are used in other countries as well, but they have not been the norm in the United States. Stigler and Hiebert, who led a videotape study of teaching in several countries as part of the Third International Mathematics and Science Study, have pointed to significant cultural differences in the practices of teachers in different countries, noting that, in contrast to teachers in many other countries, U.S. teachers are "left alone" to figure things out for themselves (Stigler and Hiebert, 1997).

Researchers who have focused on the culture of teaching in the United States have reported similar findings. Teachers in the United States have tended to work as "entrepreneurs" who value self-reliance above cooperation and who rarely engage in the kind of active mentoring relationships that have been found effective in other cultures (Little, 1990; Lord, 1994; McLaughlin and Talbert, 2001). U.S. teachers do have many opportunities for certain kinds of collaboration, such as joint planning by grade level or subject matter. However, they rarely develop the kinds of professional learning communities that have been described by researchers as the most effective teaching environments (e.g., McLaughlin and Talbert, 2001). Teachers in the United States also have a strong tradition of egalitarianism, which has often resulted in significant resistance to strategies for recognizing and rewarding those who demonstrate excellence (Little, 1990; Lortie, 2002). Where this influence is strong, administrators who would like to reward merit may face a disgruntled and resistant staff, and they tend to back down. Finally, observers have noted that those attracted to teaching tend not to be risk-takers but rather to be somewhat conservative or cautious and somewhat resistant to change (Lortie, 2002).

The national board's standards and the requirements for earning certification directly challenge these cultural norms. The standards call on teachers to challenge familiar ways of doing things, to reflect collaboratively about their practice, to publicly demonstrate their teaching, and to highlight ways in which they are more accomplished than their colleagues. The reflection and collaboration the board standards describe represent a significant departure from the established culture of teaching in the United States.

THE POLICY CONTEXT

The planning and development of the national board occurred at a time when the value of challenging and meaningful standards for students was being recognized as a critical strategy for education reform. The logic behind the national board's strategy was to set high standards for teachers as a means for improving teacher quality and, hence, student learning. The board was one part of a comprehensive strategy intended to reform the education system and help students meet the demands of an information-based society. By fostering consensus regarding what constitutes high-quality teaching and highlighting and rewarding teachers who demonstrate those standards, the board was expected to have a significant impact on the overall caliber of U.S. teachers. By expanding expectations about what constitutes good teaching, the board was expected to bring teaching into the ranks of the true professions, improve its capacity to attract and retain high-quality personnel, all of which would serve to improve student learning.

The policy climate in which this evaluation is now being conducted is different in significant ways. A basic tension is now evident between two different ways of thinking about the question of teacher quality (Kraft, 2001). On one hand is a view of teachers as professional practitioners of a complex task, who should be supported in and rewarded for thinking for themselves, collaborating with colleagues, and taking responsibility for their own growth and development. This is the view that motivated the development of the national board and its standards and has grown to be widely shared in many circles (Hiebert et al., 2002; Koppich, Humphrey, and Hough, 2006; Richardson, 2001; Tucker, 1995).

On the other hand, an emphasis on standards and accountability has shifted public focus to the outcomes of teaching in which high-quality teaching is defined as that which produces student learning. The accountability movement has placed increased focus on the results from standardized tests as measures of student learning. The kinds of characteristics measured by the NBPTS assessment—such as the capacity to understand students' needs, reflect on one's practice, and collaborate with other teachers—have not been prominent in current policy approaches. While the board includes accountability for student learning as an important element of its approach, the attributes emphasized in its standards do not fit neatly into the current framing of accountability systems.

In the years since the national board was founded, states have intensified their focus on assessment results for students and measurable criteria for effective teaching, particularly in response to the No Child Left Behind Act of 2001. Increasingly, students' scores on standardized assessment have come to be viewed, especially at policy levels, as the only or best measure of the effectiveness of any educational intervention. However, this yardstick was not viewed in the same way at the time the national board was developed, and the program was not envisioned as a strategy whose primary purpose was to raise test scores. Standardized assessments do not lend themselves easily to the evaluation of the kinds of higher order skills that were at the heart of both *A Nation at Risk* and *A Nation Prepared*. The national board's conception of teaching was broad, seeking to develop teachers who, rather than drilling their students until they learned specific bodies of factual knowledge, would use their skills to challenge their students and enable them to achieve high standards considered more broadly.

Moreover, since the national board began its work, questions and debate regarding issues related to its mission—about teacher quality and preparation, teacher salaries and incentives, the influence of teachers unions, and the potential value of a range of approaches to reforming public education and improving student achievement, to name a few—have continued (e.g., Fenstermacher and Richardson, 2005). Numerous other reforms have been initiated since the board was founded, each of which has had effects on the circumstances the board has hoped to change. The national board continues to conduct its work in a complex environment, a factor we have borne in mind as we conducted our evaluation.

4

The Assessment Program

An important responsibility of the National Board for Professional Teaching Standards (NBPTS) is to operate its assessment program, although it also provides a number of services for board-certified teachers and prospective candidates. To learn about the board, its services, and the assessment process, we reviewed the information available on its web page (http://www.nbpts.org), information provided to candidates, and technical documentation about the assessment. We also visited the board's office, met with staff members, and arranged for briefings on specific topics, such as an orientation on what candidates must do as part of the certification process, an overview of the scoring process, and a review of studies that the board has funded. To learn more about the assessment and the scoring process, we arranged for a presentation by Steve Schreiner, the Educational Testing Service (ETS) staff member who leads the NBPTS portfolio scoring process, at our fifth committee meeting. At that time, we reviewed samples of the materials that teachers submit as part of their portfolio and viewed two sample videotapes.

In this chapter, we describe the board as an organization, the experience teachers undergo as they pursue board certification, the content standards that are assessed, the assessment exercises, and the scoring. We conclude the chapter with our observations from reviewing the sample portfolio materials and videotapes. The overview in this chapter is intended to provide a framework for the detailed psychometric analysis described in Chapter 5. The board now offers advanced-level certification in 25 areas. In this chapter and Chapter 5, we focus on two certificate areas, one generalist assessment (middle childhood generalist) and one subject-area assessment (middle childhood through early adolescent mathematics), for detailed examples and analysis. Our rationale for selecting these two certificate areas is explained in Chapter 5.

THE ORGANIZATION

The NBPTS is an independent, nonprofit, nonpartisan, and nongovernmental organization with a staff of approximately 60 located in Arlington, Virginia.[1] A 27-member board of directors, of whom 13 are board-certified teachers, oversees its work. During the early years of the board's work, foundations, corporations, and the federal government provided the bulk of its financial support; applicant fees now cover most of the board's operating costs.

A major responsibility of the NBPTS is the management and operation of the assessment program through which teachers earn certification. Running this program entails developing and updating standards for the 25 areas in which certification is offered and, with the assistance of the National Board's contractor, the ETS, developing, administering, and scoring the assessments.

Five standing committees (drawn from the board of directors) assist the board with its work. In addition to committees that oversee finances and other standard responsibilities, the board has an Education Committee that is responsible for identifying education reforms in which the board should involve itself and a Certification Council that develops policies related to areas in which certification is offered, standards, methods of certification, and other issues. Several groups drawn from outside the board's membership also offer support, including the Assessment Certification Advisory Panel, which advises the board on the technical aspects of its assessment; the Visiting Panel on NBPTS Research; the National Board-Certified Teachers Advisory Group (made up of 12 board-certified teachers), which reviews product plans and development; and the NBPTS President's Roundtable, a group of philanthropic, business, and community leaders who work to enhance the NBPTS profile.

The NBPTS offers a number of resources and supports for candidates and for board-certified teachers, such as a directory of teachers who have earned board certification and a state-by-state list of financial supports

---

[1]The NBPTS also employs 11 regional outreach directors who are responsible for building awareness of the program, and it has opened a facility in San Antonio, Texas, to handle customer service, candidate materials, and fee processing. Support is also provided by Candidate Subsidy Program Administrators (not NBPTS employees), who perform a variety of functions related to data collection and the disbursement of federal subsidies at the state level.

available to candidates and rewards to those who earn board certification. The board's website also provides an opportunity for board-certified teachers to network as well as a variety of information related to its work, including a list of research and other articles, press releases, advocacy pieces, links to other websites, and statistics, such as total board-certified teachers by state (http://www.nbpts.org/). A network affiliate program provides an avenue for board-certified teachers to work together and take on leadership roles in their districts and schools. Once they earn board certification, teachers are also encouraged to participate in scoring assessment exercises and to serve as mentors to other candidates. In addition, the board sponsors a national conference and exposition every other year, which provides an opportunity for board-certified teachers, candidates, and others to attend educational sessions and develop connections with education leaders. Approximately 900 people attended the 2007 conference, of whom about two-thirds were board-certified teachers.

With funding from federal and corporate sponsors, the board has also developed two programs designed to increase the diversity of the pool of board-certified teachers. The goal of the Targeted High Need Initiative program is to increase the number of board-certified teachers in high-poverty urban and rural schools. The Direct Recruiting Efforts to Attract Minorities Team highlights the importance of national board certification for minority teachers and their students.

The NBPTS has begun offering another option for educators who are interested in pursuing certification. The Take One® program (http://www.nbpts.org/products_and_services/take_one) allows teachers and counselors who are interested but not ready to commit to the certification process to submit a single portfolio entry for scoring. The board presents it as an opportunity to learn and grow as a teacher, as well as a way to sample the process. Teachers may later apply the scored portfolio entry to a complete application if they wish.

APPLYING FOR BOARD CERTIFICATION

To begin the process of earning board certification, a candidate must first establish that he or she is qualified to apply. The candidate must have completed a bachelor's degree, have completed at least three full years of teaching or counseling before beginning the application process, and have had a valid teaching or counseling license throughout that period.[2] After submitting documentation of eligibility, the candidate receives more

---

[2]A candidate who does not have a license may be eligible if he or she has been teaching in a school in which licensure is not required that is "recognized and approved to operate by the state" (http://www.nbpts.org).

detailed instructions about the procedures for completing the entire assessment. The candidate must also submit payment of the test fee, which is currently $2,500.

The assessment consists of 10 exercises administered in two parts: a computer-based assessment of content knowledge that includes 6 constructed-response exercises, and a portfolio that consists of 4 exercises. Responses to the computer-based exercises and the portfolios are scored at designated times during the year, so the time that elapses between submitting an application and receiving certification depends on the time of year the candidate initiates the process, as well as on how long he or she takes to complete the portfolios and schedule the computer-based assessment. National board staff estimate that the typical candidate spends up to 400 hours on the 10 exercises. Given the deadlines throughout the year and the volume of work to be included in the portfolios, most candidates complete the process in approximately 12 to 18 months, but the national board will allow candidates to take as long as 3 years to complete all of the requirements before voiding early scores and asking the candidate to start again.

The board offers certification in 16 content areas of specialization covering 7 age groupings, for a total of 25 individual certificates, as shown in Table 4-1. The certificate is effective for 10 years and then must be renewed.

THE CONTENT STANDARDS

In Chapter 3 we described the development of the board's five core propositions:

1. Teachers are committed to students and their learning.
2. Teachers know the subjects they teach and how to teach those subjects to students.
3. Teachers are responsible for managing and monitoring student learning.
4. Teachers think systematically about their practice and learn from experience.
5. Teachers are members of learning communities.

Although there are detailed content standards for each of the 25 fields for which certification is available, all of the certification-specific standards and assessments are based on these five core propositions. The content standards for each certification area are described in detailed booklets that are posted on the NBPTS website. Each standards document begins with an overview of the board's approach to determining and structuring its standards and then an introduction to the main issues pertaining to the certification area. All of the individual standards are presented in a two-part format: a definition of the standards, or standards statement, followed by elaboration.

In the next sections, we briefly describe the standards for these two areas of certification: middle childhood generalist and middle childhood and early adolescence mathematics (National Board for Professional Teaching Standards, 1998, 2001c).

Standards for Middle Childhood Generalist

There are 11 content standards for the middle childhood generalist certificate. Box 4-1 lists the main standards; the standards document for this certificate provides additional details (see http://www.nbpts.org/the_standards/standards_by_cert?ID=27&x=40&y=7), including an elaboration of what is intended by each. The structure is consistent across fields: a standard statement describes key aspects of accomplished practice in the certificate area in terms of "observable actions of teacher that have an impact on their students" (National Board for Professional Teaching Standards, 2001c). This statement is followed by elaboration, which provides an explanation of what accomplished teachers need to know and demonstrate in order to meet the standard.

The elaboration of the first standard for this certificate—knowledge of students—explains that middle childhood generalists who meet this standard "understand and appreciate the ways in which each student is unique as well as the commonalities of middle school students" and are "keen observers of students." The elaboration provides examples of how these attributes are demonstrated. For example, teachers who understand the developmental status of children in middle childhood "know the importance of working at a concrete level, providing material such as maps, timelines, manipulatives, and tools for organizing and interpreting data." Recognizing the importance of opportunities both to evaluate and analyze and to learn meaningful facts, such teachers "directly teach techniques for locating, retaining, and using facts." Similarly detailed elaboration is provided for each of the 11 standards.

The middle childhood generalist is expected to teach a variety of subjects so the elaboration for Standard 2—knowledge of content and curriculum—describes what such teachers need to know in six subjects (English/language arts, mathematics, science, social studies, the arts, and health) and also describes how they would be expected to use this knowledge. For example, an elaboration of this standard for English/language arts indicates that the accomplished teacher will "use a wide range of response activities, such as journals, dramatic productions, and stories, for the pur-

TABLE 4-1 Areas of National Board Certification

	Early Childhood (ages 3-8)	Middle Childhood (ages 7-12)	Early and Middle Childhood (ages 3-12)	Early Childhood Through Young Adulthood (ages 3-18+)	Early Adolescence (ages 11-15)	Adolescence and Young Adulthood (ages 14-18+)	Early Adolescence Through Young Adulthood (ages 11-18+)
Art			x				x
Career and technical education							x
English as a new language			x				x
English language arts						x	
Exceptional needs specialist				x			
Generalist	x	x					
Health Education							x

Library media

Literacy:
reading-
language arts

Mathematics

Music

Physical
education

School
counseling

Science

Social
studies-history

World
languages other
than English

SOURCE: See http://www.nbpts.org.

BOX 4-1
Content Standards for Middle Childhood Generalist

1. *Knowledge of Students.* Accomplished teachers draw on their knowledge of child development and their relationships with students to understand their students' abilities, interests, aspirations, and values.

2. *Knowledge of Content and Curriculum.* Accomplished teachers draw on their knowledge of subject matter and curriculum to make sound decisions about what is important for students to learn within and across the subject areas of the middle childhood curriculum.

3. *Learning Environment.* Accomplished teachers establish a caring, inclusive, stimulating, and safe school community where students can take intellectual risks, practice democracy, and work collaboratively and independently.

4. *Respect for Diversity.* Accomplished teachers help students learn to respect and appreciate individual and group differences.

5. *Instructional Resources.* Accomplished teachers create, assess, select, and adapt a rich and varied collection of materials and draw on other resources such as staff, community members, and students to support learning.

6. *Meaningful Applications of Knowledge.* Accomplished teachers engage students in learning within and across the disciplines and help students understand how the subjects they study can be used to explore important issues in their lives and the world around them.

7. *Meaningful Paths to Knowledge.* Accomplished teachers provide students with multiple paths needed to learn the central concepts in each school subject, explore important themes and topics that cut across subject areas, and build overall knowledge and understanding.

8. *Assessment.* Accomplished teachers understand the strengths and weaknesses of different assessment methods, base their instruction on ongoing assessment, and encourage students to monitor their own learning.

9. *Family Involvement.* Accomplished teachers initiate positive, interactive relationships with families as they participate in the education of their children.

10. *Reflection.* Accomplished teachers regularly analyze, evaluate, reflect on, and strengthen the effectiveness and quality of their practice.

11. *Contributions to the Profession.* Accomplished teachers work with colleagues to improve schools and to advance knowledge and practice in their field.

SOURCE: National Board for Professional Teaching Standards (2001c). Reprinted with permission from the National Board for Professional Teaching Standards, http://www.nbpts.org. All rights reserved.

pose of ongoing assessment" and will "incorporate their students' language strategies and skills into other areas of the curriculum." The elaboration for this standard is particularly extensive because it treats each field in turn at a similar level of detail.

Standards for Middle Childhood and Early Adolescence Mathematics

The 12 standards for middle childhood and early adolescence mathematics follow the same format as those for the middle childhood generalist (the standards document is available at http://www.nbpts.org/the_standards/standards_by_cert?ID=8&x=37&y=10). Because all of the standards derive from the board's five core propositions, the standard statements, shown in Box 4-2, identify similar goals, such as knowledge of students, tailored to the subject matter and age range targeted. For example, Standard 2 for middle childhood and early adolescence mathematics is similar but not identical to the corresponding standard for middle childhood generalists. The elaboration of this standard for the mathematics certificate addresses such issues as "the differing ways in which students process information on their path to understanding mathematics." The elaboration notes, for example, that accomplished mathematics teachers are able to "understand a student's misconception, identify the underlying rationale, and clarify the student's thinking," and also understand the developmental changes that take place between the ages of 7 and 15 and are able to "factor this developmental knowledge into their instructional planning." Such a teacher would recognize that students at the upper end of this range could tackle a complex, multistep problem, but that younger students may have more difficulty with this type of task.

THE ASSESSMENT

Assessment Center Exercises

Candidates' mastery of the content necessary for accomplished teaching in their field is assessed by means of a computer-based assessment consisting of six individual 30-minute exercises taken at a designated testing center. The board contracts with a vendor to establish centers throughout the country so that 90 percent of candidates do not need to travel more than 60 miles. Candidates can take the assessment center exercises between July 1 and June 15. The NBPTS posts scoring guides on its website to assist candidates in understanding what will be expected of them; these describe several sample exercises and provide discussion of how responses are scored (see http://www.nbpts.org/for_candidates/scoring?ID=27&x=39&y=9 for the middle childhood generalist scoring guide and http://www.nbpts.org/for_candidates/scoring?ID=8&x=38&y=8 for the early adolescence mathematics scoring guide).

These assessment exercises focus primarily on the candidates' knowledge of the content important for the area in which they seek certification, although some questions cover pedagogical strategies. For the middle child-

BOX 4-2
Content Standards for Middle Childhood
Through Early Adolescence Mathematics

CREATING A PRODUCTIVE LEARNING ENVIRONMENT

1. *Commitment to Equity and Access*
Accomplished mathematics teachers value and acknowledge the individuality and worth of each student; they believe that all students can learn and should have access to the full mathematics curriculum; and they demonstrate these beliefs in their practice by systematically providing all students equitable and complete access to math.

KNOWLEDGE OF STUDENTS, MATHEMATICS, AND TEACHING

2. *Knowledge of Students*
Accomplished mathematics teachers recognize that students are shaped by a variety of educational, social, and cultural backgrounds and experiences that influence learning. They draw on knowledge of how students learn and develop in order to understand students and to guide curricula and instructional decision.

3. *Knowledge of Mathematics*
Accomplished mathematics teachers draw on their broad knowledge of mathematics to shape their teaching and set curricular goals. They understand significant connections among mathematics ideas and the application of those ideas not only with mathematics but also to other disciplines and the world outside of school.

4. *Knowledge of Teaching Practice*
Accomplished mathematics teachers rely on their extensive pedagogical knowledge to make curricular decisions, select instructional strategies, develop instructional plans, and formulate assessment plans.

ADVANCING STUDENT LEARNING

5. *The Art of Teaching*
Accomplished mathematics teachers create elegant and powerful approaches to instructional challenges. Their practice reflects a highly developed personal synthesis of their caring for students, their passion for teaching and math, understanding of mathematics content, ability to apply math, and rich knowledge of established and innovative educational practices.

6. *Learning Environment*
Accomplished mathematics teachers create stimulating, caring, and inclusive environments. They develop communities of involved learners in which students accept responsibility for learning, take intellectual risks, develop confidence and self-esteem, work independently and collaboratively, and value math.

7. *Using Math*

Accomplished mathematics teachers help students develop a positive disposition for mathematics and foster the development of all students' abilities to use mathematics as a way to understand the world around them. They focus instruction on developing students' mathematics power by providing opportunities for students to understand and apply mathematics concepts; investigate, explore, and discover structures and relationships; demonstrate flexibility and perseverance in solving problems; create and use mathematics models; formulate problems of their own; and justify and communicate their conclusions.

8. *Technology and Instructional Resources*

Accomplished mathematics teachers are knowledgeable about and, where available, use current technologies and other resources to promote student learning in math. They select, adapt, and create engaging instructional materials and draw on human resources from the school and the community to enhance and extend students' understanding and use of math.

9. *Assessment*

Accomplished mathematics teachers integrate assessment into their instruction to promote the learning of all students. They design, select, and employ a range of formal and informal assessment tools to match their educational purposes. They help students develop self-assessment skills, encouraging them to reflect on their performance.

PROFESSIONAL DEVELOPMENT AND OUTREACH

10. *Reflection and Growth*

Accomplished mathematics teachers regularly reflect on teaching and learning. They keep abreast of changes in mathematics and in mathematical pedagogy, continually increasing their knowledge and improving their practice.

11. *Families and Communities*

Accomplished mathematics teachers work to involve families in their children's education, help the community understand the role of mathematics and mathematics instruction in today's world, and, to the extent possible, involve the community in support of instruction.

12. *Professional Community*

Accomplished mathematics teachers collaborate with peers and other education professionals to strengthen the school's program, promote program quality and continuity across grade levels, advance knowledge in the field of mathematics education, and improve practice within the field.

SOURCE: National Board for Professional Teaching Standards (1998). Reprinted with permission from the National Board for Professional Teaching Standards, http://www.nbpts.org. All rights reserved.

hood generalist certificate, the six exercises measure the ability to support reading skills, analyze student work, and integrate the arts, as well as knowledge of science, social studies, and health. For the middle childhood and early adolescence mathematics certificate, the six exercises measure candidates' understanding of six areas (algebra and functions, connections, data analysis, geometry, number and operation sense, and technology and manipulatives) with an emphasis on the capacity to draw inferences and apply knowledge to real-world circumstances (National Board for Professional Teaching Standards, 2006b,c).

For example, in a sample exercise for the middle childhood generalist certificate, the candidate is asked to imagine that he or she is working with a group of third grade students of mixed ability and to read a passage and a transcription of a student's oral reading of the passage. The candidate then responds to four prompts that explicitly ask him or her to identify errors, cite examples from the student's text to support analysis of the student's skills, describe strategies for addressing the errors, and provide a rationale for using these strategies.

An example from the early adolescence mathematics assessments shows a similar assessment approach in a different context. The scoring guide for this exercise, which covers data analysis, explains that candidates must present:

- a complete and accurate graphical representation of a given set of data;
- a meaningful interpretation of the data based on the graphical representation;
- an appropriate and accurate alternate graphical representation of the data; and
- a meaningful, accurate, and distinct interpretation of the data based on its alternate graphical representation.

For the exercise, the candidate is provided with some data on high-grossing movies. The candidate is asked to create a box-and-whisker plot to display the data, to discuss the skewing of the data, and then to produce an alternate representation of the data and answer a question about it.

Portfolio Exercises

The portfolio component of the assessment is intended to allow candidates to demonstrate their teaching practice and expertise in several ways. Most certificates require candidates to submit:

- one classroom-based entry with accompanying student work,

- two classroom-based entries that require videorecordings of inter-actions between candidates and their students, and
- one documented accomplishments entry that provides evidence of the candidate's accomplishments outside the classroom and how that work impacts student learning.

The specific instructions for these portfolio exercises are as follows (National Board for Professional Teaching Standards, 2007, p. 19):

Classroom-based entries: Each entry requires some direct evidence of practice as well as a commentary describing, analyzing, and reflecting on this evidence. This commentary requires the teacher to set the work in context and to provide the wider goals for that particular class; and provides an opportunity for the teacher to reflect critically on practice, thus, permitting the raters to see if what the teacher writes about goals or outcomes mirrors what is seen in the evidence of practice. The video, student work or other submitted artifacts, and the commentary support each other in providing evidence of a teacher's in-class practice. These three entries are specifically designed for each certificate area, though there is significant commonality in the structure of entries from certificate to certificate.
Documented accomplishment entry: The entry requires that candidates illustrate partnerships with students' families and community and development as a learner and collaborator with other professionals by submitting descriptions and documentation of activities and accomplishments in those areas that impact student learning.

All of the evidence to be included in the portfolio must be collected within the 12 months preceding the submission deadline. After initiating the application process, the candidate receives a portfolio kit that includes detailed instructions for videotaping lessons and preparing the portfolio, as well as labeling the submission, shipping, and handling other logistics. Candidates are encouraged to videotape many lessons, both to make sure they and their students are comfortable in the presence of the camera and to ensure that they have plenty of videos to choose from as they prepare the submission.

The elements of the portfolio are designed as an integrated set of evidence both of how the candidate approaches teaching and of the ways in which he or she describes, analyzes, and reflects on that practice. Instructions to candidates emphasize that the materials they submit should provide evidence of their mastery of the five core propositions, and specifically, the NBPTS standards for their certification area. Thus, one of the written entries gives the candidate an opportunity to demonstrate understanding of his or her students, the goals for the teaching shown in the accompanying videos, and the strategies he or she intended to use. Another is intended to elicit evidence of how thoughtfully the candidate reflects afterward on the teaching interactions he or she has chosen to submit.

The NBPTS raters, who work to score the materials that teachers submit, view the videos and evaluate the extent to which the candidate demonstrates the NBPTS standards for the certification area, particularly how well he or she knows the students and the subject matter, knows how to teach the subject matter, and can reflect with insight on and learn from his or her teaching experiences. These materials are supplemented with samples of students' work related to the lesson shown and additional written commentary on what that student work demonstrates and how the candidate used and responded to it.

Although the portfolios for all certification areas require the same kinds of exercises, the specific instructions to candidates are tailored for each certification area to elicit evidence that they meet the standards outlined for that field. For example, the portfolio instructions for the middle childhood generalist certificate specify that the teacher must include a videotaped lesson plus written commentary and instructional materials that demonstrate his or her ability to "sustain a classroom environment that supports students' growth, learning, social and emotional development, and emerging abilities to understand and consider perspectives other than their own through a social/history theme, issue, or topic" in the context of a social studies lesson (National Board for Professional Teaching Standards, 2006a,e). The description of a Level 4 entry for this exercise is shown in Box 4-3.

In another example, the first portfolio submission for the early adolescence mathematics certificate focuses on developing and assessing mathematical thinking and reasoning (National Board for Professional Teaching Standards, 2006d). For this entry, candidates are instructed to "demonstrate how the design and implementation of an instructional sequence or unit of study works to inform you of students' knowledge and furthers students understanding of a substantive idea in mathematics." The instructions ask them to present "evidence of your ability to plan and implement instruction to facilitate your students' understanding of an important idea in mathematics" and go on to provide details about exactly what they should submit. The description of a Level 4 entry for this prompt is shown in Box 4-4.

Scoring the Assessment

Candidates are given detailed descriptions of the criteria the raters use in evaluating both the assessment center and the portfolio exercises. Each

---

BOX 4-3
Level 4 Scoring Rubric for "Building a Classroom
Community Through Social Studies" Portfolio Entry

The Level 4 performance provides clear, consistent, and convincing evidence that the teacher is able to create a stimulating learning climate that supports students' emerging abilities to understand and consider perspectives other than their own through a social studies/history theme, issue, or topic, and to assume responsibility for their actions.

The Level 4 response provides clear, consistent, and convincing evidence that the teacher understands child development and knows the backgrounds, abilities, interests, aspirations, and values of her or his students, which is evidenced by the detailed descriptions of the students and the compelling rationale behind the strategies for encouraging students to consider a range of perspectives and to enable students to take responsibility for their own actions. There is clear, consistent, and convincing evidence that the strategies employed by the teacher foster students' emerging abilities to understand and respect individual and group differences, to consider a range of perspectives other than their own, and to assume intellectual and social responsibility. The Level 4 response provides clear evidence that the teacher can establish an equitable, accessible, and fair classroom community where students can take intellectual risks and work collaboratively. The response contains clear, consistent, and convincing evidence that the teacher can plan, organize, and facilitate students' active participation in a meaningful discussion that develops their expression of ideas and opinions, their consideration of others' points of view, and their assumption of responsibility for their own actions. There is clear evidence of the teacher's ability to engage in reflective thinking about her or his instructional practice, to support instructional decisions, to articulate a strong rationale for pedagogical actions, and to make decisions that will strengthen the quality of her or his future practice. Overall, there is clear, consistent, and convincing evidence that the teacher is able to create a stimulating learning climate that supports students' emerging abilities to understand and consider perspectives other than their own through a social studies/history theme, issue, or topic, and to assume responsibility for their actions.

SOURCE: National Board for Professional Teaching Standards (2006b). Reprinted with permission from the National Board for Professional Teaching Standards, http://www.nbpts.org. All rights reserved.

---

exercise is assigned a score ranging from 1 to 4; generally, a score of 3 represents passing performance, and a score of 2 is considered below the accomplished level. The scores on each exercise are weighted and combined as follows: each classroom-based entry exercise is weighted 16 percent, the documented accomplishment exercise is weighted 12 percent, and each of the six assessment center exercises is weighted 6.67 percent. The weighted

---

BOX 4-4
Level 4 Scoring Rubric for "Developing and Assessing
Mathematical Thinking and Reasoning" Portfolio Entry

The Level 4 performance provides clear, consistent, and convincing evidence that the teacher is able to design a sequence of learning experiences that builds on, and gives insight into, students' conceptual understanding of a substantive idea in mathematics within the context of instruction that enhances students' abilities to think and reason mathematically.

The Level 4 performance provides clear, consistent, and convincing evidence that the teacher sets high, worthwhile, and appropriate learning goals for students based on detailed knowledge of students' interest, abilities, and needs and that he or she connects the instructional sequence to these goals. The Level 4 response provides evidence that the instructional activities are placed in the larger context of instruction that is designed to enhance student learning in mathematics. The Level 4 response features clear, consistent, and convincing evidence that the instructional sequence includes activities that are sequenced and organized to develop understanding of a substantive mathematical idea as the sequence unfolds while building on students' interest and prior knowledge. The featured activities clearly and consistently promote mathematical reasoning on the part of students and are effective in eliciting responses that can affect instruction. There is clear, consistent, and convincing evidence of the teacher's deliberate intent to build students' conceptual understanding through the strength of the connections between each of the featured activities and the substantive mathematical idea as well as the connection between the two featured activities. The Level 4 response provides clear, consistent, and convincing evidence that the teacher is able to in-

---

scores are combined, producing a score scale that ranges from 1 to 400, with the passing score set at 275. Candidates who do not earn a passing score on their first attempt are allowed to persevere in their attempts to earn certification for up to 24 months after receiving the first score. These candidates may retain any scores and reattempt only those components on which they scored less than 2.75.

All submissions are scored by trained raters, who are teachers in the field for which they are scoring (they are not required to be board certified). The raters are trained using sample submissions scored in previous years, and they are overseen by experienced trainers who are also teachers in the field. The training covers not only the scoring rubric but also possible sources of bias—including, for example, the professional bias that might unconsciously influence a rater who has strong views about how particular material should be taught.

tegrate assessment into instruction and use strategies to probe and push students' mathematical thinking, particularly by providing feedback that includes targeted questions or instructive comments designed to encourage students to use and develop appropriate mathematical written communication, reasoning, and thinking. The analysis of student responses is detailed, specific, and accurate, showing differentiated insight into individual students' learning over time. The feedback and next steps provided to students are rich, detailed, and instructive, moving students toward greater understanding of the featured mathematical concept. There is clear and consistent evidence of the connections among the concept of study, the instructional activities, the analysis of student responses, and the appropriate feedback and next steps for students. There is clear, consistent, and convincing evidence of the teacher's own knowledge of mathematics and mathematics pedagogy, as shown through the selection of the concept, the way it is taught, and the teacher's analysis and response to student work. The Level 4 response offers clear, consistent, and convincing evidence that the teacher is able to accurately describe his or her own practice, analyze it fully and thoughtfully, and reflect on its implications and significance for future practice. Overall, the Level 4 performance provides clear, consistent, and convincing evidence that the teacher is able to design a sequence of learning experiences that builds on, and gives insight into, students' conceptual understanding of a substantive idea in mathematics within the context of instruction that enhances students' abilities to think and reason mathematically.

SOURCE: National Board for Professional Teaching Standards (2006b). Reprinted with permission from the National Board for Professional Teaching Standards, http://www.nbpts.org. All rights reserved.

Committee Comments on Two Video Portfolios

At our fifth meeting, committee members had the opportunity to view two samples of teachers' submissions for the portfolio exercises required for board certification in the area of adolescence and young adulthood English language arts. We reviewed both the written and videotaped materials submitted by the two teachers. To protect the teachers' privacy, we viewed these materials under secure conditions, with each teacher's identity, as well as any information that would reveal the identity of the students, obscured.[3] The presentation was intended to help us understand the certification process for candidates, the scoring, and the nature of the assessment.

---

[3]In arranging with the NBPTS to review these materials, we agreed to certain terms to protect teachers' and students' privacy. Specifically, the committee had access to these materials only during the secure review session, which was led by NBPTS staff. All materials were returned to the NBPTS at the end of the session, and any written notes were destroyed. Committee members agreed not to disclose any information that would reveal teachers' or students' identity or would reveal secure information about the test.

Despite the information we had already reviewed about the assessment and the standards, we were struck by the richness of what was captured in the videos. Reading about the portfolio exercises and the way they are scored had not fully conveyed to us the kind of information that could be learned from the videos. Readers who have had the opportunity to view videos of teachers in action, perhaps in the context of the Third International Mathematics and Science Study, may appreciate how informative they can be. Several aspects of the national board video portfolio process are worth highlighting.

During the presentation, the committee saw excerpts from the submissions of two teachers. The candidates had been asked to describe in writing the school in which they teach and the group of students shown in the taped lesson. They also discussed the purpose of the lesson, the strategies they had used, and their thoughts about how the lesson actually went. Because candidates are encouraged to videotape many hours of lessons and are completely at liberty in choosing the lessons they would like assessors to see, the tape submitted is considered to be exemplary of the candidate's practice and of the points he or she makes in the written pieces.

In arranging the presentation, we asked to see the portfolio submissions of a teacher who had passed the assessment and one who had failed, although we asked not to be told which was which before we completed our reviews. Below we provide our observations about these materials and summarize the skills each teacher demonstrated. Out of consideration for teachers' and students' privacy and to abide by the confidentiality terms to which we agreed, we do not go into explicit detail about what we observed but instead try to give the reader a general sense of the differences between the lesson presented by Teacher A, who passed, and Teacher B, who did not. To the extent possible, we connect our observations to the standards for the adolescence and young adulthood English language arts certificate (standards are available at http://www.nbpts.org/the_standards/standards_by_cert?ID=2&x=17&y=13).

Teacher A's lesson focused on a contemporary play that involved interpreting abstract material and existential ideas. In his written materials, Teacher A described the students as being generally below grade level and noted that many had learning problems. He had made this assignment because the play was relatively easy to read, even though the ideas were sophisticated and abstract. The videotaped lesson demonstrated that he was able to engage them in an extended classwide discussion of substantive themes about the reading assignment. Teacher A demonstrated a clear command of the material he was presenting to the students, and he deftly guided the conversation so that students identified the key themes in the play. He demonstrated skill at engaging all of the students in the discussion and effectively used strategies to encourage all to participate. All of the students seemed attentive during the course of the lesson, and no off-task behaviors were evident. He stimulated students to draw on their own experiences in order to understand the messages in the play.

Teacher A's written materials discussing the lesson demonstrated his self-reflection skills. He provided a thorough analysis of the positive and negative aspects of the lesson. While the lesson appeared to have been quite effective, he identified ways in which it might have been improved. This teacher's submission demonstrated his knowledge of the students and the subject matter, effective use of instructional strategies to engage students and help them learn, and the ability to create an inclusive and supportive learning environment.

Teacher B's lesson focused on a classic 19th-century novel that her students were in the process of reading. The lesson was intended to provide historical context for the novel and to tie that context to a discussion of the text. In her written submission, Teacher B had described her students as chatty but very academically able, yet the lesson seemed not to capitalize on their ability levels nor their willingness to converse. The video showed a lesson that appeared to be disjointed and uninteresting to students. Students were not engaged in the discussion, some seemed not to be on task, and many side conversations were occurring. Students did not willingly participate in the discussion, and even when called upon, their comments were not insightful with regard to the novel. Most striking were the lack of structure and haphazardness the lesson displayed and the number of times a possible discussion dwindled for lack of effective encouragement by the teacher.

The video showed that Teacher B did not seem to have a strong command of the subject matter. For example, the observations she raised about 19th-century England were trivial, and she missed opportunities to expand on their possible relevance to the events in the novel, the creation of mood, or other important points. She did not demonstrate effective strategies in engaging her students or creating an environment conducive to learning. Her written materials demonstrated a lack of insight into the positive and negative aspects of the lesson and little in the way of self-reflection. For instance, she described the discussion as successful and noted that the lesson was an effective way to introduce contextual background important for understanding the story. However, the video portrayed a class of students who were not engaged in the discussion and did not demonstrate their understanding of important points about characters in the novel. When these misunderstandings became evident—by something the students asked or stated—the teacher was not effective in correcting them, often because the student did not appear to be listening.

These two excerpts were chosen to illustrate the two score points on either side of passing, and the committee found there were clear distinctions between the two teachers' performance. The committee came away from the presentation with an impression that the process is complex and multi-dimensional, and that it allows teachers to demonstrate a level of thinking and performance that one might expect of accomplished teachers. We were also impressed by the extent to which the video portfolios captured aspects of teaching that could not be assessed with a paper and pencil assessment, such as the effectiveness of their classroom interactions with students.

We note, however, that prior to this demonstration, we were not able to get a full sense of the nature of the assessment. At the beginning of our study, no sample portfolio entries had been publicly released, and none was made available to us. Clearly the need to respect candidates' and students' confidentiality poses a challenge, but teachers who are considering applying or in the process of preparing their submissions would benefit greatly from the opportunity we were afforded in order to fully understand what is expected of them. Moreover, our reaction to the presentation demonstrated the importance of conveying the nature of the assessment to school administrators, policy makers, and others so that they better understand what is required of teachers who earn board certification.

5

The Psychometric Quality
of the Assessments

In this chapter we discuss the psychometric quality of the assessments the National Board for Professional Teaching Standards (NBPTS) uses to certify accomplished teachers. The assessments are the tools with which the board's primary goals are accomplished, and thus their psychometric quality is critical to the program's effectiveness. Our evaluation framework includes a number of other questions, but we view the psychometric evaluation as central to a review of a credentialing test. In considering the psychometric characteristics of the assessment, we address two broad questions, specifically:

Question 1: To what extent does the certification program for accomplished teachers clearly and accurately specify advanced teaching practices and the characteristics of teachers (the knowledge, skills, dispositions, and judgments) that enable them to carry out advanced practice? Does it do so in a manner that supports the development of a well-aligned test?

Question 2: To what extent do the assessments associated with the certification program for accomplished teachers reliably measure the specified knowledge, skills, dispositions, and judgments of certification candidates and support valid interpretations of the results? To what extent are the performance standards for the assessments and the process for setting them justifiable and reasonable?

As mentioned earlier, a number of professional associations concerned with measurement have developed standards to guide the development and evaluation of assessment programs (American Educational Research Association, American Psychological Association, and the National Council on Measurement in Education, 1999; National Commission for Certifying Agencies, 2004; Society for Industrial and Organizational Psychology, 2003). Although the standards they have articulated in various documents are tailored to different contexts, they share a number of common features. With regard to credentialing assessments, they lay out guidelines for the process of identifying the competencies to be assessed; developing the assessment and exercises; field-testing exercises; administering the exercises and scoring the responses; setting the passing standard; and evaluating the reliability of the scores, the validity of interpretations based on the assessment results, and the fairness of the interpretations and uses of these results. From our review of these standards, we identified a set of specific questions to investigate with regard to the development and technical characteristics of the NBPTS assessments.

With regard to the identification of the material to be assessed and the development of the assessment (Question 1), we ask:

a.   What processes were used to identify the knowledge, skills, dispositions, and judgments that characterize accomplished teachers? Was the process for establishing the descriptions of these characteristics thoughtful, thorough, and adequately justified? To what extent did those involved in the process have appropriate qualifications? To what extent were the participants balanced with respect to relevant factors, including teaching contexts and perspectives on teaching?

b.   Are the identified knowledge, skills, dispositions, and judgments presented in a way that is clear, accurate, reasonable, and complete? What evidence is there that they are relevant to performance?

c.   Do the knowledge, skills, dispositions, and judgments that were identified reflect current thinking in the specific field? What is the process for revisiting and refreshing the descriptions of expectations in each field?

d.   Are the knowledge, skills, dispositions, and judgments, as well as the teaching practices they imply, effective for all groups of students, regardless of their race and ethnicities, socioeconomic status, and native language status?

With regard to the reliability and validity of the assessment results, the methods for establishing the passing score, and test fairness (Question 2), we ask:

a. To what extent does the entire assessment process (including the exercises, scoring rubrics, and scoring mechanisms)[1] yield results that reflect the specified knowledge, skills, dispositions, and judgments?

b. Is the passing score reasonable? What process was used for establishing the passing score? How is the passing score justified? To what extent do pass rates differ for various groups of candidates, and are such differences reflective of bias in the test?

c. To what extent do the scores reflect teacher quality? What evidence is available that board-certified teachers actually practice in ways that are consistent with the knowledge, skills, dispositions, and judgments they demonstrate through the assessment process? Do knowledgeable observers find them to be better teachers than individuals who failed when they attempted to earn board certification?

This chapter begins with a discussion of the approach we took to the psychometric evaluation and the resources on which we relied. We then describe the national board's approach in relation to our two broad questions. We first address Question 1 and discuss the national board's approach to developing the standards and assessments. This is followed by a discussion of the process for scoring the assessments and setting performance standards. We then turn to Question 2 and discuss the assessment's technical characteristics, including reliability, validity, and fairness. At the end of the chapter we return to the original framework questions, summarize the findings and conclusions, and make recommendations.

COMMITTEE'S APPROACH TO THE
PSYCHOMETRIC EVALUATION

Sources of Information Reviewed

Our primary resource for information about the psychometric characteristics of the assessments is the annual reports prepared for the NBPTS by its contractor at the time, the Educational Testing Service, to summarize information related to each year's administrations, called Assessment Analysis Reports. We reviewed the three most recent sets of these reports, which provided information for administration cycles in 2002-2003, 2003-2004, and 2004-2005. The reports of the Technical Analysis Group (TAG), the body formed to provide supplementary psychometric expertise as a re-

---

[1]Although evaluation of the assessment process would ideally include consideration of eligibility and recertification requirements, we limited our focus to the actual assessments.

source for the national board, provided historical documentation about the development process and included research findings that supported decision making about the assessments. A published study by Richard Jaeger (1998), director of the TAG, provided a good deal of documentation about the psychometric characteristics of the original assessments. Several published studies by Lloyd Bond documented efforts to investigate bias and adverse impact and construct validity (Bond, 1998a,b; Bond et al., 2000). Two grant-funded studies (McColskey et al., 2005; Smith et al., 2005) provided additional information about construct validity. We also gathered information directly from current and former NBPTS staff members via presentations they made at committee meetings and their formal written responses to sets of questions submitted by the committee.[2]

Before presenting our review, we point out that obtaining technical documentation from the board was quite difficult and significantly complicated our evaluation exercises. We made a number of requests to the board, and while the Assessment Analysis Reports were readily provided, other information was more difficult to obtain. In particular, the board did not have readily available documentation about the procedures for identifying the content to be assessed and translating the content standards into assessment exercises. In March 2007, the NBPTS provided us with a newly prepared technical report in draft form (National Board for Professional Teaching Standards, 2007), presumably in response to our repeated efforts to collect information about the testing program. This additional documentation was useful but still left a number of our questions unanswered, which we explain in relevant sections of this chapter.

Scope of the Review

The national board awards certification in 25 areas, and a separate assessment has been developed for each area of specialization. An in-depth evaluation of each of these assessments would have required significantly more time and resources than were allotted for the committee's work. To confine the scope of the psychometric evaluation, we conducted the review in two steps. Initially, using information in the Assessment Analysis Reports, we conducted a broad examination of the general psychometric characteristics of all the assessments for all the certificates.

Based on the results of this broad review, we then identified two assessments to review in more detail. For these two assessments, we reviewed the TAG reports and relevant historical documentation that described how

---

[2]Just prior to the publication of this report, an edited volume by Ingvarson and Hattie (2008) became available. The volume documents the historical development of the NBPTS, but was not available in time for the committee to use in the evaluation.

decisions were made about the nature of the assessments and the types of exercises included, as well as the research conducted as part of the development process. We cite specific examples from these assessments that were relevant to our evaluation.

In selecting the assessments for the second step of our review, we considered the numbers of candidates who take each assessment, how long the assessments have been operational, and any technical information from the broad review that signaled potential problems or difficult-to-resolve issues (such as low reliability estimates). We also wanted to include both a generalist assessment and a subject-matter assessment: we selected the middle childhood generalist assessment and the early adolescence mathematics assessment. Teresa Russell, of the Human Resources Research Organization, assisted us in conducting our review of these two assessments as well as the initial broad review. See Russell, Putka, and Waters (2007) for the full report.

ARTICULATING THE CONTENT STANDARDS AND DEVELOPING THE ASSESSMENT EXERCISES

While every assessment program has its idiosyncrasies, models and norms exist for carrying out the basic steps, which include developing the content standards against which candidates are to be judged, developing the assessment exercises that will be used to judge them, administering those assessments, and scoring the candidates' responses to them. In this section we describe the procedures the national board established for conducting this work, and we note instances in which their procedures deviate markedly from established norms.[3]

Development of the Content Standards

The content standards are the cornerstone of any assessment program. In the case of the national board, the overall design of the program called for a set of assessments for each of many areas of specialization, the standards for all of which would be closely linked to the five core propositions regarding the characteristics of accomplished, experienced teachers (see the list in Chapter 4). For any given NBPTS certification area, the standards development process takes at least 12 to 18 months. As depicted in Figure 5-1, it begins when the NBPTS board of directors appoints a standards

---

[3]Throughout the report we have used the term "content standards" to refer to the outcome of the NBPTS process for identifying performance characteristics for accomplished teachers in each specialty area. This is a term commonly used in education and is used by the NBPTS. In the credentialing field, it is more common to use terms such as "content domain" or "performance domain" and to refer to the process of identifying the domain as a practice or job analysis.

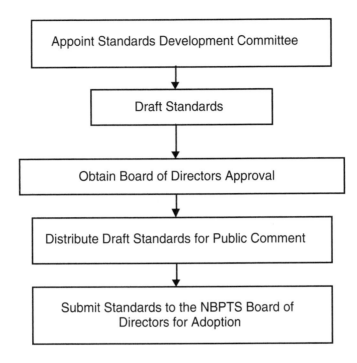

FIGURE 5-1 The NBPTS content standards development process.

committee for the particular certification area. The committee drafts and revises the standards, and the standards are then submitted to the board of directors for approval. Once approved, they are distributed for public comment and revised, then resubmitted to the NBPTS board of directors for adoption.

Composing balanced, qualified standards committees is critical to ensuring that the standards will represent important aspects of teaching in each field. The range of input sought by these committees, and the process by which they seek out and incorporate this input, will have a significant impact on the quality of the standards. According to the board's handbook (National Board for Professional Teaching Standards, 2006a), the NBPTS posts requests for nominations to the standards committees on its website, circulates the requests at conferences and meetings, and solicits nominations directly for committee members from disciplinary and other education organizations, state curriculum specialists and chief state school officers, education leaders, board-certified teachers, and the NBPTS board of directors. Committee members are selected on the basis of their qualifications and the need to balance such factors as teaching contexts, ethnicity, gender, and geographic region.

Standards committees are generally composed of 8 to 10 members who are appointed for a three-year term, subject to renewal. Committee members are teachers, teacher educators, scholars, or specialists in the relevant field. Standards committees interact with other associations and collaborate with standards committees in related fields on a regular basis. They also confer with other professionals in the field and the public on the appropriateness of the content standards and provide advice on the implementation of the certification process.

Standards committee members are expected to be up to date on the contemporary pedagogical research in their particular field, and NBPTS staff indicated that reviews of this literature (or at least, lists of articles to read) are provided to committee members prior to their first meeting. During its initial meeting, the standards committee learns about the NBPTS, the core propositions, the standards development process, and the structure of a standards development report. Members also discuss key questions about their field (e.g., What are the major issues in your field? What are some individual examples of accomplished practice in your field?).

The focus of the standards committee's discussion is to identify the characteristics of accomplished practice in their field. That is, their goal is to determine the standards that describe what accomplished teachers should know and be able to do. According to the NBPTS Technical Report (2007, p. 19), "the standards themselves do not prescribe specific instructional techniques or strategies, but emphasize certain qualities of teaching which are fundamental, such as setting worthwhile and attainable goals or monitoring student development." With regard to the portfolio, specifically, the standards allow for accomplished teaching "to be demonstrated in a variety of ways, with no single teaching strategy privileged."

An initial standards document is prepared by a professional writer, who observes the committee's discussions and translates their conclusions into draft standards. The draft standards are circulated between meetings and are the focus of the next meeting. The process of meeting, redrafting, and recirculating standards is repeated until the committee reaches consensus and decides that the standards are ready for submission to the NBPTS board of directors.

When the draft standards have been approved by the board of directors, they are released for public comment. The standards are posted on the NBPTS website and distributed directly to educators and leaders of disciplinary and specialty organizations. The public comment period lasts about 30 days. The comments are summarized and circulated to the committee, which then meets again to review the comments and revise the standards document.

The standards are submitted to the board and, after adoption, are published. They are available for download at the NBPTS website (http://www.nbpts.org). The NBPTS views the standards as living documents (National Board for Professional Teaching Standards, 2006a) and thus periodically reviews and revises them.

Development of the Assessment

The board makes extensive use of teachers in the assessment development process. The board recruits practicing teachers in the subject area and developmental level of each particular certificate—soliciting nominations from professional organizations, teachers who have been involved in previous assessment development activities, and other interested teachers who volunteer. The recruited teachers are assigned to assessment development teams, which work with the test developer to construct draft portfolio and assessment center exercises and scoring rubrics that reflect the standards for the certificate area. The development teams typically meet monthly over the course of 10 months to construct exercises and rubrics.

Most of the information we reviewed describes the development process at a general level, with details available only in the draft technical report. Even in that report, there is insufficient detail to get a clear picture of all stages of the process, nor were details regarding development of standards for specific certificates included. The first step of determining the specific content of the 10 elements of a specialty assessment is particularly vague, but results in a set of exercises that the development team judges to be an effective representation of the content standards for that specialty area. To facilitate subsequent development of alternate versions of the assessment center exercises, current practice is to develop "shells" that have both fixed and variable elements. The team also develops scoring rubrics, which anticipate the ways in which candidates might respond to the problems presented and provide guidance on how to score performance.

The exercises are pilot-tested on samples of teachers who have not participated in developing the assessment. The objectives of the pilot test are to determine (a) whether the instructions are clear, (b) whether the exercises are in need of modification, and to (c) estimate the time needed to complete the exercise. At this stage, there is insufficient statistical information on which to evaluate the exercises. Instead, the development team reviews feedback from the pilot test and conducts a type of scoring, which the NBPTS refers to as "formative scoring," to identify problems in the prompts (exercises presented to the candidates) or scoring materials and to create final scoring rubrics and other features of the scoring system. As they review responses, the assessment development team members are asked to pay particular attention to relationships between each prompt, the evidence the exercise is intended to produce, and the rubric (or scoring guide), and to identify areas in which changes need to be made. The NBPTS board of directors reviews and approves the final operational version of each set of assessment exercises before it is put into operation.

Committee Comments

Professional test standards require a systematic analysis of job requirements to determine the appropriate content for credentialing examinations. Although the original developers of the NBPTS assessments resisted the boundaries implied by traditional notions of job analysis or practice analysis, our view is that they simply used a practice analysis strategy tailored to the goals of this advanced certification program. A practice analysis typically includes both focus groups and a survey of job incumbents (in this case, teachers) to identify job requirements. The national board chose to use a consensus-based process and not a large-scale survey because its explicit goal was to define the practice of accomplished teachers as it *should be*, rather than the practice that was typical of experienced teachers.

The board focused on defining a vision of accomplished practice rather than describing the current state of teaching practice, relying on the collective judgment of the committees that develop the standards and the assessment development teams to define the practice of accomplished teachers as it should be. This seems like a reasonable approach and one that is particularly appropriate given the board's vision of accomplished practice. However, the process they use is not thoroughly documented and the translation of the general statement of the standard to a set of specific scorable exercises for each specific specialty assessment requires a significant amount of judgment on the part of the development teams, which makes it difficult for us to establish the appropriateness of each specialty assessment. The lack of documentation of the details of the process used to establish the content standards underlying specific certificates also limits the extent to which we can evaluate how well it was carried out. The content standards are written with the aid of professional writers, which results in an easily readable "vision" of accomplished practice but not one that automatically translates into an assessment plan.

With regard to the development of the content standards and assessment exercises, we conclude:

Conclusion 5-1: The process used to identify the knowledge, skills, dispositions, and judgments to be assessed was conducted in a reasonable fashion for a certification test, using diverse and informed experts. We note, however, that the process was not documented in enough detail for us to conduct a detailed review or evaluation of the process.

Conclusion 5-2: The board's articulation of the knowledge, skills, dispositions, and judgments for each assessment area, which is based on extensive input from teachers, seems to provide a defensible vision of accomplished practice. However, the definitions of accomplished practice provide very little concrete guidance to the developers of the assessments, and thus critical decisions are left to their judgment using processes that have not been well articulated either in general or for individual certificates.

THE NBPTS APPROACH TO SCORING THE ASSESSMENTS AND SETTING THE PERFORMANCE STANDARDS

Scoring of Assessments

Training the Raters

Portfolio and assessment center exercises are scored during different scoring sessions by different groups of raters (scorers).[4] Raters are not required to be board-certified teachers but must have a baccalaureate degree, a valid teaching license, and a minimum of three years of teaching experience. Current applicants for board certification are not eligible, nor are teachers who have attempted board certification but were unsuccessful. In addition, board-certified teachers who serve as raters must be currently certified in the area they are assessing. Nonboard-certified teachers must be working at least half-time in the area in which they are serving as a rater or, if retired, must have served as a rater in the past or have taught in the certificate area within the past three years. The board attempts to ensure that the raters are diverse with respect to region of the country, socioeconomic status, and race/ethnicity.

Raters go through extensive training and must qualify before participating in operational scoring. Training for those scoring portfolios lasts approximately three days; training for those scoring assessment center exercises takes one and one half days. Rater training consists of five steps: (1) acquainting raters with the history and principles of the national board; (2) acquainting raters with the mechanics and content of the scoring system, including the standards, the exercises, the rubrics, and the process; (3) in-depth examination of raters' own biases and preferences (particularly biases about ways to teach certain lessons); (4) exposure to benchmark papers (sample responses for each score point); and (5) independent scoring practice. Step three is a major focus of the scoring process and is intended to ensure that raters align their judgments with the rubric rather than their

---

[4]The NBPTS uses the term "assessors" for the individuals hired to read and score assessment exercises. For clarity, we use the more common term "raters."

own personal opinions and values about accomplished teaching practices. After completing the training process, raters score a sample of papers and must correctly assign scores in five of six cases to qualify for operational scoring. The trainers also conduct regular "read behinds," reading the responses and reviewing the scores for random samples of scorers as a further check for anomalies. Raters who show poor accuracy or consistency are given additional one-on-one training and close supervision to help them improve. Raters who continue to score inaccurately may be dismissed and are not invited to future scoring sessions. Overall, the procedures used for training the raters are in line with those used by other testing programs for scoring similar types of assessments. Ideally, however, there would be more information about how the training benchmarks are established. This is key to the proper calibration of raters.

Assigning Scores

Each of the exercises is scored using a four-point scale. Raters first assign a whole number value to the response; a plus or a minus can be attached to the whole number value to indicate quarter-point gradations in performance (for example, 3+ converts to a score of 3.25, 3– converts to 2.75, and so on). The key distinction on the score scale is between a 2 and a 3. A score of 3 represents a level of teaching that is accomplished, while a score of 2 falls below the accomplished level.

In the first year that certification is offered in a particular area, all responses are scored by two raters. In subsequent years, 25 percent of exercises are double-scored. When a response is double-scored and the two scores differ by more than 1.25 points, the discrepancy is resolved by one of the scoring trainers.

Combining Exercise Scores

The assessment as a whole has 10 components, and a compensatory model is used for determining the overall score. This means that the scores for the 10 components are combined into a total score, and that higher scores on some components can compensate for lower scores on others, to some extent. However, the scores for individual exercises are weighted to reflect the board's view of their relative importance. The board has done considerable research on the weighting scheme, and expert panels were used to make judgments about the relative importance of the various components. Overall, the expert panels judged that the classroom-based portfolio entries should be accorded the most weight, with somewhat less weight assigned to the assessment center exercises and the documentation of other accomplishments. Currently each of the three classroom-based portfolio entries is weighted by 16 percent; the documented accomplishment entry is weighted by 12 percent; and each of the six assessment center exercises is weighted by 6.67 percent.

Setting Performance Standards

Assessment programs that are used to determine whether or not someone will get a credential must have a cut score. The cut score, or passing score, is referred to as the "performance standard" because it is intended to reflect a minimum standard of performance required to earn the credential. Performance standards are generally determined by formal standard-setting procedures, in which groups of experts reach collective judgments about the performance to be required.

During the assessment development phase, TAG explored a variety of processes for determining the cut score for the NBPTS assessments. These standard-setting studies are reported in various TAG reports and documented in Jaeger (1998). Two approaches were tried initially—the "dominant profile judgment method" (Plake, Hambleton, and Jaeger, 1997) and the "judgmental policy capturing method" (Jaeger, Hambleton, and Plake, 1995)—but were replaced by an approach called the "direct judgment method." With this procedure, the standard-setting panelists are asked to make two types of judgments: (1) the relative weights to assign to the 10 components of the assessment and (2) the lowest overall score required for a candidate to receive certification. The individuals who participated in the standard setting were teachers and curriculum supervisors who had been involved with the development work for the certificate (e.g., worked with the test developer to design exercises for the various components). Additional details about the method are described in Jaeger (1998).

Originally the NBPTS convened separate, independent standard-setting sessions for each certificate, which produced different cut scores (although all were in the range of 263-284). In 1997, on the basis of feedback from teachers and others, the NBPTS decided to establish a uniform passing score of 275 for all certificates. The rationale for this decision is documented in memos to the NBPTS board of directors (J. Kelly, June 2, 1997, and June 6, 1997). Essentially, this total reflects the fact that a score of 3– (e.g., 2.75) represents accomplished teaching (as described earlier); thus a score of 2.75 on each of 10 exercises would yield the cut score of 275.[5] The cut scores continue to be based on the overall score; however, there are no minimum

---

[5]The documentation about this indicates that the cut score is actually 263, which is equivalent to 2.63 on each exercise. To compensate for measurement error and to reduce the number of false negatives, the decision was made to add 12 points to this cut score, which produced a cut score of 275. The constant of 12 points is added to each candidate's total scaled score.

scores set for each exercise. The NBPTS has carried out studies to confirm the continued use of this cut score, and reports are included in their draft Technical Report (National Board for Professional Teaching Standards, 2007).

Committee Comments

With regard to the procedures for setting the performance standards, we acknowledge all the effort that went into devising a procedure for setting standards on an assessment that was quite innovative when it was first developed (because it combined portfolio-based exercises and computer-based constructed-response exercises). The procedures seem to be well thought out and consistently implemented. We note, however, that the pass rates are low and may have an impact on the low participation rate, an issue that is discussed further in Chapter 6. That is, any teacher who decides to attempt board certification has only a 50-50 chance of passing on the first attempt. As we have noted, the NBPTS adjusted the cut scores in 1997 to make them consistent across assessments and to limit the impact of false-negative misclassifications; thus it is clear that the NBPTS considers the cut score to be adjustable when warranted. Given the structure of the assessment and the general approach taken in 1997, a case could be made for setting the passing score at 250, halfway between the average scores of 2 and 3. A candidate who earned a score of 3 on every component would be consistently "accomplished," whereas a candidate with a score of 2 on every exercise would fall 1 point short of being accomplished on every exercise.

We recognize, however, that setting performance standards requires careful consideration of a variety of measurement and policy issues, and we do not think it is within our purview to make recommendations to the NBPTS with regard to raising or lowering the cut score. We do draw the following conclusion:

Conclusion 5-3: The passing score was derived in an innovative but reasonable way, particularly given that the performance standard is embedded in the four-point exercise scoring system. Given the low pass rate and the relatively low reliability of the assessments, we suggest that NBPTS reevaluate the passing score.

TECHNICAL CHARACTERISTICS: RELIABILITY, VALIDITY, AND FAIRNESS[6]

Reliability

Reliability refers to the reproducibility of assessment scores; that is, the degree to which individuals' scores remain consistent over repeated administrations of the test. In the case of national board certification, it is important that the total scores reflect the level of skill of the candidates being assessed and not ancillary factors, such as rater characteristics or the conditions of observation. Reliability coefficients indicate the extent to which each candidate's total scores tend to remain the same across scorers, exercises, and the conditions of the observation.

Procedures for developing, administering, and scoring tests are all standardized to help increase reliability. Nevertheless, assessments are imperfect. Some error is random and beyond the control of the test developer (such as noise outside a testing room or a candidate's state of mind when performing an exercise). Other sources of error are easier to identify and can be attributable to different conditions of measurement, such as differences among the raters scoring the responses or the exercises comprising the assessment. There are two particularly important reliability issues for the NBPTS assessments. One is that they require candidates to provide complex responses that must be scored by humans (as opposed to tests that only require candidates to select a response and can be scored by machines). Thus, error can be introduced during the scoring process itself by any inconsistency in the way that raters assign scores.

The second possible source of error is that, despite the complexity of the domain being assessed, each exercise gets a single score, and thus the assessment essentially operates as a 10-item test, with 6 of the items devoted to an assessment of knowledge and skills needed in the areas of teaching being evaluated. This design has two implications. First, it is difficult to dem-

---

[6]A basic issue relevant to the technical quality of assessments is the maintenance of consistent standards over time. In large standardized testing programs, this issue is typically addressed by statistically equating scores from different test forms. However, we note that, for a number of reasons, it is generally not possible to statistically equate scores on performance tests. Thus our evaluation of the technical characteristics does not explicitly address equating methods. Two general approaches have been taken to address this problem (Linn, 1993). The first method, statistical moderation, can be applied in cases in which a closely related objective test, which can be statistically equated, has also been administered to at least some of the candidates. By equating the objective test scores across administrations and scaling the performance test scores to the objective test, one can indirectly link ("equate") the assessments across administrations (years). In this case, this tactic is not feasible. The alternative to statistical moderation requires training and calibration of the raters to maintain consistent standards, which is feasible for the NBPTS assessments.

onstrate that a performance domain has been adequately covered when the number of problems posed to candidates is so small. Second, as we discuss later, test scores based on small numbers of scorable parts are inherently less reliable than those that are based on larger numbers. For example, a 20-item test will almost invariably be more reliable than a 10-item test.

The impact of errors associated with the scoring process or with the particular set of exercises that a teacher takes can be estimated using generalizability analyses, which provide estimates of the reliability of the scores when these sources of error are taken into consideration. The board routinely evaluates the impact of these sources of error, which are reported as "assessor reliability" (or interrater consistency) and "exercise reliability" (or internal consistency reliability). The NBPTS uses three indices to estimate the reliability of the assessment system: an assessor reliability estimate, the adjudication rate, and an exercise reliability estimate. The first two of these indices involve the consistency of scores across scorers. The third index involves consistency across exercises and includes rater inconsistency as one source of error (because the different exercises are evaluated by different raters). Each is discussed below.

Interrater Consistency

If all responses were scored by all raters, the estimation of interrater consistency would simply indicate the extent of agreement across the raters. This, of course, cannot be done for a number of practical reasons (e.g., the length of time such a scoring would require). Thus, estimation of rater reliability also requires some complicated procedures. For the NBPTS, a portion of the exercise is scored by two raters and a portion is scored by a single rater. The scores of both the single-scored and double-scored raters are used in estimating interrater consistency (National Board for Professional Teaching Standards, 2007).

Once the rater reliabilities are computed for each exercise, the reliability of the composite score across the 10 components is computed (with the weights of each taken into consideration). Table 5-1 shows the average rater reliability for the total score across 24 certificates[7] for three administration cycles (2002-2003, 2003-2004, 2004-2005). This rater reliability estimate ranged from .76 to .93, with an overall mean of .85.

We also examined the rater reliabilities for individual exercises, focusing on the early adolescent mathematics and middle childhood generalist assessments. Table 5-2 presents these reliabilities. Again, for each exercise, the reliabilities reported here are the average of the reliability estimates for

---

[7]At the time we conducted our psychometric review, data were available for 24 certificates. The NBPTS now offers certification in 25 areas, recently adding an assessment in health.

TABLE 5-1 Estimates of Reliability and Decision Accuracy Across Three Administration Cycles

Statistic	2002-2003			
	M	SD	Min	Max
Total score				
N	508	655	28	2,557
Mean (M)	264	10	244	281
Standard Deviation (SD)	40	4	34	49
Reliability (exercise formula)	.68	.06	.56	.76
Reliability (assessor formula)	.84	.04	.76	.91
Percent of exercise scores adjudicated	3.7	1.0	2.0	5.7
Probability of false-negative decisions				
Reliability (exercise formula)	.09	.02	.05	.14
Reliability (assessor formula)	.07	.02	.04	.10
Probability of false-positive decisions				
Reliability (exercise formula)	.10	.02	.06	.14
Reliability (assessor formula)	.06	.02	.04	.10

NOTE: Reliabilities computed with the "exercise" formula are internal consistency estimates similar to coefficient alpha (Jaeger, 1998) and are likely to be conservative. The assessor reliability estimates represent an upper bound on the reliability. "NA" means that the reliability was not available in NBPTS reports. Twenty-five percent of the exercises are scored by two

the three administration cycles. The rater reliability estimates ranged from .51 to .94, with higher estimates reported for the early adolescent mathematics assessment.

To place these values in context, we compared them with those reported for other assessments. A meta-analysis of assessment center validities (Arthur, Day, McNelly, and Edens, 2003) reported an average assessor reliability of .86 across six studies.[8] In her book chapter on assessment centers, Tsacoumis (2007) reported rater reliabilities from two assessment centers, each including four job simulations. The average single-rater reliabilities ranged from .54 to .86, with the majority being more than .70. Reynolds (1999) reported results of role play assessor reliabilities for two managerial assessment center studies. Single-rater reliabilities ranged from .63 to .79 and two-rater reliabilities were between .73 and .88. Reported reliabilities

---

[8]The authors did not report whether this was a multirater or single-rater reliability.

2003-2004				2004-2005				Grand
M	SD	Min	Max	M	SD	Min	Max	Mean
481	512	54	1,967	480	516	57	1,954	490
261	9	239	276	260	7	244	274	262
39	4	32	48	40	4	33	48	40
.69	.05	.62	.78	.70	.05	.63	.80	.69
.86	.03	.79	.91	.86	.04	.78	.93	.85
3.4	1.0	1.8	6.2	2.9	0.9	1.6	5.2	3.3
.09	.03	.02	.13	.09	.02	.03	.12	.09
.06	.02	.01	.08	.06	.01	.04	.09	.06
.10	.02	.07	.18	.09	.01	.07	.12	.10
.06	.01	.03	.09	.06	.01	.03	.08	.06

assessors. Exercise scores are adjudicated if assessors disagree by 1.25 points or more on a single exercise. False-negative decisions occur when a candidate who should be certified is denied certification. False-positive decisions occur when a candidate who should not be certified receives certification.

for performance assessments from educational or credentialing programs have been variable. In a review of the psychometric characteristics of performance assessments, Dunbar, Koretz, and Hoover (1991) reported inter-rater reliabilities ranging from .33 to .91 across nine studies. The highest reliabilities were attributable to the use of clearly specified rubrics; the lowest reliabilities were found when such rubrics were not used.

Adjudication Rates

Estimating the adjudication rate is straightforward. As noted above, a portion of the exercises are scored by two raters. When the scores assigned by the two raters differ by 1.25 points or more, the case is flagged for adjudication by a scoring leader or more experienced rater. The adjudication rate is thus a simple index of absolute agreement between two raters.

The committee reviewed data from three administration cycles and

TABLE 5-2 Average Rater Reliability Across Three Administration Cycles (2002-2005) for Early Adolescence Mathematics and Middle Childhood Generalist

Exercises	Type	Average Reliability
Early adolescence mathematics		
Developing and assessing mathematical thinking and reasoning	Portfolio	.65
Instructional analysis: whole class mathematical discourse	Portfolio	.57
Instructional analysis: small group mathematical collaboration	Portfolio	.67
Documented accomplishments: contributions to student learning	Portfolio	.63
Median portfolios		.66
Algebra and functions	Assessment	.94
Connections	Assessment	.80
Data analysis	Assessment	.85
Geometry	Assessment	.86
Number and operations sense	Assessment	.94
Technology and manipulatives	Assessment	.73
Median assessment center exercises		.86
Middle childhood generalist		
Writing: thinking through the process	Portfolio	.59
Building a classroom community through social studies	Portfolio	.53
Integrating mathematics with science	Portfolio	.54
Documented accomplishments: contributions in student learning	Portfolio	.58
Median portfolios		.56
Supporting reading skills	Assessment	.53
Analyzing student work	Assessment	.54
Knowledge of science	Assessment	.62
Social studies	Assessment	.56
Understanding health	Assessment	.51
Integrating the arts	Assessment	.59
Median assessment center exercises		.55

24 certificates. As shown in Table 5-1, on average, the adjudication rate was 3.3 percent (for the 25 percent of cases that were double-scored). There are no published data that can be used to assess this rate. The adjudication rate of 3.3 percent is not large in absolute terms, but the difference (1.25 points) that triggers adjudication in this program is quite large relative to the four-

point score scale. The inconsistencies indicated by the adjudication rates are not unusual in performance and portfolio assessments requiring judgmental subjective scoring, but they do highlight the difficulty of achieving adequate reliability using these methods.

Internal Consistency Reliability[9]

The most commonly used approach to estimating the reliability of the overall score on an assessment that includes a number of separately scored elements is based on the consistency among the scores on the separate parts. These reliability estimates are often referred to as "internal consistency estimates of reliability" because they use observed statistical relationships (e.g., observed correlations) among the parts of the tests to estimate the relationship that would be found if two independent versions of the assessment could be administered to the same examinees. Since the relationship between the separate forms of the assessment cannot generally be observed, this parameter is estimated by extrapolating from the observed internal relationships among the parts of the assessment.

In assessments that involve multiple tasks of the same kind (e.g., a multiple-choice test consisting of a number of multiple-choice questions or an essay test with a number of essay questions that have the same weight in the assessment), the extrapolation from the internal characteristics of the assessment (e.g., the correlations among scores on the separate tasks) to the internal-consistency reliability of the total assessment can be fairly simple and can employ standard formulas (e.g., coefficient alpha). For assessments such as those used for the NBPTS, which involve a number of different kinds of tasks with different weights assigned to the different tasks, this kind of analysis becomes more idiosyncratic and more difficult.

The NBPTS estimates the overall internal-consistency reliability using an estimate developed by Cronbach and reported in Jaeger (1998) and National Board for Professional Teaching Standards (2007). The approach is complicated and involves performing multiple regressions in which the scores on nine of the exercises are used to predict the score on the tenth. This process is repeated, with each of the 10 exercises in turn treated as the dependent variable.[10] A conceptually similar procedure is used to estimate the reliability of the weighted total score across assessment exercises. The

---

[9]NBPTS documents use the term "exercise reliability" to refer to internal consistency estimates.

[10]That is, the scores on each exercise are used as measures of a dependent variable, and this dependent variable is regressed on examinees' scores for all of the other exercises in the assessment. The standard error of estimate associated with the regression is then used as an estimate of the standard error of measurement (SEM) for the exercise, and in turn, the reliability of the exercise is estimated from the SEM.

reader is referred to Jaeger (1998) or Russell, Putka, and Waters (2007) for additional details about this process.

Because each exercise is scored by a different set of scorers, the internal consistency estimates reflect variability in scores across raters as well as variability in scores across exercises. In the terminology of generalizability theory, the random errors due to variability across raters are confounded with the random errors associated with variability across exercises. Assuming that different sets of raters are assigned to each exercise, the internal-consistency estimates incorporate both sources of error and can be taken as a reasonable overall estimate of the reliability of the total scores.

Using the Assessment Analysis Reports provided by the NBPTS, we reviewed reliability information for three administration cycles (2002-2003, 2003-2004, 2004-2005). Table 5-1 reports the internal consistency reliability estimates for the total score. In this table, the reliability estimates were averaged across the 24 certificates for each administration cycle, and the final column reports the average across all three cycles.

The average reliability for the total score across 24 certificates for three administration cycles was .69. For high-stakes testing programs, it is generally recommended that the reliability be above .80 or .90 (Guion, 1998). In practice, the rule of thumb is typically applied to measures of internal consistency, which would involve the same sources of error (variability over exercises) as the NBPTS exercise reliability. This reliability of about .70 is fairly low for a high-stakes testing program. However, it is generally the case that scores based on assessments that use portfolio and constructed-response formats tend to be less reliable, in part, because they have fewer exercises. For example, the reliability estimate for the Armed Services Vocational Aptitude Test Battery 35-item word knowledge subtest is .89 (Palmer, Hartke, Ree, Welsh, and Valentine, 1988). If the word knowledge subtest had only 10 items, its estimated reliability would be .61.

Generally, the most direct and effective way to improve internal-consistency reliability is to increase the length of the assessment by adding more assessment exercises. This would clearly be difficult and expensive for both the candidates and the NBPTS. An alternative approach is to improve the quality of the individual assessment exercises and the scoring in ways that tend to enhance the internal consistency among the exercises. This is also difficult to do while maintaining the complexity and authenticity of the exercises and the scoring of the exercise performances.

A compromise approach involving the replacement of some assessment exercises by a number of shorter assessment exercises could improve internal consistency reliability without incurring much additional cost and without interfering with the relevance and representativeness of the exercises. It would not be easy to shorten or simplify the portfolios without also making them less representative of the performances of interest. However, it might be possible to enhance the reliability of the assessment center exercises by including a larger number of shorter assessment exercises. Assuming that the exercises are evaluated by different raters, this change would help to control errors due to the sampling of exercises and of raters. Generalizability theory could provide a useful framework for examining how to improve precision without changing what is being assessed.

We also examined the reliability estimates for individual exercises on the middle childhood generalist and the early adolescence mathematics assessments. Table 5-3 summarizes this information. The internal consistency reliability estimates reported in this table are, for each exercise, the average of the reliability estimates for the three administration cycles. These reliabilities for the individual exercises are, in essence, reliabilities for tests with a single item and thus would be expected to be very low. For the early adolescence mathematics assessments, the exercise reliabilities tend to be lower for the portfolios than for the assessment center exercises. The reverse is true for the middle childhood generalist, in which the reliabilities for the portfolio exercises tend to be higher than for the assessment center exercises.

Estimating Decision Accuracy

The accuracy with which the assessments identify which candidates should pass and which should not is at the heart of the assessment challenge for a certification program, and two types of decision errors can occur. False-negative decision errors occur when a candidate who should be certified (i.e., has a true score at or above the cut score) is denied certification. False-positive decision errors occur when a candidate who should not be certified receives certification. A variety of procedures exist for monitoring decision accuracy. The NBPTS uses a procedure developed by Livingston and Lewis and described in Jaeger (1998), which takes into account the reliability of the assessment, the distribution of overall scores, the minimum and maximum possible score, and the performance standard (or cut score) on the assessment.

Table 5-1 reports the probability of false-negative and false-positive decisions based on the two ways for estimating reliability. On average, across administration cycles and certificates, the false-negative rates were 6 percent (based on rater reliability) and 9 percent (based on internal consistency reliability). To get a rough idea of the effect of misclassifications for the NBPTS system overall, these probabilities can be applied to actual examinee data. Across three administration cycles, 35,359 candidates completed the NBPTS assessments, 13,218 of whom were ultimately certified and 22,041 of whom were not. Application of the false-negative rate indicates that between 1,322 and 1,984 candidates should have been certified but were

TABLE 5-3 Average Internal Consistency Reliability (R_{xx}) Estimates for Assessment Exercises Across Three Administration Cycles (2002-2005) for Early Adolescence Mathematics and Middle Childhood Generalist

Exercises	Type	Average R_{XX}
Early adolescence mathematics		
Developing and assessing mathematical thinking and reasoning	Portfolio	.21
Instructional analysis: whole class mathematical discourse	Portfolio	.14
Instructional analysis: small group mathematical collaboration	Portfolio	.20
Documented accomplishments: contributions to student learning	Portfolio	.17
Algebra and functions	Assessment	.48
Connections	Assessment	.27
Data analysis	Assessment	.23
Geometry	Assessment	.34
Number and operations sense	Assessment	.37
Technology and manipulatives	Assessment	.27
Median		.25
Middle childhood generalist		
Writing: thinking through the process	Portfolio	.21
Building a classroom community through social studies	Portfolio	.19
Integrating mathematics with science	Portfolio	.21
Documented accomplishments: contributions in student learning	Portfolio	.19
Supporting reading skills	Assessment	.12
Analyzing student work	Assessment	.12
Knowledge of science	Assessment	.07
Social studies	Assessment	.09
Understanding health	Assessment	.14
Integrating the arts	Assessment	.14
Median		.14

not (that is, between 6 and 9 percent of 22,041). The false-positive rates were 6 percent (based on rater reliability) and 10 percent (based on exercise reliability). Application of the false-positive rate indicates that between 793 and 1,322 of the candidates who were certified should not have been (that is, between 6 and 10 percent of 13,218). While the rates of misclassification are similar for false positives and false negatives, the false-negative rate

TABLE 5-4 Impact of Average Decision Accuracy Across Three Administration Cycles (2002-2005) for Early Adolescence Mathematics and Middle Childhood Generalist

	False-Negative Decisions			False-Positive Decisions		
	Probability	Number Failing	Decision Errors	Probability	Number Passing	Decision Errors
Early adolescence mathematics						
Exercise reliability	.07	1,000	67	.09	462	40
Assessor reliability	.04	1,000	43	.05	462	22
Middle childhood generalist						
Exercise reliability	.11	4,076	448	.10	2,211	221
Assessor reliability	.08	4,076	326	.07	2,211	155

has a greater impact because more candidates who attempt to earn board certification fail than pass. The false positives and false negatives are fairly high, which reflect reliability estimates that are not particularly high. The error rates based on interrater reliability estimates are higher than those for the internal consistency reliability estimates because the former includes one source of error (variability over raters), whereas the latter includes two sources of error (variability over raters and exercises).

Assuming that the intent is to generalize across both exercises and raters, the error rates (false positives and false negatives) based on the internal consistency estimates would be more appropriate than the error rates based on the interrater reliability.

We examined the decision accuracy specifically for the early adolescent mathematics assessments and the middle childhood generalist (see Table 5-4). Again, these rates are averaged across the three administration cycles. Overall, the rates for these two certificates are in the same range as the averages reported above.

Committee Comments

Our review of the methods used by the NBPTS to evaluate the reliability of its assessments and of the estimated reliabilities of these assessments suggests several possible improvements. First, we note that the internal-consistency reliabilities are low relative to generally accepted standards for high-stakes assessments.[11] Although we recognize that the national board has adopted a policy of emphasizing the authenticity and validity of its assessments rather than their reliability, we think that some improvement in the reliability of the assessments could probably be achieved without much loss in authenticity or validity and with relatively little increase in the operating costs of the assessments. For example, the board might consider adding a few short-answer or objective questions to the computer-based portion of the assessment.

Second, the methods being used to evaluate the reliability of their assessments are relatively sophisticated, but they are also relatively unconventional, complicated, and over 10 years old. It would be useful for the board to convene a technical advisory group to review these methods in light of current developments in psychometrics. Such a panel may decide that, given the design of the national board assessments, the current methods are optimal, but the issue is worth revisiting.

In any assessment that requires judgment in scoring (e.g., essays, performance tests, portfolios), it is useful to check on the consistency with which different raters apply the scoring rubrics. Even if the assessment exercises and scoring rubrics are carefully developed and the raters are thoroughly trained, there is likely to be some variability, and this variability is likely to increase as the complexity of the exercises increases (and the NBPTS exercises call for complex performances). Any variability in scores for a candidate across raters is generally treated as a source of random error, and the magnitudes of such random errors are reflected in lower reliabilities.

Although it is not surprising that different raters might assign different scores to a teacher's performance on a complex exercise (e.g., a video of a class session), because they attend to different aspects of the performance or because they tend to value different teaching styles, such inconsistency constitutes a problem. The performance is fixed (i.e., the scorers watch the same video) and therefore differences in the scores assigned to the performance reflect characteristics of the raters, rather than characteristics of the teacher performance being assessed. In an estimate of the competency of the teacher giving the lesson, such differences tend to function as random errors. It is important to keep the magnitudes of these interrater differences small to ensure that the score a candidate receives on the assessment reflects the quality of the candidate's performances and not the luck of the draw in the assignment of raters.

A number of approaches can be used to improve interrater consistency. The most direct approach is to train or calibrate the raters to use the ru-

---

[11]We also note that as is usually the case for certification programs, the candidates are self-selected, and the resulting restriction of range causes the reliabilities to be somewhat lower than they would be in the absence of restriction in range.

bric in the same way and to apply the same standards and to subsequently monitor the consistency of the raters. The national board has given this approach considerable attention and, given the complexity of the assessment exercises, has achieved considerable success.

A second approach involves the use of shorter, simpler exercises with simple rubrics that are easier to grade consistently than long, complex exercises. This approach involves serious trade-offs if the competencies of interest in the assessment tend to be employed in complex exercises (e.g., teaching a class). Shorter, less-complex exercises are likely to be seen as less relevant to or representative of the performances of interest and therefore less valid in assessing competence in these performances. The national board has opted for a more direct and representative sampling of the performance of interest; this is a reasonable choice for an advanced certification program, but it makes it difficult to maintain high interrater consistency.

A third approach to improving interrater consistency is to have two or more raters evaluate each performance and average the resulting scores over the raters. Averaging over two or more scores tends to substantially decrease the error variance associated with variability over scorers (i.e., by "averaging out" the differences across scorers), but this approach tends to be very expensive (and we do not recommend this approach). We note that the use of two raters to evaluate some performance does substantially reduce the random error associated with rater inconsistency for these candidates.

With traditional multiple-choice tests, developers are able to use statistical data to evaluate and refine individual test items before they are used operationally. This is less feasible with assessments such as those offered by the NBPTS. Over time, however, performance data on large numbers of candidates are generated and could be used to identify exercises that exhibit relatively low reliability or disparate impact. It is not clear how closely the board tracks such "item-level" data and uses them to potentially adjust either the scoring rubrics or the content of individual exercises. We think it is advisable that they do so.

On the basis of our review, we conclude:

Conclusion 5-4: The reliability of the NBPTS assessment results is generally lower than desired for a high-stakes testing program but is consistent with expectations for a largely portfolio-based process.

Validity

As we discussed in Chapter 2, there are a several ways to think about the validity of an assessment, and several types of evidence that pertain to the validity of the national board assessments. Here we address content- and construct-based validity evidence.

Content-Based Validity Evidence

The board, with the help of its TAG, has conducted three types of studies to gather content-based validity evidence. First, Hattie (1996) conducted a detailed investigation of the processes used to develop the content standards. According to Jaeger (1998), Hattie and his colleagues examined such factors as the expertise of the individuals on the standards committees, the extent to which the development of standards had a sound scientific basis, and documentation of links between content standards and accepted theory about the nature of accomplished teaching. Jaeger indicates that the results of this review were positive, but a detailed account of the study could not be located.[12]

The second type of content-based evidence collected was based on an examination of the congruence between the assessment and its content domain. The procedures utilized for these studies are documented in Crocker (1997) and in the Technical Report (National Board for Professional Teaching Standards, 2007, Appendix 8). These studies relied on the judgments of expert panels about the appropriateness of the domain defined by the content standards for a given assessment and the degree to which the exercises and scoring represent the intended content domain. A total of 21 panels of teachers were convened, with each panel focusing on a specific certificate; each panel had between 9 and 17 participants. The panelists who participated in these exercises were experienced teachers recommended by school superintendents or state departments of education.

Specifically, the panelists were asked to evaluate the extent to which (1) the content standards described the critical aspects of the domain of teaching they were intended to represent; (2) the exercises assess the knowledge, skills, and competencies described by the content standards; (3) the rubrics focus on the knowledge, skills, and competencies described by the content standards; (4) each standard is assessed by the overall assessment; and (5) the assessment as a whole distinguishes between accomplished teachers and those who are not accomplished. According to Jaeger (1998), the findings from these studies, which were conducted on all assessments in existence at the time, indicated that the exercises and rubrics were relevant to and important for the content standards and that they effectively represented those content standards. No results are reported in the Technical Report (National Board for Professional Teaching Standards, 2007), but an example is available in Loyd (1995), which provides details about the application

---

[12]Just prior to the publication of this report, details were published in Hattie (2008).

of this method of content validation to the standards, exercises, and rubrics for the early adolescence generalist assessment.

The third type of content-based evidence focused on the scoring rubrics. For this study, panelists reviewed a series of pairs of exercise responses that had been scored as part of the operational scoring procedures. Panelists were asked to review the content standards for the assessment and to make judgments about which of each pair of responses should receive the higher score for consistency with the standards. These panelists also reviewed the rubrics and the notes that raters made while scoring responses and evaluated the extent to which these materials were representative of the content domain. Jaeger (1998) describes this study but does not report the results, saying only that the results were satisfactory and the full reports were provided to the national board.

Construct-Based Validity Evidence

The board, with the assistance of its TAG, has also collected construct-based validity evidence for the NBPTS assessments. The most extensive study involved actual classroom observations of teachers and is reported in Bond et al. (2000). In this study, the researchers sought to evaluate the extent to which board-certified teachers exhibit in their classroom practice the knowledge, skills, dispositions, and judgments that are measured by the assessment. Working with a small sample of board-certified teachers (n = 31) and unsuccessful applicants (n = 34) teaching in Delaware, Maryland, North Carolina, Ohio, and Virginia, they compared the performance of the two groups.

The researchers conducted an extensive review of the literature on teaching expertise and identified 15 key dimensions of teaching. They developed protocols to evaluate teachers on these dimensions, using classroom observations, reviews of teacher assignments and student work, interviews with students, student questionnaires that asked about classroom environment and climate and evaluated student motivation and self-efficacy, and student performance on a writing assessment.

The authors found that board-certified teachers scored higher on all of these dimensions than did the unsuccessful candidates, although some of the differences were greater than others. For example, analyses of student work indicated that 74 percent of the work samples of students taught by board-certified teachers reflected deep understanding, while 29 percent of the work samples of nonboard-certified teachers were judged to reflect deep understanding. Differences in student motivation and self-efficacy levels were negligible, as were differences in the teachers' participation in professional activities, including both collaborative activities with other professionals to improve the effectiveness of the school and efforts to engage parents and others in the community in the education of young people.

Two similar investigations were conducted as part of the grant-funded studies sponsored by the NBPTS. Smith, Gordon, Colby, and Wang (2005) built on the prior work of Bond et al. (2000), using some of the same methodologies to compare the instructional practices and resulting student work of 64 teachers from 17 states. The sample included board-certified teachers (n = 35) and teachers who were unsuccessful applicants for board certification (n = 29). The researchers evaluated each teacher's description of a unit of lessons; work samples from six randomly selected students in each teacher's classroom; and (for some of the teachers) students' responses to a writing exercise. The teachers' instructional materials and the students' work samples were evaluated for depth using a taxonomy developed by Hattie and described in the Bond et al. study (2000).

Analysis of the student work samples showed a tendency toward more depth on the part of students taught by board-certified teachers than those taught by the unsuccessful candidates, although the differences were not statistically significant. Performance on the writing assessment was statistically significant and higher for students taught by board-certified teachers than unsuccessful applicants. However, no attempt was made to control for the prior writing ability of the students (i.e., the students assigned to board-certified teachers may have been better writers from the outset), and the sample that participated in this part of the study was very small (nine board-certified teachers and nine unsuccessful applicants). Analysis of teachers' assignments showed that board-certified teachers were more than twice as likely to aim instruction at in-depth learning than were nonboard-certified teachers.

McColskey, Stronge, and colleagues (2005) also examined teachers' classroom practices, by comparing results for a sample of board-certified teachers (n = 21) and a sample of nonboard-certified teachers, who were further separated into "highly effective" (n = 16) and "least effective" (n = 14) groups based on their students' achievement test performance. Data were collected from fifth-grade teachers working in four school districts in North Carolina, two urban and two rural. The goal of the study was to observe classroom practices and gather a variety of information from the teachers, similar to the types of information collected by Bond et al. (2000) and Smith et al. (2005), but the authors had significant difficulty recruiting nonboard-certified teachers to participate. A total of 70 least effective and 70 highly effective teachers were invited, but only about a quarter of the teachers in each group agreed. In contrast, 25 board-certified teachers were invited to participate and nearly all (n = 21) agreed to participate. The relatively low participation rates for the nonboard-certified teachers introduces the potential for sampling bias into this study.

McColskey, Stronge, and colleagues evaluated teachers on 15 dimensions of teacher effectiveness. For 4 of the 15 dimensions of teacher effectiveness that were based on classroom observations, statistically significant differences favored the highly effective nonboard-certified teachers over the board-certified ones. Board-certified teachers had significantly higher ratings than the other two groups in the cognitive challenge of their reading comprehension assignments and their planning activities. The authors found no statistical differences on some of the other attributes they examined, which included classroom management and the cognitive demand of the questions asked during lessons. The selection bias associated with the recruitment of nonboard-certified teachers makes it difficult to draw firm conclusions from this study.

Criterion-Related Validity Evidence

Criterion-related validity evidence is not typically expected for certification tests. As noted earlier, certification tests are designed primarily to identify candidates who have achieved some specified level of competence over some domain of knowledge, skills, and judgments (the KSJ domain). The results are interpreted as indicating that passing candidates have achieved the specified level of competence and the failing candidates have not met the standard. The validation of this kind of interpretation generally relies mainly on evaluations of how well the content of the assessment covers the KSJ domain (content-related evidence), the reliability of the assessment, and assurance that the results are not subject to any major source of systematic errors (e.g., method effects associated with testing format or context effects). The content-related validity evidence is generally based on evaluation of the procedures used to develop and implement the assessment and by judgments about the representativeness of the final product.

The rationale for certification programs typically depends on an assumption that higher levels of competence in the KSJ domain are associated with better performance in some area of activity, and the justification for assigning consequences (positive or negative) to the results of certification assessments always depends on this kind of assumption. For example, the requirement that one pass a written test (based on knowledge of the rules of the road) and a driving test (covering basic skills) is based on the assumption that individuals who lack the knowledge and skills being evaluated would be unsafe drivers. Similarly, certification in a medical specialty will generally require that the candidate pass a written test of knowledge and judgment and completion of a residency program in which a wide variety of skills and clinical judgment have to be demonstrated. In most cases, the assumption that competence in the KSJ domain is needed for effective performance in practice is justified by expert judgment about the KSJs required in practice and by a research base that associates various activities and the KSJs needed to perform these activities with valued outcomes (i.e., avoiding accidents, curing patients). For example, we expect board-certified neurologists to know the symptoms of various neurological disorders and how to treat these disorders, and we expect them to be skilled in conducting appropriate tests and in administering appropriate treatments. We take it as a given that an individual who does not have such knowledge and skill should not be certified as a neurologist, and, at a more mundane level, we assume that a person who does not know what a stop sign looks like should not earn a driver's license.

Given this interpretation and use of certification testing, traditional criterion-related validity evidence is not necessarily required, and one does not generally examine the validity of certification tests by correlating individual test scores with a measure of the outcomes produced by the individuals. Although there are a few situations in which such evidence has been collected (e.g., Norcini, Lipner, and Kimball, 2002; Tamblyn et al., 1998, 2002), in most cases, no adequate criterion is available, and, in practice, the outcomes depend on many variables beyond the competence of the individual practitioner. Even the best driver can get into accidents, and even the best neurologist will not be successful in every case. Developing a good certification test is difficult: Developing a good criterion measure with which to validate the certification tests is typically much more difficult than developing the test. Furthermore, the use of some convenient but not necessarily adequate criterion measure (e.g., death rates, accident rates) may be more misleading than informative.

However, the requirement that competence in the KSJ domain be related to outcomes (e.g., patient outcomes, road safety) does involve a predictive component, and this predictive component may or may not be supported by empirical evidence. The predictive component involves the assumption that certified practitioners who have demonstrated competence in the KSJ domain will generate better outcomes than potential practitioners who have not achieved this level of competence in the KSJ domain. This assumption can be empirically evaluated by comparing the performance of those who passed the certification test with those who failed. If the certified practitioners produce better outcomes on average than candidates who failed the certification test, there is direct evidence for the assumption that the KSJs being measured by the certification test are relevant to the quality of practice as reflected in outcomes. If the certified practitioners do not produce better outcomes than the candidates who failed the certification test, there is evidence that the KSJs being measured by the certification test are not particularly relevant to the quality of practice outcomes. In the latter case, it may be that the KSJs are simply not major determinants of outcomes, that the certification test is not doing a good job of measuring the KSJs, or that some source of systematic error is present. For whatever reason, in this example, the pass/fail status on the test is not a good predictor of future performance in practice. Even this kind of group-level (passing versus failing candidates) evidence of predictive validity is hard to attain in many contexts, but in this case some criterion-related evidence is available, and we devote Chapter 7 to a discussion of this kind of research.

As is usually the case whenever group-level criterion data are available, the criterion for which data are available in the present context (teacher certification) is far from perfect. For all of the studies discussed in Chapter 7, the criterion is student performance on the state's standardized achievement tests used for accountability purposes. The specific criterion is student score gains (or student scores adjusted for prior achievement), which are adjusted for various student and school variables. Standardized achievement test scores capture some of the cognitive outcomes of education, but certainly not all of them. State testing programs cover a few core subjects (particularly reading and math) and tend both to focus on knowledge and skills that can be evaluated using a limited set of test formats (e.g., multiple-choice questions, short-answer questions, and perhaps writing samples) and to exclude exercises that take a long time, that involve cooperation, or that would be difficult to grade. Furthermore, these outcomes are influenced by the context of the school and the community and the previous achievement and experiences of the students. These factors add noise to the system, and although it is possible to correct for many of these factors, the statistical models used to do so are complicated and difficult to interpret (see Chapter 7). Nevertheless, states' accountability achievement tests do cover some of the desired outcomes of education in various grades and are therefore relevant to the evaluation of a certification program.

While the results vary across studies, states, and models in general, the findings indicate that teachers who achieved board certification were more effective in raising test scores than teachers who sought certification but failed. Additional details about the studies are provided in Chapter 7.

Committee Comments

The studies discussed in this chapter document efforts to validate the procedures used to identify the content standards, the extent to which assessment exercises and rubrics are consistent with the content standards and intended domain, the application of the rubrics and scoring procedures, and the extent to which teachers who become board certified demonstrate the targeted skills in their day-to-day practice. All of these studies tend to support the proposed interpretation of board certification as an indication of accomplished teaching, in that the board-certified teachers were found to be engaging in teaching activities identified as exemplary practice. These studies also provided some evidence that the work of students being taught by board-certified teachers exhibited more depth than that of students taught by nonboard-certified teachers. Although the number of studies is small, the sample sizes in all these studies are modest (as they usually are in this kind of research), and the McColskey and Stronge study had sampling problems, it is worth noting that most certification programs do not collect this kind of validity evidence. As we explained in Chapter 2, certification programs generally rely on content-based validity evidence.

With regard to the validity evidence, we draw two conclusions:

Conclusion 5-5: Although content-based validity evidence is limited, our review indicates that the NBPTS assessment exercises probably reflect performance on the content standards.

Conclusion 5-6: The construct-based validity evidence is derived from a set of studies with modest sample sizes, but they provide support for the proposed interpretation of national board certification as evidence of accomplished teaching.

Fairness

Fairness is an important consideration in evaluating high-stakes testing programs. In general, fairness does not require that all groups of candidates perform similarly on the assessment, but rather that there is no systematic bias in the assessment. That is, candidates of equal standing with respect to the skills and content being measured should, on average, earn the same test score and have the same chance of passing, irrespective of group membership (American Educational Research Association, American Psychological Association, and National Council on Measurement in Education, 1999, p. 74).

Because the true skill levels of candidates are not known, fairness cannot generally be directly examined. Instead, fairness is evaluated by gathering many types of information, some based on the processes the test developer uses to design the assessment and some based on empirical data about test performance. For instance, test developers should ensure that there are no systematic differences across groups (e.g., as defined by race, gender) in access to information about the assessment, in opportunities to take the assessment, or in the grading of the results. Test developers should attend to potential sources of bias when they develop test questions and should utilize experts to conduct bias reviews of all questions before they are operationally administered.

Test developers can examine test performance for various candidate groups (e.g., gender, racial/ethnic, geographical region) so that they can be aware of group differences, seek to understand them, and strive to reduce them, if at all possible. In addition, test developers can examine performance by group membership on individual items (e.g., using such techniques as analyses of differential item functioning). When differential functioning is found, test developers can try to identify the source of any differences and eliminate them to the extent possible. In the case of credentialing assessments, group differences are typically evaluated by examining pass rates by group.

The NBPTS takes a number of steps to ensure fairness in the testing process. During the scoring process, the raters go through an extensive bias training intended to make them aware of any biases they bring to the scoring and to minimize the impact of these biases on their scoring. In addition, the board examines differences in test performances for candidates grouped by gender and by race/ethnicity and has conducted several studies focused on investigating sources of differences.

Group Differences and Disparate Impact

Two statistical indices are typically used to indicate the extent of group differences in testing performance: the effect size and differential pass rates. The effect size (d) is the standardized difference between two groups' mean scores.[13] With regard to gender groups, women generally receive higher scores than men on all of the NBPTS assessments, although the male-female difference on the assessment center exercises is quite small. With regard to racial/ethnic group differences, whites receive higher exercise scores than other racial/ethnic groups, and effect sizes for the portfolios are smaller than those for the assessment center exercises. The average difference between the performance of whites and African Americans (across the three administration cycles and all 24 certificates) has an effect size favoring whites of .53 for the portfolios and .70 for the assessment center exercises. Although these differences are large, they are not unusual. The portfolio effect sizes, in particular, are smaller than what is typically observed for cognitively loaded tests, but this may be a statistical artifact associated with the generally lower reliability of the portfolio exercises (Sackett, Schmitt, Ellingson, and Kabin, 2001).

Table 5-5 shows the effect sizes resulting from comparing performance for whites and African Americans on individual exercises on the middle childhood generalist and early adolescence mathematics assessments. The early adolescence mathematics exercise effect sizes follow the general pattern we observed across all certificates, in which the effect sizes for the assessment center exercises (i.e., median = .73) are notably higher than

---

[13](Group 1 Mean – Group 2 Mean)/Pooled Standard Deviation.

TABLE 5-5 Average White-African American Group Differences Across Three Administration Cycles (2002-2005) for Early Adolescence Mathematics and Middle Childhood Generalist

Exercises	Type	Average Effect Size
Early adolescence mathematics		
Developing and assessing mathematical thinking and reasoning	Portfolio	.39
Instructional analysis: whole class mathematical discourse	Portfolio	.35
Instructional analysis: small group mathematical collaboration	Portfolio	.44
Documented accomplishments: contributions to student learning	Portfolio	.40
Algebra and functions	Assessment	.75
Connections	Assessment	.54
Data analysis	Assessment	.70
Geometry	Assessment	.78
Number and operations sense	Assessment	.93
Technology and manipulatives	Assessment	.67
Range		.35 to .93
Middle childhood generalist		
Writing: thinking through the process	Portfolio	.50
Building a classroom community through social studies	Portfolio	.46
Integrating mathematics with science	Portfolio	.55
Documented accomplishments: contributions in student learning	Portfolio	.51
Supporting reading skills	Assessment	.63
Analyzing student work	Assessment	.62
Knowledge of science	Assessment	.61
Social studies	Assessment	.60
Understanding health	Assessment	.61
Integrating the arts	Assessment	.62
Range		.46 to .62

those for the portfolios (i.e., median = .40). This trend also appears for the middle childhood generalist exercises, but the magnitude of the effect size difference is not as large.

The differential ratio takes into account the passing rate. It compares the percentages of individuals in two different groups who achieved a passing score (i.e., percentage of African Americans who passed versus the percentage of whites who passed). The legally recognized criterion for disparate impact is referred to as the four-fifths rule. That is, if the differential ratio is less than .80, meaning that the minority passing rate is less than four-fifths of the majority passing rate, disparate impact is said to have occurred (Uniform Guidelines on Employee Selection Procedures). It is important to note, however, that disparate impact alone does not indicate that the test is biased.

Over the three administration cycles that we analyzed, the average passing rate was 38 percent across all certificates. Passing rates for candidates grouped by race/ethnicity were 41 percent for whites, 12 percent for African Americans, and 31 percent for Hispanics. On average, across certificates, there is disparate impact for both African Americans and Hispanics, but the disparate impact is much larger for African Americans.

With regard to the two assessments studied in depth, both showed disparate impact for African Americans and, for the most part, for Hispanics as well. For the middle childhood generalist, the average overall pass rate was 35 percent across the three administration cycles. The African American and Hispanic pass rates were 12 and 21 percent, respectively, and for whites was 38 percent. For early adolescence mathematics, the average overall pass rate was 32 percent. The pass rate for whites was 32 percent; the rate for African Americans was 9 percent and that for Hispanics was 26 percent. Comparisons of these pass rates shows disparate impact in all cases except for the white-Hispanic comparison on the early adolescence mathematics assessment.

NBPTS Research on Disparate Impact

The board has been concerned about disparate impact since the early days of the program and has conducted several studies to investigate it. The TAG members, particularly Lloyd Bond (1998a,b) spearheaded most of this research. The results from Bond's studies suggest that there is no simple explanation for the white-African American difference. He found that there do not appear to be important differences between the number of advanced degrees and years of teaching experience of white and African American candidates. To investigate the possibility that disparate impact resulted in part from differing levels of collegial, administrative, and technical support, the board conducted in-depth phone interviews of candidates. In the end, the analyses suggested that the level and quality of support were not major factors in the disparate impact observed (Bond, 1998a,b).

The board also investigated the possibility that an irrelevant variable (e.g., writing ability) may be causing the disparate impact. The board identified an early adolescent generalist exercise with significant writing demands and others that did not rely so heavily on writing. They conducted analyses to assess the effects of race/ethnicity and writing demands and whether there were systematic differences in candidates' performance on the writing exercises that could be attributable to race/ethnicity. The results showed statistically significant main effects of race/ethnicity and of extent of writing demand. However, the interaction effect (of race/ethnicity by exercise writing demand) type interaction was not statistically significant, which indicated that the racial/ethnic differences could not be accounted for by the writing demand required by the exercises.

The board also conducted analyses to assess the possibility that disparate impact might be a function of rater judgments and biases. Initially, they identified a small number of cases in the scoring process in which African American and white raters evaluated the performances of the same candidates. They compared the assigned scores in relation to the rater's and candidate's race/ethnicity. Their analyses revealed that African American raters tended to be slightly more lenient overall, but they found no interaction between rater race/ethnicity and candidate race/ethnicity. That is, African American candidates who were scored low by white raters were also scored low by African American raters. Since this initial, small-sample study, the board has continued to conduct similar analyses, whenever the data and sample sizes have permitted. Results of the later efforts echo those from the early work. Thus, rater bias does not appear to be the source of disparate impact (Bond, 1998b).

Other investigations have focused on instructional styles and the NBPTS vision of accomplished practice. One study (Bond, 1998a) investigated the possibility that the teaching style most effective for African American children, who are often taught by African American teachers, is not favored on the assessment. Subpanels of a review team "read across" the portfolios and assessment center exercises submitted by candidates in a study sample (raters typically rate only one kind of exercise over the course of any given scoring session). The 15-member panel was divided into five groups of three raters. Performance materials for all 37 African American candidates in 1993-1994 and 1994-1995 for early adolescence English/language arts were distributed to the groups. Raters reviewed all 37 candidates independently and judged whether the candidate's materials contained culturally related markers that might adversely affect their evaluation of the candidate's accomplishment. Of the 37 candidates, 12 were deemed accomplished by at least one panel member. During the operational scoring, only 5 of 37 had been certified. While this study resulted in a few of the candidates who had originally failed being classified as accomplished, it did not reveal consistent differences in instructional styles for African American teachers.

Another study by Bond (1998a) considered varying views of accomplished practice as a source of group differences. A total of 25 African American teachers participated in focus group discussions (some were currently practicing and some were former teachers). They were asked to (a) discuss the scope and content of the NBPTS certification standards and note how the standards differed from their own views about accomplished practice, (b) discuss the portfolio instructions with a view toward possible sources of disparate impact, (c) apply their own weights to the early adolescence English/language arts assessment exercises, and (d) evaluate the small-group discussion exercise component for two candidates. The major conclusions that Bond (1998a) drew from the focus groups are listed below.

- Without powerful incentives, accomplished African American teachers would generally not seek NBPTS certification for fear of risking their excellent reputations.
- Constraints imposed by districts and by students may work against African American teachers (e.g., district content guides that are in conflict with NBPTS views).
- Given that academically advanced students tend to make their teachers look good, those who teach students who are seriously behind, as many African American teachers do, are forced to teach lessons that may appear trivial to raters.
- There was a concern that some principals keep African American teachers out of the loop regarding professional opportunities.

Committee Comments

On the basis of our review of differential pass rates and research on the sources of disparate impact, we conclude:

Conclusion 5-7: The board has been unusually diligent in examining fairness issues, particularly in investigating differences in performance across groups defined by race/ethnicity and gender and in investigating possible causes for such differences. The board certification process exhibits disparate impact, particularly for African American candidates, but research suggests that this is not the result of bias in the assessments.

FINDINGS, CONCLUSIONS, AND RECOMMENDATIONS

Our primary questions pertaining to the psychometric evaluation of the national board certification program for accomplished teachers are (a) whether the assessment is designed to cover appropriate content (i.e., knowledge, skills, disposition, and judgment), (b) the extent to which the assessments reliably measure the requisite knowledge, skills, dispositions, and judgment and support the proposed interpretations of candidate performance, and (c) whether an appropriate standard is used to determine whether candidates have passed or failed. Our review suggests that the program has generally taken appropriate steps to ensure that the assessment meets professional test standards.

However, we find the lack of technical documentation about the assessment to be of concern. It is customary for high-stakes assessment programs to undergo regular evaluations and to make their procedures and technical operations open for external scrutiny. Maintaining complete records that are easily accessible is necessary for effective evaluations and is a critical element of a well-run assessment program. Moreover, adequate documentation is one of the fundamental responsibilities of a test developer described in the various national test standards. We return to this point in Chapter 12, and we offer advice to the board about its documentation procedures. It was difficult to obtain basic information about the design and development of the NBPTS assessments that was sufficiently detailed to allow independent evaluation. In early 2007, the NBPTS drafted a technical report in order to fill some of the information gaps, but for the program to be in compliance with professional testing standards in this regard, this material should have been readily available soon after the program became operational and should have been regularly updated (American Educational Research Association, American Psychological Association, and National Council on Measurement in Education, 1999; Society for Industrial and Organizational Psychology, 2003). While the number of certificates makes this documentation requirement challenging, it does not eliminate the obligation. Indeed, it makes it even more imperative, as it would help ensure consistency in quality and approach across certificates.

We also found it difficult to get a reasonable picture of what is actually assessed through the assessment exercises and portfolios. Initially, released exercises and responses were not made available to us. Eventually, the board did provide sample portfolio exercises and entries, which greatly helped us to understand the assessment. Overall, we were impressed by the richness of performance information provided by the assessment, and we think that these kinds of sample materials should be more widely available, both to teachers who are considering applying or preparing their submissions and to the various NBPTS stakeholders and users of the test results, such as school administrators, policy makers, and others, so that they better understand what is required of teachers who earn board certification.

The NBPTS has chosen to use performance assessments and portfolios in order to measure the general skills and dispositions that it considers fundamental to accomplished teaching. This approach is likely to enhance the authenticity of the assessment, especially in the eyes of teachers, but it also makes it difficult to achieve high levels of reliability, in part because these assessment methods involve subjective scoring and in part because each assessment generally involves relatively few exercises. As a result, the assessments tend to have relatively low reliabilities, lower than those generally expected in high-stakes assessments—on the order of .80 or .90 (Guion, 1998).

There is a significant trade-off in this choice. The use of portfolios and performance assessments allows the national board to focus the assessment on the competencies that they view as the core of advanced teaching practice and therefore tend to improve the validity of the assessments as a measure of these core competencies. The use of these assessments may also enhance the credibility of the assessment for various groups of stakeholders. However, the use of these techniques makes it far more difficult to achieve desirable reliability levels than would be the case if the board relied on more traditional assessment techniques (e.g., performance assessments involving larger numbers of shorter exercises or, in the extreme case, short-answer questions or multiple-choice items).

The board has made a serious attempt to assess the core components of accomplished teaching and has adopted assessment methods (portfolio, samples of performance) that are particularly well suited to assessing accomplished practice. The board seems to have done a good job of developing and implementing the assessment in a way that is consistent with their stated goals. Validity requires both relevance to the construct of interest (in this case, accomplished teaching) and reliability. The NBPTS assessments seem to exhibit a high degree of relevance. Their reliability (with its consequences for decision consistency) could use improvement. We also note that the reliability estimates for the assessments tend to be reasonable for these assessment methods, although they do not reach the levels we would expect of more traditional assessment methods. The question is whether they are good enough in an absolute sense, and our answer is a weak yes; there are inherent disadvantages to the national board's assessments that come along with its clear advantages.

On the basis of our review, we offer the following recommendations. We note that these recommendations are directed at the NBPTS, as our charge requested, but they highlight issues that should apply to any program that offers advanced-level certification to teachers.

Recommendation 5-1: The NBPTS should publish thorough technical documentation for the program as a whole and for individual specialty area assessments. This documentation should cover processes as well as products, should be readily available, and should be updated on a regular basis.

Recommendation 5-2: The NBPTS should develop a more structured process for deriving exercise content and scoring rubrics from the content standards and should thoroughly document application of the process for each assessment. Doing so will make it easier for the board to maintain the highest possible validity for the resulting assessments and to provide evidence suitable for independent evaluation of that validity.

Recommendation 5-3: The NBPTS should conduct research to determine whether the reliability of the assessment process could be improved (for example, by the inclusion of a number of shorter exercises in the computer-based component) without compromising the authenticity or validity of the assessment or substantially increasing its cost.

Recommendation 5-4: The NBPTS should collect and use the available operational data about the individual assessment exercises to improve the validity and reliability of the assessments for each certificate, as well as to minimize adverse impact.

Recommendation 5-5: The NBPTS should revisit the methods it uses to estimate the reliabilities of its assessments to determine whether the methods should be updated.

Recommendation 5-6: The NBPTS should periodically review the assessment model to determine whether adjustments are warranted to take advantage of advances in measurement technologies and developments in the teaching environment.

6

Teacher Participation in the Program

The vision laid out in the national board's founding document, *A Nation Prepared* (Carnegie Task Force on Teaching as a Profession, 1986) is of a system in which board certification becomes increasingly well known, respected, and widespread. Not only would administrators be able to use certification status to guide accomplished teachers to high-needs schools, but growing numbers of board-certified teachers would assume mentoring roles and share their skills with other teachers. Moreover, the task force anticipated that board-certified teachers would be in high demand in that salary structures for teachers would provide substantial rewards for earning board certification, and that states would encourage certification and support its underlying goals in other ways. Together, all of these improvements in the profession would keep the most accomplished teachers in the classroom, have a beneficial influence on the skills of all teachers, and help to attract larger numbers of able teachers to the field.

Board certification cannot produce such effects unless there is sufficient participation in the program so that a critical mass of board-certified teachers is present in schools, districts, and states. Thus, a clear understanding of the extent of participation, the factors that influence participation, and the ways in which board-certified teachers are distributed among states, districts, and schools is a critical component of an evaluation of the program.

In this chapter, we address the third question on our framework:

Question 3: To what extent do teachers participate in the program?

Figure 2-1 shows how this question fits into our overall framework. To investigate this question, the committee identified the following subsidiary questions:

a.   How many teachers apply each year for board certification? Have there been changes in application rates over time? How do application rates compare across states and districts? What are the characteristics of teachers who apply compared with those who do not? What are the characteristics of teachers who successfully earn board certification compared with those who do not?

b.   Why do teachers choose to participate or not? What do various agencies (the board, states, school districts, teachers unions, etc.) do to encourage participation? How do these actions influence teachers' attitudes toward certification and participation in the process?

To address these questions, we relied on information from two sources. The first source was the National Board for Professional Teaching Standards (NBPTS) itself. National board staff members provided written responses to questions we submitted, as well as other information about participation rates, including an electronic version of their longitudinal candidate database for our own analyses. The second source was a research base consisting of seven studies that focused on teachers' motivations for pursuing board certification. In the sections that follow, we first examine participation patterns, comparing participation rates over time and by state and school district, as well as the characteristics of teachers who pursue board certification. We then turn to a discussion of the reasons teachers decide to obtain board certification. Additional details about the specific sources we used are provided in the relevant sections.

In the sections that follow, we use the terms "applicants," "candidates," and "participants" interchangeably, to refer to all teachers who apply for board certification by completing the entire assessment process, regardless of whether they pass the assessment or not. The term "achievers" denotes teachers who earn board certification by completing the assessment process and receive a passing score.

HOW MANY TEACHERS HAVE PARTICIPATED?

The national board provided the committee with information that we used to determine the levels of participation in the program and the characteristics of participants. The electronic data set supplied by the national board contained background characteristics for teachers who applied for and earned board certification between 1993-1994 and 2005-2006,[1] as well as information about the states in which these applicants resided and the types of schools in which they worked at the time of application. Information identifying the school districts in which teachers worked at the time of application was not included on the electronic data file because of confidentiality concerns, but the national board provided the information we needed in response to specific requests. Below we summarize the information we obtained with regard to national, state, and district participation rates, as well as the characteristics of national board participants in comparison with the full population of teachers in the United States.

National Participation Rates

The national board's assessments became operational in 1993, and since that time approximately 99,300 teachers have applied for board certification and approximately 63,800 have achieved it.[2] It is not possible to determine how many of these teachers are still teaching, and we therefore cannot determine the precise percentage of the current teacher workforce these numbers represent. However, according to data from the National Center for Education Statistics' Schools and Staffing Survey (SASS), there were just over 3.7 million teachers in the country in the 2003-2004 school years, and approximately 3.1 million (83 percent) teachers were eligible to apply for board certification.[3] The total number of applicants for board certification represents 2.6 percent of the entire teaching force and 3.2 percent of the eligible teaching force. The total number of teachers who have earned board certification represents 1.7 percent of the entire teaching force and 2.0 percent of those eligible. These rates of both participation and achievement are likely to be overestimates of their share of the workforce, since it is not likely that all of the applicants and achievers are still teaching.[4]

---

[1]Unless specified otherwise, our analyses throughout this chapter are based on data from 1993-1994 through 2005-2006 because those were the data available to us during the course of the project.

[2]These figures include the numbers for the 2006-2007 school year, which became available just prior to the release of this report.

[3]NBPTS prerequisites are that a teacher must have earned a bachelor's degree, must have completed three full years of teaching, and must have a valid license throughout that period. See Chapter 4 for further details about the eligibility requirements.

[4]In calculating the percentages, we used as the numerator the total cumulative numbers of teachers who have pursued and obtained board certification during the life of the program; there is no way to verify whether they are currently teaching or not. The denominator includes the number of licensed teachers employed in the 2003-2004 school year. It is unlikely that all of the teachers who have pursued board certification were still working as of 2003-2004, and, as a result, the participation rates we report are likely to be overestimates.

TABLE 6-1 Participation in NBPTS Certification 1993-2007

	1993-1994	1994-1995	1995-1996	1996-1997	1997-1998	1998-1999	1999-2000
Applicants[a]	542	346	520	720	1,837	5,423	6,815
Achievers[b]	177	199	219	318	924	2,969	4,728

[a]Applicants include only first-time applicants who completed the entire assessment process.

Although participation rates are low, they have increased over the years. Only 542 teachers attempted the assessment the first year board certification was offered when certification was available in two areas,[5] and just 177 were successful. Since 2001, the number of first-time applicants has been over 11,000 per year, and between 7,300 and 8,500 teachers have earned board certification each year. Table 6-1 displays the participation levels over the past 14 school years, showing the number of applicants and achievers nationwide. While the rate of growth has not been regular, the trend across the life of the program has been upward.

Participation Rates by State

Participation rates vary considerably from state to state, in part because of differences in the extent to which states encourage teachers to pursue board certification (an issue taken up in more detail later in the chapter). Table 6-2 displays the number of teachers who have applied for and earned board certification by state between 1993-1994 through 2005-2006.[6] In this table, the entry for "state" indicates the location where the teacher was employed at the time she or he pursued board certification, not where the teacher currently works.

For each state, the table shows the number of applicants and achievers as a percentage of the number of eligible teachers in the state. The percentages of eligible teachers applying range from a low of 0.2 percent in New Hampshire and Texas to a high of 21 percent in North Carolina. The percentages of teachers who earned board certification range from 0.1 percent in New Hampshire, New Jersey, and Texas to a high of nearly 13 percent in

---

[5]By 1997-1998, certification was available in seven areas; by 2000-2001, 19 areas were available; by 2005-2006, there were 24, and there are currently 25.

[6]All analyses by state are based on the electronic database we received from the NBPTS and report data for the 1993-1994 through 2005-2006 school years.

2000-2001	2001-2002	2002-2003	2003-2004	2004-2005	2005-2006	2006-2007	Total
10,121	13,886	12,313	11,894	11,688	11,007	12,221	99,321
6,508	7,897	8,211	8,067	7,300	7,807	8,547	63,847

[b]Achievers include all candidates who achieved during their three-year candidacy; hence beginning in 1997-1998, the number of achievers in a given year corresponds to first-time applicants in that given year and a portion of first-time applicants from the prior two years who did not achieve in their first attempts.

North Carolina. The majority of the board-certified teachers in the country, 66 percent, were found in seven states: California, Florida, Georgia, Mississippi, North Carolina, Ohio, and South Carolina.

Participation Rates by School Districts

There are approximately 14,000 school districts in the country and 96,513 public and private schools (http://nces.ed.gov/programs/digest/d06/tables/dt06_083.asp). If board-certified teachers were evenly spread across the country (assuming that all of the 63,800 board-certified teachers were still working), this would translate to an average of four to five board-certified teachers per school district, three for every five schools. However, participation is not even across the country and varies as much by district as by state.

The NBPTS assisted us in conducting an analysis of 13 years' worth of data (1993-1994 through 2005-2006) on the districts where teachers were employed at the time they applied for board certification. These analyses revealed that, during this 13-year period in about 8,901 school districts (64 percent),[7] there were no teachers who applied for board certification. Another 2,513 (18 percent) districts had only one or two applicants. Approximately 1,008 districts (7 percent) had between three and five applicants during this time period. In 593 districts (4 percent) there were between six and 10 teacher applicants, and in the remaining 985 districts (7 percent), 11 or more teachers applied.

With regard to the distribution of board-certified teachers, in 9,846 districts (70 percent), there were no teachers who earned board certification during this time period, and another 2,200 districts (16 percent) had only one or two teachers who became board certified during this time span. Ap-

---

[7]These figures are approximates because some candidates do not report their school district, and thus the district is unknown.

TABLE 6-2 Certification Applicants and Achievers Nationwide and by State, 1993-2006

State	Applicants[a]	Achievers[a]	Total Teachers Eligible for Board Certification[b]	Applicants as a Percentage of Eligible Teachers[b]	Achievers as a Percentage of Eligible Teachers[b]
All states	87,112	55,324	3,097,271	2.8	1.8
Alabama	1,606	1,096	50,361	3.2	2.2
Alaska	115	76	7,765	1.5	1.0
Arizona	527	346	49,792	1.1	0.7
Arkansas	1,034	585	34,929	3.0	1.7
California	5,493	3,645	273,548	2.0	1.3
Colorado	424	271	46,784	0.9	0.6
Connecticut	162	126	43,946	0.4	0.3
Delaware	496	348	7,858	6.3	4.4
District of Columbia	78	18	5,080	1.5	0.4
Florida	15,222	9,223	145,826	10.4	6.3
Georgia	3,695	2,335	94,765	3.9	2.5
Hawaii	210	125	13,482	1.6	0.9
Idaho	420	327	14,427	2.9	2.3
Illinois	3,381	1,985	137,972	2.5	1.4
Indiana	280	131	61,097	0.5	0.2
Iowa	681	527	39,045	1.7	1.3
Kansas	340	236	36,790	0.9	0.6
Kentucky	1,616	1,120	45,935	3.5	2.4
Louisiana	1,923	1,032	53,155	3.6	1.9
Maine	141	104	19,060	0.7	0.5
Maryland	1,394	823	54,617	2.6	1.5
Massachusetts	656	439	80,792	0.8	0.5
Michigan	458	213	96,307	0.5	0.2
Minnesota	422	285	60,596	0.7	0.5
Mississippi	3,600	2,550	31,729	11.3	8.0
Missouri	601	341	72,455	0.8	0.5
Montana	81	58	12,381	0.7	0.5
Nebraska	88	49	26,150	0.3	0.2
Nevada	420	277	18,324	2.3	1.5
New Hampshire	25	18	14,809	0.2	0.1
New Jersey	282	134	110,326	0.3	0.1
New Mexico	510	234	19,525	2.6	1.2
New York	1,177	690	220,229	0.5	0.3

TABLE 6-2 Continued

State	Applicants[a]	Achievers[a]	Total Teachers Eligible for Board Certification[b]	Applicants as a Percentage of Eligible Teachers[b]	Achievers as a Percentage of Eligible Teachers[b]
North Carolina	17,812	11,325	84,467	21.1	13.4
North Dakota	54	25	9,498	0.6	0.3
Ohio	4,258	2,624	135,515	3.1	1.9
Oklahoma	2,341	1,567	43,544	5.4	3.6
Oregon	346	208	27,573	1.3	0.8
Pennsylvania	460	297	128,605	0.4	0.2
Rhode Island	393	253	13,674	2.9	1.9
South Carolina	7,363	5,075	45,086	16.3	11.3
South Dakota	80	58	11,157	0.7	0.5
Tennessee	431	236	61,139	0.7	0.4
Texas	547	317	257,771	0.2	0.1
Utah	193	106	21,208	0.9	0.5
Vermont	131	90	10,308	1.3	0.9
Virginia	1,872	1,134	135,515	2.2	1.4
Washington	1,784	1,307	61,985	2.9	2.1
West Virginia	432	290	21,824	2.0	1.3
Wisconsin	607	402	73,500	0.8	0.5
Wyoming	178	77	7,149	2.5	1.1

[a]SOURCE: NBPTS data files.
[b]Based on the number of public and private school teachers in the state in 2003-2004 who had met the prerequisites for board certification. SOURCE: SASS 2003-2004.

proximately 800 districts (6 percent) had between three and five teachers who earned board certification during this time span; and 417 districts (3 percent) had between six and 10 teachers. The remaining 707 (5 percent) districts had 11 or more teachers who earned board certification.

There are some districts with fairly large concentrations of board-certified teachers, such as certain areas of North Carolina and Florida. For example, Table 6-3 shows the number of applicant and board-certified teachers for five districts in relation to the total number of teachers and schools in each district. As the table shows, applicants as a percentage of total teachers in these districts range from 7 percent in Miami–Dade County, Florida, to 16 percent in Wake County, North Carolina. The percentages of board-certified teachers range from 4 percent in Miami–Dade County to 11 percent in Wake County.

Another way to consider the concentration of board-certified teachers is in relation to the number of schools in the district. In all five districts in Table 6-3, the ratio of board-certified teachers per school exceeds the national average of three for every five schools. In these schools, the ratio ranges from about two board-certified teachers per school in Miami–Dade County to seven board-certified teachers per school in Wake County.

On the basis of our review of participation rates—nationally, by state, and by district—we present two findings:

Finding 6-1: Overall, participation rates in the NBPTS certification program are low. Approximately 3 percent of the eligible teachers in the country have pursued board certification, and approximately 2 percent of the nation's eligible teachers are currently board certified. While these participation rates are low, the number of teachers pursuing board certification has increased significantly since the program began.

Finding 6-2: The rates at which teachers apply for and earn board certification vary across states and school districts.

TABLE 6-3 National Board-Certification Applicants and Achievers Between 1993 and 2006 in Five School Districts

	Total Teachers	Total Schools	Applicants[a]		Achievers[a]	
			Number	Percentage[b]	Number	Percentage[b]
North Carolina: Charlotte– Mecklenburg[c]	8,860	167	1,359	15	889	10
Wake County[d]	9,703	153	1,574	16	1,110	11
Florida: Broward County[e]	16,756	288	1,615	10	979	6
Brevard County[f]	5,120	113	888	13	464	9
Miami–Dade County[g]	23,629	415	1,692	7	945	4

[a]SOURCE: NBPTS.
[b]Percentage of total teachers.
[c]See http://www.cms.k12.nc.us/discover/pdf/fastfactssheet.pdf.
[d]See http://www.wcpss.net/basic_facts.html.
[e]See http://www.fldoe.org/eias/flmove/broward.asp.
[f]See http://www.fldoe.org/eias/flmove/brevard.asp.
[g]See http://www.fldoe.org/eias/flmove/dade.asp.

CHARACTERISTICS OF PARTICIPANTS

Background Characteristics

The NBPTS electronic data set supplied to the committee contained background characteristics for teachers who applied for board certification between 1993-1994 and 2005-2006, based on information they provided when they registered for the assessment, together with a pass/fail variable indicating successful and unsuccessful applicants. We did not have access to teachers' scores on the assessment, and the data do not include the number of attempts teachers made before passing.

The committee examined the characteristics of teachers who decide to pursue board certification (see Perda, 2007). We compared the characteristics of applicants for board certification with those of teachers in general, using data from the SASS for 2003-2004. Table 6-4 shows the percentages of all NBPTS-eligible teachers, of national board applicants, and of teachers who successfully earned board certification by gender, race, level of education, employment setting, and grade level taught, as well as the average age and years of experience for these groups. These data indicate that, overall, national board participants are predominantly white women. More than half have a master's degree and teach at the elementary level. On average, national board participants are 40 years old and have 13 years of experience.

Table 6-4 allows comparison of the characteristics of the group of teachers who applied for board certification with the full group of NBPTS-eligible teachers. The groups differ in several ways. While teachers in general were disproportionately female (75.9 percent), the applicant group was even more so (88 percent). African Americans were slightly more prevalent among the group of teachers who applied for board certification than among the overall population of teachers (9.5 versus 7.1 percent nationally), whereas the reverse was true for Hispanics (4.0 versus 5.6 percent nationally). Teachers who applied for board certification were more likely to have a master's degree (57.1 percent) than were NBPTS-eligible teachers in the national sample (49.8 percent). Board applicants were also younger and had less teaching experience (40.6 and 12.4 years, respectively), on average, than were NBPTS-eligible teachers in the national sample (44 and 15.8 years, respectively).

Table 6-4 also shows the group distributions for teachers who successfully achieved board certification. With respect to gender, age, experience, and grade level taught, teachers who earned board certification are similar to teachers who apply. In terms of race and ethnicity, however, there are differences between these two groups.

As noted above, African Americans are overrepresented in the ap-

TABLE 6-4 Characteristics of NBPTS-Eligible Teachers in Public and Private Schools in the United States (2003-2004) and National Board-Certification Applicants and Achievers (1993-2006)

	All NBPTS-Eligible Teachers[a]	Board-Certification Applicants[b]	Board-Certification Achievers[b]	Success Rate[b]
Gender				
Women	75.9	88.0	88.8	64.1
Men	24.1	12.0	11.2	59.1
Race/ethnicity				
American Indian or Alaskan Native	0.5	0.8	0.6	54.9
Asian	1.2	1.1	1.1	61.3
African American	7.1	9.5	4.7	31.4
Hispanic	5.6	4.0	3.4	54.4
Pacific Islander	0.2	0.2	0.2	57.0
White, not of Hispanic origin	84.7	84.5	90.1	67.9
Multiple races, non-Hispanic	0.7	0.0	0.0	—
Highest degree earned				
Less than bachelor's	0.0	0.1	0.1	76.5
Bachelor's	49.0	38.5	35.6	58.7
Master's	49.8	57.1	60.0	66.8
Education specialist	0.0	2.7	2.7	62.9
Doctorate	1.2	1.6	1.6	62.7
Age (mean, SD)	44.0 (10.6)	40.6 (9.1)	40.3 (9.1)	
Years of teaching experience (mean, SD)	15.8 (9.9)	12.4 (7.6)	12.6 (7.6)	
Type of school setting				
Rural	18.6	31.8	31.1	68.2
Suburban	52.6	33.2	35.9	75.6
Urban	28.8	35.1	33.0	65.6
Grade level taught				
Preschool/elementary	50.1	52.4	51.8	62.7
Middle	16.9	20.8	19.8	60.6
High	26.1	26.8	28.3	67.1
Combined	7.0	0.0	0.0	—

[a]Teachers who held a bachelor's degree, had three or more years of teaching experience and were certified by their state or other accrediting or certifying body. SOURCE: SASS 2003-2004.

[b]SOURCE: NBPTS data files.

plicant group compared with their percentages in the general population of teachers, but, at 4.7 percent of those who earn certification, they are underrepresented in the successful applicant group. Column four of Table 6-4 shows the success rate for each group—a combination of the initial pass rate, based on results from the first attempt on taking the assessment, and teachers' persistence levels (teachers may retake the assessment until they obtain the required passing scores). The success rate for African American teachers is less than half that for white teachers (31.4 versus 67.9 percent).[8] A lower success rate for Hispanics (54.4 percent) also contributes to their lesser representation in the successful applicant group (3.4 percent), compared with their representation in the full applicant group (4.0 percent) and in the national sample of NBPTS-eligible teachers (5.6 percent).

Successful applicants also tend to have higher education levels than the full applicant group and the national sample of eligible teachers. The successful applicant group included fewer teachers who have only a bachelor's degree (35.6 percent) than did both the full applicant group (38.5) and the national eligible sample (49.0 percent) and higher percentages of teachers with master's degrees (60 percent) than did the full group of applicants (57.1 percent) and the national eligible sample (49.8 percent).

Board-Certified Teachers' Employment Settings

There are currently no national data sets that provide information about the locations where board-certified teachers work. The data set maintained by the NBPTS indicates only the type of school setting in which teachers worked at the time of application, and even this indicator provides minimal information (e.g., whether the school is classified as rural, suburban, or urban). As shown in Table 6-4, board applicants are fairly evenly distributed across rural, urban, and suburban schools, and the same is true for teachers who earn board certification. By contrast, the majority of the national sample of NBPTS-eligible teachers was employed in suburban schools (52.6 percent), with only 18.6 percent teaching in schools in rural areas. Beyond this, there is no existing, routinely collected, national information about where board-certified teachers work.

Two groups of researchers have investigated this issue in depth, using data collected and maintained by six states and one large school district. Using these data, Goldhaber, Perry, and Anthony (2003) and Humphrey, Koppich, and Hough (2005) compared the characteristics of employment settings for board-certified and nonboard-certified teachers. The initial

---

[8]These are *eventual* success rates, which reflect multiple attempts to pass the assessment. Thus the success rate reflects both the initial pass rate and teachers' persistence in reattempts to pass the assessment.

study by Goldhaber et al. (2003) focused on teachers working in North Carolina schools. Humphrey et al. (2005) expanded on this, studying the employment settings of board-certified teachers in the six states that employ nearly 65 percent of the board-certified teachers: California, Florida, Mississippi, North Carolina, Ohio, and South Carolina. We focus on the latter study because of its broader coverage of multiple states.

One underlying goal of board certification was to provide information that could be used in employment decisions, so that the most accomplished teachers could be placed in schools with high-needs students. Humphrey et al. (2005) investigated the extent to which this goal is being realized. The researchers classified schools according to their performance on the state's achievement tests and based on characteristics that tend to correlate with academic achievement (large numbers of minority children and children who participate in the federal free and reduced-price lunch program). The authors characterized the schools in each state as "high-poverty schools" (in which at least 75 percent of the students were eligible for free and reduced-price lunch), "high-minority schools" (in which at least 75 percent of the students are racial/ethnic minorities), and "low-performing schools" (schools with state test scores in the bottom three deciles for two of three years between 2000-2001 and 2002-2003). They reported that across all six states, 12 percent of the board-certified teachers (2,297 teachers) taught in high-poverty schools, 16 percent (3,076 teachers) worked in high-minority schools, and 19 percent (3,521 teachers) were employed in low-performing schools.

Examination of these data at the state level in six states indicates that, with the exception of California, board-certified teachers are less likely than teachers in general to work in high-poverty, high-minority, and low-performing schools (Table 6-5). These data show that, in five of the six states studied, board-certified teachers are not in abundance in the schools in which they are needed most, and they are much less likely to be in these schools than are other teachers in general. California is the exception, but the researchers attributed this to particular characteristics in Los Angeles resulting from specific policy incentives intended to encourage board-certified teachers to work in high-needs schools. Examination of the data for California with Los Angeles data excluded reveals that 26 percent of board-certified teachers work in low-performing schools, compared with 28 percent of all teachers in the state; these percentages are similar to those for teachers in general in other states.

However, it is important to point out that other research has shown that students in high-poverty, less advantaged schools are less likely than other students to be taught by high-quality teachers, regardless of how teacher quality is measured (e.g., by NBPTS certification or by other ways of measuring teacher quality such as years of experience or having an advanced

TABLE 6-5 Percentages of Board-Certified and All Teachers in High-Poverty, High-Minority, and Low-Performing Schools in Six States

State	High Poverty		High Minority		Low Performing	
	Board Certified	All Teachers	Board Certified	All Teachers	Board Certified	All Teachers
California[a]	26	27	58	45	40	33
Florida	11	17	17	22	16	25
Mississippi	18	34	16	32	11	26
North Carolina	6	11	6	13	17	27
Ohio	6	10	8	11	20	26
South Carolina	10	18	9	18	14	25

[a]The different pattern in California appears to be attributable to the Los Angeles school district. When results are reported separately for California with Los Angeles schools excluded, the patterns of percentages resemble those of other states.

SOURCE: Adapted from Humphrey, Koppich, and Hough (2005, Exhibits 3, 4, and 5). Data are for 1998 through 2003. Reprinted with permission from the National Board for Professional Teaching Standards, http://www.nbpts.org. All rights reserved.

degree) (Boyd et al., 2005; Darling-Hammond, 1987; Ingersoll, 2002, 2008; Oakes, 1990; Radenbush et al., 1998). To date, we know of no research that has investigated whether board-certified teachers are any less likely to teach in schools with high-needs students than teachers who are considered highly qualified based on other measures (e.g., years of experience, having an advanced degree). Moreover, in general, when teachers change jobs, they tend to move to more advantaged schools (Ingersoll and Perda, 2008). Obtaining board certification is likely to increase teachers' mobility, probably because it may increase their bargaining power, which would be another factor decreasing the likelihood that they will teach in high-needs schools. These issues are addressed in greater detail in Chapter 9.

WHY TEACHERS PARTICIPATE

Attempting to obtain national board certification is a significant undertaking. It costs $2,500 and generally requires an investment of roughly 400 hours over a full school year, as well as the support and assistance of colleagues and administrators. At a minimum, candidates must obtain permission to videotape their students in the classroom and recruit a colleague to operate the camera. They are also encouraged to engage colleagues in collaboration as they prepare their submissions (see, e.g., National Board for Professional Teaching Standards, 2006a). Because teachers who attempt it must be videotaped teaching lessons to their students, the fact that they are applying, and the possibility of their failing, are very public within their schools. Thus, one might wonder why a teacher would decide to undertake this endeavor.

Board certification is not a requirement for any teacher in this country. The decision is a voluntary one. Some teachers may pursue it for personal satisfaction and the sense of accomplishment. Others may seek the external recognition of their teaching. Still others may be encouraged by the administrators and supervisors in their school districts or states. States and districts differ substantially in their perspectives about board certification. Some offer significant rewards to teachers who earn the credential, while others have no means for explicitly recognizing these teachers. In the next section, we explore teachers' motivations for pursuing board certification. We begin with a review of the incentives states provide and follow this with information gathered from teachers about their reasons for becoming board certified.

State Incentives

Although states vary in their level of endorsement of national board certification, the most visible strategies they use to encourage teachers to participate are financial incentives. The national board keeps track of state and district incentives and provided us with the information displayed in Table 6-6, the main incentives offered by each state for 2004, 2005, and 2006. As can be quickly discerned from this table, the financial incentives vary considerably.

Teacher participation in the program tends to reflect these incentives. North Carolina and South Carolina, for example, in which roughly 21 percent (17,812 teachers) and 16 percent (7,363 teachers), respectively, of NBPTS-eligible teachers apply, both currently offer comparatively generous incentives. In South Carolina, the program's fees are covered by loans that are forgiven for successful candidates, and half the amount is forgiven for applicants, regardless of whether they succeed. Board-certified teachers in that state also receive a $7,500 annual salary increase for as long as they remain certified. The test fees are paid outright for teachers in North Carolina who apply for board certification, and those teachers also receive 12 percent salary increases for the life of their board certification (10 years). North Carolina candidates are also eligible for three days of release time to prepare their portfolios.

In other states, the incentives are much more modest or nonexistent, and the numbers of participants seem to reflect that. For example, Alaska, with a 2 percent participation rate (a total of 115 applicants), does not cover the fee and has no incentives. New Hampshire, which has a 0.2 percent participation rate (25 applicants), has recently discontinued the policy of subsidizing the application fee, and North Dakota, with a 0.6 percent application rate (54 applicants), offers a one-time stipend and will assist no more than 17 total candidates per year with 50 percent of the fee.

These examples illustrate the possible influence of financial incentives. The committee analyzed data about incentives and participation rates for the 2004-2005 school year, the most recent year for which complete data were available for all of the variables studied. We considered each state's history of providing incentives for the five-year period prior to the 2004-2005 school year (i.e., between 1999-2000 and 2003-2004). We conducted the analyses two ways. First, we grouped states according to the number of years during that period in which they had provided any form of financial incentive, either fee assistance or any salary bonus, regardless of the size. The average participation rate across the states that provided some sort of ongoing financial incentive over that time period was six times that of other states (Table 6-7).

Table 6-7 shows that 30 states provided incentives during at least four of the years between 1999 and 2003. In these states, 0.6 percent of teachers applied for board certification, on average. While this participation rate is still low, it is clearly higher than the 0.1 percent participation rate for states that provided incentives during three or fewer years during this time period.

The right half of the table shows participation rates by the kinds of support that was offered during the 2004-2005 school year. The average participation rate remained at 0.6 percent (or slightly higher) for states that offered a salary bonus alone or combined with fee assistance. Fee assistance alone did not seem to be associated with higher participation rates.

We also examined these data a second way by converting the financial incentive packages into dollar figures. We then expressed the financial package as a percentage of each state's average teacher salary (using 2004-2005 figures) and considered these percentages in relation to the state participation rates. This relationship is depicted in Figure 6-1 and Table 6-8.

In Figure 6-1, values on the x-axis are the sum of the amount of test fee reimbursement provided by the state and the amount of the annual bonus offered to teachers upon certification. The values are expressed as percentages of the average teacher income in each state (National Education Association, Estimates of School Statistics, 1969-1970 through 2004-2005). Values on the y-axis represent the percentage of teachers in the state who apply for board certification. The correlation between the two values is fairly high, at 0.63, which suggests a positive relationship between the financial incentives offered and the percentage of teachers who pursue board certification.

TABLE 6-6 Financial Incentives for National Board Certification Offered by States 2004-2006

State	Fee Assistance[a]		
	2004	2005	2006
Alabama	$2,500 per candidate[c]	$2,500 per candidate	$2,500 per recipient[d]
Alaska			
Arizona			
Arkansas	$2,500 per candidate	$2,500 per candidate	$2,500 per 1st-time candidate
California			
Colorado		$1,000 each for 60 candidates	$1,000 per candidate (limit implied)
Connecticut			$1,000 for 10 candidates
Delaware			Loan program
District of Columbia	$1,000 each for 20 candidates	$1,000 each for 20 candidates	$1,000 each for 1st-time candidates
Florida	$2,250 per candidate	$2,250 per candidate	$2,250 for 1st-time candidates
Georgia	$2,500 per recipient	$2,000 per candidate	$1,000 per candidate
Hawaii	$1,500 per candidate, $1,000 per recipient	Up to $3,000 per candidate	Up to $3,000 per candidate
Idaho			
Illinois	$2,000 per candidate	$2,000 per candidate	$2,000 per candidate
Indiana			$2,000 for 60 candidates
Iowa	$1,250 per candidate, plus $1,250 per recipient	$1,250 per candidate, plus $1,250 per recipient	$1,250 per candidate, plus $1,250 per recipient
Kansas	Up to $45,000 total	Fee assistance available	$1,000 per 1st-time candidate
Kentucky	$1,875 per recipient	$1,875 per recipient, plus unspecified stipend	$1,875 per recipient, plus $400 stipend
Louisiana	$2,000 per candidate	$850 per candidate	$2,000 per candidate (limited number)
Maine	Grant, unspecified	Grant, unspecified	Grant, unspecified

Salary Bonus[b]		
2004	2005	2006
$5,000 per year	$5,000 per year	$5,000 per year
$4,000 per year	$5,000 per year	$5,000 per year
$2,000 per year	$2,000 per year	$2,000 per year
12% annual increase $5,000, one time	12% annual increase $5,000, one time	12% annual increase $4,000, one time
10% annual increase; 10% increase for mentoring 10% annual increase	10% annual increase; 10% increase for mentoring 10% annual increase	10% annual increase; 10% increase for mentoring 10% annual increase
$5,000 per year	$5,000 per year	$5,000 per year
$1,000 per year $3,000 per year; $1,000 to $3,000 to mentor	$1,000 per year $3,000 per year; $1,000 to $3,000 to mentor	$1,000 per year $3,000 per year; $1,000 to $3,000 to mentor
$2,500 per year	$2,500 per year	$2,500 per year
$1,000 per year	$1,000 per year	$1,000 per year
$2,000 per year, plus pay for mentoring	$2,000 per year, plus pay for mentoring	$2,000 per year, plus pay for mentoring
$5,000 per year	$5,000 per year	$5,000 per year
		$3,000 per year

Continued

TABLE 6-6 Continued

State	Fee Assistance[a]		
	2004	2005	2006
Maryland	$1,650 each for 500 candidates from the state, plus $850 per candidate from the district	$1,650 each for 750 candidates from the state, plus $850 per candidate from the district	$1,650 each for 500 candidates from the state, plus $850 per candidate from the district
Massachusetts			
Michigan	$100,000 appropriated for fee assistance	$100,000 appropriated for fee assistance	$1,250 per candidate (limit implied)
Minnesota			
Mississippi	$2,500 per recipient	$2,500 per recipient	
Missouri	$1,875 per candidate	$1,875 per candidate	$750 for 100 candidates
Montana			
Nebraska			
Nevada	$2,000 per recipient	$2,000 per recipient	
New Hampshire	$1,000 each for 10 candidates	$1,000 each for 10 candidates	
New Jersey	Fee assistance for 175 candidates	Fee assistance for 175 candidates	$625 per candidate
New Mexico			
New York	$2,500 per candidate	$2,500 per candidate	$2,000 per 1st-time candidate
North Carolina	$2,500 per candidate	$2,500 per candidate	$2,500 per candidate
North Dakota	$1,250 each for 17 candidates	$1,250 each for 17 candidates	$1,250 each for 17 candidates
Ohio	$2,000 each for 550 candidates	$2,000 each for 400 candidates	$2,200 per 1st-time candidate
Oklahoma	$2,500 each for 200 candidates	$2,500 each for 400 candidates	$2,500 each for 400 candidates
Oregon			Subsidies available, unspecified
Pennsylvania			$1,250 each for 500 candidates
Rhode Island		$2,000 per candidate	$1,000 per candidate (limit implied)

Salary Bonus[b]		
2004	2005	2006
$4,000 per year	$4,000 per year	$4,000 per year
$6,000 per year	$6,000 per year	$6,000 per year
Career ladder advancement	Career ladder advancement	$5,000 per year
$3,000 per year	$3,000 per year	$6,000 per year
		Promotion to master teacher status
5% annual increase	5% annual increase	5% annual increase
$4,000 per year	$4,600 per year	$5,200 per year
$1,000 per year	$1,000 per year	$1,000 per year
12% annual increase	12% annual increase	12% annual increase
Stipend, unspecified	Stipend, unspecified	
$2,500 per year	$1,000 per year	$1,000 per year
$5,000 per year	$5,000 per year	$5,000 per year

Continued

TABLE 6-6   Continued

State	Fee Assistance[a]		
	2004	2005	2006
South Carolina	$1,150 per candidate, plus $1,150 per recipient	$1,150 per candidate, plus $1,150 per recipient	$1,250 per candidate, plus $1,250 per recipient
South Dakota	$2,500 per recipient	$2,500 per recipient	$2,500 per public school recipient
Tennessee			
Texas			
Utah			
Vermont	$650 each for 30 candidates	$850 each for 30 candidates	$850 each for 30 candidates
Virginia	$1,000 each for 75 candidates	$1,000 each for 75 candidates	$1,000 each for 75 candidates
Washington			$1,250 each for 500 candidates
West Virginia	$1,250 per candidate, plus $1,250 per recipient for 200	$1,250 per candidate, plus $1,250 per recipient for 200	$1,250 per candidate, plus $1,250 per recipient for 200
Wisconsin	$2,000 per recipient	$2,000 per recipient	$2,000 per recipient
Wyoming		$1,000 per candidate; $500 for retakes	$2,000 per candidate

NOTE: All incentives and the conditions for receiving them may vary from year to year due to changes in leadership and budgeting.

[a]Fee assistance is defined as those funds appropriated by states from their own budgets to help candidates meet the costs of pursuing board certification. It excludes funds provided by independent organizations and foundations.

From this examination of the effects of states' financial incentives on participation rates, we find:

Finding 6-3: Greater numbers of teachers opt to pursue board certification in states that offer significant financial incentives, such as salary increases, bonuses, payment of the NBPTS fee, and release time for the assessment activities, than in those that do not.

It is likely that such financial incentives serve as a proxy for the state's general perspective on board certification. It may be that the states that offer significant incentives also provide other types of supports that not only encourage teachers to apply but also contribute to a general climate

Salary Bonus[b]		
2004	2005	2006
$7,500 per year	$7,500 per year	$7,500 per year
$1,000 per year	$1,000 per year	$1,000 per year
	$3,000 per year	$2,000 per year
$2,750 per year	$2,750 per year	$2,750 per year
$3,500 per year	$3,500 per year	$7,000 per year
$2,500 per year	$2,500 per year	$2,500 per year
$2,250 per year	$2,250 per year	$2,250 per year
	Variable, $1,000 to $3,000	$8,000

[b]Salary bonuses are those funds appropriated by states from their own budgets to give teachers rewards or benefits for achieving board certification.
[c]Candidate = a teacher who attempts to earn board certification.
[d]Recipient = a teacher who earns board certification.
SOURCE: NBPTS.

of encouragement for the board standards and approach, but there are no systematically collected data that permit investigation of this possibility. There are studies, however, that have probed teachers' reasons for participating in the program. These studies shed some light on the role of financial incentives versus other factors that contribute to teachers' decision making.

Studies of Teachers' Decisions to Participate

A number of researchers have explored teachers' thinking about their reasons for pursuing board certification, and we found seven studies that provide evidence relevant for our evaluation. Summaries of the studies

TABLE 6-7 Relationship Between State Financial Incentives and National Board Participation

Number of Years in Which Financial Incentives Were Provided Between 1999 and 2003	Average Participation Rate Between 1999 and 2003[a]	Average Participation Rate by Type of Support in 2004-2005[a]			
		Fee Assistance and Bonus	Bonus Only	Fee Assistance Only	No Support
4 or 5 years (n = 30)[b]	0.6%	0.7% (n = 22)	0.6% (n = 4)	0.1% (n = 2)	0.3% (n = 2)
2 or 3 years (n = 7)	0.1%	0.2% (n = 3)	0.1% (n = 1)	0.1% (n = 1)	0.0% (n = 2)
1 or 0 years (n = 14)	0.1%	—	0.4% (n = 1)	0.0% (n = 2)	0.1% (n = 11)

[a]Because of data limitations, participation rates are based on the percentage of all teachers in the state, not NBPTS-eligible teachers.
[b]Number of states.

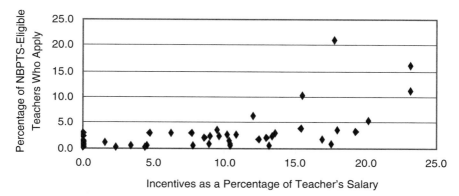

FIGURE 6-1 Percentage of teachers who apply by amount of support provided by the state, 2004-2005. Values on the x-axis are the sum of the amount of test-fee reimbursement provided by the state and the amount of the annual bonus offered to teachers upon certification. The values are expressed as the percentage of the average teacher income in the state. Values on the y-axis represent the percentage of NBPTS-eligible teachers in the state who apply for board certification. The correlation between the two values is .63.

we considered appear in Appendix A, and an overview is presented in Table 6-9. These studies use a combination of surveys, focus groups, and interviews to investigate what teachers say about their reasons for pursuing or not pursuing board certification.

Five studies examined reasons why teachers decide to pursue board certification. Two relied on small, single-state samples (Indiana Professional Standards Board, 2002; Wayne et al., 2004) and provide limited evidence. Three studies had relatively large samples—Belden (2002); Koppich, Humphrey, and Hough (2006); Sykes et al. (2006)—and we think their findings are the most generalizable. Most of the respondents in Belden (2002) said that they pursued certification because it was a personal challenge (84 percent) and provided an opportunity to strengthen their teaching (79 percent). Between 54 and 59 percent reported that they pursued certification because of the state's monetary compensations. The opportunity for career advancement was also important to more than half (53 percent), as was the prospect of receiving recognition for teaching skill (50 percent).

Sykes and his colleagues surveyed teachers in South Carolina and Ohio. These two states also have somewhat different policies regarding incentives for teachers to pursue board certification. Ohio covers most of the fee for first-time candidates and offers a $1,000 annual salary increase for teachers who earn board certification, and South Carolina will cover the whole fee for successful candidates and provides them with a $7,500 annual salary

TABLE 6-8   Financial Incentives in Relation to Average Teacher Salary and National Board Participation Rates

State	Financial Incentives[a]		Average Teacher Salary[b]
	Fee Support	Bonus	
Alabama	$2,500	$5,000	$38,863
Alaska[c]			$52,424
Arizona			$42,905
Arkansas	$2,500	$3,000	$40,495
California		$5,000	$57,876
Colorado			$44,161
Connecticut			$58,688
Delaware		$6,104	$50,869
District of Columbia	$1,000	$5,000	$58,456
Florida	$2,250	$4,108	$41,081
Georgia	$2,500	$4,652	$46,526
Hawaii	$2,500	$5,000	$44,273
Idaho		$2,000	$42,122
Illinois	$2,000	$3,000	$55,629
Indiana			$46,851
Iowa	$2,500	$2,500	$40,347
Kansas	$2,500	$1,000	$39,190
Kentucky	$1,875	$2,000	$41,002
Louisiana	$2,000	$5,000	$38,880
Maine			$40,940
Maryland	$1,650	$4,000	$52,331
Massachusetts			$54,596
Michigan	$2,500		$55,693
Minnesota			$46,906
Mississippi	$2,500	$6,000	$36,590
Missouri	$1,875	$5,000	$38,971
Montana		$3,000	$38,485
Nebraska		(Career ladder step)	$39,456

Incentives as a Percentage of Salary		Percentage of Eligible Teachers in the State[d]	
Bonus	Fee and Bonus	Applicants	Achievers
12.9	19.3	3.2	2.2
		1.5	1.0
		1.1	0.7
7.4	13.6	3.0	1.7
8.6	8.6	2.0	1.3
		0.9	0.6
		0.4	0.3
12.0	12.0	6.3	4.4
8.6	10.3	1.5	0.4
10.0	15.5	10.4	6.3
10.0	15.4	3.9	2.5
11.3	16.9	1.6	0.9
4.7	4.7	2.9	2.3
5.4	9.0	2.5	1.4
		0.5	0.2
6.2	12.4	1.7	1.3
2.6	8.9	0.9	0.6
4.9	9.5	3.5	2.4
12.9	18.0	3.6	1.9
		0.7	0.5
7.6	10.8	2.6	1.5
		0.8	0.5
	4.5	0.5	0.2
		0.7	0.5
16.4	23.2	11.3	8.0
12.8	17.6	0.8	0.5
7.8	7.8	0.7	0.5
		0.3	0.2

Continued

TABLE 6-8   Continued

| State | Financial Incentives[a] | | Average Teacher Salary[b] |
	Fee Support	Bonus	
Nevada	$2,000	$2,170	$43,394
New Hampshire	$1,000		$43,941
New Jersey	$2,500		$56,600
New Mexico		$4,000	$39,328
New York	$2,500	$3,333	$56,200
North Carolina	$2,500	$5,198	$43,313
North Dakota	$1,250	(stipend)	$36,449
Ohio	$2,000	$1,000	$48,692
Oklahoma	$2,500	$5,000	$37,141
Oregon			$50,790
Pennsylvania			$52,700
Rhode Island			$53,473
South Carolina	$2,300	$7,500	$42,207
South Dakota	$2,500	$2,000	$34,040
Tennessee			$41,527
Texas			$41,009
Utah			$39,965
Vermont	$650		$44,535
Virginia	$1,000	$5,000	$44,763
Washington		$3,500	$45,712
West Virginia	$2,000	$2,500	$43,466
Wisconsin	$2,500	$2,500	$38,360
Wyoming			$40,392

[a]Incentives are for the 2004-2005 school year.

[b]Average salary for the 2004-2005 school year. SOURCE: *National Education Association, Estimates of School Statistics,* 1969-1970 through 2004-2005.

[c]A blank indicates that no financial incentive was offered.

[d]Based on number of public and private school teachers in the state in 2003-2004.

Incentives as a Percentage of Salary		Percentage of Eligible Teachers in the State[d]	
Bonus	Fee and Bonus	Applicants	Achievers
5.0	9.6	2.3	1.5
	2.3	0.2	0.1
	4.4	0.3	0.1
10.2	10.2	2.6	1.2
5.9	10.4	0.5	0.3
12.0	17.8	21.1	13.4
(not specified)	3.4+	0.6	0.3
2.1	6.2	3.1	1.9
13.5	20.2	5.4	3.6
		1.3	0.8
		0.4	0.2
		2.9	1.9
17.8	23.2	16.3	11.3
5.9	13.2	0.7	0.5
		0.7	0.4
		0.2	0.1
		0.9	0.5
	1.5	1.3	0.9
11.2	13.4	2.2	1.4
7.7	7.7	2.9	2.1
6.5	13.0	2.0	1.3
5.8	10.4	0.8	0.5
		2.5	1.1

TABLE 6-9 Studies Examining Teachers' Reasons for National Board Participation

Study	Population Studied	State(s)	Sampling Method
Barfield and McEnany (2004)	NBCTs asked why teachers do not participate	MT	Sent to all NBCTs in the state
Belden (2002)	NBCTs	CA	Sent to all NBCTs in the state
Indiana Professional Standards board (2002)	NBCTs	IN	Sent to all NBCTs in the state
Koppich, Humphrey, and Hough (2006)	NBCTs	CA, FL, MS, NC, OH, SC	Stratified random sample
Moore (2002)	Nonparticipants asked why teachers do not participate	TN – 2 counties	Cluster sampling

Sample Size, Response Rate	Methods	Findings	Issues Affecting Validity of the Findings
31; responses from 22 (71%)	Mail survey	- Time commitment and cost - Lack of administrator support - Fear of not being successful - Harassment of teachers who have become certified	Small sample. In appropriate sample: NBCTs were asked to speculate about their peers' reasons for not participating
785; responses from 519 (68%)	Mail survey, focus groups	- Personal challenge - Opportunity to strengthen teaching - Monetary compensation - Career advancement and recognition	All survey questions were worded positively
71; responses from 32 (48%)	Mail survey, focus group	- Improve effectiveness - Intrinsic motivation to advance - External validation of their teaching	Small sample
1,136; responses from 654 (75%)	Mail survey	- Improve student learning - Financial compensation - Increase the credibility of one's teaching - Career advancement - Influence change at the school	No concerns
700; responses from 448 (64%)	Survey	- Negative opinion of the program, but also poorly informed about it - Paperwork and time commitment - Skepticism about the process - Fear of being ostracized by non-NBCTs	No NBCTs in the counties studied; unclear how much respondents knew about the NBPTS

Continued

TABLE 6-9 Continued

Study	Population Studied	State(s)	Sampling Method
Sykes et al. (2006)	NBCTs	OH, SC	
Wayne et al. (2004)	NBCTs, unsuccessful applicants, and nonparticipants	CA, FL, MD	Unclear

increase. This survey was part of a much more comprehensive study of the impacts of board certification; we highlight here only the findings relevant for this aspect of our evaluation. The authors asked survey respondents why they decided to pursue certification. Factors given the strongest ratings were financial compensation, the opportunity for professional development, and the opportunity to serve in leadership roles. The rankings of these factors were slightly different in the two states—teachers in South Carolina, the state with the more generous incentives, ranked financial compensation much higher than did Ohio teachers. The opportunity for professional development was given similar weight by teachers in both states.

Koppich et al. (2006) surveyed teachers in six states—California, Florida, Mississippi, North Carolina, Ohio, and South Carolina—which together, at the time, accounted for 65 percent of the board-certified teachers in the country. As with Sykes et al., the survey delved into a number of issues besides reasons for participating in the NBPTS, and we highlight here only the relevant findings. Koppich and her colleagues found that the top three motives for pursuing board certification were to improve student learning (95 percent), to achieve the potential for increased financial compensation (90 percent), and to obtain external validation for the quality of one's teaching (88 percent). Slightly fewer than half also reported that they pursued board certification because of the possibility of advancing their careers without leaving teaching (45 percent) and the opportunity to influence changes at their schools (44 percent). The authors report that focus

Sample Size, Response Rate	Methods	Findings	Issues Affecting Validity of the Findings
1,500; responses from 1,153 (77%); 566 from SC and 587 from OH	Survey	- Financial compensation - Opportunity for professional development - Opportunity to serve in leadership roles	No concerns
86; 40 NBCTs, 32 unsuccessful applicants, 14 nonparticipants	Phone interviews	- Validate teaching capabilities - Increase professional status - Financial incentives important but not the primary motive	Small sample, unclear how obtained; sample too small to examine responses by group

group discussions and interviews corroborated these findings, with most board-certified teachers saying that they viewed the credential as evidence of personal achievement and that they decided to pursue it out of a desire to prove that they are accomplished practitioners.

Together, the findings from these three studies suggest that financial incentives are important factors in teachers' decisions to pursue board certification, but not the sole factor. Generally, it seems that the three principal motivators are financial incentives, the desire to improve their effectiveness, and the desire to obtain external validation and recognition of their capabilities. These findings are similar to those reported in the two smaller scale surveys (Indiana Professional Standards Board, 2002; Wayne et al., 2004).

In contrast, only two studies have examined reasons why teachers choose not to pursue board certification (Barfield and McEnany, 2004; Moore, 2002). Barfield and McEnany surveyed board-certified teachers in Montana about the reasons other teachers do not participate. The sample was fewer than 25 teachers, who were asked to speculate about their non-board-certified colleagues' motivations, so the results must be viewed with caution. Moore (2002) surveyed over 400 teachers who had the minimum qualifications to pursue board certification but who had not done so. However, all the teachers surveyed worked in two counties in Tennessee, neither of which had any board-certified teachers; thus, there is no way to know whether the respondents actually understood what board certification involves. Despite these methodological problems, the two studies report similar findings. In both, the respondents commented on the extent of work involved and the time commitment, saying that these factors, along with the expense, were obstacles to participation. The respondents also voiced some skepticism about the benefits of board certification, commenting that teachers who earned the credential were "harassed" (Barfield and McEnany) or "ostracized" (Moore) by other teachers.

None of the seven studies addressed the issue of minority participation in the NBPTS program. Although the participation rates for racial/ethnic minority teachers generally reflect their relative representation among NBPTS-eligible teachers (i.e., racial/ethnic minorities represent about 15 percent of NBPTS-eligible teachers and 15 percent of NBPTS applicants), their absolute numbers are quite small. Over the 13-year time span represented in Table 6-4 (between 1993-2004 and 2005-2006), only roughly 13,000 minority teachers participated in the program. Furthermore, while racial/ethnic minority teachers comprise about 15 percent of the NBPTS-eligible applicant pool, fewer than 10 percent of the group achieved board certification, which amounts to roughly 5,500 teachers. To date, the only study that has explored the issue of minority teacher participation was a small-scale study by Bond (1998a), which was discussed in Chapter 5. Bond's focus group discussions with 25 African American teachers revealed that they were reluctant to pursue board certification out of fear of performing poorly and concern about the academic abilities of their students (which would be highlighted on the videotapes). They also reported that they were not kept informed regarding professional opportunities, such as board certification.

NATIONAL BOARD EFFORTS TO ENCOURAGE PARTICIPATION

We queried the NBPTS about its efforts to encourage teachers to pursue board certification. The board staff includes 10 regional outreach directors who are responsible for developing strategies to expand awareness of the board in their assigned geographic regions, encouraging policy makers to provide fee support and/or incentives and promoting NBPTS products and services. The board's primary efforts focus on media coverage of board-certified teachers and the board's position on issues relating to board certification and teacher quality. They feature teachers' stories in education-related publications and in newspapers and also advertise in organizational publications (e.g., the American Federation of Teachers, the National Education Association, the Educational Testing Service, the National Association of Black School Educators). The board uses its national conference for board-certified teachers to raise awareness as well. When the conference occurs in Washington, DC, one day is designated Hill Day, and participants go to Capitol Hill to meet with various U.S. representatives. The board also recently implemented its Take One program, which allows teachers to get a taste of the certification process by completing and submitting a single portfolio entry. The entry is scored and eligible teachers can bank the score for credit if they later decide to complete the full certification process within a designated time period. The board also has efforts under way to recruit minority candidates, which were described in Chapter 4.

We are not aware of any efforts the board has made to collect information from state policy makers or teachers regarding their awareness of the NBPTS, their opinion of its value, or its relevance to their needs. If it has not been conducted, such market research could be of considerable value to board staff.

CONCLUSIONS AND RECOMMENDATIONS

Our examination of participation in the certification program reveals several clear points. First, application rates are low but steadily increasing. To date, approximately 3 percent of the 3.1 million NBPTS-eligible teachers in this country have attempted to become board certified, and approximately 2 percent of the nation's eligible teachers have earned board certification. Second, participation in the program is quite variable across the country. In four states, participation rates are more than triple the national rate (Florida, Mississippi, North Carolina, and South Carolina), but in many others, the participation rate is equal to, or lower than, the national rate. There are five school districts that have seen fairly high participation, with over 460 board-certified teachers in each, but in 64 percent of the school districts in the country, there were no applicants, and in 70 percent of the districts there were no teachers who earned board certification.

The link between the incentives offered by states and participation in the program appears to be quite strong, suggesting that teacher participation is related to the degree to which states and districts encourage it. However, teachers report that while financial incentives are a consideration in their decision making, they also pursue board certification for personal reasons, primarily for the professional accomplishment and the desire to validate their teaching skills. Little is known about the opinions of teachers who have not chosen to participate or who participated and were unsuccessful. Information about the opinions of these latter two groups would be useful in understanding the likely future participation of teachers in board certification. Furthermore, the absolute numbers of racial/ethnic minority teacher participants are low, but little is known about the reasons why they do not pursue board certification. Research on this issue would be useful to help inform recruitment efforts.

There are other important questions about participation that cannot be answered with the existing data. Most important, no existing data sets make it possible to determine exactly where board-certified teachers work. We can identify where teachers were employed at the time of application, but we do not know what teachers do after becoming board certified—even whether they stay in their original school or transfer elsewhere. Thus, we cannot evaluate the distribution of board-certified teachers across the country. This is a topic we return to in Chapter 9, where we address teachers' career paths.

From the committee's examination of participation patterns, it is not clear whether the board should be judged successful at creating a significant cadre of advanced certified teachers, and we spent considerable time debating what, if any, conclusions to draw and recommendations to make. On one hand, the founders of the NBPTS never expected that all teachers in the country would become board certified. They intended the credential to create an upper echelon in the profession, with only the most accomplished teachers attaining this level. If the upper echelon was interpreted to mean the top 10 percent of teachers, one might expect that eventually roughly 400,000 teachers would become board certified. If one were to assume that all of the current total of 63,800 board-certified teachers were still teaching, the NBPTS would be about one-sixth of the way toward achieving this goal.

On the other hand, the founders did expect that there would be an ever-increasing number of these accomplished teachers, in sufficient supply that administrators could call on them to perform in leadership roles, and that this cadre would influence the professional development of other teachers. In many places, the current numbers of board-certified teachers and annual applicant and success rates are not sufficient to realize these objectives. However, in a few districts, the numbers are approaching levels likely to be sufficient for the program to have the intended effects.

Judgments about the program should be based on a complete examination of its benefits and costs. The other aspects of our evaluation framework all bear on this kind of judgment, so we reserve our overarching conclusions for the final chapter of this report. At this point we draw two conclusions about participation, based on the information that we have reviewed:

Conclusion 6-1: Although the number of teachers who have obtained certification is small relative to the population of eligible U.S. teachers, the total has grown since the program began and is now over 63,800. Participation varies significantly by state and district, however; in a few districts, participation rates are approaching levels likely to be sufficient for the program to have the intended effects.

Conclusion 6-2: States that offer financial incentives for attempting and achieving board certification are likely to have more teachers that apply and succeed in the program.

In addition, we note that the existing data about the teachers who have gone through the board-certification process are scant. For example, it is not currently possible to determine what teachers have done after completing the process, what happened to teachers who did not pass the assessment, how many board-certified teachers are currently employed, or where board-certified teachers currently work. We encourage the NBPTS to establish data collection systems that allow for investigation of these issues. Thus we recommend:

Recommendation 6-1: The NBPTS should implement and maintain a database of information about applicants and their career paths. This effort should include routine, annual data collection as well as specially designed studies. The data collected should provide information about what teachers have done after going through the certification process, what has happened to teachers who did not pass the assessment, how many board-certified teachers are currently employed, where board-certified teachers currently work, and what jobs they do.

7

The Impact of Board-Certified Teachers on Student Outcomes

The National Board for Professional Teaching Standards (NBPTS) set out to accomplish a number of broad goals, all intended to transform the teaching profession in this country. By reshaping the teaching field, expanding the opportunities available to teachers, and articulating the standards for accomplished teaching, the national board envisioned having a significant impact on the quality of teachers and teaching and, consequently, on student learning (National Board for Professional Teaching Standards, 1991). The board emphasized that ultimately all of these goals were directed at improving student learning. In keeping with this objective, Congress specifically asked that the committee's evaluation consider the impact of national board certification on student outcomes. Accordingly, our evaluation framework asks:

> **Question 4: To what extent does the advanced-level certification program identify teachers who are effective at producing positive student outcomes, such as learning, motivation, school engagement, breadth of achievement, educational attainment, attendance, and grade promotion?**

Figure 2-1 shows how this aspect of the evaluation fits within the committee's framework, displaying our model of the ways a certification program for accomplished teachers could affect the teaching profession and the way our evaluation questions map onto this model. We identified two issues to investigate and to provide evidence of the extent to which board certification has an impact on student learning. Specifically:

a. How does achievement compare for students taught by board-certified and nonboard-certified teachers, after controlling for other factors? Are the differences meaningful? Do students taught by board-certified teachers have higher achievement or achievement gains than those taught by nonboard-certified teachers? Do student gains persist into the future?

b. How do other student outcomes (such as motivation, breadth of achievement, attendance rates, promotion rates) compare for students taught by board-certified and nonboard-certified teachers?

The majority of studies that estimated effects of national board certification focus on student achievement (our Subquestion a). We located only one study that addressed other outcomes such as those listed in Subquestion b. The bulk of this chapter therefore addresses the findings from studies of student achievement. At the end of the chapter, we discuss other types of student outcome measures and propose research that should be considered in future investigations.

This chapter has five sections. In the first, we discuss issues related to using scores on standardized achievement tests as the outcome variable. The studies use sophisticated statistical methods, and in the second section, we discuss issues that bear on this kind of research and provide explanations of some of the technical terminology. The third section reviews studies of the impact of board certification on student achievement and our analyses of this topic. The fourth section describes the only study we located that examined student outcomes other than performance on achievement tests. The chapter closes with a discussion of conclusions that can be drawn from this evidence base and the types of research needed to fill gaps in what is known.

USING ACHIEVEMENT TEST SCORES AS THE OUTCOME VARIABLE

Nearly all the research discussed in this chapter uses student scores on standardized achievement tests as the measure of the impact of board certification. Using test scores in this way has a long history in research, and in the current federal accountability system established under the No Child Left Behind Act, test scores are the primary indicator of whether schools are making "adequate yearly progress."

However, test scores as measures of achievement are not universally accepted as measures of student learning. Committee members from different disciplines had differing views about test scores as measures of learning outcomes and the types of inferences that are appropriate from the results. For example, economists routinely use achievement test scores as indicators of student learning, understanding that the scores are not perfect as indicators of learning but are the best quantitative measures available for statistical analyses (e.g., Rivkin, Hanushek, and Kain, 2005). Achievement test scores, in particular, have been found to be correlated with other outcomes, such as high school completion, college enrollment and completion, job status, future earnings, and other measures of success (e.g., Carnevale, Fry, and Lowell, 2001; Chiswick, Lee, and Miller, 2002; Jencks et al., 1979; McIntosh and Vignoles, 2001; Sewell, Hauser, and Featherman, 1976; Tyler, Murnane, and Willett, 2000).

Psychometricians, who are trained in the processes and methods for developing tests, focus on whether test scores are valid measures of learning and whether interpretations drawn about them are appropriate. In the present context, achievement tests have not been developed for the purpose of evaluating the effectiveness of teachers' instructional practices. Tests developed specifically to assess teaching could look different from those used for measuring student achievement.

Furthermore, among teachers and teacher educators, test scores are viewed as, at best, only correlated with student learning. Teachers are familiar with curriculum and state and local standards and how tests relate to them, and they are aware that tests capture only a portion of what they teach and what students learn. They know that exceptional students can perform poorly on tests and low-performing students can do well on tests. They know that tests vary in the extent to which they assess critical thinking, problem solving, and higher order thinking skills.

Many of the skills that the national board requires teachers to demonstrate are not reflected by what is evaluated on standardized achievement tests. For example, to become board certified in the middle childhood generalist area, teachers need to demonstrate that they can establish a caring and stimulating learning environment, that they respect individual differences, that they use a rich and varied collection of materials in their teaching, that they provide multiple paths to learning, and that they provide students with situations when they can apply what they have learned (National Board for Professional Teaching Standards, 2001c). All this is in addition to demonstrating their understanding of the subject matter, the curriculum, and pedagogy.

In evaluating the body of research covered in this chapter, the committee was cognizant of the limitations as well as the different disciplinary perspectives. Throughout this report, we have attempted to portray a balanced perspective of this research and the use of student test scores for these purposes.

METHODOLOGICAL ISSUES

The question of whether board-certified teachers are more effective than nonboard-certified teachers is formally a question of whether a student who had a board-certified teacher learns more than if he or she had a non-board-certified teacher. Asked in this way, the question cannot be answered because the same student cannot be taught at the same time by a board-certified teacher and a nonboard-certified teacher. This problem—of not being able to observe results as they would occur under the "counterfactual" situation—commonly arises in studying the effectiveness of interventions. In medical research, for example, individuals cannot simultaneously take a pharmaceutical treatment and take the placebo treatment.

Researchers have devised a variety of methods for addressing the problem of not having a counterfactual situation for comparison purposes. These methods focus on creating a comparison group that is similar with respect to all relevant characteristics to the treatment group, allowing the researchers to infer that posttreatment differences are attributable to the treatment and not to other differences between the groups. The most powerful way to create equivalent groups is with random assignment of subjects to treatment and comparison groups. However, random assignment of students to board-certified teachers has not often been done (although we review the findings from one such study below) because it is difficult to accomplish in real-life situations.

Three issues arise when random assignment is not used: (1) if students are not randomly assigned to teachers, they may differ systematically; for example, board-certified teachers may have students with higher than average achievement and motivation to learn; (2) if teachers are not randomly assigned to schools, some of the observed achievement differences between board-certified and nonboard-certified teachers may be attributable to differences in their schools; and (3) if teachers are not randomly assigned to pursue board certification, teachers who do and do not receive certification may differ systematically. We explore these three issues below and discuss how various studies have addressed them.

Nonrandom Assignment of Students to Teachers

If students are not randomly assigned to teachers, the effects of board certification may be either underestimated or overestimated to the extent that teachers are systematically assigned students who are below or above average. For example, if board-certified teachers are typically assigned above-average students, comparing test scores may suggest board-certified teachers are more effective than nonboard-certified teachers when in fact all that is true is that the students they have been assigned have higher achievement levels (and would have them even if taught by a nonboard-certified teacher).

The studies we reviewed used two strategies to estimate the effects of board certification in the absence of random assignment of students to teachers. Some used a covariate adjustment approach, which uses statistical controls for measured preexisting characteristics of students, such as gender, race/ethnicity, economic circumstances, and prior achievement.[1] A shortcoming of this approach, however, it is that it is limited by the characteristics that have been measured and are available (e.g., in the data set). That is, if measures of characteristics such as gender, race, or economic circumstances are not available, no statistical control of them can be implemented. Thus, covariate adjustment approaches might not control for all preexisting conditions. Even prior achievement may not fully account for all preexisting conditions because the tests are not perfectly reliable and because other circumstances may change that may affect the predictive power of prior achievement.

Other researchers used student fixed effects models to take prior conditions into account. Theoretically, student fixed effects models control for all the time-invariant characteristics of students (e.g., characteristics that are stable over time), whether or not direct measures of those characteristics are available. They do so by subtracting a student's mean value over time from each of his or her own data points. What remains, then, is the student's *trajectory* over time (up or down), which can be related to the student's changing experiences (for example, whether she or he has a board-certified teacher in one year and not the next).

Student fixed effects models operate by allowing each student to serve as his or her own control. In the present context, the model estimates the average achievement for each student and determines the extent to which each student's achievement in a given year deviates from this expected average achievement.[2] These deviations can then be compared when students are taught by board-certified teachers and when they are taught by nonboard-certified teachers.

---

[1]Controls for prior achievement are particularly important in this approach. The studies we reviewed controlled for prior achievement in two different ways. Some included prior achievement as a covariate, and others subtracted prior achievement from subsequent achievement so that the outcome reflects a gain score rather than an achievement level. These approaches make different assumptions about the relation between pretests and posttests (gain scores assume that pretests and posttests have a one-to-one relationship; covariate adjustments do not make this assumption), and both approaches are widely used with neither clearly preferred over the other. Several studies presented results based on both approaches.

[2]This is typically done by creating an "indicator" variable (or "dummy variable") for each student in the analysis. Further information about this kind of "dummy coding" is provided in Pedhazur (1982, pp. 274-279). Mathematically, this is the same as subtracting each student's mean over time from the achievement estimate for the current year.

Student fixed effects models offer more rigorous adjustments for pre-existing conditions than covariance adjustment models because they account for unobserved characteristics (whereas covariance adjustments take into account only observed, measured variables). However, they demand data on students from multiple time points, and they do not take account of un-observed conditions that may change over time. Also, fixed-effects models rely on information from students whose experiences change over time; a student who always had a board-certified teacher, or who never had a board-certified teacher, would contribute no information to the fixed-effects model.[3]

Nonrandom Assignment of Teachers to Schools

Schools may differ in their ability to attract or retain board-certified teachers. For example, board-certified teachers may be more often found in schools serving advantaged communities. If so, underlying differences in school characteristics may be confounded with differences arising because of board certification.

Studies we reviewed used two methods for taking into account nonran-dom assignment of teachers to schools. Some used school-level covariates to adjust for preexisting conditions likely to be related to achievement, such as the percentage of students participating in the free and reduced-price lunch program, the percentage of minority students, and prior information about student achievement at the school. However, as discussed above, covariate adjustment approaches can control only for preexisting differences in characteristics that have been measured and are available.

Other studies included school fixed effects, which are analogous to the student fixed effects model discussed above. School fixed effects models control for all stable characteristics of the school, whether or not direct measures of those characteristics are available. They do so by subtracting each school's mean over time from each school's yearly mean, thus creating a school's trajectory over time. As with student fixed effects models, this allows each school to serve as its own control and, in the present context, measures the extent to which the school's achievement in a given year deviates from its average over time.[4] For the studies discussed in this chapter, the school fixed

---

[3]There is also evidence that student fixed effects models do not rule out biases that may result from unobserved time-varying characteristics of students that may affect the assignment of students to teachers (Rothstein, 2008).

[4]As with student fixed effects models, this is typically done by creating an "indicator" vari-able (or "dummy variable") for each school in the analysis. Further information about this kind of "dummy coding" is provided in Pedhazur (1982, pp. 274-279). Mathematically, this is the same as subtracting each school's mean over time from the school's achievement estimate for the current year.

effects model essentially compares board-certified and nonboard-certified teachers in the same school. That is, they determine the average achievement trajectory for each school and compare deviations from this trajectory for board-certified teachers and nonboard-certified teachers.

School fixed-effects models share the same limitations as student fixed effects models. They control for school characteristics that are stable over time, under the assumption that these characteristics will have the same effects on performance in one year as in a subsequent year. As with student fixed effects models, they cannot control for characteristics that vary over time, such as when the school district boundaries are altered so that the composition of the student body changes markedly. School fixed effects models require at least two years of data for each school, and preferably three or more years of data, and therefore rely on the existence of large-scale longitudinal data sets.

Nonrandom Assignment of Teachers to National Board-Certification Status

The decision to pursue board certification is voluntary, and, as a result, teachers are not randomly assigned to become board certified. Teachers thus "self-select" into board-certified and nonboard-certified status. Simply comparing achievement of students of board-certified and nonboard-certified teachers can mix differences related to board certification and differences related to characteristics of teachers who chose to become board certified. The studies we reviewed used two methods for controlling for these preexisting differences among teachers. Some relied on covariate adjustment procedures using teacher-level covariates, such as years of experience, level of education, and teacher-licensure test scores to control for prior differences among teachers. Again, the downside to the use of covariance adjustment is that it relies on characteristics for which measures are available.

Others used teacher fixed effects, which are analogous to student fixed effects and school fixed effects models described above. Teacher fixed effects models use teachers as their own controls. They estimate the average growth trajectory for each teacher's students (e.g., the average across all students taught by a given teacher) and analyze the deviations from this average.[5] Teacher fixed effects models can be used to examine whether these deviations are associated with the teacher's board-certification status.

---

[5]As with models that use student fixed effects or school fixed effects, this is typically done by creating an "indicator" variable (or "dummy variable") for each teacher in the analysis. Further information about this kind of "dummy coding" is provided in Pedhazur (1982, pp. 274-279). Mathematically, this is the same as subtracting each teacher's mean over time from the teacher's achievement estimate for the current year.

These models share the shortcomings noted above for school and student fixed effects models. They require at least two years of data for each teacher and, thus, rely on the existence of large-scale longitudinal data sets.

Most of the studies we reviewed examined whether board certification distinguished more effective from less effective teachers (often referred to as a signaling effect). This question is important because a major goal of the program is to retain the most effective teachers in the teaching field and many states offer salary increases to teachers who become board certified. This question can be addressed by knowing each teacher's board-certification status.

Several studies we reviewed also attempted to determine whether board certification makes teachers more effective, an issue that economists refer to as a human capital effect. Addressing this question requires that the dataset contain information on teachers before and after they participated in the board certification process, and organized in such a way that the timing of earning board certification can be determined. Four studies had the needed information on teachers before and after they participated in the board-certification process, making it possible to assess whether going through the certification process increases a teacher's effectiveness.

Nesting of Students Within Classrooms

Conventionally, students are grouped in classrooms, and classes are taught by a single teacher. Researchers refer to this structure as nesting or clustering of students within classrooms. This clustering needs to be considered in designing the research approaches because students in a class are generally more like each other than students in different classes. Students in a classroom share a common learning environment and a common teacher, which causes their test scores to be somewhat positively correlated. If these correlations are not taken into account in the statistical models, estimates of teacher effects will seem to be more precise than they really are, leading to false conclusions about statistical significance.

Researchers handle this in different ways. Some create statistical models that reflect the nesting of students in classrooms, such as hierarchical or multilevel models. Others use a statistical correction procedure. This procedure corrects for the fact that the estimates of teacher effects are overly precise. The procedure estimates "robust standard errors," resulting in correct estimates of statistical significance. When the nesting is not addressed, tests of statistical significance are biased such that effects may be found to be statistically significant when in fact they are not.

STUDIES OF STUDENT PERFORMANCE
ON ACHIEVEMENT TESTS

Ten studies that we reviewed used student achievement test data to evaluate the effects of board-certified teachers on test scores. Some studies found positive effects of board certification, and some found no effects. The findings are sensitive to model specification, how comparison teachers are identified, the timing of the comparison—before certification, after certification, or during the certification process—and the nature of the test score used as the outcome.

In reviewing these studies, we attempted to get an overall sense of the evidence about the relationship between board certification and student learning and the extent to which the findings are consistent across studies. Because our initial review revealed some discrepancies in the findings, we looked closely at the methodologies used by each researcher to consider the extent to which methodological choices contributed to differences in findings. We solicited the assistance of two researchers (Daniel McCaffrey and Steven Rivkin) to help us with this review. We asked our reviewers to help sort out the methodological differences, summarize the findings, and identify unanswered questions. The goal of their work was to identify a set of analyses that would be appropriate for the various data sets and would help to disentangle the methodological issues from the findings. We also had two teams of researchers carry out the analyses: one team (Timothy Sass and Douglas Harris) for the Florida data set, and the other team (Helen Ladd and associates) for the North Carolina data set.

The next section highlights the main findings from the reviewed studies to give readers a sense of whether findings are statistically significant and consistent across analyses and statistical models. The reader is referred to Appendix A for additional details about the findings, to McCaffrey and Rivkin (2007) for a thorough critique of the studies, and to the original papers for a complete presentation of the approaches and findings.

Review of Existing Studies

Of the 10 studies that we reviewed, three relied on relatively small samples. McColskey et al. (2005) analyzed data for 25 board-certified teachers in North Carolina; Stone's (2002) study consisted of data for 16 board-certified teachers in Tennessee; and Vandervoot, Amrein-Beardsley, and Berliner (2004) focused on data for 35 self-selected board-certified teachers in Arizona. The committee judged that these small sample sizes combined with other methodological limitations made it difficult to draw conclusions from the studies. We focus below on the seven studies that relied on larger samples of teachers and more sophisticated analytic approaches. Table 7-1 provides a brief overview of each.

The studies used a range of approaches to control for differences among students, teachers, and schools and for dealing with the issue of students nested within classrooms. We first discuss the study that used random assignment and then discuss the studies that used statistical controls to compensate for the fact that they did not use random assignment.

Most of these studies were very comprehensive, reporting results for numerous comparisons based on a variety of statistical models. In this review, we attempt to give the reader a general sense of the findings by characterizing the effects in terms of statistical significance. For ease of presentation, we do not specify the exact level of statistical significance (i.e., the p-values reported by the authors), but in all cases, effects we refer to as "statistically significant" met a criteria of $p < .05$. Additional details about the studies and summaries of effect sizes are provided in Appendix A.

Random Assignment of Teachers to Classrooms

Cantrell et al. (2007) is the only study that used a form of random assignment. Using data for students and teachers in the Los Angeles Unified School District, the researchers assigned teachers randomly to classrooms of students. To conduct the assignment, researchers worked with the NBPTS to identify applicants for board certification, some of whom had earned board certification and others who had not. Each applicant was matched with a nonapplicant comparison teacher in the same school and grade. Classrooms were then randomly assigned to teachers. Two additional samples of board-certified and nonboard-certified teachers were identified to allow the researchers to study the effects of random and nonrandom assignment on the results. The researchers classified applicants as passed, failed, or withdrawn and compared achievement test results for the students taught by each of these groups and students taught by the nonapplicants. The findings for the three groups indicate that applicants who received board certification were more effective than those who applied but failed, and the differences were statistically significant. There were small differences in effectiveness between board-certified teachers and nonapplicants, but these differences were not statistically significant. The results for the nonexperimental sample showed the same patterns, but the effect sizes were much smaller.

Studies Using Statistical Adjustments to Account for Nonrandom Assignment

Six of the seven studies used fixed effects models and/or covariates to adjust for differences in school, teacher, and student characteristics

TABLE 7-1 Studies Examining the Relationship Between Board Certification and Student Achievement

Study	Grades/ Content Area(s)	Years	State/District
Cantrell et al. (2007)	3rd-5th; reading, math	2003-2005	Los Angeles
Cavaluzzo (2004)	9th-10th; math	2000-2003	Miami–Dade County
Clotfelter, Ladd, and Vigdor (2006)	3rd-5th; reading, math	1994-2004	NC
Clotfelter, Ladd, and Vigdor (2007)	5th; reading, math	1999-2000	NC

Groups Compared	Statistical Models	Findings	Issues Affecting Interpretations of the Findings
- NBCTs - Unsuccessful applicants - Nonparticipants	Experimental	Differences between NBCTs and nonapplicants were not significant. Differences between NBCTs and unsuccessful applicants were significant.	No concerns.
- NBCTs - Current applicants - Unsuccessful applicants - Nonparticipants	Education production function	Students of NBCTs made highest gains followed in order by those taught by nonparticipants and those taught by unsuccessful candidates. Differences were statistically significant.	Standard errors did not account for nesting; when corrected, effect sizes may not be statistically significant.
- NBCTs - Future NBCTs - Current applicants - Nonparticipants	Education production function	NBCTS were more effective than others in reading and math. Effectiveness declined during year of application. Comparisons prior to and post certification showed mixed results.	Standard errors did not account for nesting; when corrected, effect sizes may not have been statistically significant.
NBCTs and nonparticipants	Various	NBCTs more effective in reading than other teachers; not in math.	Evaluating the effectiveness of NBCTs was not the primary purpose of the study.

Continued

TABLE 7-1 Continued

Study	Grades/ Content Area(s)	Years	State/District
Goldhaber and Anthony (2007)	3rd-5th; reading, math	1996-1999	NC
Harris and Sass (2006)	3rd-10th; reading, math	1999-2004	FL
Sanders, Ashton, and Wright (2005)	5th-8th; reading, math	1999-2003	2 districts in NC: Wake and Charlotte–Mecklenberg

NOTE: The outcome measure for all studies was the state's achievement test used for account-ability purposes. Harris and Sass used two different outcome measures, but results reported here are for the state accountability test. All studies included student, teacher, and school

Groups Compared	Statistical Models	Findings	Issues Affecting Interpretations of the Findings
- NBCTs - Unsuccessful applicants - Nonparticipants	Education production function	NBCTs were more effective in reading, but not in math. Comparison of NBCTs at various stages, showed that future NBCTs were more effective than other teachers. Current applicants showed a decline in effectiveness. During the first year of certification, NBCTs were more effective than other teachers. Results for 2+ years postcertification were inconsistent.	Standard errors did not account for nesting; when corrected, effect sizes may not have been statistically significant.
- NBCTs - Applicants - Nonparticipants	Education production function	NBCTs were more effective in reading than others, not in math. Effectiveness declined during the various stages, postcertification effectiveness never reached levels of precertification effectiveness.	Standard errors did not account for nesting, but most effects were not statistically significant.
- NBCTs - Future NBCTs - Current applicants - Nonparticipants	Hierarchical linear model; compared four models	Results varied by model. Author's preferred model showed few statistically significant effects for NBCTs.	Analyses conducted separately by grade level, which reduced power. Likely that the sample size was small.

characteristics as statistical controls, although the nature of these variables differed across studies. NBCTs = national board-certified teachers.

(Cavaluzzo, 2004; Clotfelter, Ladd, and Vigdor, 2006, 2007a,b; Goldhaber and Anthony, 2007; Harris and Sass, 2006). All six compared gains in test scores of students taught by board-certified teachers to gains in scores for students taught by nonboard-certified teachers who were otherwise qualified to pursue board certification (i.e., were licensed to teach and had at least three years of teaching experience). Two of the studies (Cavaluzzo; Goldhaber and Anthony) also compared test score gains of students taught by successful and unsuccessful applicants for board certification. Four of the studies also examined more specific comparisons of effects for teachers (1) before they became board certified (called "future board-certified teachers"), (2) while they were going through the application process, (3) in the year during which board certification was achieved, and (4) more than one year after achieving board certification. These comparisons addressed the question of whether teachers raised test scores more after earning board certification.

With respect to comparisons of the effectiveness of teachers who successfully earned board certification and those who were unsuccessful, Cavaluzzo and Goldhaber et al. reported similar findings: Board-certified teachers were more effective than teachers who had not applied, and teachers who had not applied were more effective than teachers who had applied and were unsuccessful. Differences between these groups of teachers were statistically significant in both studies, but the magnitudes of the coefficients differed both between the two studies and within each study (when estimated using different statistical models). The pattern is similar to findings in the Cantrell et al. study in that teacher applicants who were successful were more effective than teacher applicants who were unsuccessful. However, Cantrell et al. found no statistically significant differences between board-certified teachers and nonapplicants, whereas the differences between these two groups were statistically significant in the Cavaluzzo and Goldhaber et al. studies.

The studies also investigated the extent to which board-certified teachers raised test scores more as they went through the certification process. The findings for teachers in North Carolina (Clotfelter, Ladd, and Vigdor, 2006, 2007a,b; Goldhaber and Anthony, 2007) were more positive with regard to the effects of board certification than the findings for teachers in Florida (Harris and Sass, 2006). However, even in North Carolina, the findings were not consistent across subjects, grade level, different groupings of teachers, or different choices of statistical models.

Goldhaber and Anthony (2007) reported that students of board-certified teachers had larger gains in reading but not math, and students of future board-certified teachers had the largest gains. Students showed losses in the year teachers were going through the certification process (that is, students of current applicants had smaller gains than students of other teachers).

Students of teachers in their first year after board certification had larger gains than students of other teachers. Students of board-certified teachers after their first year of being certified in some cases had larger gains than students of other teachers and in some cases had smaller gains, depending on the subject area and the statistical model. The study did not correct for clustering of students within classrooms, so tests of statistical significance may be positively biased (that is, effects that are identified as statically significant may not be if adjustments for clustering were performed). Also, the authors compared different groups of teachers in various stages of board certification, which means that unobserved differences in teacher cohorts could explain part of the observed differences.

Clotfelter, Ladd, and Vigdor (2006) found that reading scores were higher for students of board-certified teachers compared with those of nonboard-certified teachers (math scores were not higher). A later study (Clotfelter, Ladd, and Vigdor, 2007a) expanded the years of data included, the grades covered, and the categories of board certification status and reported positive and statistically significant relationships between board certification and student achievement in both reading and mathematics. Their analyses of effects at various stages of board certification showed smaller effects in the year of application, similar to the findings in Goldhaber and Anthony (2007). Their comparisons of effectiveness prior to and after certification were inconsistent, however; depending on the model and the content area, they differed in size, direction, and statistical significance. A third study by these authors (Clotfelter, Ladd, and Vigdor, 2007b) focused on high school students. They found positive and statistically significant effects on student achievement across subject areas.[6] They also found that board-certified teachers improved in their effectiveness when their students' gains were compared from the precertification period to the postcertification period.

While the Cavaluzzo study focused on two high school grades in Miami–Dade County, Harris and Sass (2006) expanded the analyses to the entire state of Florida and included elementary through high school grades. The author also used two outcome measures: scores from the state's accountability test and scores from the state's norm-referenced test. The results differed depending on which outcome measure was studied, a finding that has been documented in other studies (e.g., Lockwood et al., 2007). Findings from the basic comparison of board-certified teachers and nonboard-certified teachers varied depending on the outcome measure. For the norm-referenced test, the effects associated with board certification were

---

[6] At the high school level, students are tested only once in each subject, so models of student fixed effects over time cannot be estimated. Instead, the authors estimated fixed-effects models of student achievement across subjects.

negative and not statistically significant for both reading and mathematics. For the accountability test, the effects associated with board certification were positive for reading and math and statistically significant for reading. Overall, the effect sizes were smaller than those estimated using North Carolina data.

Harris and Sass' examination of the impact of board certification by the various stages of the process yielded a complex set of results depending on the content area and the test used as the outcome measure. When scores from the norm-referenced test were the outcome measure, the results seemed to suggest a decline in effectiveness across the three time periods of board certification such that achievement tended to be higher for future board-certified teachers before they were certified than after becoming certified. Results were mixed when the accountability test was the outcome variable. In this case, decreases in effectiveness were evident across the three time periods, but effectiveness tended to increase beyond the first year after certification, which we speculate may indicate that it takes some time for teachers to implement what they learn from the board-certification process.

This study did not adjust for classroom clustering of students, but few of the findings were statistically significant. In this case, the adjustment is less of an issue because adjusting for clustering would only reduce statistical significance further.

Sanders, Ashton, and Wright (2005) used hierarchical linear modeling techniques to examine the effects of the board certification on student achievement. The study divided teachers into four groups: (1) current board-certified teachers, (2) future board-certified teachers, (3) applicants who failed to be certified, and (4) teachers with no NBPTS involvement. The analyses restricted the comparisons to current board-certified teachers and each of the other three groups. The study relied on data for only two school districts in North Carolina, and the sample sizes are not specified. While these two school districts have larger concentrations of teachers who participate in the NBPTS than other districts in the country, the sample sizes in this study were necessarily smaller than in the studies that used data for the entire state of North Carolina (e.g., Clotfelter et al., 2006; Goldhaber and Anthony, 2007). In addition, the researchers conducted analyses separately for five grades, which reduced the number of teachers on which estimates were based and thereby reduced the statistical power of the analyses to detect effects.

Nonetheless, this study makes an important contribution in that the researchers studied the effects of different model specifications on the results. The authors fit four models, designed to make explicit comparisons to those used by Cavaluzzo (2004) and by Goldhaber and Anthony (2007). Two models replicated those used in the prior studies, which did not account for the clustering of students within classroom. Two other models accounted for this clustering by including random effects for teachers. Random effects capture systematic differences in performance that are shared by students taught by a particular teacher but that are unrelated to any measured teacher or student characteristic already in the model. This effect allowed the researchers to compare the variability of teachers within a specific classification (e.g., variability among board-certified teachers) with the variability of teachers across classifications (e.g., variability between board-certified teachers and nonapplicants).

The findings varied considerably depending on the model. The models that replicated those used by Cavaluzzo and by Goldhaber et al. tended to find statistically significant effects, particularly in reading, whereas the models that accounted for clustering by including random effects uncovered few statistically significant effects. The implication is that accounting for classroom clustering may be an important feature of the models for estimating variances correctly. However, the size of the effects revealed by Sanders, Ashton, and Wright was not dissimilar to those reported by other researchers. Sanders, Ashton, and Wright's disaggregation by grade level reduced sample sizes, reducing power and making it more difficult to identify significant effects, irrespective of the clustering issue.

Synthesis of the Research Findings

The literature review above was intended to describe findings from research on the relationship between national board certification and student test scores. Studies that compared test score gains for students of teachers who were and were not successful in earning board certification consistently found statistically significant differences between the two groups. Results from comparisons of test score gains for students of board-certified teachers and nonapplicants were less consistent.

The studies differed along many dimensions that affect attempts to draw conclusions from them. They used different samples of teachers and classified teachers differently into NBPTS participation groups. Consequently, in some studies the comparison group was teachers who had failed to achieve certification, and in some studies it was all nonboard-certified teachers, which included nonparticipating teachers as well as teachers who had failed to obtain board certification. The studies used different characteristics of students, teachers, classes, and schools as explanatory variables. The studies also differed in the way they measured test score differences, some using gains and some using the current test score with the previous score(s) as a covariate. Given the extent of differences among studies, it is impossible to assess which findings are robust and which are consequences of methodological choices.

As described earlier, the committee had two teams of researchers carry out a set of analyses appropriate for the various data sets and to help disentangle the methodological issues from the findings. The findings from these supplemental analyses are described below.

Results of Supplemental Analyses with Florida and North Carolina Data Sets

The two teams of researchers used a common set of specifications to analyze Florida and North Carolina data. The analyses used data for the 2000-2001 through 2003-2004 school years and examined reading and math performance for fourth and fifth graders, the two grades common between the two data sets. School, teacher, classroom, and student characteristics that were common to both data sets were included in the analyses. Two general classification schemas were used. They first classified teachers into two groups—ever-board-certified and not-ever-board-certified—to examine the signaling effects associated with board certification. They then classified teachers according to the stage of their participation: (1) current board-certified teacher; (2) current applicant for board certification; (3) future board-certified teacher (that is, not currently board certified but would attain certification in the future); and (4) no participation with the NBPTS. This analysis investigated the extent to which teachers improved test scores as they progressed through the certification process.

The researchers ran six alternative models that reflected the methodological variations observed in the studies we reviewed. Two strategies were used to estimate score increases (gain score model and covariate model) and two methods were used to handle preexisting group differences (student fixed effects and school fixed effects). The results are shown in Table 7-2.

The results indicate that the findings are more sensitive to context (i.e., the state) than to model specification. Consistent positive and statistically significant effects for board-certified teachers in North Carolina are evident for both reading and mathematics. The magnitude of the effects varied with model specification, but the sign and significance did not. In Florida, the effects on reading achievement were positive and statistically significant for all but one model, although the effects were smaller than in North Carolina. For mathematics, the Florida estimates were small and not statistically significant.

Results for the model that we judged to be strongest appear in columns 7 and 8 of Table 7-2. This model used the gain score as the outcome measure and estimated both student and school fixed effects. The results indicate that, compared with other teachers, board-certified teachers in

North Carolina raise test scores about 7 percent of a standard deviation[7] more in math and 4 percent of a standard deviation more in reading. In Florida, board certification is associated with a smaller increase of about 1 percent of a standard deviation in mathematics and about 2 percent of a standard deviation in reading. The coefficients for Florida were not statistically significant.

Table 7-3 allows comparison of the results from our analyses to those for prior studies that were based on a variety of different models (as described in the final column of the table). They generally show effect sizes in the same range as our commissioned analyses (roughly 5 to 7 percent of a standard deviation in mathematics and 4 to 6 percent of a standard deviation in reading), with the exception that our analyses of Florida tended to produce lower effect sizes.

The bottom portion of Table 7-2 shows the relationship between board certification and student achievement at different stages of the certification process (the second schema). Several observations can be made about these results. For North Carolina, future board-certified teachers appear to be more effective before becoming board certified, raising test scores 5 percent more in math and 2 percent more in reading than other teachers. The decline in effectiveness reported in other studies is evident during the application year. After teachers earn board certification, they reach similar levels of effectiveness as prior to the process, raising test scores by 8 percent of a standard deviation in math and 4 percent of a standard deviation in reading.

In Florida, the coefficients were smaller and most were not statistically significant. The exceptions were in math, in which teachers who were currently board certified raised test scores by 2 percent of a standard deviation more than other teachers. Also, in reading, teachers who would later become board certified appeared to raise their students' test scores 4 percent of a standard deviation more than other teachers.

Comparison of Teachers Who Passed and Teachers Who Failed

The data sets we used for these analyses did not contain the information needed to compare the effectiveness of teachers who attempted to earn board certification and were successful and those who failed. The data needed for this comparison must be obtained directly from the NBPTS and requires some careful matching of state-level records with NBPTS records. Four sets of researchers worked with the NBPTS to obtain the needed data,

---

[7]Reporting the results in terms of the percentage of a standard deviation is a way of placing the effects on the same metric. This allows researchers to compare effects from different models, analyses, and data sets.

TABLE 7-2 Estimated Effects of National Board Certification on Mathematics and Reading Scores in Florida and North Carolina

	Math	Reading	Math	Reading
FLORIDA				
Schema 1				
Ever certified	.00	.01[b]	.01	.02
	(.008)[a]	(.005)	(.006)	(.007)
Schema 2				
Certified in the future	.00	.02	−.01	.05
	(.012)	(.010)	(.015)	(.014)
Certified in current year	−.01	.01	−.01	−.01
	(.013)	(.011)	(.017)	(.016)
Certified in prior year	.01	.01	.01	.01
	(.009)	(.007)	(.011)	(.009)
NORTH CAROLINA				
Schema 1				
Ever certified	.05	.03	.07	.04
	(.005)	(.004)	(.006)	(.005)
Schema 2				
Certified in the future	.05	.02	.06	.04
	(.010)	(.009)	(.015)	(.012)
Certified in current year	.03	.02	.04	.02
	(.013)	(.009)	(.014)	(.012)
Certified in prior year	.06	.03	.07	.04
	(.006)	(.004)	(.007)	(.006)
Model	gain score		gain score	
Student fixed effects	no		yes	
School fixed effects	no		no	

[a]Standard errors appear in parentheses.
[b]Bold value are statistically significant, $p < .05$.
SOURCE: McCaffrey and Rivkin (2007, Table 4).

and their studies report effect sizes for each of these two groups of teachers. Examining the differences in effectiveness between these two groups provides a cleaner comparison because it eliminates any biases presented by the fact that teachers self-select to pursue board certification. Differences between the two groups thus speak to the ability of the assessment to identify more effective teachers, an issue often addressed in the context of criterion-related validity evidence as discussed in Chapter 5.

Cantrell et al. (2007), Cavaluzzo (2004), Goldhaber and Anthony (2007), and Sanders, Ashton, and Wright (2005) permit this comparison. The results from all four of these studies show that teachers who successfully earned board certification were more effective than those who were

Math	Reading	Math	Reading	Math	Reading	Math	Reading
.00	.01	.01	.02	.02	.02	.01	.02
(.007)	(.006)	(.009)	(.008)	(.006)	(.005)	(.006)	(.005)
-.00	.02	-.01	.04	.01	.02	-.00	.02
(.012)	(.010)	(.015)	(.015)	(.011)	(.010)	(.011)	(.010)
-.02	.01	.01	-.01	.01	.01	-.01	.01
(.013)	(.011)	(.018)	(.017)	(.013)	(.011)	(.012)	(.010)
.01	.01	.02	.01	.03	.02	.02	.02
(.009)	(.007)	(.011)	(.010)	(.008)	(.006)	(.008)	(.007)
.05	.02	.07	.04	.06	.03	.05	.02
(.005)	(.004)	(.007)	(.006)	(.005)	(.004)	(.005)	(.004)
.04	.02	.08	.05	.04	.02	.04	.01
(.011)	(.009)	(.016)	(.012)	(.011)	(.009)	(.010)	(.008)
.03	.02	.05	.02	.03	.03	.03	.02
(.013)	(.009)	(.015)	(.013)	(.012)	(.009)	(.012)	(.009)
.05	.02	.08	.04	.06	.04	.05	.03
(.006)	(.005)	(.008)	(.007)	(.006)	(.004)	(.006)	(.004)
gain score		gain score		lagged score		lagged score	
no		yes		no		no	
yes		yes		no		yes	

unsuccessful; furthermore, teachers who were unsuccessful were less effective than teachers who did not attempt board certification. The magnitude of the effects differs from study to study, however, with the effect sizes reported by Cantrell et al. slightly larger than those reported in the other studies. Table 7-4 presents the effect sizes reported in each study when comparing teachers who passed with teachers who failed. The results from Cantrell et al. indicate that teachers who passed raised their students' achievement about .20 of a standard deviation more in both math and reading than teachers who failed. In the other studies, the differences in effectiveness were about .10 in math (range of .09 to .13) and about .04 in reading (range of .03 to .05).

TABLE 7-3 Summary of Effect Sizes from Different Models: Board Certified Versus Never Applied

Study	Math	Reading	Model
Cavaluzzo	.074	—	School fixed effects, gain score
Cantrell et al.	.046	.060	Random assignment of students to teachers, lagged achievement
Florida committee analyses	.003	.015	Student, school fixed effects, gain score
Goldhaber and Anthony	.050	.040	Covariate, gain score
North Carolina committee analyses	.067	.038	Student, school fixed effects, gain score
Sanders, Ashton, and Wright[a]	.070	.036	HLM,[b] lagged achievement
Sanders, Ashton, and Wright[c]	.054	.058	HLM, teacher random effects, lagged achievement

[a]Data from Sanders, Ashton, and Wright, Table 3A, average effect sizes across grades for board certified versus never applied.
[b]HLM = Hierarchical linear modeling.
[c]Data from Sanders, Ashton, and Wright, Table 3B, average effect sizes across grades for board certified versus never applied.

TABLE 7-4 Summary of Effect Sizes: Successful National Board Applicants Versus Unsuccessful Applicants

Study	Math	Reading	Model
Cantrell et al.	.219	.194	Random assignment of students to teachers, lagged achievement
Cavaluzzo	.100	—	School fixed effects, gain score
Goldhaber and Anthony	.090	.050	Student fixed effects, gain score
Sanders, Ashton, and Wright[a]	.134	.038	HLM,[b] lagged achievement
Sanders, Ashton, and Wright[c]	.102	.032	HLM, teacher random effects, lagged achievement

[a]From Sanders, Ashton, and Wright, Table 3A, average effect sizes across grades for board certified versus failed.
[b]HLM = Hierarchical linear modeling.
[c]From Sanders, Ashton, and Wright, Table 3B, average effect sizes across grades for board certified versus failed.

Interpreting the Effects

The coefficients reported above, even when statistically significant, are small in an absolute sense. For example, in North Carolina an improvement of 8 percent of a standard deviation in math translates to roughly 1 point on the test that has a mean score of 150. To help evaluate the magnitude of these effects, we investigated the effect size for a hypothetical advanced-level certification process that relies solely on value-added estimates derived from student test scores. We refer to this hypothetical process as "pure value-added certification."

To our knowledge, no one has seriously proposed a pure value-added certification process, but there is substantial policy interest in value-added approaches, and many people have proposed approaches to certification or licensure that involve some role for value-added measures. A pure value-added certification process might seem appealing because, by design, it would certify the teachers who produce high value-added estimates, but at the same time it has serious drawbacks. There are four critical caveats to the implementation of a pure value-added certification process. First, there are unresolved technical issues about whether current value-added approaches can reliably identify the value-added estimate that should be attributed to individual teachers. Second, comparisons based on a pure value-added system are problematic in that the comparison selects teachers based on the outcome on which comparison will be done. Regression to the mean will lead the group selected to perform lower in the following year. Third, value-added approaches require the use of standardized tests that are unavailable for many grades and subjects in many states. Finally, in all proposed certification approaches that rely on value-added methods, the value-added estimates are combined with other measures. Although the use of additional measures is likely to increase the reliability and validity of the ultimate certification decision, it would also *reduce* the measured value-added difference between certified and noncertified teachers below the difference we will calculate for a pure value-added certification system. Therefore, although the pure value-added certification process that we discuss here is useful for making comparisons with other approaches to advanced certification, this kind of system could not be fully implemented in practice without resolving these caveats.

A pure value-added certification process would have to determine where to draw the line between the teachers who are awarded board certification and those who are not. Table 7-5 gives results for three possible ways of doing this: choosing the top 25 percent, the top 50 percent, or the top 75 percent of all teachers. Using two different estimates of the size of quality differences across teachers, the table provides the size of the effect in student value-added (compared with an average teacher) that would be associated with teachers who pass and teachers who fail in the pure value-added certification process.

Table 7-5 shows that in a pure value-added certification system, the size of the effects for teachers who pass and teachers who fail crucially depends on how many teachers are selected. If only the top 25 percent of teachers is selected, then the teacher who passes is much better than an average teacher—with an effect size of 0.32. In contrast, if the top 75 percent of teachers is selected, the effect size for teachers who pass is reduced to 0.11.

To compare the pure value-added certification process portrayed in Table 7-5 to national board certification, we need to know whether national board certification is attempting to identify teachers who more closely correspond to the top 25 percent, the top 50 percent, or the top 75 percent of all teachers. Although we do not know the true quality of the teachers who apply for national board certification, we do know that roughly 60 to 65 percent of the teachers who apply are ultimately successful. We also know that teachers who fail the assessment are less effective than average teachers, and that the negative effect size for teachers who fail is about as large as the positive effect size for teachers who pass. Considering this information, the selection rule of choosing the top 50 percent for the pure value-added certification system seems like the closest match to the selectivity of national board certification.

Our supplemental analyses of Florida and North Carolina data produced certification effect sizes for board-certified teachers that average roughly 0.04. This certification effect can be compared with the effect of 0.20 for a pure value-added certification system that chooses the top 50 percent of all teachers to receive certification. Comparison of the two effect sizes indicates that national board certification captures one-fifth of the value-added effect that would be produced by a pure value-added certification process.

Taken together, the results from our additional analyses lead us to articulate three findings and a conclusion:

TABLE 7-5 Certification Effects for a Pure Value-Added Certification

Selection Rule	Effect Size for Teachers Who Pass	Effect Size for Teachers Who Fail
Top 25%	0.32	−0.11
Top 50%	0.20	−0.20
Top 75%	0.11	−0.32

NOTE: Effect sizes estimated from the teacher quality distribution estimate of 0.25 standard deviation of student value added for a 1 standard deviation difference in teacher quality in Texas (see Hanushek, Kain, O'Brien, and Rivkin, 2005).

Finding 7-1: Fourth and fifth graders taught by board-certified teachers in North Carolina show higher gains on the state's accountability test than those taught by other teachers. The effects are in the range of 4 to 5 percent of a standard deviation in reading and 7 to 8 percent of a standard deviation in mathematics, and they are statistically significant.

Finding 7-2: Fourth and fifth graders taught by board-certified teachers in Florida show slightly higher gains on the state's accountability test in reading than those taught by other teachers. The effects are in the range of 2 to 4 percent of a standard deviation. In mathematics, the effects are indistinguishable from zero.

Finding 7-3: In Los Angeles, similar achievement test gains in mathematics and reading were made by third through fifth graders taught by board-certified teachers and by teachers who had not applied for board certification. Achievement gains were statistically significantly lower for students taught by teachers who attempted to obtain board certification but were unsuccessful as compared with those taught by teachers who were board certified.

Conclusion 7-1: Students taught by teachers who are board certified make slightly higher achievement test score gains than do those taught by teachers who have not applied for board certification. The magnitude of the effects varies for reading and math and by state or jurisdiction. Students taught by teachers who have attempted board certification but were unsuccessful make smaller gains than those taught by board-certified teachers or teachers who have not applied for board certification.

The evidence is clear that national board certification distinguishes more effective teachers from less effective teachers with respect to student achievement. The differences are small (and not entirely consistent) in absolute terms, but when considered in terms of teacher value-added contributions to achievement, they are substantively meaningful.

STUDIES OF OTHER STUDENT OUTCOMES

Our search of the literature identified one study that measured the effects of board certification on students using outcomes other than achievement test scores. Helding and Fraser (2005) compared board-certified and nonboard-certified teachers at 13 high schools in Miami–Dade County in terms of classroom environment and student attitudes as well as achievement. The researchers used questionnaires to measure students' perceptions about their science classes and their attitudes about science. The results from these questionnaires, along with each student's science score on Florida's state accountability test, were compared for students taught by board-certified and nonboard-certified teachers. Results generally favored the board-certified teachers, with their students having more positive attitudes and higher science scores.

There are important limitations to these findings, however. The way in which teachers were recruited to participate in the study may have introduced biases, and no efforts were made to control for differences between students assigned to board-certified teachers and nonboard-certified teachers. The authors did not adjust for classroom clustering; thus the significance tests they performed overstate the differences between board-certified and nonboard-certified teachers. This study is described in more detail in Appendix A.

CONCLUSIONS AND RECOMMENDATIONS

Our search of the literature base revealed 11 studies on the relationship between board certification and outcomes for students, far more than we found for any other question on our evaluation framework. For the most part, however, the studies were based on data from only three states—most studied teachers and students in North Carolina, three drew their samples from Florida, and one used data from California (Los Angeles). The only exceptions were two relatively small-scale studies conducted in Arizona and Tennessee that had serious methodological limitations. Furthermore, nearly all focused on achievement test results in mathematics and reading, and most restricted their samples to students and teachers in the elementary grades. We are hesitant to generalize these findings to students and teachers in other states, subjects, and grades.

The committee noted two paths that future research might take. One path would be replication of the Florida and North Carolina studies in more states, content areas, and grades. The committee recognizes, however, that when moving beyond the elementary grades, each student is taught by many teachers, which complicates the teacher attribution that is needed for this kind of research. Furthermore, many states may not have the extensive administrative data sets of teachers and students that are maintained in Florida and North Carolina.

The second path is to examine other student outcomes. Test scores are a narrow conception of student learning, and the standardized test data currently available are primarily scores on tests designed to measure mastery of state content standards, not teaching skills. It may be that the skills board-certified teachers have to demonstrate have impacts on other outcomes that are not detected on accountability tests. We encourage different approaches to the research that focus on different outcomes.

Regardless of the path, longitudinal analyses of test scores for large samples of students need to be balanced with smaller scale studies that use different methods or outcomes. Cantrell et al. (2007) provides one example of a smaller scale study that used random assignment and allowed the researchers to draw more valid conclusions. Helding and Fraser (2005) demonstrate an example of a study that expanded the kinds of outcomes to student attitudes and motivation. In addition, some of the validation studies discussed in Chapter 5 were based on classroom observations and reviews of student work. In these studies, the researchers evaluated the complexity of teachers' assignments, the quality of student work samples, and the depth of students' questions during classroom discussions. These are examples of other measures that might be considered.

We therefore make the following recommendations:

Recommendation 7-1: To the extent that existing data sets allow, we encourage replication of studies that investigate the effects of board-certified teachers on student achievement in states besides North Carolina and Florida, in content areas beyond mathematics and reading, and in grades beyond the elementary levels. Researchers pursuing such studies should work with the national board to obtain the information needed to study the effects of teachers who successfully obtained board certification as well as those who were unsuccessful.

Recommendation 7-2: We encourage studies of the effects of board-certified teachers on outcomes beyond scores on standardized tests, such as student motivation, breadth of achievement, attendance rates, and promotion rates. The choice of outcome measures should reflect the skills that board-certified teachers are expected to demonstrate. Such research should be conducted using sound methodologies, adequate samples, carefully controlled conditions, and appropriate statistical analyses.

8

The Effects of the Certification
Process on Practice

The founders of the National Board for Professional Teaching Standards (NBPTS) anticipated that board certification would have a positive effect on the quality of teaching in this country. They envisioned that articulating the standards for accomplished teaching and recognizing teachers who meet these standards would result in large-scale improvements in the practice of teaching (Carnegie Task Force on Teaching as a Profession, 1986; National Board for Professional Teaching Standards, 1991). In these documents, the founders suggest that improvements will be realized by such mechanisms as making the standards available to teacher preparation programs and by having a growing cadre of board-certified teachers in schools throughout the country who can implement better practices and share their skills with other teachers. While the founding documents do not specifically envision that individual teachers' practice will improve directly as a consequence of the certification process itself, more recent NBPTS publications make this claim. For instance, in "I Am a Better Teacher" (National Board for Professional Teaching Standards, 2001a, p. 1), the board states that "the certification process helps teachers improve their teaching."

Considering the time required by the assessment and the depth and complexity of the tasks involved, it seems reasonable to expect some impact on the practices of those who complete the process. While it is not typical to assume that simply taking a test would improve the skills the test intends to measure, the national board's assessment is somewhat unique in this regard. Applicants for board certification are expected to analyze, dissect, and reflect on the lessons they include in their portfolio. The activities involved in preparing for the assessment and in assembling the portfolio itself may present candidates with an opportunity to develop and hone their teaching strategies. Therefore, in our evaluation framework, we investigate whether going through the NBPTS certification process could have an impact on a teacher's practices and ultimately on student learning. The question that we take up in this chapter is whether there is any evidence that this occurs.

Question 5: To what extent do teachers improve their practices and the outcomes of their students by virtue of going through the advanced-level certification process?

Figure 2-1 shows where this piece of the evaluation fits within the committee's framework, displaying our model of the ways a certification program for accomplished teachers might influence the teaching profession and the way our evaluation questions map onto this model. To respond to this aspect of the evaluation, we identified three subsidiary questions to investigate. Specifically:

a. To what extent do teachers who go through the certification process improve their teaching practices and classroom climate, regardless of whether they become board certified?
b. Do teachers who obtain board certification become more effective at increasing student achievement in ways that are evident in their students' achievement scores?
c. Do teachers have a greater impact on other student outcomes (e.g., higher student motivation, higher promotion rates) after they obtain certification than they did before they were certified?

Our literature review revealed that little research has addressed these questions, and the evidence that is available is not conclusive. In this chapter, we discuss the available evidence on each of the subquestions and the limitations of the findings, and we propose ways to improve upon the existing research base. We begin with Subquestion b because the studies that address this question were just discussed in Chapter 7. We then move to Subquestion a, for which there were two studies that objectively evaluated the impact of the process on teachers' practices (Darling-Hammond and Atkin, 2007; Lustick and Sykes, 2006) and four survey-based studies that provide self-reports from teachers about their perceptions of the impacts of the assessment on their practices (Indiana Professional Standards Board, 2002; National Board for Professional Teaching Standards, 2001a,d; Yankelovich Partners, 2001). We found no studies that addressed Subquestion c. Table 8-1 provides a summary of the studies discussed in this chapter.

TABLE 8-1 Professional Development Effects of the National Board-Certification Process

Study	Grades/ Content Area(s)	Years	Sample Size	State(s)
Studies of Impacts on Student Achievement				
Clotfelter, Ladd, and Vigdor (2006)	3rd-5th; reading, math	1994-2004	All teachers in the state	NC
Clotfelter, Ladd, and Vigdor (2007b)	High school		All teachers in the state	NC
Goldhaber and Anthony (2007)	3rd-5th; reading, math	1996-1999	All teachers in the state	NC
Harris and Sass (2006)	3rd-10th; reading, math	1999-2004	All teachers in the state	FL
Studies of Impact on Teachers' Practices				
Darling-Hammond and Atkin (2007)	Middle and high school; math and science		16 teachers, 9 applicants and 7 nonparticipants	CA

Groups Compared	Findings	Issues Affecting Interpretations of the Findings
- NBCTs - Future NBCTs - Current applicants - Nonparticipants	Effectiveness declined during year of application. Comparisons prior to and post certification showed mixed results.	Standard errors did not account for nesting; when corrected, effect sizes may not have been statistically significant.
- NBCTs - Future NBCTs - Current applicants - Nonparticipants	Effectiveness increased from precertification period to postcertification period. No decline was evident during the application year.	No concerns.
- NBCTs - Unsuccessful applicants - Nonparticipants	Comparison of NBCTs at various stages showed that future NBCTs were more effective than other teachers. Current applicants showed a decline in effectiveness. During the first year of certification, NBCTs were more effective than other teachers. Results for 2+ years postcertification were inconsistent.	Standard errors did not account for nesting; when corrected, effect sizes may not have been statistically significant.
- NBCTs - Applicants - Nonparticipants	Effectiveness declined during the various stages, postcertification effectiveness never reached levels of precertification effectiveness.	Standard errors did not account for nesting, but most effects were not statistically significant.
Applicants and nonparticipants	Teachers who went through the certification process improved their formative assessment practices more than the nonparticipants.	Very small sample, produced in large part by attrition. No information provided about the teachers who dropped out of the study.

Continued

TABLE 8-1 Continued

Study	Grades/ Content Area(s)	Years	Sample Size	State(s)
Indiana Professional Standards Board (2002)	N/A	2001	71; responses from 32 (48%)	IN
Lustick and Sykes (2006)	Science (adolescent and young adult)	2001-2004	188 teachers	National
NBPTS (2001a)	N/A	September 2001	10,700; responses from 5,641 (53%)	National
NBPTS (2001d)	N/A	Teachers board certified between 1994 and 1999	600; responses from 235 (40 percent)	National

Groups Compared	Findings	Issues Affecting Interpretations of the Findings
Only studied NBCTs	Respondents said the process made them more effective. The emphasis on reflection helped them with their lesson planning.	Small sample, low response rate.
Pretest group = applicants before going through the certification process; Posttest group = applicants after going through the certification process	Teachers in the posttest group performed better than those in the pretest group on simulated NBPTS-like tasks after going through the actual certification process.	Questions about the extent to which performance on the tasks generalizes to classroom practice.
Teachers who completed the certification process	Teachers reported that the process helped them: - Develop stronger curricular skills - Improve ways to evaluate learning - Improve interactions with students - Collaborate better with other teachers - Incorporate state content standards in teaching. Most reported it was a good professional development experience. Most thought it made them better teachers.	Sample included teachers who were unsuccessful, but results not reported for this group. Sampling methodology is questionable. No evaluation of the extent to which the sample represented the population. Results described in an advocacy piece. Few details are provided.
Only studied NBCTs	NBCTs reported that the process - Was better than any other professional development process - Had a greater impact than receiving the credential itself - Positively affected their teaching practices - Caused them to become more reflective.	Results reported in an advocacy piece with few details about the methodology. No evaluation of the representativeness of the sample.

Continued

TABLE 8-1 Continued

Study	Grades/ Content Area(s)	Years	Sample Size	State(s)
Yankelovich Partners (2001)	N/A	Nov. 2000- Jan. 2001	4,800; responses from 2,186 (45%)	National

NOTE: N/A = Not available; NBCTs = National Board-Certified Teachers.

IMPACT OF BOARD CERTIFICATION ON STUDENT GAINS ON ACHIEVEMENT TESTS

In Chapter 7, we discussed results from studies that compared achievement test gains for the students of board-certified teachers who were at different stages in the certification process—before pursuing board certification, during the application process, and after becoming board certified. Goldhaber and Anthony (2005) and Clotfelter, Ladd, and Vigdor (2006, 2007b) examined these staged effects for teachers in North Carolina, and Harris and Sass (2006) examined them for teachers in Florida.

Three of these studies (Clotfelter, Ladd, and Vigdor, 2006; Goldhaber and Anthony 2005; Harris and Sass, 2006) generally found that teachers who eventually earned board certification were more effective from the outset at increasing their student's test scores than other teachers, but the studies did not provide evidence of improved effectiveness after becoming board certified. Moreover, some results implied that teachers were *less* effective after attaining board certification than before. Results for the most recent study (Clotfelter, Ladd, and Vigdor, 2007b), which focused on high school students and teachers, were somewhat different, showing statistically significant differences (p < .05) when teachers' effectiveness was compared before and after becoming certified.

As discussed in Chapter 7, because of methodological differences among the studies, we conducted supplemental analyses to better understand the actual effects. The additional analyses used data for Florida and North Carolina, the only states that maintain longitudinal data that allow for such analyses, and focused on the grades, subject areas, and variables that were common to the two states. The results from our supplemental analyses were also inconclusive, some showing that teachers were slightly

Groups Compared	Findings	Issues Affecting Interpretations of the Findings
Only studied NBCTs	Board certification increased their credibility in the profession and made them feel more confident in their abilities. Board certification was associated with improved respect.	Low response rate; no indication of how representative the respondents were of the sample.

more effective at increasing their students' test scores after completing the process than before going through it and some showing no differences in pretest and posttest effectiveness (see Table 7-2).

While the Florida and North Carolina data sets offer the advantage of providing longitudinal data with a wide array of variables and large sample sizes, the analyses are exploratory in nature. That is, they are based on comparisons of precertification and postcertification effectiveness, without an underlying hypothesis about how or why improvements in effectiveness might occur and when they might become apparent. For example, it may be that teachers need a year or two to implement what they learn from the process, such that improvements in effectiveness would not be immediately apparent. Florida's state data allowed for a preliminary exploration of this idea.

In supplemental analyses with the Florida data, the researchers were able to split the postcertification stages into one year postcertification and two or more years postcertification. They conducted these analyses for reading and mathematics in three grade spans (elementary, middle, and high school). The results for mathematics showed a slight trend toward improvements in effectiveness across the two postcertification stages, but the increases were generally less than a .03 change in effect sizes (e.g., for high school mathematics the effect size was .00 during the first year postcertification and .03 afterward). The results for reading were smaller and not consistent across the three grade spans.

Again, these analyses were exploratory, taking advantage of existing data systems. We think it would be useful for researchers to develop hypotheses about what teachers might learn from the certification process, how they might implement these newly formed skills and practices, and when improvements in practice should become evident. This kind of research would require a more focused, theory-based approach that begins with a conception of what teachers might learn and how they might incorporate this information into their classroom practices, followed by the collection of data designed specifically to evaluate these hypotheses. We think that this approach should be considered in collecting evidence to evaluate the impact of teachers' practices on student outcomes, as well as on other outcomes.

TEACHERS' PRACTICES BEFORE AND AFTER NBPTS PARTICIPATION

Two studies took a different approach to evaluating the impact of the certification process on teachers by focusing directly on their performance. As with the studies just discussed, these two also do not provide definitive findings about improvements in teachers' skills as a result of the certification process. However, we describe the approaches taken in each study because we think the methodologies have merit and should be considered in future research.

Lustick and Sykes (2006) compared teachers' performance before and after completing the assessment for the adolescent and young adult science credential. The study used simulated NBPTS-like portfolio exercises created by the researchers. To accomplish the data collection, the researchers sent each of the 118 participants, who had been randomly assigned to treatment groups, a sealed packet containing the exercises. The researchers conducted a phone interview during which each teacher opened the sealed packets and responded to the exercises. The exercises consisted of five assignments. Two of them asked teachers to describe their own experiences, much like what is required on the actual assessment. Three assignments involved reviewing materials that the researchers sent, including a videotaped lesson, a written scenario of a lesson, and a sample of student work. Their responses were recorded, transcribed, and scored by trained NBPTS assessors following the standard NBPTS rubric.

For this study, teachers were assigned randomly to either a pretest or a posttest group, with the pretest group taking the simulated assessment prior to going through the actual board-certification process and the posttest group participating in the study afterward (but before receiving results from the NBPTS). Analyses revealed that the posttest group scored statistically significantly (p < .05) higher than the pretest group.

The authors have since accumulated information on the actual assessment results for the participants (personal communication with first author, February 2, 2007). As is typical for the general pool of all NBPTS applicants, about half of the teachers in each group passed. The researchers compared the performance of unsuccessful teachers in the pretest and in the posttest group with the performance of successful teachers in the pretest and posttest groups. Analyses indicated that both teachers who passed and teachers who failed showed gains on the simulated exercises, suggesting that even teachers who are not successful learn from the process.

This study, while methodologically sound, focused on what teachers would do under certain hypothetical situations, but it did not evaluate teachers' performance in the classroom. Darling-Hammond and Atkin (2007) examined teachers' actual classroom practices. This study focused on the impact of the certification process on the classroom practices of middle and high school mathematics and science teachers. The authors recruited teachers interested in becoming board certified and randomly assigned them to two groups. The NBPTS group went through the certification process during the time period of the study, while the comparison group postponed their application for board certification. The researchers followed the teachers for three years and collected data at specific stages of the application process: one year prior to pursuing board certification, the year of candidacy, and the year after candidacy.

Attrition became a significant issue for this study, however. About 60 teachers initially expressed interest in participating, but in the end only 16 completed the study and only nine went through the certification process. This attrition rate is so high that it calls into question the validity of the findings, but we highlight the study because the approach is one that we encourage.

For this study, teachers submitted videotapes of lessons, written responses to questions about the videotaped lessons, and student work samples from the unit that was videotaped. They also participated in interviews and surveys about their assessment practices. The focus of the collected information was on the ways that teachers use formative assessment practices in their daily teaching, including the types of assessments, the use of assessment results for planning instruction, and the feedback given to students. The researchers designed a rubric that was used to score the submitted information.

The researchers found that the NBPTS group used a wider range of assessment methods and questioning strategies in class discussions that elicited more complete explanations from students. They were better able to integrate their assessments with ongoing instruction. Overall, the NBPTS group showed consistent improvement in their assessment practices during the course of the study.

It is not known what effect attrition had on the findings from this study. Some of the teachers dropped out of the study after the first or second year, and partial information was collected on them. The authors did not report any results for these teachers, however, so we cannot evaluate how this affected the results. For example, it is not known if the teachers who dropped out tended to be systematically weaker or stronger than other teachers in the group (the first author did not respond to our queries about this). For this reason, the committee thinks that no strong conclusions can be drawn from this study. Nonetheless, the researchers' focus on actual classroom practice and the kinds of information they collected permitted a rich set of analyses.

The approaches used in these two studies are the kinds of strategies that we encourage. We think these methodologies, when carried out in a scientifically sound way with sufficient numbers of appropriately selected participants, are likely to be the most fruitful ways to investigate the impact of the certification process on teachers. In our judgment, these studies suggest that teachers learn from the certification process, but the evidence base at this point is simply too thin to draw any firm conclusions from these findings.

WHAT DO TEACHERS REPORT ABOUT THEIR EXPERIENCES?

As our review makes clear, there is very little empirical evidence about the impact of the certification process on teachers' practices and effectiveness. In the absence of studies that objectively evaluate the effects of the process on teachers' practices, we turned to other sources. One way to find out if teachers learn from the experience is simply to ask them.

Our literature review identified four survey-based studies that asked teachers about their experiences after completing the certification process. Three were large-scale national surveys sponsored by the NBPTS (National Board for Professional Teaching Standards, 2001a,d; Yankelovich Partners, 2001), and one was a small-scale survey of board-certified teachers in Indiana (Indiana Professional Standards Board, 2002). The findings from these surveys were generally positive. Teachers tended to report that the certification process was a worthwhile professional development activity that improved their teaching practices and stimulated them to become more reflective, a practice that is encouraged in the NBPTS standards.

However, these surveys were not conducted in a way that would best address the questions in our evaluation framework. What is needed to evaluate the impact of the certification process on teachers is to collect data on a pretest and posttest basis to compare responses before and after going through the process. These surveys collected information only after teachers had successfully completed the process. Thus, while they provide some basic information about teachers' perceptions of the effects of the process, the results cannot be used to make inferences about changes in their practices attributable to the process itself.

There were additional limitations to these studies. Results from the survey of board-certified teachers in Indiana were based on a sample of only 32 teachers (Indiana Professional Standards Board, 2002). Details about the NBPTS-authored studies are lacking. The results from two of the surveys (National Board for Professional Teaching Standards, 2001a,d) are presented in advocacy pieces intended to promote the program, and the discussion of the findings is neither fully detailed nor objective. The report on the third survey (Yankelovich Partners, 2001) consists of only a tally of the survey responses with little or no discussion of the methodology or findings. These shortcomings made it impossible to draw independent judgments about the validity of the findings.

We would like to have conducted our own survey or possibly a more in-depth study that evaluated teachers' perceptions of the process before and after going through it, but we had neither the time nor the resources for such an undertaking. Instead, we arranged for several small-scale focused conversations to follow up on findings reported in these surveys. As noted in Chapter 2, we held a structured discussion with teachers who serve on the National Research Council's (NRC's) Teacher Advisory Council, of which four were board-certified, and we organized a panel discussion with three board-certified teachers at one of our meetings. The teachers involved in these discussions were not intended to be representative samples of any kind but simply to provide an opportunity for committee members to hear teachers discuss the NBPTS process and to ask them questions about its effects on their teaching.

The findings from these discussions generally confirmed those reported in the surveys. The board-certified teachers who spoke with us made positive remarks about the process. They thought it was a worthwhile professional development experience that had significant impacts on their teaching. They said that after becoming board certified, they tended to adopt the reflective practices toward teaching that the board endorses. The remarks made by one of the panelists, Sara Eisenhardt, a board-certified elementary teacher in Cincinnati, Ohio, are typical of those made by other board-certified teachers:

> Sara Eisenhardt commented that one consequence of going through the board-certification process is that she learned to be more "strategic" in her teaching. She said that the focus on reflective teaching was critical and opened her eyes to new teaching methodologies. Before participating in the program, she had not thought of teaching in this way and had not learned how to discuss student work and to reflect on how effective her instruction had been. As a result of the national board process, she learned to be more focused in her lesson planning, to better evaluate students' learning and how well the lesson went, and to strategically plan for the next day's lesson. She is now actively involved in support programs for teachers going through the process and in revamping the school system's professional development activities for teachers.

In our judgment, the survey results combined with our own conversations with teachers provide some evidence, albeit weak, that teachers who have successfully earned board certification find the process to enhance their practices.

Finding 8-1: Self-report information from teachers who have successfully completed the board-certification process indicates that they tend to be positive about the experience. Board-certified teachers report that the process provides a professional development experience for them and has positive influences on their teaching practices, helping them become reflective of their teaching and their instructional decisions. However, no empirical research has yet been conducted to corroborate this self-report information.

CONCLUSIONS AND RECOMMENDATIONS

It is difficult to draw any firm conclusions from the research discussed in this chapter. The survey results and our own discussions with teachers suggest that teachers learn from the process, but we cannot ignore the fact that this information is entirely subjective. For one thing, it is limited to teachers who were successful in their attempt to earn board certification. It is not surprising that individuals who successfully complete a lengthy and difficult process feel positive about it, and it would be quite worrisome if these teachers reported negative perceptions of the process. In addition, the surveys were conducted only after teachers earned their credentials, making it impossible to evaluate changes in their attitudes, ideas, and perspectives as a consequence of going through the process. Also, we were particularly reluctant to draw conclusions from the four surveys discussed in this chapter because of methodological problems associated with each one.

Nevertheless, we see an important role that survey data could play in addressing this aspect of the evaluation framework. First, surveys should be conducted both before and after the process, either by tracking the same group of teachers over time or by gathering pretest and posttest data from equivalent groups. Second, teachers who did not pass on the first attempt need to be included, and their results should be examined separately.

We encourage the NBPTS and other researchers to conduct such surveys. The board could easily implement such data collections as a routine part of the testing process, as is done by many other testing organizations. Test-takers could be required to respond to a questionnaire at the time they register for the assessment and again after completing the assessment center exercises. This is a straightforward way to collect a wealth of information. Other data collection efforts could be focused at later stages of the process, such as shortly after receiving the assessment results, a year later, and so on, and they could be combined with data collections to address other aspects of our evaluation. This kind of data collection need not be on the full population of test-takers but a carefully selected random sample. In developing these questionnaires, conducting these surveys, and reporting the results, we encourage the NBPTS to consult with experts to avoid the methodological problems associated with their past surveys (see Appendix A).

We also hesitate to draw firm conclusions about the effects of the certification process on teachers' practices. The findings from Lustick and Sykes and from Darling-Hammond and Atkin are suggestive, but each study has limitations. Together they represent a first step in such investigations, but more research is needed before definite conclusions can be made. We think that this line of research holds promise, however, and encourage researchers and the NBPTS to pursue it. We recognize that such studies are difficult undertakings and recruiting participants can be a challenge. Nevertheless, studies such as these allow for more in-depth analyses of teachers' practices and a better understanding of any impacts of the board-certification process.

At this stage, we cannot say whether any learning that teachers acquire from the process translates into higher achievement test scores for their students. The findings from existing studies are contradictory. Despite the fact that the most recent Clotfelter, Ladd, and Vigdor (2007b) paper found improvement in teachers' effectiveness, we note that the improvement is not large, and it is likely that any positive effects reported in future studies will also show only small effects. There may be several reasons for this.

First, it is important to remember that the national board did not set out to develop a means for raising students' test scores. The board laid out a mechanism for professionalizing teaching, one consequence of which was to improve teachers' practice, thereby improving student learning.

The board's discussions of accomplished practice suggest the kinds of behaviors that advanced-level teachers may demonstrate. They suggest that teachers who become board certified may be better able to engage their students. Their lessons may be more structured and better focused. They may provide more appropriately geared lessons that build on their students' experiences and interests, and they may learn to continually adjust their lessons to meet their students' needs. As a result of board certification, teachers may develop a new enthusiasm for their teaching and thus better stimulate their students.

If these are the sorts of skills that teachers develop, however, they may not manifest themselves as higher scores on standardized achievement tests. Standardized achievement tests generally measure a fairly narrow set of skills and knowledge. They are typically paper and pencil tests that require students to demonstrate what they know through written responses. Some students are disadvantaged by these assessments and would provide more in-depth information about what they know through interviews or other, more hands-on mechanisms. Standardized tests often do not assess higher order critical thinking skills and cannot measure enthusiasm for learning. Furthermore, as we laid out in Chapter 7, there are many methodological issues associated with conducting studies that focus on students' standardized test scores that may depress potential effects.

In our judgment, the existing research does not provide documentation that the certification process enhances teachers' skills at improving students' achievement test performance. Neither does it refute this claim. At this stage, the available research focuses only on reading and mathematics achievement in two states and primarily in the elementary grades. These studies are exploratory in nature and not based on a theory of the ways in which the certification process might impact teachers' effectiveness or when these impacts are likely to be evident. We think it is premature to conclude that these findings would generalize to all other states, content areas, and grades. We think there is a need for replication of these studies in other states, grades, and content areas, but we do not want to see all resources invested in such studies. We therefore encourage multiple avenues for research.

Large-scale studies that use standardized test performance as the outcome measure are relatively easy to conduct when these tests are routinely given to all students and the data are maintained in state databases. These resources offer an efficient means for conducting such studies. However, such studies should not be the only kind conducted. We encourage researchers to find ways to evaluate students' performance on other measures that are more aligned with the skills that the board emphasizes, such as assessments of critical thinking skills or evaluations of students' attitudes toward a given subject. These studies combined with surveys and research that directly evaluates teachers' classroom practices should provide a more complete picture of the impacts of the certification process.

We therefore make the following recommendations for additional research:

Recommendation 8-1: We encourage the NBPTS and other researchers to undertake research to investigate the effects of the process on the candidates. The studies should use pretest-posttest and longitudinal designs and should allow for comparison of responses from successful and unsuccessful candidates.

Recommendation 8-2: We encourage the NBPTS and other researchers to pursue more mixed-method studies, using both quantitative and qualitative research methods, to examine the effects of board certification on teachers' practices. These studies should examine a variety of measures and a variety of student outcomes. Such research should be conducted using sound methodologies, adequate samples, and appropriate statistical analyses.

Recommendation 8-3: Researchers should work with the NBPTS to obtain the information needed to study the relationships between board certification and student achievement across the various stages of board certification. These studies should examine the impacts of the certification process on teachers' effectiveness in increasing their students' test scores and specifically should examine effects for the years subsequent to the receipt of board certification. To the extent that existing data sets allow, we encourage replication of studies in states besides North Carolina and Florida and in subjects beyond elementary reading and mathematics.

9

The Impact of Certification on
Teachers' Career Paths

A fundamental reason for establishing the National Board for Professional Teaching Standards (NBPTS) and offering advanced-level certification
was to make the teaching profession more appealing for high-performing
teachers, thus encouraging them to remain in it. Hiring difficulties and the
loss of good teachers are significant problems in many jurisdictions. Well-
prepared, experienced teachers—particularly math and science specialists
who are likely to have other higher paying career options—are in short
supply. Experienced teachers often find that the only way to advance in
their careers is to move out of the classroom and become administrators or
to leave teaching entirely. Teaching has also been less likely to attract the
most successful students from top undergraduate programs, in part because
of comparatively low pay scales, lower prestige, and flat career trajectories
(National Commission on Teaching and America's Future, 2003).

The committee addressed the possibility that a program that offers
advanced-level certification for teachers could make the field more at-
tractive and thus mitigate these problems. In Chapter 2, we posited that
such a program might be expected to improve the conditions that affect
teachers' career decisions in several ways. Such a program could help to
professionalize the field, lead to higher pay for teachers who obtain board
certification, lead to expanded opportunities for leadership in the field, and
increase their satisfaction with their careers. Such improvements could, in
turn, impact the career paths of teachers. Once again, we turn to Figure
2-1 for a visual display of how these factors could interact to improve the
teaching profession.

Our evaluation framework focused on career paths for teachers with this question:

Question 6: To what extent and in what ways are the career paths of both successful and unsuccessful candidates affected by their participation in the program?

To respond to this aspect of the evaluation, we identified three specific issues to investigate with regard to teachers' career paths:

a.   What are the typical career paths for teachers? Does the career path change for those who obtain advanced certification? What are the effects on the career paths of teachers who attempt to become certified but who are unsuccessful?
b.   Do departure rates differ for board certified and nonboard-certified teachers with regard to leaving teaching (attrition), including those who leave classroom teaching for other jobs in schools (transition)?
c.   Does the program have any effects on teacher mobility within the teaching field? Does it encourage teacher mobility in ways that are beneficial for lower performing students or in ways that contribute to inequities—for example, do board-certified teachers move out of urban areas to wealthy suburban districts?

Our literature review quickly revealed there are very few studies that have examined the job transitions and career changes teachers make after becoming board certified. One study (Goldhaber and Hansen, 2007) examined teachers' mobility patterns in North Carolina, and one question on the survey administered by Sykes et al. (2006) asked teachers about their future plans. In addition, follow-up surveys to the 1993 Baccalaureate and Beyond Longitudinal Survey (B&B) collected information that allowed some basic comparison of career paths for board-certified and nonboard-certified teachers, and we conducted analyses of these data. We expected to be able to draw from the results from another national data collection, the Schools and Staffing Survey, which includes an item on board certification, but a flaw in the question rendered the data unusable. We describe the problems in more detail later in this chapter.

Our analyses combined with the results from prior research provide some basic information about teachers' longevity in the field and about teacher mobility. We were unable to locate any information that deals with teachers' transitions out of the classroom to other positions in K-12 education.

We begin this chapter with an explanation of the challenges of conducting studies on teachers' career paths and the kinds of data that are available. We then turn to the issue of the kinds of career decisions that teachers make and discuss what is known about turnover rates (Subquestion b) and about the effects of teacher mobility (Subquestion c). For the most part, our analysis left us with many questions that need to be answered by additional studies, and we conclude the chapter with suggestions for the kinds of data that need to be collected.

CHALLENGES IN STUDYING TEACHERS' CAREER PATHS

One way to examine teachers' career path decisions is to simply ask them about the decisions they have made and the reasons for them. Surveys and interviews can be used for this, although obtaining an adequate sample and following teachers over time can be an arduous undertaking. Another possibility is to use existing data from large-scale administrative data systems. Currently, there are three potential sources for such information—data systems maintained by states and two surveys of teachers conducted by the U.S. Department of Education. We discuss the benefits and limitations of each below.

State-Level Data Systems

Some states maintain administrative data systems on teachers, their characteristics, and their teaching assignment. When linked longitudinally, these systems allow the tracking of teachers from the time they are first hired in the state throughout their education careers in the public school system in that state. Such data systems can also provide information on the types of schools in which teachers are employed. These data are useful for investigating patterns of teacher mobility within the state and, depending on the type of information maintained, possibly on transitions to nonteaching positions in the state's public school system as well.

When a teacher leaves the state's public school system, however, the tracking ceases. Thus these systems usually provide little or no information on these departures. Of those who left the state's public school system, state data systems generally cannot distinguish whether the teacher moved to a teaching job in a private school (in or out of the state), moved to a teaching job in a public school in another state, or left K-12 teaching entirely. As a result, examining attrition from the teaching field usually requires national data.

Schools and Staffing Survey

One national source for studying teacher attrition and retention is the Schools and Staffing Survey (SASS), administered by the National Center for Education Statistics (NCES) of the U.S. Department of Education. To date, five independent cycles of SASS have been completed: 1987-1988, 1990-1991, 1993-1994, 1999-2000, and 2003-2004. SASS is an unusually large survey. Each cycle of SASS administers survey questionnaires to a random sample of about 53,000 teachers, 12,000 principals, and 4,500 districts, representing all types of teachers, schools, districts, and all 50 states.

The most recent (2003-2004) survey asked teachers about board certification, but the question was ambiguous. It asked teachers if they "have taken any of the following tests?" and the list included "an exam for NBPTS." Initial analyses of the responses to this question revealed that approximately 540,000 teachers (roughly 14.5 percent of all teachers in the sample) indicated they had earned this credential. This figure differs sharply from the numbers of board-certified teachers in the country reported by the NBPTS, which as of 2004, was approximately 40,217. This suggests that the vast majority of survey respondents misunderstood this question. Thus, as of this writing, the SASS database cannot be used to compare attrition or retention rates for board-certified and nonboard-certified teachers.

Baccalaureate and Beyond Longitudinal Study

A second national data collection effort by NCES, the Baccalaureate and Beyond Longitudinal Study of 1993 (B&B 93:03), focuses on the postbaccalaureate experiences of college students who graduated in 1992-1993. Potential sample members were identified through the cross-sectional National Postsecondary Aid Study of 1993. The subsample eligible for the B&B 93:03 study consisted of approximately 11,200 college graduates who received their bachelor's degrees between July 1992 and June 1993. Students eligible for the B&B study were asked questions about their plans for the future, particularly expectations for employment and graduate education. Follow-up studies were conducted in 1994, 1997, and 2003, and information was obtained about postbaccalaureate experiences, including information about employment experiences, such as occupation, salary, and job satisfaction.

A unique focus of the B&B 93:03 follow-up was on graduates who had considered or entered teaching. Approximately 2,000 of the college graduates in the sample had taught at some point between 1993 and 2003. These teachers were asked about preparation, initial licensure, grades and subjects taught, job satisfaction, and reasons for staying in or leaving teaching.

The 2003 follow-up included, for the first time, a question about national board-certification status. Respondents who had previously indicated that they were licensed to teach at the K-12 level were asked "if they were working toward or had already earned a national board certificate (issued by the National Board for Professional Teaching Standards (NBPTS))." Of those who were asked, 45 indicated that they were working toward board certification and 104 said they had obtained board certification (roughly 7.5 percent). While this is a very small sample, it does provide some information that can be used to compare retention in teaching for board-certified and nonboard-certified teachers. The data set does not contain any information about the schools in which teachers were employed or the types of teaching assignments they held. Thus, this data set cannot be used to study teacher mobility at the national level.

TEACHER TURNOVER

Retention and Attrition

A large body of research documents the extent of teacher attrition from the profession. A recent estimate based on the SASS data indicated that approximately 6 percent of teachers leave the profession each year (Ingersoll, 2001, p. 521). Approximately 33 percent of teachers leave within the first three years of teaching and 46 percent leave within the first five years (Ingersoll, 2002b, cited in National Commission on Teaching and America's Future, 2003). When asked about their reasons for leaving the profession, nearly half (49 percent) reported dissatisfaction or pursuit of another job (Ingersoll, 2001). For those who reported that they were dissatisfied with the profession, the top reasons they cited were poor salary, lack of student motivation, inadequate administrative support, and student discipline problems.

These data address attrition for all teachers, and few data sources contain the kind of information needed to compare attrition rates for board-certified and nonboard-certified teachers. Sykes et al. (2006) reports survey results that addressed this issue. One survey question, which was intentionally worded to be similar to a question posed on the SASS questionnaire, asked respondents: "How long do you plan to continue teaching?" The researchers compared the responses of their board-certified respondents from Ohio and South Carolina with those of all teachers surveyed in SASS 1999-2000. Their results are presented in Table 9-1.

These results, while hardly definitive, suggest that board-certified teachers in these two states are more likely than other teachers to indicate that they plan to remain in teaching and less likely to indicate that they plan

TABLE 9-1 Comparison of the Reponses of Board-Certified and All Teachers to the Survey Question: How Long Do You Plan to Continue Teaching?

State	As long as I am able to:		I plan to leave teaching as soon as I can:	
	Board-Certified Teachers[a]	All Teachers[b]	Board-Certified Teachers[a]	All Teachers[b]
Ohio	52%	38%	0.2%	2%
S. Carolina	49%	35%	0.2%	5%

[a]Based on Sykes survey of teachers in Ohio (n = 587) and South Carolina (n = 566).
[b]Based on SASS 1999-2000 results for 1,525 teachers.
SOURCE: Data excerpted from Sykes et al. (2006, Table 4). Reprinted with permission from the National Board for Professional Teaching Standards, http://www.nbpts.org. All rights reserved.

to leave teaching. To further explore this issue, we conducted a small-scale analysis of the B&B data set.

The B&B 93:03 data set followed 1993 college graduates for 10 years. Of those 1993 college graduates who had gone into teaching, the 2003 follow-up obtained information on whether they were still doing so as of 2003 and on whether they had ever attained board certification. The B&B includes 204 teachers who indicated that they were board certified. Because this is such a small sample from a single cohort (the class of 1993), we would expect its composition to differ from those in the NBPTS database of all teachers who ever applied and obtained board certification.[1] For example, we found that 6.7 percent of the B&B 93:03 sample obtained board certification, compared with less than 2 percent of all teachers in the nation. Moreover, the B&B 93:03 sample contains a greater proportion of men (25.7 versus 11.2 percent from the NBPTS database), fewer whites (84.6 versus 90.1 percent in the NBPTS database), more African Americans (7.8 versus 4.7 percent in NBPTS database), and fewer teachers with advanced degrees (42.6 versus 61.6 percent in NBPTS database). Not surprisingly considering the timing of the survey, the B&B sample is younger (on average 35.2 versus 40.3 years) and less experienced (8.9 versus 12.6 years in the NBPTS database). The B&B 93:03 sample also has a greater proportion of teachers working in elementary schools (61.9 versus 51.8 percent in the NBPTS database).

Despite these differences between the two data sets, we used the B&B 93:03 to examine the attrition rates between 1993 and 2003 for board-

---

[1]Chapter 6 provides additional details about the NBPTS data set that we used for these analyses.

certified and nonboard-certified teachers. While the majority of teachers in the B&B 93:03 began teaching in 1993 or 1994, some did not do so until subsequent years. We therefore estimated attrition rates separately for teachers depending on when they entered the teaching profession (those who began teaching between 1993 and 1995 and those who began teaching between 1996 and 1999). If teachers were no longer teaching in 2003, they were labeled as "leavers," and those who remained in teaching were labeled as "stayers."

Table 9-2 presents the attrition rates for the two groups of teachers, separated by when they entered teaching and their board certification status. Overall, attrition rates were lower, at a statistically significant level (p < .05), for the B&B 93:03 sample of board-certified teachers than for the nonboard-certified teachers. For those who began teaching between 1993 and 1995, 31.8 percent of board-certified teachers had left teaching by 2003 compared with 35.6 percent of the nonboard-certified teachers. For teachers who entered the field between 1996 and 1999, 26 percent of the board-certified teachers had left teaching by 2003 compared with 34 percent of those without board certification. These analyses are described in additional detail in Perda (2007).

It is important to point out that these analyses were descriptive in nature and do not allow us to conclude that obtaining board certification

TABLE 9-2 Teacher Attrition Rates by 2003 National Board-Certification Status

	Stayers	Leavers	Total Teachers	Attrition Rate
Board-Certified Teachers:				
Started initial teaching job between 1993 and 1995	6,073	2,838	8,911	31.8%
Started initial teaching job between 1996 and 1999	1,703	599	2,302	26.0%
Nonboard-Certified Teachers:				
Started initial teaching job between 1993 and 1995	94,541	52,275	146,816	35.6%
Started initial teaching job between 1996 and 1999	31,619	16,288	47,907	34.0%

SOURCE: Perda (2007, Table 10), based on data from B&B 93:03.

caused teachers to stay in the field longer. The fact that board-certified teachers were less likely to leave the profession does not necessarily imply that the process of going through certification increased their attachment to the profession. Indeed, standard human capital theory shows that workers who intend to remain in a profession longer are more likely to undertake costly activities to enhance their skills (Ben-Porath, 1967). Put differently, teachers who feel strongly tied to teaching as a career are the most likely to find board certification worthwhile. In this sense, board certification may provide administrators with a signal of teachers' preexisting commitments to remain in the profession.

Mobility and Transition

Goldhaber and Hansen (2007) investigated the impact of board certification on the job transitions and career paths of teachers employed in North Carolina. Their primary sample included most of those who taught in the state public schools between the 1996-1997 and 1999-2000 school years, and they restricted the analyses to teachers who had at least three years of experience (and were thus eligible for board certification) but less than 30 years of experience (to eliminate mobility due to retirement). This teacher sample was tracked over an eight-year period from 1997 to 2003, and data were obtained on several types of job transitions during this period: (1) moving to another teaching position at a different public school within the same district; (2) moving to another teaching position in another public school district within the state; (3) leaving the North Carolina public school system. As with other state databases, the data used in this study provided no information on whether those in the latter category—leaving the North Carolina public schools—had moved to a public school job out of state, had moved to a private school job in or out of the state, or had left teaching entirely. This is an important limitation because it means the study could not specifically isolate the influence of board certification on attrition from the teaching occupation.

For the above three job transitions included in the database, the analyses made several comparisons: (1) those who obtained board certification versus those who had not; (2) those who had never applied for board certification versus those who had applied; and (3) among those who had applied, the analysis compared successful applicants with unsuccessful applicants. Because those who apply for board certification may be different than those who never apply, the latter comparison among successful and unsuccessful applicants is especially useful to mitigate selection bias. In addition, the analyses were broken out by teachers' experience level and by race, because the data showed differences among these groups in the likelihood of passing and in the impact of obtaining board certification. As a result of these many groupings—by type of transition, by board certification status, by experience, and by race—there were many permutations of possible comparisons in the results.

The analyses used competing-risks models to estimate the hazard (i.e., probability) of an individual experiencing each of the types of job transitions, after controlling for a series of teacher and school characteristics. To further mitigate selection bias, the analyses also used a quasi-experimental method—regression-discontinuity analyses—in the comparisons of the successful applicants with unsuccessful applicants. This method was used to estimate the effects of successfully passing the NBPTS assessment on two outcomes: (1) the likelihood of experiencing one of the above three job transitions and (2) on the characteristics of the new schools to which they moved.

The results of the analyses showed that, overall, those who obtained board certification had more mobility than those who were not board certified. However, the analyses also showed that these differences lay not so much with those who had never applied for board certification (the majority of teachers in the state), but rather, the differences in mobility were primarily found among those who had applied: between the successful applicants and unsuccessful applicants.

A more nuanced picture emerged when comparing the latter two groups. Although the coefficients were not always statistically significant across the different teacher experience levels, the direction of the signs was consistent. Those who passed the assessment and obtained the certification were more likely to move between schools and districts and more likely to leave the North Carolina public school system than were those who applied but did not pass the assessment. A different picture also emerges depending on the race of the teacher. For successful African American applicants, the results indicate that board certification has little impact on career mobility.

EFFECTS OF MOBILITY

In Chapter 6, we presented results from a study by Humphrey, Koppich, and Hough (2005) that described the characteristics of the schools in which board-certified teachers work in six states. Their results documented that board-certified teachers are not equitably distributed across schools in these states (with the possible exception of the Los Angeles school district) and tend to work in schools with higher achieving, advantaged students.

Inequality in the distribution of the most qualified teachers is not a new finding. Numerous studies have shown that higher poverty, more disadvantaged schools have less qualified, less experienced, lower scoring teachers (e.g., Boyd, Lankford, Loeb, and Wyckoff, 2005; Stinebrickner, Scafidi, and Sjoquist, 2003). In short, data have long documented that there is an unequal distribution of high-quality teachers, regardless of the criteria used to define teacher quality (e.g., years of experience, master's degrees, undergraduate subject-matter major, or board certification). Moreover, in general when teachers change teaching jobs, they tend to move to more advantaged schools (Ingersoll and Perda, 2008). Hence, along with the issue of an unequal distribution of board-certified teachers, there is the related question of how teacher mobility impacts their distribution.

Humphrey et al. (2005) did not establish where teachers were working before they become board certified and, thus were unable to investigate whether teachers move to (or away from) schools with high-needs students after earning board certification. However, Goldhaber and Hansen (2007) did examine this issue. Their analysis compared the nature of the school moves made by those who earned board certification compared to teachers who were unsuccessful applicants. The school characteristics the authors examined included the percentage of enrolled students in poverty, the percentage of minority students, per-pupil expenditures, and median housing values in the district. The authors reported the results separately for white and African American teachers.

For white teachers, the results were generally weak. There was some consistency in the direction of the sign of the coefficients; that is, white board-certified teachers tended to move to schools with fewer students in poverty and fewer minority students than did unsuccessful applicants. However, most of the coefficients were neither statistically nor substantively significant. For example, there was generally less than a 1 percent difference between successful and unsuccessful applicants in terms of the percentages of students in poverty at the schools to which they moved, and differences in the range of 1 to 2.5 percent in the percentages of minority students at their new schools.

For African American teachers, the results were also generally weak, with the exception of the percentages of minority students at the schools to which board-certified teachers moved. That is, compared to unsuccessful applicants, African American board-certified teachers tended to move to schools with fewer minority students, and the differences were generally large and statistically significant. With regard to the other school characteristics studied (percent of students in poverty, per-pupil expenditures, and median housing values), differences were not significant, and the sign of the coefficients was not consistent.

Thus, the Goldhaber and Hansen study indicates that for white teacher applicants, obtaining board certification is associated with a substantial increase in career mobility at all levels (interschool, interdistrict, and out of the state system), but it is not clear whether their new schools were definitively different from those to which otherwise equal teachers moved. For African American teacher applicants, the results indicate that board certification has little impact on career mobility, but it has a fairly substantial impact on the racial composition of the schools to which they moved.

CONCLUSIONS AND RECOMMENDATIONS

The available research on career paths suggests that teachers who earn board certification may remain in the field longer than teachers who do not earn it. It also suggests that teachers who earn board certification become more mobile, and we speculate that they may possibly use the certification as a means for leaving the state to work elsewhere. We note that these are tentative conclusions based on the results from two studies and our own analyses. The findings need to be corroborated before any solid conclusions can be drawn.

The available evidence is clearly insufficient to answer the questions we posed in our evaluation framework. While some sources document aspects of the career path, these sources do not allow comparisons between board-certified and nonboard-certified teachers. Given that a major objective of the NBPTS is to provide a means for encouraging teachers to remain in the profession, we think it is important to study the career paths of board-certified teachers as well as the impact the credential has had on teachers' career decisions.

We understand that the NBPTS has recently begun to investigate this issue and is in the process of collecting information from board-certified teachers about their current employment status. We did not have the opportunity to review plans for this analysis, but we encourage the board to pursue this avenue of research using scientifically sound sampling procedures, instrument design, and analytical methodology. One way to conduct such research would be to identify a specific time frame and select a random sample of teachers who applied for board certification (both successfully and unsuccessfully) during that time frame. It might be advisable to oversample teachers from specific groups, such as racial/ethnic minorities. A questionnaire could then be distributed to the sample to inquire about the career options they have pursued since applying for board certification. Comparisons of responses for successful and unsuccessful candidates would address questions about the impact of the credential on career paths.

Specifically, we recommend:

Recommendation 9-1: The NBPTS and other researchers should study the subsequent career choices of teachers who have applied for board certification. The information they collect should be analyzed for successful and unsuccessful candidates separately so the correlation between board certification and career choice can be evaluated. Studies that track teachers over long periods should also be used to test whether the process alters career choices. The data collected should include information about the extent to which state or district policies influenced the respondents' career choices.

We also encourage further investigation of the impact of board certification on teachers' career choices using national data sets, such as SASS. As a first step, we recommend that NCES further investigate the problems with the question on the SASS questionnaire, which asked respondents about their board-certification status. If the problems are indeed caused by the wording of the question, we suggest that alternative wordings of this question be pilot-tested before operational use to ensure that accurate information is collected when the survey is repeated. We also encourage education researchers to conduct analyses at the state level using procedures such as those employed by Goldhaber and Hansen (2007). Both national and state-level studies should consider a broad set of events in teaching careers in order to distinguish the effects of board certification from those of other kinds of career enhancements (such as obtaining an advanced degree or a promotion). Together these kinds of research could vastly improve understanding of the impact of board certification on teachers' careers. On this point, we specifically recommend:

Recommendation 9-2: The National Center for Education Statistics should amend the Schools and Staffing Survey so that it collects information about respondents' board certification status. In designing the survey questions on this topic, the National Center for Education Statistics should pilot-test alternate versions to ensure that respondents will accurately understand the question.

Recommendation 9-3: Researchers should use the data available from state-level data systems to expand the evidence on the mobility of board-certified teachers. These studies should use methodologies that permit comparisons of teachers' career choices before and after becoming board certified and should compare the choices of unsuccessful applicants for board certification, teachers who successfully obtained the credential, and teachers who did not apply for board certification.

10

The Effects of Certification
on the Education System

In *A Nation Prepared,* the Carnegie Task Force on Teaching as Profession documented their conviction that the overall quality of the nation's teaching force needed to be improved, and they endorsed the creation of the National Board for Professional Teaching Standards (NBPTS) as one mechanism for accomplishing these changes. Task force members hoped that the influence of the NBPTS would reach well beyond any impact that individual board-certified teachers might have on their students. They hoped that the board's standards for accomplished teaching would be widely influential and that the demand for board-certified teachers would lead to improvements in working conditions for all teachers. The founders envisioned (Carnegie Task Force on Teaching as a Profession, 1986; National Board for Professional Teaching Standards, 1991):

- A growing cadre of board-certified teachers would serve as leaders in their schools and districts, working to improve instruction and sharing their expertise with other teachers through informal collegial relationships, formal mentoring activities, and participation in professional development programs.
- Schools, districts, and states would value board-certified teachers. They would use the standards defined by the board as a guide in hiring and making teaching assignments and would work to provide teaching environments conducive to the national board approach.
- Teacher preparation programs would focus on the standards articulated by the national board and be influenced by its portfolio-

based assessment format, so that entry-level teachers would learn the foundational skills that lead to accomplished practice.

- Professional development and inservice programs for teachers would focus on national board standards and practices. Eventually all teachers—not just those who became board certified—would learn the skills and practices endorsed by the board.

In the context of program evaluation, these sorts of far-reaching impacts are referred to as "spillover effects," although that term is not intended to imply that they are extraneous or unimportant. They are also sometimes referred to as systemic or secondary effects or externalities (Rossi, Lipsey, and Freeman, 2004). In this chapter, we evaluate the extent to which spillover effects are evident. These kinds of effects were important elements in the overall goal the task force hoped to achieve with its multipronged reform approach. It is important to note, however, that the task force cautioned that none of its proposed strategies (of which the assessment-based certification program was one) "will succeed unless all are implemented" (Carnegie Task Force on Teaching as a Profession, 1986, p. 57).

This chapter addresses our seventh question:

Question 7: Beyond its effects on candidates, to what extent and in what ways does the certification program have an impact on the field of teaching, the education system, or both?

Figure 2-1 shows where this question fits within our evaluation framework. We identified several kinds of influence an advanced-level certification program for teachers might have and framed specific questions about them:

a. What are the effects of having one or more board-certified teachers in a school or district?
b. Has the board-certification program had any effects on:
   - the course content, methods of preparation, and assessments used in teacher education programs or
   - the content of and strategies used in inservice training and professional development for practicing teachers?
c. Has the board-certification program had any effects on the applicant pool for teacher education programs? Since the board came into existence, have there been changes in the numbers of individuals entering teacher education programs or the characteristics of the applicants?
d. Has the existence of board certification had an impact on the allocation of teachers across districts and schools? Has the program

been a useful tool for increasing the numbers of accomplished teachers in high-needs schools?

We begin with a discussion of the challenges associated with this aspect of our evaluation. We then discuss what can be learned from the existing studies, which primarily relate to Subquestion a, and we close the chapter with our conclusions.

THE CHALLENGES OF EVALUATING SPILLOVER EFFECTS

Evaluating systemic change is difficult in any context. Systems are complex, and the many factors that may affect outcomes interact in complicated ways. Detecting and isolating effects is correspondingly complex because researchers cannot manipulate conditions or use experimental controls, as is done in other kinds of research. Without these tools, it is usually not possible to isolate a single factor as the cause of any observed change. Thus, for example, if we were to observe a change in the content of teacher education programs, it would be nearly impossible to attribute it directly to the NBPTS or any action it has taken.

Researchers may see signs that particular changes have occurred but lack suitable indicators with which to measure them. For example, suppose that board-certified teachers were indeed influencing their colleagues in a positive way or that increasing numbers of teacher education programs were relying on NBPTS standards in developing their curricula. How would one measure such change? The changes may be so gradual that they are difficult to detect, or there may be very few reliable criteria to use in calibrating the "before" and the "after" effects.

Systemic change also happens slowly, whether the desired change is the reduction of a behavior linked to public health problems or a shift in the culture of a large organization. It takes time for each element of a system to respond to an intervention and for the relationships among different elements to adapt, and it takes time to change behavior. Education is no exception, and those who study education reform have written about the challenge of engaging each of the necessary partners (teachers, administrators, state and local political leaders, etc.) in enacting changes, and also about the inertia that reformers often face (see, e.g., Datnow and Stringfield, 2000; Fullan, 2007; Goertz, Floden, and O'Day, 1995). Schools and teachers have their own cultures, traditions, and habits. Educators must operate within a complex network of rules, regulations, and policies imposed by the district, the state, and the federal government, all of which may interfere further with efforts to introduce change. Many observers of education reform have pointed to the difficulty of bridging the critical gap between presenting prescriptions for improvement and affecting teachers' day-to-day practice (e.g.,

Stevenson and Stigler, 1992; Tyack and Cuban, 1996). The title *Tinkering Toward Utopia*, which describes generations of reforms that have passed lightly over the surface of public education without fundamentally changing it, is an apt phrase to describe the imperviousness of educational institutions to change (Tyack and Cuban, 1996).

For the Carnegie task force's vision to be realized, fairly dramatic changes would be needed in how teachers do their work and in how they think about their roles. Yet teachers as a group have tended to be reluctant to stand out or to seem to claim that they are superior in some way to their colleagues. Lortie (2002), among others, has described teachers as viewing their field in an egalitarian way and as resisting professional status distinctions. As we discussed in Chapter 3, teachers in the United States also tend to have an individualistic orientation, in contrast to those in other countries. They tend to work in isolation and determine for themselves what is best for their students. Although schools create opportunities for certain kinds of collaboration, such as meetings for those teaching a particular grade level or subject matter, U.S. teachers rarely observe one another in the classroom or critique one another's practice (Little, 1990; Lord, 1994; McLaughlin and Talbert, 2001). Yet the national board prizes collaboration and reflection and also identifies and rewards exemplary teachers. Their goal is to create an occupational status distinction that places teachers who earn the credential above other teachers. Thus the board faced an uphill climb as it set out to alter fundamental aspects of the way U.S. teachers approached their practice.

Despite the challenges of investigating spillover effects, we have included these questions in our evaluation for several reasons. First, the board clearly viewed stimulating systemic change in the field of teaching as a critical goal. Second, we think that spillover effects are important, even if they are difficult to pinpoint. Including them in our evaluation allowed us to step away from detailed technical questions to consider broader questions about the program's impact and significance that we think are an important aspect of this evaluation. Finally, although little research is available on spillover effects associated with the NBPTS, we think it is possible to conduct this kind of research. These kinds of studies take time. Researchers must plan in advance to take advantage of opportunities to collect data, and they must wait for longitudinal data to accumulate. We think that evidence of spillover effects could be collected, if studies based on thoughtful hypotheses and well-planned data collection were undertaken.

AVAILABLE EVIDENCE

Among the NBPTS-related studies, we identified three that provided information relevant to spillover effects, although they focus only on the issue addressed by our Subquestion a: Koppich et al. (2006), Yankelovich Partners (2001), and Sykes et al. (2006). Key characteristics of these studies are highlighted in Table 10-1, and more complete descriptions appear in Appendix A.

Two of these studies are very comprehensive and make use of multiple methods for obtaining and analyzing data. Koppich, Humphrey, and Hough (2006) studied the impact of board certification in six states, focusing on what board-certified teachers do after becoming certified and what it takes for them to make a difference in a school. They collected data using a mail survey of board-certified teachers, focus groups, interviews, and site visits to 18 selected case study schools. Sykes and colleagues (2006) report findings from three interrelated studies of board-certified teachers and their influence in their school systems. The studies include a school-level survey, a state-level survey, and a four-school field study of teachers in South Carolina and Ohio.

The third study offers less robust evidence. An NBPTS survey (Yankelovich Partners, 2001) queried teachers about the types of activities in which they participated after earning the credential. We were hesitant to draw any firm conclusions from this survey because the report consists only of a tally of the survey responses and provides minimal discussion of the methodology and findings.

No research has been done on the impact of the NBPTS standards on teacher preparation or teacher professional development. A full-scale study of this issue would have been beyond the scope of our evaluation and would have required far more time and resources than were available. However, as described in Chapter 2, we held a panel discussion at our third meeting at which we heard testimony from three teacher educators with regard to this issue. While their commentary provides only anecdotal accounts of the kinds of influences that NBPTS standards might have, we think that they provide a basis for conceptualizing additional research in this area.

EFFECTS OF HAVING BOARD-CERTIFIED TEACHERS IN SCHOOLS

Findings from surveys conducted by Sykes et al. (2006) and Yankelovich Partners (2001) provide some evidence that board-certified teachers participate in mentoring and leadership activities within their school system. In both studies, the majority of survey respondents indicated that they are involved in such activities as mentoring other teachers, serving as team leaders in their schools, developing curriculum materials for the school system, providing professional development activities, and supporting other national board candidates as they undergo the certification process. Sykes et al. also report that teachers' participation in such activities seems to increase over time once teachers obtain board certification, although they note that the more experienced teachers in a school system are typically the ones given leadership roles in any case. One point that cannot be discerned from these studies is the extent to which earning the credential caused teachers to participate in such activities. There is no evidence in Sykes et al. as to how active teachers were in leadership activities prior to becoming board certified, but the majority of respondents to the surveys by Yankelovich Partners (2001) and Koppich et al. (2006) said that they had participated in these kinds of activities prior to earning the credential. Thus, it may be that teachers who decide to pursue board certification are those who are already leaders in the school system, and that the credential simply signals their leadership skills.

The case studies conducted by Koppich et al. and Sykes et al. provide additional insights about board-certified teachers' experiences in their school systems. Taken together, the results from these two studies indicate that, in the regions studied, board-certified teachers are not having the desired effects in their school systems.

Koppich and her colleagues asked board-certified teachers about the support they received from their administrators and the ways in which their skills are used. Overall, they found little evidence of schools relying on board-certified teachers to serve as mentors or in leadership positions. They found that many of the board-certified teachers were teaching in situations that were not supportive of efforts to take on a leadership role or to move beyond the conventional obligations of classroom teaching. The authors report that more than 90 percent of the teachers surveyed said they were no more influential than other teachers on such matters as selecting curriculum and materials, advising on professional development programs, teacher hiring and evaluation, advising on budget, and determining the focus of school reform efforts.

Interviews with board-certified teachers and their colleagues led the authors to conclude that there is a culture of "individualism and egalitarianism that remains alive in the profession." Board-certified teachers reported that they are often given the cold shoulder by nonboard-certified teachers, and nearly 43 percent agreed that "my school culture is not welcoming of teachers stepping into leadership positions." The authors found that board-certified teachers actually go to considerable lengths to downplay any distinctions between themselves and their nonboard-certified colleagues, sometimes even concealing the fact that they have earned the credential. In one school, the authors found that board-certified teachers actually declined requests to participate in leadership activities, despite encouragement from the principal. At this school, there was a history of negative attitudes toward board-certified teachers. The board-certified teachers said they were

TABLE 10-1 Studies Examining Effects on the Teaching Profession and the Education System

Study	Population Studied	State(s)	Sampling Method
Koppich, Humphrey, and Hough (2006)	NBCTs, their colleagues, their administrators	CA, FL, MS, NC, OH, SC	Stratified random sample
Sykes et al. (2006)	NBCTs	OH, SC	
Yankelovich Partners (2001)	NBCTs who earned certification in 1999	Nationwide	Sent survey to all; sample consisted of those who responded by a specific date.

willing to lead professional development activities elsewhere but not at their own school with the colleagues with whom they worked each day.

Sykes and his colleagues reported similar findings from their case studies. The teachers they interviewed reported that they did not interact with each other about their instructional practices, and board certification was not emphasized. The teachers who had obtained board certification were

Sample Size, Response Rate	Methods	Findings	Issues Affecting Validity of the Findings
1,136; responses from 654 (75%)	Mail survey, interviews, focus groups, 18 case studies	- Little evidence that schools rely on NBCTs as leaders or mentors. - More than 90% of NBCTs report they are no more influential than other teachers.	No concerns.
1,500; responses from 1,153 (77%); 566 from SC and 587 from OH	Mail survey, focus groups, interviews, case studies	- Majority of NBCTs participate in leadership activities. - NBCTs and non-NBCTs are reluctant to say that certification signals special competence. - Principals are reluctant to favor NBCTs.	No concerns.
4,800; responses from 2,100 (45%)	Mail survey	- Majority participate in mentoring and leadership activities. - Most had done so prior to becoming board certified.	Report is a tally of survey responses; no details are provided about methodology or findings. Sampling methods were questionable.

generally positive about the experience, although they were reluctant to state that board certification signaled a level of competence that set them apart from their colleagues. The nonboard-certified teachers tended to think there was no difference between those who were board certified and themselves, sometimes citing stories of well-qualified teachers who tried and did not pass or less qualified teachers who passed. Principals also noted that they were careful about how they made assignments, not wanting to seem to favor the board-certified teachers or to engender resentment from those who were not board certified.

Among the 18 case studies conducted by Koppich and colleagues, one stood out as an example of what the founders of the national board likely had in mind. At this elementary school in North Carolina, both the principal and assistant principal were board certified. They enacted a number of changes designed to promote the goals of the certification process. This began with encouragement at the district level for all teachers to pursue certification—the district sponsored weekly and monthly meetings and training sessions and provided other supports. The administrative staff at the school took the lead in changing the school's teaching culture to one of shared learning and growth, altering the school schedule to allow time for collaborative work and redefining teaching as a public activity in which observation and constructive critique were the norm. However, although this elementary school achieved considerable success with its program, including significant gains in student achievement, it was a "rare bird," according to the authors.

Koppich et al. also cited the ways that Cincinnati public schools made use of national board certification as part of their efforts to create a career ladder for teachers. Their description (p. 15) of this process, paraphrased below, provides another portrait of the factors that seem to be necessary to make board certification a significant benefit in a school or system.

> In Cincinnati, the creation of the lead teacher position has opened up new roles and opportunities for board-certified teachers. When *A Nation Prepared* was first released, the school system used the report to guide their attempts to professionalize teaching. Administrators developed a teacher career ladder that included a lead teacher position, with the goal of creating professional leadership roles for teachers that would allow them to remain in the classroom. The school system defined roles for the lead teachers, including such responsibilities as department head, team leader, curriculum specialist, staff development specialist, and peer evaluator. Lead teachers served on committees that made decisions about instruction and resource allocation and on intervention teams for low-performing schools. Initially, the school system used its own assessment procedures but adopted board certification when it became available as a means for earning lead teacher status. Earning board certification is not a requirement for becoming a lead teacher, but having the credential increases a teacher's chances of receiving this designation.

EFFECTS ON TEACHER PREPARATION

The Carnegie task force intended that the national board-certification program and its standards for accomplished teachers would have a significant influence on the preparation of new teachers (Carnegie Task Force on Teaching as a Profession, 1986). They hoped that teacher preparation programs would coordinate their standards with those of the national board and be influenced by the portfolio-based approach, and that entry-level teachers would learn the foundational skills that lead to accomplished practice. Thus, the committee sought information about whether the national board certification program has had any effects on the content, methods of preparation, and assessment of candidates in initial teacher education programs or in advanced programs for teachers, such as master's degree programs.

Two organizations that influence the content of teacher preparation programs have worked to align their standards with those of the national board. The Interstate New Teacher Assessment and Support Consortium (INTASC) was established in 1987 to promote collaboration among states seeking to reform teacher preparation and teacher licensing with the aim of improving the quality of the teaching force. The organization is a consortium of state education agencies (34 states are current members) and professional educational organizations (including the national board, National Council for Accreditation of Teacher Education [NCATE]), and the two largest teachers unions). It defines curriculum standards for programs that prepare beginning teachers, which are aligned with those of the national board (http://www.ccsso.org/projects/Interstate_New_Teacher_Assessment_and_Support_Consortium/).

The NCATE, an alliance of 33 professional groups (including the NBPTS as well as teacher educator organizations, teachers unions, and other organizations), promotes high-quality teaching through the accreditation of schools, colleges, and departments of education. NCATE's standards for teacher education programs are also aligned with those of the national board. Because of the intentional alignment of the standards of these three groups, some have called INTASC, NCATE, and the NBPTS the "three-legged stool" of teacher quality (Bradley, 1997). These efforts lay the groundwork for the NBPTS standards to impact teacher preparation, but there is no research to document the extent of the board's influence on the content of teacher preparation programs or the standards of individual programs.

We explored this issue with the teacher educators at our June 2006 meeting and heard anecdotal accounts of the ways in which the NBPTS standards have been used to make changes at two institutions. Mary Futrell, dean the school of education at George Washington University, served on the original board of directors for the NBPTS and was a strong supporter of the program. She persuaded her faculty to look at the three sets of standards (NBPTS, NCATE, and INTASC) in relation to their curricula. They considered the ways in which their program incorporated the NBPTS standards and what would be needed to bring their program in line with them.

Although she encountered considerable resistance, Futrell said, she was eventually able to persuade the faculty to revise the curriculum to bring it in line with the standards, and the five NBPTS propositions (see Chapter 4) are now explicitly incorporated into the curriculum. In addition, teachers enrolled in the university's graduate special education program are required to assemble a portfolio that is graded on the basis of the NBPTS standards. Their faculty also now work with teachers at a low-performing school in Northern Virginia to help them improve their practices and to encourage them to become board certified.

Carol Matern, on the faculty of the teacher preparation program at Indiana University–Purdue University, Indianapolis, became board certified several years ago. She found the certification process to be an exceptional professional development experience. Since earning board certification, she has worked to incorporate NBPTS standards into the courses she teaches. She relies on the standards when preparing her course syllabi, and she explicitly includes reflective writing, analysis of videotaped lessons, and collaborative discussions in her graduate courses for teachers.

Although these accounts are clearly anecdotal and describe very localized changes, they indicate the kinds of influences the NBPTS standards can have. They also suggest that both commitment to the NBPTS approach by program administrators and institutional leadership are needed for the board standards to have a noticeable influence on teacher education programs. We caution, however, that these anecdotal accounts did not provide an indication of how representative these changes might be of education programs at other universities, and no data have been collected to indicate the extent to which the more than 1,200 teacher education programs in the United States have been influenced by the NBPTS standards.

CONCLUSIONS AND RECOMMENDATIONS

At present, little research has been conducted on the extent to which the national board is having spillover effects. At the same time, there is evidence from two investigations that board-certified teachers are having very limited impact in their school systems. The teachers studied by Koppich and by Sykes were reluctant to accept status distinctions in their field. Perhaps out of reluctance to violate an egalitarian tradition in the field, those who earn the credential tend to keep quiet about it, and those who are not board certified minimize its value. These studies also provide glimpses of the circumstances that are necessary for board-certified teachers to have a marked impact, such as engaged administrators at the school and district level who provide leadership opportunities and a shared commitment to changing the teaching culture in a school.

Another factor limiting the systemic impact of the NBPTS is the low number of board-certified teachers. Even if all of the 63,800 teachers who have earned board certification were still teaching, this translates to only an average of three board-certified teachers for every five schools and about 2 percent of all the 3.7 million members of the current teaching force. Except in a few districts, the numbers of board-certified teachers are likely to be too small for them to have an impact on their school systems.

With regard to the other areas in which spillover effects may have occurred, there simply is no research to draw from. For example, there have been no systematic attempts to evaluate the content of teacher preparation programs to see if changes related to the national board have occurred over the past decade. Such research is difficult to carry out, but it is not impossible. Studies could evaluate the content of course syllabi or curriculum standards and note changes that occur over time. Surveys of administrators of teacher preparation programs could also shed light on these issues. These kinds of studies may not use the stringent kinds of methodologies that would allow one to attribute any detected changes directly to the NBPTS, but they would provide the beginnings of a research base on these questions. We think that such studies lie within the purview of the NBPTS. The board established these goals from the outset and should implement the kinds of research that would make possible evaluation of the extent to which these goals have been realized. Late in our evaluation process, the board embarked on this kind of study, and we encourage the completion of this investigation.

There is also no way for us to evaluate the impacts of the national board on professional development programs for teachers because no research has examined the extent to which the NBPTS standards have influenced inservice programs. This type of research could also be conducted. Researchers who have studied the effects of professional development on instruction have found ways to characterize different kinds of professional development, to identify theoretical approaches, and to examine the effects of different approaches on teachers' classroom practice (Desimone et al., 2002; Garet et al., 2001; Guskey, 2003; Hawley and Valli, 1999; Porter et al., 2000; Wilson and Berne, 1999). This body of work provides research models that could be useful in efforts to trace the influence of the NBPTS approach on professional development programs. This literature also indicates that a consensus seems to be emerging about the key features that make professional development effective, such as opportunities for teachers to work as a group and to develop their learning over an extended period of time; opportunities for active learning; a focus on content; and links among the professional development activities, the curricula with which the teachers are working, and the standards they are using. These newer findings regarding professional development seem to reinforce many of the elements recommended by the national board.

Our evaluation framework also includes questions about the impact of the program on the characteristics of teachers who enter the profession. At present there are no data that could be used to address this question. No data have been collected to ascertain whether applications to schools of education have increased since board certification became available or whether the characteristics of applicants have changed over time.

The final question in our framework dealt with the allocation of teachers across schools. We were interested in the extent to which principals and administrators use board certification status to assign teachers to high-needs schools or classrooms with the most challenging students. We were not able to answer this question either. In Chapters 6 and 9 we described the problems with the existing data systems (i.e., that there are no ways to determine where teachers currently work or to track their placements on a national level), and we refer the reader to those sections of the report for details about the problems with data collection in these areas.

Investigating spillover effects caused us to consider what might look different if states, districts, and schools around the country had actively embraced the board certification program from the start. As Chapter 6 discusses, this has not happened, except in a few places. There is a stark contrast between the particularly ambitious goals of the Carnegie task force and the very modest spread of the national board certification program. We could find no studies or evidence to answer questions about why the national board has not become more deeply ingrained in the U.S. education system, but it is clear that systemic effects go hand in hand with the volume of certified teachers.

Having reviewed the evidence on all of these questions, we think that board-certified teachers are unlikely to have a significant impact without broader endorsements by states, districts, and schools of the NBPTS goals for improving professional development, setting high standards for teachers, and actively using the board-certified teachers in leadership roles. Furthermore, we think that the NBPTS program is unlikely to have broad systemic effects on the field of teaching unless greater numbers of teachers become board certified and the Carnegie task force's other recommendations—for creating a more effective environment for teaching and learning in schools, increasing the supply of high-quality entrants into the profession, and improving career opportunities for teachers—are implemented.

Our review of the evidence led us to draw the following conclusion:

Conclusion 10-1: There is not yet sufficient research to evaluate the extent to which the NBPTS is having systemic impacts on the teaching field and the education system.

11

The Cost-Effectiveness of Certification as a Means of Improving Teacher Quality

The congressional bill that authorized the National Research Council to conduct this evaluation contained specific language requesting consideration of the extent to which certification by the National Board for Professional Teaching Standards (NBPTS) is a cost-effective method for improving teacher quality. While this is a challenging question to address, we understand why it has been posed. Although the board got its start from private funding, since 1991 it has received considerable federal money to support its work. Given the federal dollars invested in the program, it is reasonable for Congress to ask if the investment has been wise.

To respond to this aspect of the committee's charge, our evaluation framework includes the following question:

Question 8: To what extent does the advanced-level teacher certification program accomplish its objectives in a cost-effective manner, relative to other approaches intended to improve teacher quality?

As before, we refer to Figure 2-1 for our model of the kinds of impacts that an advanced-level certification program for teachers might have. The question we address in this chapter does not explicitly appear in the model, but we regard it as an overarching question about the net effect of the various impacts of an advanced-level certification program, when considered in the context of the costs of the program. Addressing Question 8 requires us to summarize the benefits of the NBPTS, consider its costs, and compare the resulting cost-effectiveness with that of other interventions designed to improve teacher quality. We identified the following issues to investigate and to provide evidence about the cost-effectiveness of the national board's certification program, specifically:

    a. What are the benefits of the certification program?
    b. What are the costs associated with the certification program?
    c. What other approaches have been shown to bring about improvement in teacher quality? What are their costs and benefits?

It is important to note that the existing research base for such an inquiry is inadequate. The cost side is not the issue. Although there have not been extensive examinations of the costs associated with the NBPTS, a relatively coarse consideration of costs is sufficient for the task at hand. Rather, it is the benefits side of the analysis that is the problem. Furthermore, while the evidence about the benefits of the NBPTS is inadequate for a thorough cost-effectiveness evaluation, even less is known about the benefits of other interventions to improve teacher quality. As a result, the kind of cost-effectiveness comparison one would like to perform, and as stated in our charge, is not possible at this time. Despite the inadequacies in the evidence base, we lay out the issues to the extent that available research and data allow. In the sections that follow, we first consider the benefits, the costs, and the resulting cost-effectiveness of board certification as a route to improving teacher quality. We then examine the available information about the cost-effectiveness of four comparison interventions.

BENEFITS ASSOCIATED WITH THE PROGRAM

Before considering the specific benefits of the NBPTS, we step back to consider the ways in which an intervention intended to improve teacher quality might operate. There are three kinds of benefits such an intervention might produce:

    1. Identifying highly skilled teachers.
    2. Improving the practices of teachers who go through the program.
    3. Improving the quality of teachers throughout the education system, keeping accomplished teachers in the field, and attracting stronger teacher candidates in the future.

We note here that simply identifying highly skilled teachers provides no direct benefit, and therefore the first benefit requires that some action be taken once highly skilled teachers are identified. For example, administrators and policy makers could implement incentives for teachers who are identified as highly skilled, either to encourage them to remain in teaching or to encourage them to work in traditionally difficult-to-staff schools. Teachers identified as highly skilled could also be used as a way of identifying instructional leaders who could then support other teachers and thus pass their skills onto other practitioners. We also point out that this benefit is one that is often claimed by programs that offer advanced-level certification in other fields, such as nursing or medicine: identification of highly skilled practitioners is the first step in realizing the benefits offered by a program that recognizes advanced practice. It is not necessarily a benefit in and of itself, but it serves as the foundation for other potential benefits. Moreover, the actual process of defining advanced practice can make a significant contribution to the field.

While the three benefits are interrelated, they differ in critical ways. For example, it is possible for an intervention to produce one of these benefits without providing the other two. In the context of a program like the NBPTS, it is easy to see that the program may produce the benefit of identifying highly skilled teachers without improving the teaching ability of the candidates as they go through the certification process or improving the quality of teachers throughout the education system. This result can occur if the certification process itself does not provide candidates with new skills or if the resulting certification is not used by the system in a way that changes what teachers are taught, who enters and stays in teaching, and who leaves, thus having no impact on overall quality.

Other interventions designed to improve teacher quality may focus entirely on one of these kinds of benefits and not at all on others. For example, inservice professional development is intended to improve teacher quality directly (Benefit 2) without providing a means for identifying highly skilled teachers (Benefit 1). However, increasing teacher pay is an intervention intended to improve teacher quality throughout the education system (Benefit 3) without directly identifying highly skilled teachers (Benefit 1) or directly improving the teaching ability of any particular teachers (Benefit 2).

Of course, improving the teaching quality of teachers throughout the system (Benefit 3) is presumably the ultimate goal of an intervention focused on teacher quality, and it is reasonable to assume that identifying highly skilled teachers (Benefit 1) or improving the teaching abilities of teachers going through a program (Benefit 2) are just two intermediate routes to achieving that ultimate goal. However, it is important to consider these two intermediate benefits separately, because their mechanisms for influencing teacher quality throughout the system differ. A certification program that improves the practices of teachers who participate in it (Benefit 2) will directly increase the quality of those teachers who participate, as long as the participants continue to be teachers, which will have a larger system impact to the extent that many teachers participate. However, a program that identifies highly qualified teachers without directly improving their teaching practices will require that the certification be used by the education system in some way that produces the benefit of increasing teacher quality throughout the system. In the next sections, we examine the evidence related to each of these benefits.

Benefit 1: Identifying Highly Skilled Teachers

With respect to the NBPTS program's ability to identify high-quality teachers, the available evidence shows that the board's certification program does identify skilled practitioners, whether defined in terms of teachers' skills or students' achievement. The content- and construct-based validity evidence, discussed in Chapter 5, indicates that the assessment is measuring the knowledge and skills it is intended to measure, which were judged to represent accomplished teaching. The findings from value-added analyses addressed in Chapter 7 demonstrate that the assessment is identifying high-quality teachers with respect to their effectiveness at raising tested student achievement in mathematics and reading—an important, though incomplete, indicator of teacher success.

Most of the investigations described in Chapter 7 report results based on comparisons of board-certified teachers with all other teachers in the system, a comparison that confounds the ability of the assessment to identify high-quality teachers with the particular quality mix of their nonboard-certified colleagues. These investigations show that board-certified teachers produce gains in student achievement that are, on average, about a 0.04 standard deviation larger than their nonboard-certified colleagues (ranging from 0.01 to 0.08 in our analyses of North Carolina and Florida). The size of this difference is roughly one-half to one-fifth of the difference in value-added between teachers in the top and bottom halves of the distribution (see Chapter 7).

Thus, while based on a limited conception of student achievement reflected by standardized test scores, the findings from value-added analyses show that the NBPTS certification process does in fact identify teachers of higher quality. We emphasize that NBPTS certification identifies highly qualified teachers as determined by value-added analyses of standardized test scores, without the certification decision being determined by those test scores themselves. We highlight this point here because this is in contrast to a certification process, like that being considered for the American Board for Certification of Teacher Excellence's (ABCTE) Distinguished Teacher[SM] program, in which value-added measures are a component of certification decisions. In this latter case, it would not be unexpected to find that teachers who earn board certification are more effective at raising their students' achievement test scores, since that is part of the basis for the certification decision. The fact that teachers who earn NBPTS certification are effective at improving their students' achievement test scores beyond those who do not earn certification is an important finding, because student test score gains are not considered in awarding certification. These measures, board certification and results from value-added analyses, are independent, imperfect proxies of high-quality teaching, but their overlap provides some evidence that they are both capturing some aspect of this quality.

Benefit 2: Improving the Practices of Teachers Who Participate

The findings discussed in Chapter 8 show that there is some evidence that teachers' practices improve after going through the certification program, although at present this evidence is weak and the results are mixed. Survey results indicate that candidates who go through the process report it to be a valuable experience. Some empirical research shows that candidates, even those who fail, may improve their ability to perform tasks similar to those used for the assessment. Other studies suggest that teachers are less effective at raising students' test scores while going through the process and, in some cases, may continue to be less effective after earning certifications. In our estimation, the evidence with regard to this benefit is not yet conclusive, and we hesitate to draw firm conclusions from the available studies. Existing research is in need of replication in other states with other samples, other criteria, and using a variety of quantitative and qualitative methods.

Benefit 3: Improving the Quality of Teachers
Throughout the Education System

As shown in Figure 2-1, there are several different ways in which the NBPTS certification program could lead to improvements throughout the education system. Specifically, the program could

3a. improve the teaching practices of individual teachers who go through the process, whether or not they pass (a benefit that was also addressed above);
3b. encourage skilled teachers who become board certified to continue practicing longer;
3c. lead to assigning board-certified teachers to leadership roles that allow them to help improve the teaching of nonboard-certified teachers;
3d. improve the sorting of teachers across job assignments by identifying highly skilled teachers and targeting incentives to encourage teachers to take positions in difficult schools;
3e. encourage potentially effective teachers to enter the teaching field

(i.e., because of the recognition and monetary rewards offered by advanced-level certification); and

3f. change the teaching profession via the process and result of defining excellence in teaching.

Aside from improving the practices of individual board-certified teachers (Benefit 2/3a), these mechanisms for improving teaching quality throughout the education system require that advanced-level certification be used in effective ways that capitalize on the skills recognized by the credential. The evidence summarized in Chapters 6, 9, and 10 suggests that this is not currently being done.

It has been hypothesized that board certification—and the recognition and extra pay associated with it—would encourage high-quality teachers to continue for a longer period of time in the classroom (Benefit 3b) and would lead to more effective use of their skills through assignment of board-certified teachers to work in hard-to-staff schools (Benefit 3d). The evidence discussed in Chapter 9 is simply too limited to draw any firm conclusions about this.

Although there is the possibility that the presence of board-certified teachers could improve the practices of their nonboard-certified colleagues (Benefit 3c), the studies discussed in Chapter 10 suggest that this is currently not happening. Not only are there few examples of schools in which board-certified teachers are used in a formal way as mentors to improve the practice of their nonboard-certified colleagues, but there is also disturbing (if anecdotal) evidence that in some schools the ethos of equality across the faculty leads board-certified teachers to conceal their status from their colleagues.

Furthermore, although it seems possible that the vision of accomplished teaching put forth by the NBPTS has influenced some aspects of the teacher preparation system, it is likely to be impossible to demonstrate how significant this influence has been. This does not mean that this impact has not occurred only that it is difficult to measure.

In considering the impact of the NBPTS on the education system, it is important to distinguish the effect that board certification can have on the system on its own from effects that require other actors in the system to use board certification as a lever for change. If it were established that board certification acted to improve teacher quality directly (Benefit 2/3a), then no help from other actors in the system would be necessary. But mechanisms that require pay increases, recognition, mentoring roles, or tailored teaching assignments (i.e., assigning board-certified teachers to hard-to-staff schools) all require the participation of other actors besides the NBPTS. It is clear that board certification has been used as a policy lever in some states, such as North Carolina, by adopting an institutional orientation toward supporting teachers to acquire board certification and by providing financial support for going through the process and financial rewards for teachers who earn the credential. However, there are no examples of states that have systematically used board certification status as a way to identify qualified teachers to act as mentors to improve the teaching practices of other teachers in their school or district, and there are no examples of states that have systematically assigned board-certified teachers to work in the more difficult schools.

We note that considerable effort went into the process of identifying the standards for the NBPTS assessment. As described in Chapter 3, this effort brought a wide and diverse set of perspectives together, and currently the board's standards are reflected both in the standards for undergraduate teacher training and in the accreditation standards for schools of education. However, there have not been any systematic studies to evaluate the impacts of these efforts, particularly in a way that could be used in a cost-effectiveness analysis. As a result, it is important to acknowledge not only that there is limited research related to the benefits of board certification, but also that there has been inadequate experience with using board certification as a policy lever for improving teacher quality. The following conclusion summarizes our synthesis of the effectiveness of board certification as a route toward improving teaching quality:

Conclusion 11-1: There is evidence from both a psychometric review of the assessment process and analysis of student achievement test results that board certification identifies highly qualified teachers. There is no conclusive evidence that teachers improve their practices by going through the certification process, and there is essentially no evidence that certification or the existing recognition and financial incentives awarded to board-certified teachers in some states are sufficient to substantially increase their tenure as teachers. However, the ability of board certification to identify highly qualified teachers suggests that it offers a potential policy lever for increasing teaching quality throughout the system if it were used in ways that have not yet been tried on a large-scale systematic basis, such as by using board certification in hiring, promotion, and assignment decisions; systematically using board-certified teachers as mentors or as teacher leaders; or by targeting incentives to encourage board-certified teachers to work in the more difficult schools.

COSTS ASSOCIATED WITH THE PROGRAM

The costs associated with the NBPTS program include the following, which are incurred for each teacher who applies for board certification: (1) the cost of running the assessment program; (2) the time for the candidate to prepare the materials and go through the assessment process; (3) the time (or cost) for any mentors or other assistance to candidates as they are going through the process; and (4) the bonuses that are paid to successful candidates by the states and local school districts that provide such bonuses.

Ideally, one wants to measure all of the above costs, but there are poor or virtually no data on some of these items, such as the costs borne by mentors or other teachers who help the applicant. However, these costs are probably minor compared with the main costs, which include the costs of running the assessment program, the time of the applicant to prepare the materials, and the bonuses for board-certified teachers. In addition, for the purposes of comparing the cost-effectiveness of different mechanisms for improving teacher quality, it is likely that the available data on both the effectiveness and the costs will be fairly coarse for most of the options, so it is likely that a coarse cost analysis for board certification is not only the best we can do but perhaps also all that is needed. Below we provide estimates of each of these costs.

Costs of Running the Assessment Program

The test fee, which is currently $2,500, provides one estimate of the costs of the NBPTS assessment program per applicant. However, this estimate does not account for the full costs of running the program; in 2005, with roughly 12,000 applications and a test fee of $2,300, the test fee generated roughly $28 million out of total income for the NBPTS of $42 million (personal communication, Joseph Aguerrebere, August 7, 2006). Another estimate of the cost of the assessment program per applicant would be to divide the total costs for the organization across all the applicants, with the justification that the assessment program is essentially the organization's only product. Adding in the institutional costs for maintaining the organization and regularly updating the assessments spreads those fixed costs over all current applicants. This gives the average per-applicant cost for running the assessment program at its current size, but it is important to note that that average cost would be smaller if there were more applicants over whom to spread the institutional costs (or higher if there were fewer applicants). In 2005, using the average per-applicant cost that includes these institutional costs, this would produce an estimate 50 percent higher than the test fee alone. To allow for some uncertainty in the appropriate costs to assign, we use the range of $2,500-$4,000.

In some cases the cost of the test fee ($2,500) is covered by the applicants and in other cases it is covered by the state, the local district, or (indirectly) by the federal government. That is, the federal government currently provides funding to states for teacher improvement efforts, and some states draw from this funding to support bonuses for teachers who earn board certification. During the 2005-2006 school year, 36 of the 51 states (including the District of Columbia) provided some sort of fee assistance. Nine of these states covered the full fee for applicants, although some impose limitations, such as the number of applicants allowed per year or a requirement that the candidate pass. Ten of the states paid most of the fee ($2,000-2,250), and 16 offered partial assistance of $1,250 or less.

Note that the cost of running the assessment process does not include the development costs of the NBPTS, which were roughly $200 million (Hannaway and Bischoff, 2005)[1] and covered by a mix of public and private sources. Since that cost is money already spent, it is inappropriate to include it in an analysis of the ongoing cost-effectiveness of the program as a means for increasing teacher quality. However, in a later section, we discuss the nature of the country's $200 million investment in the research and development leading to board certification and consider the cost-effectiveness of that investment.

Cost to Applicants for Preparing for the Assessment

Cohen and Rice (2005) estimate that candidates spend approximately 400 hours during the assessment process—preparing their portfolio and preparing for and taking the assessment center exercises. In addition, they estimate that candidates spend approximately $350 on supplies related to the preparation of their portfolio submission.

In most cases, the time cost to the applicants is likely to be largely unreimbursed so that the applicant bears the cost of preparing her or his own portfolio. However, in some states or districts, candidates can obtain release time for preparing their materials, which shifts the costs from the applicant to the state or local government. Assuming an average salary with benefits of $60,000 and a 1,600-hour work year, the 400-hour time cost for applicants to prepare their portfolios would translate into $15,000 of salary and benefits, if the preparation time were fully reimbursed.[2] In the 2005-2006 school year, six states offered teachers release time while preparing for the assessment. However, even in these states, the amount of time allotted for assessment preparation ranges from two to five days, which is far below the

---

[1] Hannaway and Bischoff (2005) estimate the costs of research and development to be $200 million, which includes both direct and indirect costs. The NBPTS estimates the costs to be somewhat less, approximately $125 million, which excludes some of the costs for outreach, recruitment, support, and other overhead.

[2] The average salary without benefits for 2004-2005 was $47,750 in current dollars (http://nces.ed.gov/programs/digest/d06/). Hess (2004) cites an unreferenced figure of 26 percent of salary for the cost of benefits for teachers and an estimate of 38 weeks of work per year at 45 hours per week (http://www.hoover.org/publications/policyreview/3438676.html).

average time teachers spend in preparation. Thus, essentially the full cost of the preparation time is currently borne by the applicants themselves.

Costs of Mentors and Support Programs

The NBPTS estimates that approximately 80 percent of candidates participate in a support program of one kind or another, although the basis for this figure is unclear and the kind of support offered by these programs varies considerably across jurisdictions. In some school systems, support is provided in a relatively informal manner, such as weekly meetings among the candidates with mentorship provided by teachers who are already board certified. These informal support programs are relatively inexpensive. Other school systems have more formal support programs, which can be much more costly.

To some extent, the availability of board-certified teachers in the jurisdiction influences the kind of support that is offered. In districts in which board certification is encouraged, there tend to be more board-certified teachers, which means there is an available resource of teachers who can both lobby for funding for support programs and offer their services in assisting teacher candidates. In districts with fewer board-certified teachers, candidates may be on their own as they assemble their portfolios. In cases in which candidates obtain informal mentoring and support from their colleagues in preparing their materials, it is plausible that the cost of such support is likely to be in the form of unreimbursed time for the mentors. Without having any firm basis for evaluating this cost, we speculate that it might range from 10 to 40 hours. If reimbursed, the above estimates of salary and hours suggest that this mentoring time would cost roughly $400-$1,500, and so we use a cost of $1,000 for informal support.

Cohen and Rice (2005) conducted an analysis of the costs of four formal support programs. The services offered by these programs varied widely as did the number of participants served. The authors report that program-related costs per participant were $1,000 (60 participants), $2,600 (100 participants), $5,600 (70 participants), and $11,200 (9 participants). They indicated that some of this variability in costs is explained by the economy of scale realized by the larger programs and some is a function of design. Not all candidates participate in such formal programs of support, and only scant data are available on the prevalence of such programs. We judged the highest cost ($11,200) to be an outlier and not typical of the kinds of support offered throughout the country. Based on the above, we estimate the typical cost of support to be between $1,000 and $5,000, whether formally or informally provided.

Costs of Salary Bonuses to Board-Certified Teachers

The salary bonuses for successful candidates that some states provide come in a variety of forms.[3] Sometimes they are expressed as a percentage of the base salary, sometimes as a promotion on the state's career ladder, and sometimes as a specific amount of money. During the 2005-2006 school year, 36 states (including the District of Columbia) provided such bonuses, and they ranged from a low of $1,000 per year (in five states) to a high of $7,500 per year (in one state). The average bonus generally ranged between $3,000 and $5,000 per year, with a median value of $2,100.

Overall Cost per Applicant

Table 11-1 summarizes the overall costs associated with applying for board certification. Because the time costs of candidates and mentors may not be reimbursed, they are included in the table as both dollar costs and hours. The costs for a successful applicant in the year of application thus total roughly $20,000, if all costs are converted into dollars. Since roughly half of all candidates are successfully certified and since certification lasts for 10 years, this means that the application costs for every two applicants can be spread over 10 years of teaching by a single board-certified teacher, resulting in a cost of $4,000 per year of certified teaching.[4] To obtain the total cost per year of certified teaching, we need to add the per-year cost of the salary bonuses, roughly $3,000-$5,000, to the per-year cost of a successful application, resulting in a cost of $7,000-$9,000 per year of certified teaching. Roughly half of this cost is paid for by the candidates themselves, on average, mostly in the form of their unreimbursed time in preparing for the assessment. If the cost of the unreimbursed time for candidates is excluded, the costs are roughly $4,000-6,000 per year of certified teaching.

---

[3]It is important to distinguish between the cost to society and the cost to the public. For the cost to society, we include the teachers' unreimbursed time to prepare but not the costs of the salary incentives that are a benefit to the teacher; for the cost to the public, we exclude the teachers' unreimbursed time to prepare but include the costs of the salary incentives. As a result, the two different types of costs should be roughly the same.

[4]($20,000 × 2)/10. The calculation in the text understates the eventual pass rate, which is closer to 60-65 percent, and overstates the period of time the board-certified teachers teach, which is unknown but is certainly less than the full 10 years that the NBPTS certificate lasts. For the purposes of the rough cost calculation that we are performing here, we assume that the understated pass rate and the overstated period of teaching will approximately cancel each other out, with the net result that roughly 10 years of certified teaching results from every two applications. In addition, we ignore the effects of time discounting even though the costs and benefits occur over an extended period of time; given the coarseness of the figures that are available about both the benefits and the costs, this additional refinement would not appreciably affect the result.

TABLE 11-1 Costs Associated with National Board Certification

Type of Cost	Cost	Who Pays
Running the assessment process	$2,500-$4,000	Candidate or state (NBPTS subsidy)
Cost to applicants of preparing the materials	$15,350 (or 400 hours and $350)	Candidate or state
Mentors and support programs	$1,000-$5,000	Mentor or state
Salary bonuses	$3,000-$5,000 per yr	State

COST-EFFECTIVENESS OF THE PROGRAM

To estimate the cost-effectiveness of the NBPTS program, we combine the information on the benefits and the information on the costs from the preceding two sections. As stated in Conclusion 11-1, there is no conclusive evidence yet that board certification directly improves the teaching practices of candidates or that it has led to the improvements across the educational system in the ways enumerated (in Benefits 3a through 3f). As a result, there is little evidence that we can use for a cost-effectiveness analysis. However, board certification does offer a way of identifying high-quality teachers, and the difference between board-certified teachers and nonapplicants reported in value-added analyses provides a quantitative estimate that can be used in cost-effectiveness analyses. As stated above, in order for the difference in effectiveness signaled by board certification to have an effect, it must be used. Below, to estimate the cost-effectiveness of the program, we develop a hypothetical example of a policy intervention that required all experienced teachers to become board certified. This hypothetical example allows us to use the results from value-added analyses to explore the overall impact of such a policy on system-wide teacher effectiveness.

Evidence from value-added analyses suggests that board-certified teachers produce student achievement test scores that are 0.04 standard deviation[5] higher than those produced by the average nonapplicant. We consider this in the context of a hypothetical policy in which all teachers were required to become board certified (which admittedly is both untried and, at present, unrealistic). If this were the case and all students were instructed by board-certified teachers, this intervention would potentially offer a way to increase student achievement by 0.04 standard deviation on average (per

---

[5]This means 4 percent of a standard deviation. Thus, if the test's standard deviation was 25, 4 percent of a standard deviation would be 1 score point.

year). The costs of the current system suggest that the public cost of this intervention might be roughly $7,000-$9,000 per year of certified teaching if the candidates' time is reimbursed, or $4,000-$6,000 if it is not. This is a cost of $1,750-$2,250[6] per 0.01 standard deviation increase per class per year if the candidates' time is reimbursed, or $1,000-$1,500[7] if it is not.

We reiterate that because the empirical research leading to our estimate of 0.04 of a standard deviation gain in test scores finds that board-certified teachers are this much more effective on average, both before and after undergoing the certification process, we caution that this should not be interpreted as a benefit that is *caused* by the NBPTS process alone. Rather, the cost-effectiveness is calculated with respect to a policy that combines board certification with a requirement that all teachers obtain that certification—it is the *combination* of board certification and the mandatory requirement that would hypothetically have the cost-effectiveness that we have calculated. It is important to note that the hypothesized policy intervention of requiring all teachers to become board certified goes beyond our current experience with the program and would require careful examination and experimentation before anyone should consider the adoption of such a policy.

COMPARISONS WITH OTHER MECHANISMS FOR IMPROVING TEACHER QUALITY

Estimates of cost-effectiveness are difficult to interpret in isolation. For a cost-benefit analysis, in which the benefits of an intervention are monetized, it is possible to determine whether the benefits are greater than the costs. In contrast, in cost-effectiveness analyses, the benefit of the intervention is not necessarily monetized, often because of uncertainty or disagreement about the appropriate monetary value to place on the benefit. In this case, it is necessary to compare the resulting cost-effectiveness of the intervention with other mechanisms for achieving the benefits.

For the NBPTS, it is important to note that there are no other operating programs that offer advanced-level certification for teachers on a national, large-scale basis (although there are local programs for acknowledging accomplished teachers, for example in Cincinnati and California). However, three comparison interventions seem to offer an appropriate comparison: (1) the Distinguished Teacher[SM] credential to be offered by ABCTE, (2) master's degrees, and (3) inservice professional development.

Despite the difficulties of assessing the cost-effectiveness of these interventions to improve teacher quality, the resulting analysis can offer an

---

[6] $7,000/4 and $9,000/4.
[7] $4,000/4 and $6,000/4.

instructive comparison with the cost-effectiveness of board certification. In each case, these interventions are focused on improving the teaching quality of practicing teachers. It would be possible to extend the range of comparisons to interventions related to improving the quality of beginning teachers or to interventions related to improving student learning but not specifically focused on improving teacher quality. However, we chose to focus our set of comparisons on the interventions most closely aligned with the goals of the NBPTS and the request of Congress in evaluating its cost-effectiveness. Because many people are familiar with the example of class-size reduction and the original Student/Teacher Achievement Ratio experiment in Tennessee that suggested the potential effectiveness of that intervention, we also briefly discuss the cost-effectiveness of class-size reduction as a basis for comparison with board certification.

In the sections that follow, we briefly summarize information about the benefits and the costs of the three interventions related to teacher quality, as well as the intervention of class-size reduction.

ABCTE Distinguished Teacher[SM] Program

The ABCTE is developing an advanced-level certification program that, when operational, would serve as an alternative to NBPTS certification. Since data from an operational program are not yet available, an assessment of the benefits and costs of the program must be speculative. Some information about ABCTE's planned approach to designing its advanced-level certification allows us to make some observations about its benefits and costs in comparison to those of NBPTS certification.

The original plan for the program (which has since been altered) was to base certification decisions on two requirements: teachers would have to pass a computer-based test of subject matter, and they would have to demonstrate a measurable impact on the gains of their students on achievement tests. These two features would allow the ABCTE Distinguished Teacher[SM] program to offer an instructive contrast to board certification.

On one hand, the use of computer-based testing alone is likely to be substantially cheaper than the combined portfolio and computer-based assessment used in the NBPTS process. On the other hand, the requirement that teachers demonstrate a measurable impact on student test scores means that the ABCTE certification would have to be limited to teachers who teach in the grades and subject areas in which standardized tests are routinely used and available for statistical comparison. The NBPTS approach offers certificates in a wide array of areas for which standardized tests of students may not be available (e.g., art, career and technical education, English as a new language, exceptional needs, health education, library media, music, physical education, school counseling, world languages).

It is not clear how a value-added approach would be adapted to include advanced-level certificates in these areas.

These two contrasting features of the original ABCTE Distinguished Teacher[SM] program allow us to lay out some logical implications of this design. With respect to the potential benefits of the program, there are some critical implications. The restriction of the program to the grades and subject areas that are routinely tested would severely limit efforts to use this advanced-level certification to identify high-quality teachers and to use certification as a policy lever to improve teacher quality throughout the system. Given the existing grades and subject areas in which standardized tests are routinely available, the original approach of ABCTE would limit its coverage to less than half of the current teaching pool, depending on the state.[8] Not only would this directly limit the ability of the program to identify high-quality teachers, but it would also make it very difficult politically to offer incentives because they could not be made available to all teachers. Note that these limitations would apply to any model for teacher certification or selection that relied on value-added approaches.

While there are no existing approaches that focus solely on value-added methodologies, we point out that such an approach downplays the importance of teachers' practices. That is, it is possible for teachers to use practices, such as explicit "teaching to the test," that may produce increases in test scores but do not represent exemplary practice.

At the same time, the original ABCTE Distinguished Teacher[SM] program offered a potential advantage on the cost side by substituting a less expensive testing process that would probably have resulted in a lower test fee than for NBPTS certification. However, it is important to consider the implications of this cost reduction in relation to the overall costs of NBPTS certification shown in Table 11-1. The NBPTS cost of processing an assessment ($2,500-$4,000 per applicant) results in a cost per year of certified teacher of $500-$800[9] out of the total cost of NBPTS certification of $5,000-$8,000[10] per year of certified teaching. The majority of the costs associated with NBPTS certification result from candidates' time in preparing the assessment materials and from the salary bonuses offered to successful candidates. The only way to substantially reduce the costs of an advanced certification program is to reduce one of these two costs—but it is difficult to see how ABCTE could effectively reduce either one of those costs and still be a viable program. That is, teachers need a reason to pursue board certification, most likely some type of extrinsic incentive, such as

---

[8]See http://nces.ed.gov/programs/digest/d04/tables/dt04_065.asp?referrer=list.

[9]($2,500 × 2)/10; ($4,000 × 2)/10.

[10]($2,500 × 2); ($4,000 × 2), since it takes approximately two applicants to get one board-certified teacher.

the bonuses in place for NBPTS certification. Furthermore, the assessment needs to be of sufficient substance that it serves as a reasonable basis for awarding advanced-level certification; if the assessment is challenging, candidates will have to spend time preparing for it (although the preparation time may not be as long as the estimated 400 hours required to assemble the NBPTS portfolio). As a result, it seems likely that the total costs of the ABCTE Distinguished Teacher^{SM} program, as originally designed, would not have been substantially lower than that of NBPTS certification. This discussion is also somewhat hypothetical, however, in that the ABCTE has made changes to its original design making it more similar to the NBPTS approach.

Recently, the ABCTE Distinguished Teacher^{SM} program has indicated that it is expanding its assessment criteria by exploring the possibility of incorporating ratings of three classroom observations in certification decisions as well as a supervisor's rating. This change could affect both the costs and the benefits of the program. Classroom observations are quite costly to conduct, systematize, and score; thus, this potential change could increase costs of the ABCTE Distinguished Teacher^{SM} program compared with the original vision. However, as noted above, most of the cost involved with certification is not in the cost for processing the assessment itself, so this increase in cost is not likely to be a critical problem. It is also possible that the ABCTE might decide that classroom observation could be used in place of test score gains for subjects and grades in which standardized tests are not available. This is, of course, purely speculative, but if it were the case, it could potentially remove a severe limitation of the ABCTE Distinguished Teacher^{SM} program as a policy lever for improving teacher quality. Note, however, that it would also move the program to becoming more similar to NBPTS certification.

Thus, as originally planned, the ABCTE presented a slightly less expensive alternative to NBPTS certification, but we are unsure how it would be made available to all teachers. The new version carries the same restriction and is likely to result in costs similar to those of the NBPTS.

Obtaining a Master's Degree

Another alternative mechanism for improving teacher quality is to encourage teachers to pursue additional coursework beyond that completed for the undergraduate degree. Most states require graduate coursework to maintain the teaching credential, and some require teachers to earn a graduate degree within a certain amount of time after entering the school system. The salary structure typically considers both experience and graduate coursework in determining a teacher's pay, with a substantial increase associated with earning a master's degree. Thus, we can examine the benefits associated with earning a master's degree in relation to the costs as a means for comparing our cost-effectiveness estimate for the NBPTS.

Benefits of a Master's Degree

Over the past 30 years, approximately 25 studies have compared achievement test performance for students taught by teachers with and without a master's degree (for a summary, see Harris and Sass, 2007). The results from these studies are mixed. The majority found that teachers with master's degrees are not any more effective than teachers with bachelor's degrees at improving their students' achievement, and, in some cases, teachers with master's degrees were less effective. However, six of these studies did report statistically significant positive effects associated with having a master's degree (Betts et al., 2003; Dee, 2004; Ferguson and Ladd, 1996; Goldhaber and Brewer, 1997; Monk, 1994; Nye et al., 2004), more so in comparing the effects on math performance than on reading. Only two studies (Betts et al., 2003; Ferguson and Ladd, 1996) reported statistically significant effects for reading.

Two studies of teachers and students in North Carolina by Clotfelter, Ladd, and Vigdor (2006, 2007b) permit direct comparison of the effects of board certification and of master's degrees on student achievement. In their study focused on the elementary grades, Clotfelter et al. (2006) report that teachers with a master's degree produce achievement test gains similar to or slightly lower than teachers with bachelor's degrees, while the effects associated with national board certification were between 0.02 and 0.03 of a standard deviation. In their high school study (Clotfelter, Ladd, and Vigdor, 2007b), the authors report that teachers with a master's degree improve their student's performance by 0.005 of a standard deviation more than teachers with a bachelor's degree. Again, this is lower than the effect they report for board certification status, which was 0.051.

It is important to recognize that there are some likely explanations for the poor showing of benefits from master's degrees. One explanation relates to the fact that teachers take their graduate coursework over a period of time, and thus the effects may occur gradually over the period during which the coursework is taken. Attaining the degree is just one step in the course-taking process, and there may not be large effects associated with getting past this final hurdle. Another explanation relates to the characteristics of the group of teachers with bachelor's degrees that serves as the comparison group in these analyses. The comparison group may include teachers who are on the path toward obtaining their master's degree, and their own teaching may be affected by the courses they have taken. These kinds of analyses encounter the same sorts of confounds that we described in Chapter 7 for comparisons of board-certified and nonboard-certified teachers.

A final explanation relates to the nature of master's degree programs. There are as many conceptions of master's degree programs for teachers as there are institutions of higher education in this country. A master's degree may be awarded after completion of a comprehensive course of study at an accredited institution. Graduate programs are also available through alternate and less formal mechanisms, such as online courses, courses offered through the school system, and continuing education credit awarded for participation in various professional development activities. Thus, when a teacher obtains a master's degree, it is not clear what body of knowledge or set of skills has been acquired. In contrast, while there are at least 50 different implementation models for the NBPTS program, the assessments are standardized. That is, all teachers pursuing a given certificate must demonstrate mastery of the same knowledge, content, and dispositions. Obtaining the title of board-certified teacher generally means the same thing regardless of the jurisdiction in which the teacher is employed. This stands in stark contrast to what is signified by obtaining a master's degree.

Costs of a Master's Degree

To summarize the cost of a master's degree, we use cost categories that are similar to three of the categories for board certification, omitting the cost of mentoring. In place of the cost of the assessment process, there is the cost of providing the graduate program. This is the tuition for graduate school combined with the subsidy to tuition provided by public and private endowment support. The full cost of study is relatively similar across public and private universities and is roughly $40,000 per year. Thus for a one- or two-year master's degree, the cost is $40,000 or $80,000 (Knapp et al., 1990, in Cohen and Rice, 2005).[11] It is likely, however, that this is an overestimate of the actual annual costs because teachers typically pursue graduate degrees on a part-time basis, attending courses in the evenings and during the summer.

The second cost category is the cost of the time for the candidate, in this case the candidate for a master's degree. Here the required time might be estimated as 30 weeks of full-time study for each year of the master's degree, corresponding to roughly 1,200 hours for the candidate. Given a median cost of a teacher's annual salary of approximately $48,000 (http:// nces.ed.gov/programs/digest/d06/) and benefits at approximately 26 percent for 1,600 hours of work (Hess, 2004), this translates into a cost of roughly

---

[11]Cohen and Rice (2005) estimate that the cost of a full-time masters program is $71,000 over two years of time. This estimate is in 2003 dollars. When converted to 2008 dollars, the cost increases to $83,500.

$45,000 per year of graduate study.[12] The third cost category is the annual salary bonus for teachers with a master's degree. Nationally, this bonus is roughly $7,000 per year.[13]

The up-front cost of obtaining a master's degree is $85,000 per year. If we assume that the degree takes an average 1.5 years to obtain and that teachers teach 25 years after obtaining it, then the resulting cost per year for obtaining the degree is roughly $5,000 if the time for teachers to study is reimbursed, $2,500 if it is not.[14] Adding to this the cost of the average annual salary bonus, the result is a rough estimate of $12,000 per year of teaching for a teacher with a master's degree if the time for teachers to study is reimbursed, $9,500 of it is not.

For master's degrees, the evidence about benefits is too mixed to allow us to produce a cost-effectiveness figure that can be compared with the $1,000-$2,250 cost per 0.01 standard deviation increase in student achievement that was based on our hypothetical example of requiring all teachers to become board certified. The cost per class-year of a teacher with a master's degree is roughly the same as the cost per class-year of a teacher who is board certified. As noted in the previous section, however, the available evidence does not consistently indicate that teachers with master's degrees are more effective than teachers without them.

Inservice Professional Development of Practicing Teachers

Inservice professional development programs are generally intended to help teachers implement new curriculum, new pedagogy, new procedures, and conceivably a combination of all three. For example, if a district were putting in place a new middle school math curriculum with an online formative assessment component, teachers are likely to need to learn the new curriculum, learn and practice the teaching methods it required, and learn how to manage the assessment system. This sort of professional development is different from the NBPTS process, which might be considered as a point-in-time demonstration of professional competence. In contrast, most inservice professional development has an instrumental purpose. As described in the benefit section above, inservice training offers a means for improving the quality of all teaching without going through the process of identifying highly skilled practitioners.

---

[12][$48,000 + ($48,000 × .26)] × (1,200/1,600).

[13]This cost is estimated as the median difference, controlling for experience level, between the average salary for teachers with a BA degree and the average salary for teachers with an MA degree. Salaries for teachers with a BA degree can be found at: http://nces.ed.gov/programs/digest/d07/tables/dt07_073.asp?referrer=list. Salaries for teachers with an MA degree can be found at: http://nces.ed.gov/programs/digest/d07/tables/dt07_074.asp?referrer=list.

[14]($85,000 × 1.5)/25 years if time is reimbursed, or ($40,000 × 1.5)/25 years, if it is not.

However, there is little research that provides the kind of information needed for an evaluation of the cost-effectiveness of inservice professional development. This is not to say that there is no research on inservice training for teachers, only that it has not produced the information needed for a cost-effectiveness analysis that can be compared with the cost-effectiveness of NBPTS certification. A common way to evaluate the benefits of professional development is in terms of participants' satisfaction or other qualitative measures. We were able to locate only three studies that evaluated professional development in terms of quantitative measures: a recent study by Harris and Sass (2007) that used Florida's state data about inservice training in value-added analyses, as well as two earlier studies (Angrist and Lavy, 2001; Jacob and Lefgren, 2004). The results from all three studies suggest there are only weak value-added benefits (i.e., the strongest effect in Harris and Sass analysis was 0.001 standard deviation, which was statistically significant) associated with teachers' professional development activities.

Similarly, there is little research that documents the costs of inservice professional development in a way that can be used in a cost-effectiveness evaluation. Currently, the federal government provides funding to school districts that can be allocated for professional development. The funding is provided through the No Child Left Behind legislation, which stipulates that 15 percent of any district's Title I allocation be directly invested in teacher professional development. In addition, districts receive federal Title II grants that are specifically targeted for professional development. Because the federal portion of a district's budget is not likely to exceed 5 to 6 percent of the total, the likelihood is that the federal contribution for professional development would be less than 1 percent of a district's operating budget. And in many cases a substantial portion of those funds could be directed to salaries for those who provide professional development. It is difficult, however, to directly connect this funding to specific inservice training activities in a way that would be useful for a cost-effectiveness evaluation.

Cost estimates of other types of professional development activities are also provided in Cohen and Rice (2005). They evaluated nine other professional development programs. Their findings indicated that per-participant costs (in 2003 dollars) ranged from a low of $1,438 for the Connecticut Beginning Educator Support and Training program to a high of $14,000 for the Leadership Institute in St. Paul, Minnesota, with a median value of roughly $3,100. The studies that Cohen and Rice utilized are fairly dated, ranging from 1994 to 2001, and they provide no estimates of benefits. Given the state of the literature base at the current time, we are unable to derive a cost-effective estimate associated with inservice professional training for teachers.

Evaluations of the Effects of Class-Size Reduction

A considerable amount of research has focused on the costs and benefits associated with class-size reduction policies, and we draw on those estimates to compare with the effectiveness of the NBPTS. The two interventions are, of course, not directly comparable. Class-size reduction in and of itself provides a means to produce improvement in student learning. National board certification provides a means to identify the more effective teachers, but, as described earlier, additional actions are required to realize the benefits. Nevertheless, the comparison can be instructive when considering situations in which policy makers must decide how to allocate funding. The funding could be used to hire additional (presumably effective) teachers so that students can be assigned to smaller classes. Alternatively, the funding could be used to encourage teachers to pursue board certification so that the more effective teachers are identified and their skills used. A comparison can help to understand which is the better investment of funds.

There have been several attempts to implement class-size reduction policies. In 1985, the state of Tennessee initiated a policy targeted at reducing the student-teacher ratio in classes. The state implemented the policy as an experiment designed to examine the effects on achievement of assigning students to classes with smaller numbers of students. Students entering kindergarten were assigned at random to either a small class (13-17 students) or a regular class (22-26 students). Teachers were randomly assigned to the classes. Students remained in their original experimental assignment (small versus large class) over the course of four years (K-3), with a follow-up data collection in seventh grade (Finn and Achilles, 1999).

The results from this experiment indicated that students in the smaller classes performed better than those in the larger classes, with effect sizes ranging from 0.15 to 0.25. Given an estimated average annual cost of $60,000 per teacher (for salary plus benefits), this is roughly a $30,000[15] cost per year for a lower class size (e.g., reducing the class size from 24 to 16 students) for a benefit of roughly 0.20 standard deviation. This converts to a cost of $1,500[16] per 0.01 standard deviation increase per class per year.

This can be compared with our estimates of the effectiveness of national board certification (under the hypothetical situation in which all teachers are required to become board certified). Superficially, the two estimates are approximately equal: NBPTS certification results in a smaller effect (0.04 versus 0.20) but also at a lower cost ($2,000-$8,000 versus

---

[15]With teacher pay at $60,000, a class size of 24 costs $2,500 per child. A class size of 16 costs $3,750 per child. The difference ($1,250) is the additional cost per student of class size reduction. The total cost is then $1,250 × 24.

[16]$30,000/(0.20/0.01).

$30,000 per classroom). The resulting cost-effectiveness is similar for the two interventions: $500-$2,000[17] for mandatory NBPTS certification versus $1,500 for class-size reduction per 0.01 standard deviation increase per year per class.[18] We caution, however, that the two interventions are not directly comparable because class-size reduction actually caused the increase, whereas the NBPTS example is hypothetical and would require additional policy actions to produce such an increase.

The effectiveness estimates from Tennessee's controlled experiment ultimately helped persuade a number of policy makers to adopt class-size reduction as an educational intervention in other states. Continuing studies of the effects of class-size reduction have led to substantial revisions in the estimates of the effectiveness of this intervention when implemented as a statewide policy. For example, results from the study of class-size reduction policy in California revealed that the effects were statistically significant but quite small, in the range of 0.05 to 0.08 of a standard deviation (Bohrnstedt and Stecher, 2002; Stecher, Bohrnstedt, Kirst, McRobbie, and Williams, 2001). In part, this was a consequence of the limited supply of experienced, high-quality teachers that were required to implement the policy.

Evaluating the Research and Development Investment in the NBPTS

Approximately $200 million (see footnote 2) was spent on the research and development that went into developing the assessments that now constitute the NBPTS certification program. Eleven private organizations funded the board during its developmental years. The Carnegie Foundation was the largest supporter, providing approximately $1 million per year for 11 years. Other funding sources included the Ford Foundation, the DeWitt Wallace-Reader's Digest Fund, the Lilly Endowment, the Pew Charitable Trusts, the Atlantic Philanthropies, Xerox, IBM, DuPont, AT&T, and Chrysler (Hannaway and Bischoff, 2005). The board began receiving federal support in 1991, under the first President Bush, which increased substantially under President Clinton. According to Hannaway and Bischoff, between 1987 and 2002, the board received over $100 million in federal funding and an equivalent amount from other sources.

In evaluating this research and development investment of $200 million (see foonote 2), it is useful to provide some other figures related to teaching to put the investment in perspective. As noted in Chapter 6, there are roughly 4 million teachers in grades K-12, of whom approximately 64,000 have become board certified. The annual salary and benefits for these

---

[17]($2,000/4); ($8,000/4).

[18]These costs for class-size reduction do not include the facility costs of providing additional classrooms.

teachers total roughly $240[19] billion each year. When administrative and other costs for K-12 education are added to the cost of teachers' salaries, the total cost of K-12 education is slightly more than $500 billion per year (http://nces.ed.gov/programs/digest/d04/tables/dt04_029.asp?referrer=list).

Compared with the annual cost of K-12 education, the $200 million (see foonote 2) investment in the NBPTS is small, representing less than 0.04 percent of the cost of K-12 education for a single year. Considering the larger goal of NBPTS, which was to transform the profession of teaching by articulating a conception of accomplished teaching and developing an assessment for identifying accomplished teaching, the $200 million (see foonote 2) cost of the investment does not seem like a high price to pay. To date the NBPTS has not been able to bring about the transformation in teaching that was hoped for two decades ago, although it has produced an innovative certification process that does in fact identify accomplished teachers. However, in evaluating research and development costs, it is important to remember that any single research and development effort is a calculated gamble with an uncertain chance of success. It is inappropriate to evaluate the initial investment decision with the knowledge available now that the NBPTS has not brought about the transformation it hoped to achieve. Instead, we have to look at the decision that was made at the time when no one knew whether or not the NBPTS would be successful in transforming the profession of teaching. If we consider that choice, it is probably fair to say that from the beginning the likelihood was probably low that the project would have truly been able to transform the profession of teaching. At the same time, however, the educational payoff, if the project had achieved the unlikely result of transforming teaching, could have been very high indeed. And the gamble in the NBPTS was not undertaken lightly but represented a bold and serious effort by many leaders in education research and policy. For a serious research and development gamble that had a chance to transform teaching, even with a low probability, it does not seem excessive to have invested 0.1 percent of the cost of K-12 education for a single year.

It is also useful to compare the $200 million (see foonote 2) investment in the NBPTS with the size of the annual research and development investment in K-12 education. Although the cost of K-12 education is quite high, the level of investment in research and development for K-12 education is quite low, relative to the rate of research and development spending in many other sectors of the economy. The annual investment in research and development for K-12 education is on the order of $1.3 billion per

---

[19]$60,000 in salary and benefits × 4 million teachers.

year.[20] Thus, although the investment in the NBPTS is small compared with the overall annual cost of K-12 education, it is large compared with the annual investment in research and development for K-12 education. Still, if the investment in research and development investment for the NBPTS represented 15 percent of all research and development for K-12 education for a single year—that does not seem a high price to pay for a program that was a serious effort to bring about a transformation in teaching quality. For comparison, the Gates Foundation has invested roughly $650 million in its small high schools program (Hendrie, 2004).

The above calculation considers the costs that the federal government and private foundations invested in the NBPTS to get the program up and running. A more expansive consideration of costs might treat the entire program as an experiment and count the costs of certifying roughly 64,000 teachers as part of the ultimate cost of conducting that experiment. Earlier we saw that the cost per year of certified teaching is roughly $6,000, resulting in a total cost of $300 million over the 64,000 teachers. This cost clearly dominates the initial $200 million investment itself (see footnote 2). However, if the entire $500 million cost is seen as representing nothing more than a serious research and development gamble to bring about a transformation in teaching quality, it is probably fair to say that the gamble was still a reasonable one to take.

It is important to note that this discussion about the research and development investment in the NBPTS has been stated from the perspective of the original decision 20 years ago to make a serious commitment to developing this particular vision of transforming teaching quality for K-12 education. Evaluating whether or not that initial decision two decades ago was an appropriate investment in research and development is entirely different than evaluating the current decision about whether or not to continue to invest in the program. The decision about whether to continue to invest in the NBPTS going forward must rest on evidence that its continuing presence is helping to improve K-12 education.

CONCLUSIONS

In this chapter, we have attempted to address the final aspect of our charge, which was significantly complicated by the limited evidence base. There was insufficient evidence on which to base a thorough cost-

---

[20]This figure is the sum of the 2008 budget allocations for the Department of Education's Institute of Education Sciences ($546.1 million) and for the National Science Foundation's Education and Human Resources ($725.5). Details about the Department of Education's budget can be found at: http://www.ed.gov/about/overview/budget/budget09/summary/appendix4. pdf. Details about the National Science Foundation's budget can be found at: http://www.nsf. gov/about/budget/.

effectiveness evaluation of the NBPTS, primarily due to a lack of research documenting benefits. We note that it was not necessarily the case that there is evidence of no benefits, but that the evidence base is simply too thin, and findings from research that has been conducted are in need of corroboration. For example, research on the effects of board certification on teachers' longevity in the field and studies of the extent to which the certification process improves their effectiveness (as described in Chapters 8 and 9) have the potential to yield estimates of benefits that could be used in future cost-effectiveness evaluations. It was also not possible to compare the effectiveness of the NBPTS with other mechanisms for improving teacher quality—such as alternative kinds of advanced-certification programs for teachers, encouraging teachers to pursue master's degrees, and providing inservice professional development—because of a lack of information on both the costs and benefits of these activities. While our cost analysis suggests that the annual per-teacher costs associated with board certification are probably lower than annual per-teacher costs of obtaining a master's degree, a sufficient number of rigorous studies was not available to allow us to compare the benefits of these two interventions in a meaningful way. Thus, we conclude:

Conclusion 11-2: At this time, it is not possible to conduct a thorough cost-effectiveness evaluation of the NBPTS because of the paucity of data on the benefits of the program and on both the costs and benefits of other mechanisms intended to improve teacher quality. Such an evaluation should be undertaken if and when the necessary evidence becomes available.

Because of the lack of evidence for a thorough cost-effectiveness evaluation, we undertook a somewhat speculative approach to considering the cost-effectiveness of the NBPTS. We laid out three kinds of potential benefits. To date, the existing research provides evidence of only one of these benefits: identification of high-quality teachers. We pointed out that this benefit cannot be realized without some additional action that makes use of the skills of board-certified teachers, and we explored the hypothetical example of requiring all experienced teachers to become board certified. While this is a policy that has not yet been tried, tested, or debated, we think it is worth considering, possibly on a localized basis for all teachers or teachers in some schools. Given the substantial investment that has already been made in the NBPTS certification program, it is important to consider not only the cost-effectiveness of NBPTS certification as a realized mechanism for improving teacher quality, but also its potential if it were to be used more actively by states as a policy lever for improving teacher quality throughout the education system.

12

Overall Evaluation

Our review of the National Board for Professional Teaching Standards (NBPTS) required that we consider the program from a variety of perspectives and explore several complex technical questions in detail. In Chapters 5 through 11, we examined each of the questions in our evaluation framework on its own merits. In this final chapter, we step back to consider all of the pieces of evidence together and to offer several overall conclusions about the program. We begin by summarizing the key conclusions and recommendations related to each element of the evaluation framework. We then present our overall conclusions about the board and the role it can play in improving teacher quality.

FINDINGS AND RECOMMENDATIONS

Psychometric Characteristics of the Assessment

From our review of the assessments themselves and the development process, we find that, in general, high standards have been followed. The initial design and development process was extensive, and some of the most renowned measurement experts in the country had considerable input. The process was carried out carefully and in a transparent manner. The development of standards and assessments for a wide array of teaching specialty areas is a significant accomplishment.

Since the program has become operational, however, attention to psychometric matters seems to have become routinized, and somewhat less attention is being paid to issues that were critical during the development stage. This might be expected as a testing program matures and evolves. However, perhaps in part because of staff turnover and a change in location, historical documentation about the assessment has been difficult to locate. We initially encountered significant difficulty in obtaining documentation that was sufficiently detailed to allow us to evaluate the development of the standards and the design of the assessments, although we note that the board eventually provided most of the information we needed to conduct our review.

We found this deficiency to be particularly troublesome as we explored the content-related validity evidence for the national board assessment. Ordinarily, the primary focus in an evaluation of a credentialing assessment is content-related validity evidence—that is, the evidence that the assessment measures the knowledge and skills it is intended to measure, based on the content standards that guide the development of the assessment. Content-related validity evidence, such as documentation of how the content standards were established, who participated in the process, what the process involved, and how the content standards were translated into test items, was the most difficult for us to obtain from the NBPTS.

The NBPTS is unusual in that its mission includes policy reform goals as well as the operation of an assessment program. However, in our opinion, the assessment is its primary responsibility. Ongoing evaluation of an assessment program is critical to maintaining its quality and credibility, and providing thorough documentation that is easily accessible to outside evaluators is a critical element of this process. The NBPTS should be able to readily provide documentation that demonstrates that its assessments are developed, administered, and scored in accord with high standards, such as those laid out in the standards documents for credentialing assessments. We note that during the course of our evaluation, the NBPTS has begun developing a technical guide, and we encourage the NBPTS to finalize this document and make it available to researchers and others interested in learning about the technical attributes of the assessments.

Our key recommendations relating to the assessment itself are as follows:

Recommendation 5-1: The NBPTS should publish thorough technical documentation for the program as a whole and for individual specialty area assessments. This documentation should cover processes as well as products, should be readily available, and should be updated on a regular basis.

Recommendation 5-2: The NBPTS should develop a more structured process for deriving exercise content and scoring rubrics from the content standards and should thoroughly document application of the process for each assessment. Doing so will make it easier for the board to maintain the highest possible validity for the resulting assessments and to provide evidence suitable for independent evaluation of that validity.

Recommendation 5-3: The NBPTS should conduct research to determine whether the reliability of the assessment process could be improved (for example, by the inclusion of a number of shorter exercises in the computer-based component) without compromising the authenticity or validity of the assessment or substantially increasing its cost.

Recommendation 5-4: The NBPTS should collect and use the available operational data about the individual assessment exercises to improve the validity and reliability of the assessments for each certificate, as well as to minimize adverse impact.

Recommendation 5-5: The NBPTS should revisit the methods it uses to estimate the reliabilities of its assessments to determine whether the methods should be updated.

Recommendation 5-6: The NBPTS should periodically review the assessment model to determine whether adjustments are warranted to take advantage of advances in measurement technologies and developments in the teaching environment.

Teacher Participation in National Board Certification

The board's founders envisioned that NBPTS certification would become a widely recognized credential, that districts and states would value board-certified teachers, and that the numbers of certified teachers would grow. The founders expected that board-certified teachers would become a significant presence, helping to increase the influence of the board standards by serving as leaders and mentors to other teachers. From the 1993-1994 school year, when the program began operation, to the 2006-2007 school year, 99,300 teachers have attempted to earn board certification, and 63,800 teachers have been successful.

These numbers represent approximately 3 percent of the 3.1 million NBPTS-eligible teachers in the country, and it is likely that some of those who obtained board certification will have retired or allowed their certification to lapse. While NBPTS participants represent a small fraction of the teachers in this country, the absolute volume of teachers who have pursued board certification is considerable. Moreover, the numbers of participants have increased over the life of the program, from 550 applicants in the first year to 12,200 during the 2006-2007 school year. Still, it is worth noting that the original target set by the board was to identify the top 10 percent of teachers. If the board had met that goal, approximately 400,000 teachers would currently be certified. Assuming that all of the 63,800 teachers who had obtained board certification by 2006-2007 were still teaching, the NBPTS would be about a sixth of the way toward achieving this goal.

Participation rates are not even across the country. Overall, the number of board-certified teachers translates to three for every five of the 96,513 schools in the country. However, there are higher concentrations in some districts, such as Wake County, North Carolina, with an average of seven board-certified teachers per school, and Broward County, Florida, with an average of two per school. There are other disparities as well. More teachers from advantaged schools participate, and the absolute numbers of minority teachers participating are low.

The popularity of board certification varies dramatically from state to state, as does the degree to which states and districts encourage it. We were not able to find any research on the factors that influence the thinking of state policy makers about encouraging teacher participation. However, some states offer financial incentives to teachers—covering the $2,500 test fee and offering sizable salary increases to those who are successful—and they have higher participation rates than states that offer no incentives. In four states that have consistently offered financial incentives—Florida, Mississippi, North Carolina, and South Carolina—between 10 and 21 percent of NBPTS-eligible teachers have attempted to become board certified, well over the national rate of about 3 percent. In the seven states that have not offered incentives over the past few years—Alaska, Arizona, Massachusetts, Minnesota, Tennessee, Texas, and Utah—the participation rate ranges from 0.2 to 1.5 percent of NBPTS-eligible teachers.

On the basis of our review of the available data, we have drawn two conclusions and make one recommendation.

Conclusion 6-1: Although the number of teachers who have obtained certification is small relative to the general population of U.S. teachers, the total has grown since the program began and is now over 63,800. Participation varies significantly by state and district; however, in a few districts, participation rates are approaching levels likely to be sufficient for the program to have the intended effects.

Conclusion 6-2: States that offer financial incentives for attempting and achieving board certification are likely to have more teachers that apply and succeed in the program.

Recommendation 6-1: The NBPTS should implement and maintain a database of information about applicants and their career paths. This effort should include routine, annual data collection as well as specially designed studies. The data collected should provide information about what teachers have done after going through the certification process, what has happened to teachers who did not pass the assessment, how many board-certified teachers are currently employed, where board-certified teachers currently work, and what jobs they do.

Impacts of the National Board-Certification Process

Our framework examines the various kinds of impacts the NBPTS could have on students, in terms of their learning; on the teachers who participate, in terms of their professional growth and their career paths; and on the education system itself, through board-certified teachers' influence on their colleagues, school systems, and teacher training programs. This task was more difficult than we had anticipated because, as we have reiterated throughout this report, little valid evidence is available. The dearth of evidence was somewhat of a surprise because numerous studies have been conducted on the impacts of the NBPTS. However, many were based on such small sample sizes, or suffered so severely from selection bias, attrition, or other methodological problems, that it was impossible to draw solid conclusions from their findings. These problems were evident in studies conducted by the board itself, some funded by its research grant program, and some conducted independent of the board. The more quantitatively sophisticated large-scale studies were narrower in scope, focusing solely on one of the issues in which we were interested, student achievement as measured by standardized tests. This left us little evidence with which to answer the questions in our framework. Nevertheless, we scoured the studies for findings that we judged to be valid, given the methodology used; supportable, based on the evidence collected; and reasonable, given the limitations of the study.

Impacts on Outcomes for Students

The question of how the program is related to student outcomes can be considered in two ways. First, passing the certification process may act as a signal of preexisting teaching effectiveness. Second, the process of becoming board certified may *cause* a teacher's classroom effectiveness to improve. These questions related to student outcomes have generated the largest number of research studies, with most focusing on the question of whether board certification acted as a signal of preexisting teaching effectiveness.

Nearly all of these studies compare the achievement test scores of students taught by board-certified and nonboard-certified teachers; few compare other student outcomes, such as motivation, student engagement, breadth of achievement, attendance, or promotion.

We focused on studies that controlled for school and student variables related to student achievement. As a group, these studies show that the students of board-certified teachers performed better than students taught by nonboard-certified teachers (the magnitude of the differences is on the order of 0.02 to 0.08 of a standard deviation). The studies demonstrate that board certification is a signal that teachers with this credential are more effective than other teachers at raising their students' test scores.

Few studies examined the extent to which the certification process caused teachers' effectiveness to improve, and the findings from these studies were mixed. We note that certification programs are not typically designed to improve the performance of those who apply (i.e., passing a certification test typically does not in and of itself improve performance), and certification programs are not typically evaluated on this issue. However, the impact of the certification process is a relevant issue and it is included in our framework.

While the studies examining the effects of board-certified teachers on their students' achievement are generally scientifically sound, there are some caveats to consider. First, much of the research draws on data from two states (Florida and North Carolina) and one district (Los Angeles), and the studies focus primarily on achievement in reading and math for third through fifth graders. We do not know the extent to which these findings can be generalized to other jurisdictions, content areas, and grades.

Second, the studies define student learning in a narrow way. Standardized tests of student achievement are not designed to assess the sorts of higher order critical thinking skills that teachers following the board's content standards would be encouraged to focus on. The NBPTS content standards are based on a view of learning in which the focus is on engaging students as active learners. Teachers do this by building on students' experiences and interests and engaging them in activities that are purposeful and meaningful. Given the diversity in students' backgrounds, teachers must continually adjust their plans in order to meet students' needs while simultaneously building on their strengths. This kind of teaching demands thoughtful decision making, which depends, in turn, on a teacher's ability to reflect on his or her practice. This approach to teaching may be very effective and yet not be reflected as higher scores on tests designed to measure basic math and reading skills.

On the basis of our review of the impacts on outcomes for students, we make the following recommendations:

Recommendation 7-1: To the extent that existing data sets allow, we encourage replication of studies that investigate the effects of board-certified teachers on student achievement in states besides North Carolina and Florida, in content areas beyond mathematics and reading, and in grades beyond the elementary levels. Researchers pursuing such studies should work with the national board to obtain the information needed to study the effects of teachers who successfully obtained board certification as well as those who were unsuccessful.

Recommendation 7-2: We encourage studies of the effects of board-certified teachers on outcomes beyond scores on standardized tests, such as student motivation, breadth of achievement, attendance rates, and promotion rates. The choice of outcome measures should reflect the skills that board-certified teachers are expected to demonstrate. Such research should be conducted using sound methodologies, adequate samples, and appropriate statistical analyses.

Impacts on Participating Teachers' Professional Development

The evidence pertaining to this question is scant. Only two studies directly investigate what teachers may learn in the course of the process. While the results suggest that teachers learn from the process, the studies were small in scope and the findings are in need of replication. Several other studies compare the effectiveness of teachers in North Carolina and Florida in terms of their students' reading and mathematics achievement test scores before, during, and after earning board certification. As noted above, the findings from these studies are mixed.

Results from surveys and our own discussions with board-certified teachers indicate that teachers are positive about the experience. Teachers who successfully completed the process report that it is a professionally rewarding experience, and that learning about the board's notion of reflective practice alters their approach to instruction. We note, however, that this evidence is both subjective in nature and collected after the fact. There are no studies that collected baseline data about teachers before going through the process, making it impossible to attribute any findings to the process itself. In fact, while several surveys found that the majority of board-certified teacher respondents say that they participate in leadership activities and mentor other teachers, they also found that these teachers participated in these activities prior to earning board certification. Others reported that administrators discouraged board-certified teachers from assuming responsibilities beyond their primary role of classroom instruction. Furthermore, there are no studies that evaluate the impact of the process on teachers who are unsuccessful.

On the basis of this review, we find that there is not sufficient evidence to draw firm conclusions. We make the following recommendations for additional research:

Recommendation 8-1: We encourage the NBPTS and other researchers to undertake research to investigate the effects of the process on the candidates. The studies should use pretest-posttest and longitudinal designs and should allow for comparison of responses from successful and unsuccessful candidates.

Recommendation 8-2: We encourage the NBPTS and other researchers to pursue more mixed-method studies, using both quantitative and qualitative research methods, to examine the effects of board certification on teachers' practices. These studies should examine a variety of measures of teachers' practices and a variety of student outcomes. Such research should be conducted using sound methodologies, adequate samples, and appropriate statistical analyses.

Recommendation 8-3: Researchers should work with the NBPTS to obtain the information needed to study the relationships between board certification and student achievement across the various stages of board certification. These studies should examine the impacts of the certification process on teachers' effectiveness in increasing their students' test scores and specifically should examine effects for the years subsequent to the receipt of board certification. To the extent that existing data sets allow, we encourage replication of studies in states besides North Carolina and Florida and in subjects beyond elementary reading and mathematics.

Impact on Teachers' Career Paths

A significant goal for an advanced-level certification program is to make the teaching field more appealing to the best teachers and encourage them to stay in it. Goals for the national board include helping to professionalize the field; motivating districts and states to raise salaries for accomplished teachers; motivating districts and states to provide expanded opportunities for leadership in the field; and increasing accomplished teachers' satisfaction with their careers.

Very little information is available to answer questions about this kind of impact. Only one existing study examined teachers' longevity in the field, and the findings were based on teachers' responses to a few survey questions. We conducted analyses of data from the Baccalaureate and Beyond data set, but the sample of teachers included in these analyses was small. Nevertheless, the survey findings suggest that board-certified teachers are more likely than teachers in general to indicate that they plan to remain in teaching, and the results from our own analyses indicate that board-certified teachers do actually stay in teaching at higher rates than other teachers. However, neither the existing study nor our analyses permit causal inferences; that is, they do not indicate whether the NBPTS process causes teachers to stay in the field longer or whether the teachers who choose to become board-certified are already more likely to remain in the profession, regardless of whether they earn certification.

A third study considered whether acquiring board certification increases the mobility of teachers within the profession. Data from one state (North Carolina) show that those who successfully obtain board certification tend to move from one teaching job to another at higher rates than do unsuccessful applicants. These data also indicate that when they move, board-certified teachers are likely to move to teaching assignments with more advantaged conditions, such as schools with higher student achievement levels or fewer poverty-level students. However, it is not clear that this tendency is any more prevalent for board-certified teachers than for other teachers with excellent qualifications.

We caution that only tentative conclusions can be based on the limited evidence. The available research and existing databases did not allow us to answer many of our questions about teachers' career paths. However, we think that there are many ways that data could be collected to address this question. Two viable approaches are through the national board itself and through the School and Staffing Survey managed by the National Center for Education Statistics, which has attempted to obtain such information but needs to revise and clarify its questions on this issue. Our primary finding is that research is needed in this area.

Recommendation 9-1: The NBPTS and other researchers should study the subsequent career choices of teachers who have applied for board certification. The information they collect should be analyzed for successful and unsuccessful candidates separately so the correlation between board certification and career choice can be evaluated. Studies that track teachers over long periods should also be used to examine whether the process alters career choices. The data collected should include information about the extent to which state or district policies influenced the respondents' career choices.

Recommendation 9-2: The National Center for Education Statistics should amend the Schools and Staffing Survey so that it collects information about respondents' board certification status. In designing the survey questions on this topic, The National Center for Education Statistics should pilot-test alternate versions to ensure that respondents will accurately understand the questions.

Recommendation 9-3: Researchers should use the data available from state-level data systems to expand the evidence on the mobility of board-certified teachers. These studies should use methodologies that permit comparisons of teachers' career choices before and after becoming board certified and should compare the choices of unsuccessful applicants for board certification, teachers who successfully obtained the credential, and teachers who did not apply for board certification.

Impacts on the Education System

The Carnegie task force envisioned that the board's influence would reach well beyond any impact that individual board-certified teachers might have on their students. However, there is very little basis for conclusions about whether or not the board has had impacts on the education system, such as improved working conditions for all teachers, influence on the practice of nonboard-certified teachers, or changes in teacher preparation or professional development. These sorts of far-reaching effects are difficult to measure or evaluate in any context, in part because they tend to occur very slowly and to involve complex interactions among the elements of the system.

The foundation for these kinds of impacts has not yet been established, however. Results from qualitative studies indicate that school systems are not making the best uses of their board-certified teachers. Principals and other school administrators sometimes discourage board-certified teachers from assuming responsibilities outside the classroom. Principals worry about showing favoritism toward board-certified teachers and downplay the significance of the credential. Some board-certified teachers report that they conceal their credential so as not to seem to be showing off. These kinds of findings indicate that board certification is simply not widely accepted as a signal of excellence or as an expected way for a teacher to progress professionally.

Despite these negative reports, there are isolated cases in which board-certified teachers are rewarded, used effectively, and offered new opportunities. In these instances, administrators and other teachers are aware of and respect the board-certification process, and board-certified teachers are used as mentors, team leaders, and organizers of professional development activities. In these situations, board certification appears to be viewed as part of a broader commitment to improving professional development and meeting higher standards for teachers.

We think that board-certified teachers are unlikely to have a significant impact without broader endorsements by states, districts, and schools of the NBPTS goals for improving professional development, setting high standard for teachers, and actively using the board-certified teachers in leadership roles. Furthermore, we think that the board certification program is unlikely to have broad systemic effects on the field of teaching unless greater numbers of teachers become board certified and the Carnegie task force's other recommendations—for creating a more effective environment for teaching and learning in schools, increasing the supply of high-quality entrants into the profession, and improving career opportunities for teachers—are implemented.

Our review of the evidence led us to draw the following conclusion:

Conclusion 10-1: There is not yet sufficient research to evaluate the extent to which the NBPTS is having systemic impacts on the teaching field and the education system.

Cost-Effectiveness

The final aspect of our evaluation was to examine the cost-effectiveness of the national board's certification program as a means of improving teacher quality. Our review revealed that, at present, the research base needed to support a cost-effectiveness evaluation of the NBPTS is inadequate. Making a rough calculation of the costs of the program is relatively straightforward, but evaluating its benefits presented significant problems because of a lack of data.

Advanced-level certification of teachers has the potential to offer three kinds of benefits: (1) it can provide a systematic way of identifying high-quality teachers; (2) the process itself can provide a means for teachers to improve their practices; and (3) it can enhance teaching as a career, keeping better teachers in the field and attracting better teacher candidates in the future. The evidence that we have to date suggests that NBPTS certification does provide a means for identifying highly skilled teachers. However, the existing evidence base does not provide sufficient information to assess the latter two benefits.

Simply identifying high-quality teachers provides no direct benefit unless the signal of quality is used in some way. For example, administrators and policy makers could implement incentives for teachers who are identified as highly skilled, either to encourage them to remain in teaching or to encourage them to work in traditionally difficult-to-staff schools. Board certification could also be used as a way of identifying instructional leaders who could then support other teachers and thus pass on their skills to them. While some of these policies have been implemented (e.g., salary bonuses provided to teachers who obtain board certification, providing financial incentives to teach in schools with high needs students), the policies were not implemented in a way that allows an examination of their impacts. One of the most important benefits that might result from the program, keeping high-quality teachers in the profession, could not be evaluated because the necessary data have not been collected. With the exception of isolated instances, there is no evidence that the signal of quality provided by board certification is being used to encourage board-certified teachers to work in difficult schools or to mentor other teachers.

Cost-effectiveness estimates are best understood by comparing them to estimates for other similar interventions. Three interventions that could serve as comparison with the cost-effectiveness of NBPTS are: (1) the American Board for Certification of Teacher Excellence's current plans for certifying distinguished teachers^{SM}, (2) encouraging teachers to pursue master's degrees, and (3) providing inservice professional development. Our cost analysis suggested that the annual per-teacher costs associated with board certification are likely to be lower than the annual per-teacher costs of obtaining a master's degree. However, the evidence about the benefits of master's degrees is too mixed to be able to derive a cost-effectiveness estimate that could be compared with that of board certification. For the other two possible comparisons, even less is known. Thus we conclude:

Conclusion 11-2: At this time, it is not possible to conduct a thorough cost-effectiveness evaluation of the NBPTS because of the paucity of data on the benefits of the program and on both the costs and benefits of other mechanisms intended to improve teacher quality. Such an evaluation should be undertaken if and when the necessary evidence becomes available.

CONCLUDING OBSERVATIONS

The board set out to transform the teaching field in the United States and has been innovative in its approach to this challenge. Its effort to articulate standards for accomplished teaching brought diverse voices to the table, individuals who had never before sat together and discussed the components of excellent teaching—including policy makers, education researchers, teacher union leaders, teachers, and others. In this sense, the process through which these standards for accomplished teaching were developed was innovative, as were the standards themselves. The standards captured a complex conception of accomplished teaching and stimulated thinking about what teachers should know and be able to do. The portfolio-based assessment developed to measure teachers' practice according to these standards pushed the measurement field forward.

The board faced significant obstacles. To accomplish its goals, the board needed to alter deeply entrenched norms and views in the teaching field. Several well-established traditions in teaching were directly antithetical to the NBPTS goals. Structural elements of the field, including typical modes of teacher preparation and professional development as well as state and local policies—and union positions—regarding hiring, compensation, and tenure, for example, in some ways fit poorly with the approach advocated by the NBPTS. Perhaps more important, traditions of egalitarianism and conceptions of instruction as an autonomous and independent activity have been deeply ingrained among teachers. Yet the board's goals called for recognition and rewards for teachers who demonstrate their skills at collaborating with others and make an effort to distinguish themselves from their colleagues by meeting a high standard.

Moreover, measuring the outcomes of teaching (e.g., student learning) plays a much more visible role in education policy today than it did when the national board was established, with the result that expectations for reform efforts have been framed in new ways. The Carnegie task force intended that a transformed teaching profession would naturally improve student learning, but they did not envision this improvement solely or even primarily in terms of increases in students' scores on standardized achievement tests (Carnegie Task Force on Teaching as a Profession, 1986). The NBPTS was part of the strategy for addressing the significant disadvantages to students, teachers, and schools brought about by the perceived second-class status of teaching. The design of the national board's assessment reflected a view of teachers as professional practitioners. The desired outcome was framed as producing teachers who:

- are committed to students and their learning,
- know the subjects they teach and how to teach them,
- take responsibility for managing and monitoring student learning,
- think systematically about their practice and learn from experience, and
- serve as members of learning communities.

Over the years since the board began its work, the policy climate has shifted. Increasingly, students' scores on standardized assessments have become the key components of accountability systems with rewards and sanctions for schools and teachers. The current policy focus on concrete measures of accountability, while not inherently at odds with the national board's original goal of professionalizing teaching, reflects a markedly different conception of what constitutes excellent teaching.

The NBPTS has the potential to make a valuable contribution to efforts to improve teacher quality, together with other reforms intended to create a more effective environment for teaching and learning in schools, increase the supply of high-quality entrants into the profession, and improve career opportunities for teachers. Our review of the research, however, suggests that there is not yet compelling evidence that the existence of the certification program has had a significant impact on the field, teachers, students, or the education system. We note, however, that much of the research needed to evaluate these impacts has not been conducted, in part because the necessary data have not been collected. Moreover, revolutionary changes of the kind the board's founders envisioned would be expected to develop over decades, not years. The founders also intended, as we have repeatedly stressed, that the certification program would be supported by an array of other reforms, many of which have not been implemented. This evaluation thus provides an opportunity to take stock of what has worked well and what has not and to consider changes that are needed to respond to the current policy environment.

We summarize our findings with the following conclusion:

Conclusion 12-1: At its outset, the National Board for Professional Teaching Standards was innovative. Its contribution in three areas is particularly noteworthy: (1) its vision and overall plans for professionalizing the teaching field, (2) the nature of the assessment it developed and the impact it has had on the measurement field, and (3) the development of standards for 25 certificates and assessments for each. However, participation rates are low and few of the other elements of the Carnegie task force's plan, which were to have worked with the certification program, have been carried out.

Moreover, for the board to realize its potential, several key changes in its operation and approach are needed. We judged it to be beyond the scope of our evaluation to make policy recommendations regarding the board's future, so we present these as suggestions to the board leadership. We think that, if the board is to build on its accomplishments and thrive as a means of improving teacher quality in the United States, it will need to attend to the following:

1. The NBPTS must be sure that it conducts its work according to the highest standards for assessment programs, and that its operations are accessible to external scrutiny. Our review reveals that the board has not devoted the same energy that went into the original assessment design into ongoing evaluation of how that design has worked over time or found ways to modify that design in response to problems, such as low reliabilities on some assessments.
2. To be a trusted institution that can have widespread influence, the NBPTS needs to carefully distinguish between objective research and advocacy. In conducting and reporting on its own research and in presenting the research of others, the board should be careful to adhere to scholarly standards.
3. The NBPTS should pursue an ongoing research agenda to evaluate progress toward its goals. The board has ready access to data

relevant to some of the questions we pose in this report (e.g., Does board certification increase retention in the field? What effects does the program have on teachers who are unsuccessful in earning board certification?). We encourage the board to work with researchers to undertake studies of these kinds of questions using scientifically sound, methodologically strong procedures.

4.   The NBPTS should periodically review its assessment model, both to evaluate how it has worked in practice and to adapt to changes in the policy environment and advances in research. As part of such ongoing evaluation efforts, the board should consider whether adjustments are needed in the types of information used as the basis for certification, which might include classroom observations, objective tests of content knowledge, or measures of student performance.

5.   The NBPTS should continue to invest in its larger mission of influencing the teaching field in broad, comprehensive ways.

The national board has produced a viable program for assessing teachers and certifying those who meet its high standards. Data have not been collected to permit evaluation of the extent to which the board has met the other goals it identified, such as creating a more effective environment for teaching and learning in schools, increasing the supply of high-quality entrants into the profession, and improving teacher education and continuing professional development. However, it is important to point out that these are goals that depend on other actors. The board cannot compel states and districts to encourage teachers to participate, to structure teaching schedules to encourage collaboration, or to provide teachers with opportunities to advance professionally as they develop their expertise. The board has no means of influencing teachers' salaries, which have not been brought in line with those in other fields with comparable demands, nor any means of altering teacher preparation or professional development programs.

The board may have done an exemplary job of trying to engage others in these goals, but we had no basis on which to evaluate this aspect of their work and we did not attempt to do so. We do think, however, that is not too late to implement studies to evaluate progress toward these goals. The standards for accomplished teachers have been established, and they were developed to reflect broad consensus regarding what constitutes exemplary teaching. A significant investment has been made in developing the assessment program, and it is operational. It is a ready tool at a time when concern about improving teacher quality is among the issues at the top of the education policy agenda.

In our opinion, the national board has offered a thoughtful approach to serious problems with the way the U.S. education system selects and prepares its teachers and the conditions in which our teachers do their work. Given the magnitude of the problems the board addressed and the lack of systematic data collection systems on such issues as teacher mobility and the career paths of board-certified and nonboard-certified teachers, the lack of evidence of its impact does not necessarily indicate that the board is not having an impact. For the program to have the intended impacts on the teaching field, improvements will be needed, both in the operational aspects of the program and in the evidence collected, as we have recommended throughout this report. The board cannot achieve these goals alone, however. Meeting these ambitious goals will also require a serious commitment by education policy makers to the other recommendations made by the Carnegie Task Force on Teaching as a Profession.

References

Abbott, A. (1988). *The system of professions: An essay on the division of expert labor.* Chicago: University of Chicago Press.

American Board for Certification of Teacher Excellence. (2007). *Elements of the American Board Distinguished Teacher^SM.* Available: http://www.abcte.org/masterteacher/ [accessed November 20, 2007].

American Educational Research Association. (2006). *Standards for reporting on empirical social science research in AERA publications.* Washington, DC: Author.

American Educational Research Association, American Psychological Association, and National Council on Measurement in Education. (1999). *Standards for educational and psychological testing.* Washington, DC: Author.

Angrist, J.D., and Lavy, D. (2001). Does teacher training affect pupil learning? Evidence from matched pairings in Jerusalem public schools. *Journal of Labor Economics, 19*(2), 343-369.

Angus, D.L. (2001). *Professionalism and the public good: A brief history of teacher certification.* Washington, DC: Thomas B. Fordham Foundation.

Arthur, W., Day, E.D., McNelly, T.L., and Edens, P.S. (2003). A meta-analysis of the criterion-related validity of assessment center dimensions. *Personnel Psychology, 56*(1), 125-154.

Baber, A. (2007). *State-level testing requirements for teacher certification.* Available: http://www.ecs.org/clearinghouse/72/92/7292.pdf [accessed November 20, 2007].

Ballou, D., and Podgursky, M. (2000). Gaining control of professional licensing and advancement. In T. Loveless (Ed.), *Conflicting missions: Teachers unions and educational reform.* Washington, DC: Brookings Institution.

Barfield, S.C., and McEnany, J. (2004). *Montana's national board certified teachers' views of the certification process.* Unpublished article, Montana State University-Billings.

Belden, N. (2002). *California teachers' perceptions of national board certification.* Santa Cruz, CA: Center for the Future of Teaching and Learning.

Ben-Porath, Y. (1967). The production of human capital and the life cycle of earnings. *Journal of Political Economy, 75*(4), 352-365.

Betts, J.R., Zau, A.C., and Rice, L.A. (2003). *Determinants of student achievement: New evidence from San Diego.* San Diego: Public Policy Institute of California.

Bohrnstedt, G.W., and Stecher, B.M. (Eds.). (2002). *What we have learned about class size reduction in California.* Sacramento: California Department of Education.

Bond, L. (1998a). Culturally responsive pedagogy and the assessment of accomplished teaching. *Journal of Negro Education, 67*(3), 242-254.

Bond, L. (1998b). Disparate impact and teacher certification. *Journal of Personnel Evaluation in Education, 12*(2), 211-220.

Bond, L., Smith, T., Baker, W.K., and Hattie, J.A. (2000, September). *The certification system of the National Board for Professional Teaching Standards: A construct and consequential validity study.* Greensboro: University of North Carolina, Center for Educational Research and Evaluation. Available: http://www.nbpts.org/resources/research/browse_studies?ID=16 [accessed November 20, 2007].

Boyd, D., Lankford, H., Loeb, S., and Wyckoff, J. (2005). Explaining the short careers of high achieving teachers in schools with low performing students. *American Economic Review, 95,* 166-171.

Bradley, A. (1997). Accreditors shift toward performance. *Education Week, 17*(9). Available: http://www.edweek.org/ew/articles/1997/10/29/09ncate.h17.html [accessed November 26, 2007].

Cantrell, S., Fullerton, J., Kane, T.J., and Staiger, D.O. (2007). *National board certification and teacher effectiveness: Evidence from a random assignment experiment.* A paper developed under a grant from the Spencer Foundation and the U.S. Department of Education. Available: http://harrisschool.uchicago.edu/Programs/beyond/workshops/ppepapers/fall07-kane.pdf [accessed May 2008].

Carnegie Task Force on Teaching as a Profession. (1986). *A nation prepared: Teachers for the 21st century.* Hyattsville, MD: Carnegie Forum on Education and the Economy.

Carnevale, A.P., Fry, R.A., and Lowell, B.L. (2001). Understanding, speaking, reading, writing, and earnings in the immigrant labor market. *The American Economic Review, 91*(2), 159-163. Papers and Proceedings of the Hundred Thirteenth Annual Meeting of the American Economic Association, May.

Carr-Saunders, A.M., and Wilson, P.A. (1964). *The professions.* Oxford, England: Clarendon Press.

Cavalluzzo, L.C. (2004, November). *Is national board certification an effective signal of teacher quality?* Alexandria, VA: CNA Corporation. Available: http://www.nbpts.org/resources/research/browse_studies?ID=11 [accessed November 20, 2007].

Chiswick, B.R., Lee, Y.L., and Miller, P.W. (2002, March). *Schooling, literacy, numeracy and labor market success.* (IZA Discussion Paper No. 450.) Bonn, Germany: Institute for the Study of Labor (IZA). Available: http://ssrn.com/abstract=305369 [accessed July 2008].

Clotfelter, C., Ladd, H.F., and Vigdor, J.L. (2006, Fall). Teacher-student matching and the assessment of teacher effectiveness. *Journal of Human Resources, 41*(4), 778-820. Available: http://www.nber.org/papers/w11936 [accessed June 2008].

Clotfelter, C., Ladd, H.F., and Vigdor, J.L. (2007a, March). *How and why do teacher credentials matter for student achievement?* Working paper 2. National Center for Analysis of Longitudinal Data in Education Research. Available: http://www.caldercenter.org/PDF/1001058_Teacher_Credentials.pdf [accessed November 27, 2007].

Clotfelter, C., Ladd, H.F., and Vigdor, J.L. (2007b, September). *Teacher credentials and student achievement in high school: A cross-subject analysis with student fixed effects.* Available: http://www.caldercenter.org/PDF/1001104_Teacher_Credentials_HighSchool.pdf [accessed November 27, 2007].

Clotfelter, C.T., Ladd, H.F., and Vigdor, J.L. (2007c). Teacher credentials and student achievement: Longitudinal analysis with student fixed effects. *Economics of Education Review, 26*(6), 673-682.

Cohen, C.E., and Rice, J.K. (2005, August). *National board certification as professional development: Design and cost.* Arlington, VA: National Board for Professional Teaching Standards.

Crocker, L. (1997). Assessing content representativeness of performance assessment exercises. *Applied Measurement in Education, 10*(1), 83-95.

Darling-Hammond, L. (1987). Teacher quality and equality. In P. Keating and J.I. Goodlad (Eds.), *Access to knowledge.* New York: College Entrance Examination Board.

Darling-Hammond, L., and Atkin, J.M. (2007, March). *Influences of national board certification on teachers' classroom assessment practices.* Unpublished paper, Stanford University.

Datnow, A., and Stringfield, S. (2000). Working together for reliable school reform. *Journal of Education for Students Placed at Risk, 5*(1 & 2).

Dee, T. (2004). Teachers, race, and student achievement in a randomized experiment. *Review of Economics and Statistics, 86*(1), 195-210.

Desimone, L.M., Porter, A.C., Garet, M.S., Yoon, K.S., and Birman, B.F. (2002). Effects of professional development on teachers' instruction: Results from a three-year longitudinal study. *Educational Evaluation and Policy Analysis, 24*(2), 81-112.

Dilworth, M.E., Aguerrebere, J.A., and Keller-Allen, C. (2006). *National Board for Professional Teaching Standards initial thoughts on the reauthorization of the No Child Left Behind Act.* Excerpts from unpublished manuscript, May. Available: http://www.nbpts.org/resources/research [accessed November 20, 2007].

Dunbar, S.B., Koretz, D., and Hoover, H.D. (1991). Quality control in development and use of performance assessments. *Applied Measurement in Education, 4*(4), 289-304.

Durkheim, E. (1956). *Education and sociology.* (Translated with an introduction by S.D. Fox.) Glencoe, IL: Free Press.

Education Commission of the States. (2004). *ECS report to the nation: State implementation of the No Child Left Behind Act.* Denver, CO: Author.

Fenstermacher, G.D., and Richardson, V. (2005). On making determinations of teacher quality. *Teachers College Record, 107*(1), 186-213.

Ferguson, R.F., and Ladd, H.F. (1996). How and why money matters: An analysis of Alabama schools. In H.F. Ladd (Ed.), *Holding schools accountable: Performance based reform in education.* Washington, DC: Brookings Institution.

Finn, J.D., and Achilles, C.M. (1999). Tennessee's class size study: Findings, implications, misconceptions. *Educational Evaluation and Policy Analysis, 21*(2), 97-109.

Freund, M., Russell, V., and Kavulic, C. (2005, May). *A study of the role of mentoring in achieving certification by the National Board for Professional Teaching Standards.* Available: http://www.nbpts.org/resources/research/browse_studies?ID=19 [accessed July 2008].

Friedman, M. (1995). *Public schools: Make them private.* CATO Institute Briefing Papers. Washington, DC: CATO Institute.

Fullan, M. (2007). *The new meaning of educational change.* New York: Teachers College Press.

Garet, M.S., Porter, A.C., Desimone, L., Birman, B.F., and Yoon, K.S. (2001). What makes professional development effective? Results from a national sample of teachers. *American Educational Research Journal, 38*(4), 915-945.

Goertz, M.E., Floden, R., and O'Day, J. (1995). *Studies of education reform: Systemic reform.* Available: http://www.ncela.gwu.edu/pubs/reports/systemwideconf/sysreform.pdf [accessed November 20, 2007].

Goldhaber, D., and Anthony, E. (2007). Can teacher quality be effectively assessed? National board certification as a signal of effective teaching. *Review of Economics and Statistics, 89*(1), 134-150.

Goldhaber, D., and Brewer, D. (1997). Why don't schools and teachers seem to matter? Assessing the impact of unobservables on educational productivity. *Journal of Human Resources, 32*(3), 505-523.

Goldhaber, D., and Hansen, M. (2007). *National board certification and teacher career paths: Does NBPTS certification influence how long teachers remain in the profession and where they teach?* Arlington, VA: National Board for Professional Teaching Standards. Available: http://www.nbpts.org/resources/research/browse_studies?ID=184 [accessed November 27, 2007].

Goldhaber, D., Perry, D., and Anthony, E. (2003). *Making the grade: Who applies for and earns advanced teacher certification?* Washington, DC: Urban Institute.

Goodlad, J. (1994). *Educational renewal: Better teachers, better schools.* San Francisco: Jossey-Bass.

Guion, R.M. (1998). *Assessment, measurement and prediction for personnel decisions.* Mahwah, NJ: Lawrence Erlbaum Associates.

Guskey, T.R. (2003). What makes professional development effective? *Phi Delta Kappan, 84*(10), 748-763.

Hannaway, J., and Bischoff, K. (2005, April). *Philanthropy and labor market reform in education: The case of the National Board for Professional Teaching Standards and Teach for America.* Prepared for American Enterprise Institute Conference, With the Best of Intentions: Lessons Learned in K-12 Education Philanthropy. Available: http://www.aei.org/event959 [accessed October 2007].

Hanushek, E.A., Kain, J.F., O'Brien, D.M., and Rivkin, S.G. (2005, February). *The market for teacher quality.* National Bureau of Economic Research. Available: http://www.nber.org/papers/w11154 [accessed November 27, 2007].

Harris, D.N., and Sass, T.R. (2006, August). *The effects of NBPTS-certified teachers on student achievement.* Arlington, VA: National Board for Professional Teaching Standards. Available: http://www.nbpts.org/resources/research/browse_studies?ID=139 [accessed November 27, 2007].

Harris, D.N., and Sass, T.R. (2007, February). *Teacher training, teacher quality, and student achievement.* Available: http://www.caldercenter.org/PDF/1001059_Teacher_Training.pdf [accessed November 27, 2007].

Hattie, J. (1996, April). *Validating the specification of a complex content domain.* Paper presented at the annual conference of the American Educational Research Association, New York.

Hattie, J. (2008). Validating the specifications for teaching. Applications to the National Board for Professional Teaching Standards' assessments. In L.C. Ingvarson and J. Hattie (Eds.), *Assessing teachers for professional certification: The first decade of the National Board for Professional Teaching Standards* (pp. 93-112). Amsterdam: Elsevier/JAI Press.

Hawley, W., and Valli, L. (1999). The essentials of effective professional development: A new consensus. In L. Darling-Hammond and G. Sykes (Eds.), *Teaching as the learning profession: Handbook of policy and practice* (pp. 127-150). San Francisco: Jossey-Bass.

Helding, K.A., and Fraser, B.J. (2005, April). *Effectiveness of national board certified teachers in terms of attitudes, classroom environments and achievement among secondary science students.* Paper presented at the annual meeting of the American Educational Research Association, Montreal, Canada.

Hendrie, C. (2004). High schools nationwide pairing down. *Education Week,* June 16.

Hess, F.M. (2004, April-May). *Teacher quality, teacher pay.* Available: http://www.hoover.org/publications/policyreview/3438676.html [accessed May 28, 2008].

Hiebert, J., Gallimore, R., and Stigler, J.W. (2002). A knowledge base for teaching profession: What would it look like and how can we get one? *Educational Researcher, 31*(5), 3-15.

Humphrey, D.C., Koppich, J.E., and Hough, H.J. (2005). Sharing the wealth: National board certified teachers and the students who need them most. *Education Policy Analysis Archives, 13*(18). Available: http://epaa.asu.edu/epaa/v13n18/v13n18.pdf [accessed June 2008].

Indiana Professional Standards Board. (2002, Spring). *Status of national board certified teachers in Indiana*. Indianapolis: Author. Available: http://www.nbpts.org/resources/research/browse_studies?ID=26 [accessed November 27, 2007].

Ingersoll, R. (2001). Teacher turnover and teacher shortages: An organizational analysis. *American Educational Research Journal, 38*(3), 499-534.

Ingersoll, R. (2002a). Teacher quality and educational inequality: The case of Title 1 schools. In M. Wang and K. Wong (Eds.), *Efficiency, accountability, and equity issues in Title I schoolwide program implementation* (pp. 149-182). Greenwich, CT: Information Age Press.

Ingersoll, R. (2002b). The teacher shortages: A case of wrong diagnosis and wrong prescription. *NASSP Bulletin, 86*(631),16-31.

Ingersoll, R. (2008). Teacher quality, educational inequality, and the organization of schools. In A.R. Sadovnik, J. O'Day, G. Bohrnstedt, and K. Borman (Eds.), *No Child Left Behind and the reduction of the achievement gap: Sociological perspectives on federal educational policy* (pp. 153-175). New York: Routledge.

Ingersoll, R., and Perda, D. (2008). [National data on the destination schools of teacher transfers and movers.] Unpublished raw data.

Ingvarson, L.C., and Hattie, J. (Eds). (2008). *Assessing teachers for professional certification: The first decade of the National Board for Professional Teaching Standards*. Amsterdam: Elsevier/JAI Press.

Jacob, B.A., and Lefgren, L. (2004). The impact of teacher training on student achievement: Quasi-experimental evidence from school reform efforts in Chicago. *Journal of Human Resources, 39*(1), 50-79.

Jaeger, R.M. (1998). Evaluating the psychometric qualities of the National Board for Professional Teaching Standards' assessments: A methodological accounting. *Journal of Personnel Evaluation in Education, 12*(2), 189-210.

Jaeger, R.M., Hambleton, R.L., and Plake, B.S. (1995, April). *Eliciting configural performance standards through a sequenced application of complementary methods*. Paper presented at the annual meeting of the American Educational Research Association, San Francisco.

Jencks, C., Bartlett, S., Corcoran, M., Crouse, J., Eaglesfield, D., Jackson, G., McClelland, K., Mueser, P., Olneck, M., Schwartz, J., Ward, S., and Williams, J. (1979). *Who gets ahead? The determinants of economic successes in America*. New York: Basic Books.

Joint Committee on Standards for Educational Evaluation. (1994). *The program evaluation standards: How to assess evaluations of educational programs, 2nd edition*. Thousand Oaks, CA: Sage.

Keller, B. (2006). NBPTS upgrades profession, most agree, despite test-score letdown. *Education Week, 25*(40), 1-14.

Knapp, J.L., McNergney, R.F., Herbert, J.J., and York, H.L. (1990). Should a master's degree be required of all teachers? *Journal of Teacher Education, 41*(2), 27-37.

Koppich, J.E., Humphrey, D.C., and Hough, H.J. (2006). Making use of what teachers know and can do: Policy practice, and national board certification. *Education Policy Analysis Archives, 15*(7), 1-30.

Kraft, N.P. (2001). Standards in teacher education: A critical analysis of NCATE, INTASC, and NBPTS (A Conceptual Paper/Review of the Research). In J. Kincheloe and D. Weil (Eds.), *Standards and schooling in the United States: An encyclopedia*. Santa Barbara, CA: ABC-CLIO.

Labaree, D.F. (2000). On the nature of teaching and teacher education: Difficult practices that look easy. *Journal of Teacher Education, 51*(3), 228-233.

Labaree, D.F. (2004). *The trouble with ed schools*. New Haven: Yale University Press.

Ladd, H., Sass, T.R., and Harris, D.N. (2007). *The impact of national board certified teachers on student achievement in Florida and North Carolina*. Paper prepared for the Committee on Evaluation of Teacher Certification by the National Board for Professional Teaching Standards. Available: http://www7.nationalacademies.org/bota/NBPTS-MTG4-Sass-paper.pdf [accessed November 27, 2007].

Levine, A. (2006). *Educating school teachers*. Washington, DC: Education Schools Project.

Lewis, C., and Tsuchida, I. (1998). A lesson is like a swiftly flowing river: Research lessons and the improvement of Japanese education. *American Educator*, Winter, 12-17, 50-52.

Linn, R.L. (1993). Linking results of distinct assessments. *Applied Measurement in Education, 6*(1), 83-102.

Little, J.W. (1990). The persistence of privacy: Autonomy and initiative in teachers' professional relations. *Teachers College Record, 91*(4), 509-536.

Lockwood, J.R., McCaffrey, D.F., Hamilton, L., Stecher, B., Le, V., and Martinez, F. (2007). The sensitivity of value-added teacher effect estimates to different mathematics achievement measures. *Journal of Educational Measurement, 44*(1), 47-67.

Lord, B. (1994). Teachers' professional development: Critical colleagueship and the role of professional communities. In N. Cobb (Ed.), *The future of education: Perspectives on national standards in America*. New York: College Board.

Lortie, D.C. (2002). *Schoolteacher* (2nd edition). Chicago: University of Chicago Press.

Loyd, B. (1995, February). *Content validation of the National Board for Professional Teaching Standards early adolescence generalist assessment* (technical report). Arlington, VA: National Board for Professional Teaching Standards.

Lucas, C.J. (1999). *Teacher education in America*. New York: St. Martin's Press.

Lustick, D., and Sykes, G. (2006). National board certification as professional development: What are teachers learning? *Education Policy Analysis Archives, 14*(5). Available: http://epaa.asu.edu/epaa/v14n5 [accessed March 1, 2006].

Marcoulides, G.A. (1990). An alternative method for estimating variance components in generalizability theory. *Psychological Reports, 66*(2), 379-386.

McCaffrey, D.F., and Rivkin, S.G. (2007). *Empirical investigations of the effects of national board teacher standards certified teachers on student outcomes*. Paper prepared for the Committee on Evaluation of Teacher Certification by the National Board for Professional Teaching Standards. Available: http://www7.nationalacademies.org/bota/NBPTS-MTG4-McCaffrey-Paper.pdf [accessed November 27, 2007].

McColskey, W., Stronge, J.H., Ward, T.J., Tucker, P.D., Howard, B., Lewis, K., and Hindman, J.L. (2005, June). *Teacher effectiveness, student achievement, and national board certified teachers*. Arlington, VA: National Board for Professional Teaching Standards. Available: http://www.nbpts.org/UserFiles/File/Teacher_Effectiveness_Student_Achievement_and_National_Board_Certified_Teachers_D_-_McColskey.pdf [accessed June 2008].

McIntosh, S., and Vignoles, A. (2001). Measuring and assessing the impact of basic skills on labour market outcomes. *Oxford Economic Papers, 53*, 453-481.

McLaughlin, M.W., and Talbert, J.E. (2001). *Professional communities and the work of high school teaching*. Chicago: University of Chicago Press.

Monk, D.H. (1994). Subject area preparation of secondary math and science teachers and student achievement. *Economics of Education Review, 13*(2), 125-145.

Moore, J.W. (2002, December). *Perceived barriers to the National Board for Professional Teaching Standards certification.* Unpublished dissertation, East Tennessee State University.

Murray, F.B. (2001). From consensus standards to evidence of claims: Assessment and accreditation in the case of teacher education. *New Directions for Higher Education, 2001*(113), 49-66.

National Board for Professional Teaching Standards. (1991). *Initial policies and perspectives of the National Board for Professional Teaching Standards* (3rd edition). Detroit: Author.

National Board for Professional Teaching Standards. (1998). *Middle childhood through early adolescence/mathematics standards.* Arlington, VA: Author. Available: http://www.nbpts.org/the_standards/standards_by_cert?ID=8&x=36&y=5 [accessed November 26, 2007].

National Board for Professional Teaching Standards. (1999). *What teachers should know and be able to do.* Arlington, VA: Author.

National Board for Professional Teaching Standards. (2001a). *I am a better teacher.* Arlington, VA: Author. Available: http://www.nbpts.org/resources/research/browse_studies?ID=25 [accessed November 27, 2007].

National Board for Professional Teaching Standards. (2001b). *Middle childhood generalist standards.* Arlington, VA: Author. Available: http://www.nbpts.org/the_standards/standards_by_cert?ID=27&x=47&y=6 [accessed November 26, 2007].

National Board for Professional Teaching Standards. (2001c). *NBPTS middle childhood generalist standards* (2nd edition). Arlington, VA: Author. Available: http://www.nbpts.org/the_standards/standards_by_cert?ID=27&x=51&y=10 [accessed November 20, 2007].

National Board for Professional Teaching Standards. (2001d). *The impact of national board certification on teachers: A survey of national board-certified teachers and assessors. An NBPTS research report.* Arlington, VA: Author. Available: http://www.nbpts.org/resources/research/browse_studies?ID=23 [accessed November 20, 2007].

National Board for Professional Teaching Standards. (2001e). *National board certification candidate survey.* Arlington, VA: Author.

National Board for Professional Teaching Standards. (2006a). *2006 guide to national board certification.* Arlington, VA: Author. Available: http://www.nbpts.org/UserFiles/File/51049_web.pdf [accessed November 20, 2007].

National Board for Professional Teaching Standards. (2006b). *Middle child generalist scoring guide, effective 2006.* Arlington, VA: Author. Available: http://www.nbpts.org/for_candidates/scoring?ID=27&x=59&y=3 [accessed November 20, 2007].

National Board for Professional Teaching Standards. (2006c). *Early adolescence mathematics scoring guide, effective 2006.* Arlington, VA: Author. Available: http://www.nbpts.org/index.cfm?t=downloader.cfm&id=464 [accessed November 26, 2007].

National Board for Professional Teaching Standards. (2006d). *Early adolescence mathematics portfolio instructions.* Arlington, VA: Author. Available: http://www.nbpts.org/for_candidates/the_portfolio?ID=8&x=63&y=10 [accessed November 26, 2007].

National Board for Professional Teaching Standards. (2006e). *Middle childhood generalist portfolio instructions.* Arlington, VA: Author. Available: http://www.nbpts.org/for_candidates/the_portfolio?ID=27&x=63&y=8 [accessed November 26, 2007].

National Board for Professional Teaching Standards. (2006f, May). *Standards development handbook.* Arlington, VA: Author.

National Board for Professional Teaching Standards. (2007, March). *Technical report: Draft.* Arlington, VA: Author.

National Commission for Certifying Agencies. (2004). *Standards for the accreditation of certification programs.* Washington, DC: National Organization for Competency Assurance.

National Commission on Excellence in Education. (1983). *A nation at risk: The imperative for educational reform*. Washington, DC: U.S. Department of Education.

National Commission on Excellence in Education. (1984). *A nation at risk: The full account*. Portland, OR: USA Research.

National Commission on Teaching and America's Future. (2003). *No dream denied: A pledge to America's children*. Washington, DC: Author.

National Council for Accreditation of Teacher Education. (2004). *NCATE at 50: Continuous growth, renewal, and reform*. Available: http://www.ncate.org/documents/15YearsofGrowth.pdf [accessed November 2007].

National Council on Teacher Quality. (2004). *Searching the attic: How states are responding to the nation's goal of placing a highly qualified teacher in every classroom*. NCTQ Reports. Available: http://www.nctq.org/nctq/publications [accessed November 2007].

National Research Council. (2001). *Testing teacher candidates: The role of licensure tests in improving teacher quality*. Committee on Assessment and Teacher Quality, K.J. Mitchell, D.Z. Robinson, B.S. Plake, and K.T. Knowles (Eds.). Board on Testing and Assessment, Center for Education, Division of Behavioral and Social Sciences and Education. Washington, DC: National Academy Press.

National Research Council. (2002). *Scientific research in education*. Committee on Scientific Principles for Education Research, R.J. Shavelson and L. Towne (Eds.). Center for Education, Division of Behavioral and Social Sciences and Education. Washington, DC: National Academy Press.

Norcini, J.J., Lipner, R.S., and Kimball, H.R. (2002). Certifying examination performance and patient outcomes following acute myocardial infarction. *Medical Education, 36*, 853-859.

Nye, B., Spyros, K., and Hedges, L.V. (2004). How large are teacher effects? *Educational Evaluation and Policy Analysis, 26*(3), 237-257.

Oakes, J. (1990). *Multiplying inequalities: The effects of race, social class, and tracking on opportunities to learn mathematics and science*. Santa Monica, CA: RAND Corporation.

Palmer, P., Hartke, D.D., Ree, M.J., Welsh, J.R., and Valentine, L.D. (1988). *Armed services vocational aptitude battery (ASVAB): Alternative forms reliability (Forms 8, 9, 10 and 11)*. (AFHRL-TP No. 87-48.) Brooks Air Force Base, TX: Air Force Human Resources Laboratory.

Pedhazur, E.J. (1982). *Multiple regression in behavioral research*. Ft. Worth, TX: Harcourt Brace Jovanovich.

Perda, D. (2007, June). *Who are the national board certified teachers?* Paper prepared for the Committee on Evaluation of Teacher Certification by the National Board for Professional Teaching Standards.

Plake, B.S., Hambleton, R.K., and Jaeger, R.M. (1997). A new standard-setting method for performance assessments: The dominant profile judgment method and some field test results. *Educational and Psychological Measurement, 57*, 400-411.

Porter, A.C., Garet, M.S., Desimone, L., Yoon, K.S., and Birman, B.F. (2000, October). *Does professional development change teaching practice? Results from a three-year study*. Report to the U.S. Department of Education, Office of the Under Secretary, on Contract No. EA97001001 to the American Institutes for Research. Washington, DC: Pelavin Research Center.

Raudenbush, S., Fotiu, R., and Cheong, Y. (1998). Inequality of access to educational resources. *Educational Evaluation and Policy Analysis, 20*, 253-267.

Reynolds, D.J. (1999). *Assessing the assessor: Understanding the reliability of assessor judgment*. Paper presented at the 27th International Congress on Assessment Center Methods, Orlando, FL.

Richardson, V. (Ed.). (2001). *Handbook of research on teaching* (4th edition). Washington, DC: American Educational Research Association.

Rivkin, S.G., Hanushek, E.A., and Kain, J.F. (2005, March). Teachers, schools, and academic achievement. *Econometrica, 73*(2), 417-458.

Rossi, P.H., Lipsey, M.W., and Freeman, H.E. (2004). *Evaluation: A systematic approach.* Thousand Oaks, CA: Sage.

Rotherham, A. (2004, March). *Opportunity and responsibility for national board certified teachers.* Progressive Policy Institute Policy Report. Washington, DC: Progressive Policy Institute.

Rothstein, J. (2008, April). *Unobserved heterogeneity, fixed effects, and causal inference.* Paper presented at the National Conference on Value-Added Modeling, Madison, WI.

Russell, T., Putka, D., and Waters, S. (2007, October). *Review of the psychometric quality of the national board assessments.* Paper prepared for the Committee on Evaluation of Teacher Certification by the National Board for Professional Teaching Standards.

Sackett, P.R., Schmitt, N., Ellingson, J.E., and Kabin, M.B. (2001). High stakes testing in employment, credentialing, and higher education: Prospects in a post-affirmative action world. *American Psychologist, 56,* 302-318.

Sanders, W.J., Ashton, J.J., and Wright, S.P. (2005). *Comparison of the effects of NBPTS-certified teachers with other teachers on the rate of student academic progress.* Arlington, VA: National Board for Professional Teaching Standards. Available: http://www.nbpts.org/resources/research/browse_studies?ID=15 [accessed November 27, 2007].

Schön, D.A. (1983). *The reflective practitioner: How professionals think in action.* New York: Basic Books.

Scriven, M. (1991). *Evaluation thesaurus* (4th edition). Thousand Oaks, CA: Sage.

Sedlak, M., and Schlossman, S. (1986). *Who will teach? Historical perspectives on the changing appeal of teaching as a profession.* Center for the Study of the Teaching Profession, RAND Corporation.

Sewell, W.H., Hauser, R.M., and Featherman, D.L. (Eds.). (1976). *Schooling and achievement in American society.* New York: Academic Press.

Shulman, L.S., and Sykes, G. (1986). *A national board for teachers? In search of a bold standard.* Paper prepared for the Task Force on Teaching as a Profession. Carnegie Forum on Education and the Economy. New York: Carnegie Corporation.

Smith, T.W., Gordon, B., Colby, S.A., and Wang, J. (2005). *An examination of the relationship between depth of student learning and national board-certification status.* Arlington, VA: National Board for Professional Teaching Standards. Available: http://www.nbpts.org/UserFiles/File/Applachian_State_study_D_-_Smith.pdf [accessed June 2008].

Society for Industrial and Organizational Psychology. (2003). *Principles for the validation and use of personnel selection procedures.* Bowling Green, OH: Author.

Stecher, B.M., Bohrnstedt, G.W., Kirst, M., McRobbie, J., and Williams, T. (2001). Class-size reduction in California: A story of hope, promise, and unintended consequences. *Phi Delta Kappan, 82*(9), 670-674.

Stevenson, H.W., and Stigler, J.W. (1992). *The learning gap: Why our schools are failing and what we can learn from Japanese and Chinese education.* New York: Simon & Schuster.

Stigler, J., and Hiebert, J. (1997). Understanding and improving mathematics instruction: An overview of the TIMSS video study. *Phi Delta Kappan, 79*(1), 14-21.

Stinebrickner, T., Scafidi, B., and Sjoquist, D. (2003). *The relationship between school characteristics and teacher mobility.* Unpublished manuscript, University of Western Ontario, Department of Economics.

Stone, J.E. (2002). *The value-added achievement gains of NBPTS-certified teachers in Tennessee: A brief report.* Johnson City, TN: Education Consumers Clearinghouse. Available: http://www.education-consumers.com/briefs/stoneNBPTS.shtm [accessed June 2008].

Sykes, G., and Wilson, S. (1988). *Professional standards for teaching: The assessment of teacher knowledge and skills.* Charleston, WV: Appalachia Educational Laboratory.

Sykes, G., Anagnostopoulos, D., Cannata, M., Chard, L., Frank, K., McCrory, R., and Wolfe, E. (2006). *National board-certified teachers as organizational resource.* Arlington, VA: National Board for Professional Teaching Standards. Available: http://www.nbpts.org/resources/research/browse_studies?ID=174 [accessed November 27, 2007].

Tamblyn, R., Abrahamowicz, M., Brailovsky, C., Grand'Maison, P., Lescop, J., Norcini, J., Girard, N., and Haggerty, J. (1998). Association between licensing examination scores and resource use and quality of care in primary care practice. *Journal of the American Medical Association, 280*(11), 989-996.

Tamblyn, R., Abrahamowicz, M., Dauphinee, W.D., Hanley, J.A., Norcini, J., Girard, N., Grand'Maison, P., and Brailovsky, C. (2002). *Journal of the American Medical Association, 288*(23), 3019-3026.

Tom, A.R. (1984). *Teaching as a moral craft.* New York: Longman.

Tsacoumis, S. (2007). Assessment centers. In D.L. Whetzel and G.R. Wheaton (Eds.), *Applied measurement: Industrial psychology in human resources management.* Mahwah, NJ: Lawrence Erlbaum.

Tucker, M. (1995). *A nation prepared: Teachers for the 21st century.* Report of the Carnegie Forum on Education and the Economy's Task Force on Teaching as a Profession. In D.N. Planck (Ed.), *Commissions, reports, reforms, & educational policy.* Westport, CT: Greenwood Publishing Group.

Tyack, D., and Cuban, L. (1996). *Tinkering toward utopia: A century of public school reform.* Cambridge, MA: Harvard University Press.

Tyler, J.H., Murnane, R.J., and Willett, J.B. (2000, May). Estimating the labor market signaling value of the GED. *Quarterly Journal of Economics, 115*(2), 431-468.

U.S. Department of Education. (2001). *Public law print of the No Child Left Behind Act of 2001.* Available: http://www.ed.gov/policy/elsec/leg/esea02/index.html [accessed July 2007].

U.S. Department of Education, Office of Postsecondary Education. (2006). *The Secretary's fifth annual report on teacher quality: A highly qualified teacher in every classroom.* Washington, DC: Author.

Vandervoort, L.G., Amrein-Beardsley, A., and Berliner, D.C. (2004). National board certified teachers and their students' achievement. *Education Policy Analysis Archives, 12*(46).

Walsh, K., and Jacobs, S. (2007). *Alternative certification isn't alternative.* Thomas B. Fordham Institute, National Council on Teacher Quality. Available: http://www.heartland.org/pdf/22264.pdf [accessed June 2008].

Wang, J., and Paine, L.W. (2003). Learning to teach with mandated curriculum and public examination of teaching as contexts. *Teaching and Teacher Education, 19*(1), 75-94.

Wayne, A.J. (2002). Teacher inequality: New evidence on disparities in teachers' academic skills. *Education Policy Analysis Archives, 10*(3). Available: http://epaa.asu.edu/epaa/v10n30/ [accessed July 2008].

Wayne, A., Chang-Ross, C., Daniels, M., Knowles, K., Mitchell, K., and Price, T. (2004). *Exploring differences in minority and majority teachers' decisions about and preparation for NBPTS certification.* Arlington, VA: SRI International.

Wilensky, H.L. (1964). The professionalization of everyone? *American Journal of Sociology, 70*(2), 137-158.

Wilson, S.M., and Berne, J. (1999). Teacher learning and the acquisition of professional knowledge: An examination of research on contemporary professional development. *Review of Research in Education, 24*, 173-209.

Appendix A

Reviews of Studies That Provided Evidence for the Evaluation

This appendix provides additional details about the studies that provided the bulk of the evidence for our evaluation. Box A-1 presents the primary questions on our evaluation framework, and for each study, we describe the specific relevance to the framework as well as the general purpose, the participants, and the findings. Also, for each study we provide a comment section that highlights the primary contributions of the study as well as any concerns the committee had about the methodology that affected the weight we placed on the findings. We hope that these comments will assist researchers with future investigations intended to build on this body of research.

Barfield, S.C., and McEnany, J. (2004). *Montana's national board-certified teachers' views of the certification process.* Unpublished article, Montana State University-Billings.

Relevance to evaluation framework: Question 3 (Chapter 6).

Purpose: The authors sought to determine why more teachers in Montana had not pursued board certification.

Subjects/participants: National board-certified teachers (NBCTs) in Montana.

Methodology and findings: Barfield and McEnany queried NBCTs in Montana about their certification experience. In spring 2003, the authors distributed surveys to the 31 NBCTs in the state and received responses from 22 (71 percent response rate). The survey instrument was adopted

---

BOX A-1
The Committee's Evaluation Framework

Question 1: To what extent does the certification program for accomplished teachers clearly and accurately specify advanced teaching practices and the characteristics of teachers (the knowledge, skills, dispositions, and judgments) that enable them to carry out advanced practice? Does it do so in a manner that supports the development of a well-aligned test?

Question 2: To what extent do the assessments associated with the certification program for accomplished teachers reliably measure the specified knowledge, skills, dispositions, and judgments of certification candidates, and support valid interpretations of the results? To what extent are the performance standards for the assessments and the process for setting them justifiable and reasonable?

Question 3: To what extent do teachers participate in the program?

Question 4: To what extent does the advanced-level certification program identify teachers who are effective at producing positive student outcomes, such as learning, motivation, school engagement, breadth of achievement, educational attainment, attendance rates, and grade promotion?

Question 5: To what extent do teachers improve their practices and the outcomes of their students by virtue of going through the advanced-level certification process?

Question 6: To what extent and in what ways are the career paths of both successful and unsuccessful candidates affected by their participation in the program?

Question 7: Beyond its effects on candidates, to what extent and in what ways does the certification program have an impact on the field of teaching, the education system, or both?

Question 8: To what extent does the advanced-level certification program accomplish its objectives in a cost-effective manner, relative to other approaches intended to improve teacher quality?

---

from one used by the National Board for Professional Teaching Standards (NBPTS) in their survey of candidates in fall 2001 (National Board for Professional Teaching Standards, 2001e). The authors sought to determine why more teachers in Montana had not pursued board certification and thus added questions to the instrument to ask the respondents if they knew other teachers who were interested in earning board certification but had not yet done so.

Reasons for not pursuing board certification included the time commitment, the cost, the support required to complete the process (e.g., the videotaping and portfolio assembly), and lack of administrator support. The respondents also said teachers were concerned about the consequences. For example, they said some teachers thought it was very public and too risky, some were fearful of not being successful, and some had observed harassment of teachers who do become certified.

Comments: This study is one of the few that address nonparticipation in the program, and the findings are useful in that regard. However, the sample for this study was very small, and the participants may not have been the most appropriate to query about the questions in which the investigators were most interested. That is, it would have been better to ask nonparticipants why they had not pursued board certification instead of asking NBCTs to speculate about their nonparticipating colleagues. This provides a first step in learning about reasons for not participating, and the findings could serve as a basis for future studies with nonparticipants.

Belden, N. (2002). *California teachers' perceptions of national board certification.* Santa Cruz, CA: Center for the Future of Teaching and Learning.

Relevance to evaluation framework: Question 3 (Chapter 6); Question 6 (Chapter 8); Question 7 (Chapter 10).

Purpose: The author sought to gather information about teachers' reasons for pursuing board certification.

Subjects/participants: NBCTs in California.

Methodology and findings: Beldon surveyed all NBCTs in California (n = 785) in summer 2001 and received responses from 519 (68 percent response rate). A focus group discussion was also held in June 2001 in Sacramento; comments from this activity are incorporated into the paper. The survey asked NBCTs about their motivations for pursuing certification and the effects of the process on them and their teaching. It also gathered information about the type of school in which the NBCTs work.

Most respondents said that they pursued certification because it was a personal challenge (84 percent) and provided an opportunity to strengthen their teaching (79 percent). Between 54 and 59 percent reported that they pursued certification to receive the state's monetary compensations. The opportunity for career advancement was also important to more than half (53 percent), as was the prospect of receiving recognition of one's teaching qualities (50 percent).

Comments: Strengths of this study are its large sample size and response rate, relative to other studies of this nature, as well as the use of focus groups to follow up the survey results. An issue that should be considered in interpreting the findings is that all survey questions are all worded positively;

there is no opportunity for a respondent to say the process did not have an effect on his or her teaching. The only exception is the question: "Do you feel that the certification process made you a much better teacher, somewhat better, or did not impact your practice?" The inclusion of both positively and negatively worded questions would have increased the objectivity of the survey and would have helped the researchers to detect problems with response sets (i.e., the tendency for respondents to respond in a given way or to select what he or she regards as an acceptable response).

Bond, L., Smith, T., Baker, W.K., and Hattie, J.A. (2000, September). *The certification system of the National Board for Professional Teaching Standards: A construct and consequential validity study.* Greensboro: University of North Carolina, Center for Educational Research and Evaluation.

Relevance to evaluation framework: Questions 1 and 2 (Chapter 5).

Purpose: This study was a validity investigation that sought to evaluate the extent to which teachers who achieved board certification exhibited the assessed knowledge, dispositions, skills, and judgments as part of their actual classroom practices.

Subjects/participants: Participants were first-time candidates who had attempted certification in one of two areas: early adolescence English language arts and middle childhood generalist. The sample included 65 teachers working in Delaware, Maryland, North Carolina, Ohio, or Virginia, 31 NBCTs and 34 non-NBCTs.

Methodology and findings: The authors used a two-pronged approach to investigate the validity of the NBPTS. They first attempted to validate the qualities assessed on the NBPTS assessments through a literature review. They reviewed the literature and tried to identify the dimensions of accomplished teaching. Then they observed teachers who had participated in the NBPTS assessment and rated them on the identified dimensions.

Through their literature review, they identified 15 dimensions: (1) use of knowledge; (2) identifying essential representations: deep representations; (3) identifying essential representations: problem solving; (4) setting goals for diverse learners: improvisation; (5) setting goals for diverse learners: challenge of objectives; (6) guiding learning through classroom interactions: classroom climate; (7) guiding learning through classroom interactions: multidimensional perception; (8) guiding learning through classroom interactions: sensitivity to context; (9) monitoring learning and providing feedback; (10) monitoring learning and providing feedback: test hypotheses; (11) respect for students; (12) passion for teaching and learning; (13) motivation and self-efficacy; (14) outcomes of lessons: surface and deep; and (15) outcomes of lessons: achievement. They then developed protocols for evaluating each of the dimensions. Dimensions 1 through 13 were evaluated by observing teachers in their classrooms; Dimensions 14 and 15 involved review of student work and achievement.

To identify the sample, the authors used performance results for teachers who had taken the NBPTS assessments. Using the NBPTS score data, they grouped teachers as follows: (1) total score at least 1.25 standard deviations (SDs) below the cut score; (2) total score between 0.25 and 0.75 SDs below the cut score; (3) total score between 0.25 and 0.75 SDs above the cut score; and (4) total score at least 1.25 SDs above the cut score. They used this strategy to maximize the possibility of detecting differences among the groups. The list of teachers who fell into each group was randomized, and teachers were recruited until a sufficient number was obtained for the particular group.

Ultimately, between 15 and 17 candidates were recruited for each group. Teachers' performance with regard to these dimensions was evaluated through a variety of mechanisms, including classroom observations, reviews of teacher assignments and students' work, interviews with students, student questionnaires that asked about classroom environment and climate and evaluated students' motivation and self-efficacy, and students' performance on a writing assessment.

With regard to Dimensions 1 through 13, the results from classroom observations revealed that NBCTs scored higher on all of these dimensions than did the non-NBCTs; the differences were statistically significant ($p < .05$) on 11 of the 13 dimensions.

Analyses of student work indicated that 74 percent of the work samples of students taught by NBCTs reflected deep understanding, while 29 percent of the work samples of non-NBCTs were judged to reflect deep understanding. On the writing tasks, the mean was slightly higher for students taught by NBCTs than by non-NBCTs, but the differences were not significant ($p > .05$).

Differences between NBCTs and non-NBCTs were negligible with regard to student motivation and self-efficacy levels. The authors also compared teachers on their participation in professional activities, including (1) collaborative activities with other professionals to improve the effectiveness of the school and (2) to engage parents and others in the community in the education of young people. Again, differences between NBCTs and non-NBCTs were negligible.

Comments: This is a comprehensive study that examines construct-based validity evidence for the assessments for two NBPTS certificates. It draws from the literature on effective teaching to develop protocols for evaluating teachers and then compares teachers' ratings on these protocols with their performance on the NBPTS. Studies of this nature are challenging to carry out. One issue with this study is that the authors' description of the sampling procedures is somewhat vague. The report indicates that they recruited teachers via phone calls, and they provide the verbatim protocol for recruiting teachers, but they do not provide any details about this process. They do not specify how many calls were required in order to obtain the necessary numbers of participants for each of the four NBPTS score groups or whether it was more difficult to fill any of the groups. It would have been useful to know how representative the participating samples of teachers were of the full set of individuals identified for each score group.

Cantrell, S., Fullerton, J., Kane, T.J., and Staiger, D.O. (2007, April 16). *National board certification and teacher effectiveness: Evidence from a random assignment experiment.* Unpublished paper. A paper developed under a grant from the Spencer Foundation and the U.S. Department of Education. Available: http://harrisschool.uchicago.edu/programs/beyond/workshops/ppepapers/fall07-kane.pdf [accessed May 2008].

   Relevance to evaluation framework: Question 4 (Chapter 7).
   Purpose: The authors examined the relationships between board certification and student achievement.
   Subjects/participants: NBPTS applicants and non-NBPTS applicants teaching grades 3-5 in the Los Angeles Unified School District during the 2003-2004 and 2004-2005 school years.
   Methodology and findings: In this study, the authors were able to implement random assignment of classrooms to teachers. To accomplish this, NBPTS provided them with a list of applicants for board certification. Each applicant in the sample was matched with a nonapplicant comparison teacher in the same school and grade (comparison teachers had at least three years experience); 99 pairs of teachers participated. Classrooms were randomly assigned to teachers in this "experimental sample" (although students were not randomly assigned to classrooms). Another "nonexperimental sample" of NBPTS applicants and nonapplicants was also identified to allow the researchers to study the effects of random and nonrandom assignment.
   Analyses used the covariate model (lagged achievement test score) and the gain score model, as well as a set of student characteristics, classroom peer characteristics, and fixed effects for school by grade by administrative track by year. The NBPTS certification status variables included passed, failed, or withdrawn. The researchers obtained assessment results for the teacher applicants, which included both the pass/fail score and the numeric scores on each of the components of the assessment. They examined the extent to which different weightings of the component scores altered the relationship between certification status and students' test score gains.
   The authors found that teachers who applied for board certification but were unsuccessful were less effective than nonapplicant teachers. The

coefficients for the unsuccessful group were always negative—specifically, with the covariate model, –.17 for math and –.13 for reading; and with the gain score model, –.36 for math and –.21 for reading. Comparison of the coefficients for teachers who achieved board certification and teachers who were unsuccessful revealed that the differences were statistically significant (or approached significance with p = .05). They summarize this finding saying that the board-certified teachers outperformed the unsuccessful applicants by 0.2 standard deviations in math and language arts. No statistically significant differences were found in comparisons of NBCTs and nonapplicants.

The results for the nonexperimental group demonstrated the same patterns, but the effect sizes were smaller.

Comments: This study makes a significant contribution in its use of random assignment of students to teachers, which helps to control for preexisting differences among the groups of students assigned to board-certified and nonboard-certified teachers. By randomly assigning students to teachers, the study removed many of the potential threats to the validity of inferences about the effectiveness of NBCTs. In addition, the study restricted the comparison teachers to those with at least three years of teaching experience to make them more like the NBCTs. However, it was not able to match more closely in terms of experience and it did not include years of experience as a control variable in the analyses. So it is possible the NBCTs and their matched pair teachers might differ in terms of experience. The authors also report some student switches after assignment (less than 15 percent) that might also have affected the results.

Cavalluzzo, L.C. (2004, November). *Is national board certification an effective signal of teacher quality?* Alexandria, VA: CNA Corporation. Available: http://www.nbpts.org/resources/research/browse_studies?ID=11 [accessed November 20, 2007].

Relevance to evaluation framework: Question 4 (Chapter 7).

Purpose: The author examined the relationships between board certification and student achievement.

Subjects/participants: Students of NBCTs and non-NBCTs teaching 9th and 10th grade mathematics in Miami–Dade County, Florida, during the 2000-2001 to 2002-2003 school years. The sample included 107,997 students and 2,137 teacher-years. It includes all the NBCTs teaching the selected grades during the chosen school years. Student scores on the state's end of grade accountability test (the Florida Comprehensive Assessment Test, Sunshine Standards Tests) provide the measure of student outcomes.

Methodology and findings: The author used education production function methods to study differences between the outcomes of students taught by NBCTs, current NBPTS applicants, teachers who applied for but did not receive NBPTS certification, and other teachers. The covariates used in the models are detailed student background variables, including grade level, age, gender, race/ethnicity, English language proficiency, participation in free or reduced price meal programs, grade retention, gifted status, special education status, school suspensions, days absent, grade point average, math effort and conduct, and whether the students' math class was above, below, or at grade level.

The models also included teacher background variables: whether or not the teacher is teaching in the subject area of certification, the salary step (as a measure of years of experience), certification status, whether or not the teacher has a graduate degree, and the selectivity of the teacher's undergraduate college or university.

The production function used a linear model that included these variables and the student's prior year math score to predict current scores. Some models also included variables measuring school attributes, and others included school fixed effects—that is, indicator variables for each school that equal 1 if the student attended the school and 0 otherwise. Scores from 9th and 10th grade students were combined into a single data set and fit to a single model.

The author found that after adjusting for all the variables mentioned above, the test scores of students whose teachers were NBCTs were statistically significantly higher than students whose teachers had no participation with NBPTS. Similarly, students whose teachers were currently NBCT applicants scored statistically significantly higher than students whose teachers had no participation with NBPTS; students whose teachers applied for NBPTS certification but failed to be certified scored statistically significantly lower than students whose teachers had no participation with NBPTS. For the author's preferred model, the effect sizes were about 0.07 (standard deviations) for NBCTs, 0.02 for current applicants, and –0.02 for teachers who failed to receive certification. These results were relatively insensitive to variations in the model, including the use of student fixed effects instead of using prior year scores as a covariate.

Comments: This study is one of the few that focus on high school students and teachers. The study used a large sample of students and explored several different models, which helps to evaluate the consistency of findings across models. One concern with this study is that the analysis does not account for the fact that student test scores are nested within classes, within schools. Given that the effect sizes are small, it is very likely that many would not be statistically significant if this clustering was accounted for.

A second concern is that the model does not account for the course content, and NBCTs might not be teaching courses with the same content as other teachers. This could result in the confounding of content and NBCT effects. There is no discussion of course content, so the possible extent of bias cannot be assessed. Course content is particularly important with high school mathematics students because the content is highly differentiated across courses but the tests are not course specific.

Clotfelter, C.T., Ladd, H.F., and Vigdor, J.L. (2007, March). *How and why do teacher credentials matter for achievement?* Working paper 2. National Center for Analysis of Longitudinal Data in Education Research. Available: http://www.caldercenter.org/PDF/1001058_Teacher_Credentials.pdf [accessed November 27, 2007].

Relevance to evaluation framework: Question 4 (Chapter 7); Question 5 (Chapter 8).

Purpose: The study examines the relationships between student achievement and board certification status.

Subjects/participants: North Carolina students in grades 3, 4, and 5 for the 1994-1995 to the 2003-2004 school years and their teachers.

Methodology and findings: In this study, the authors model the relationship between a variety of teacher characteristics and student achievement test scores. The study used a production function approach and a series of alternative specifications for the model. To motivate their model, the authors first introduce a simplified model for student achievement with the assumption that the effects of teacher quality on student achievement were the same at every grade level and were constant across all years of the study. In addition, they assumed that these effects decay at a constant rate every year. This yields a structural model for current-year test scores as an additive linear function of the prior achievement score and current-year teacher inputs. The authors used this model to motivate five more complex models that they then fit to the data to estimate the effects of various teacher attributes on student achievement.

The first model was a simple value-added model with current-year score as the outcome or the dependent variable, and the explanatory variables in the model included prior-year score and time-invariant and time-varying teacher, classroom, and student characteristics. The authors extended this model by adding school fixed effects, so that the effects of teacher characteristics were measured by variation within schools and differences in the student populations across schools were not confounded with the estimates of the effects of teacher characteristics. The third model used student gain scores as the dependent variable, rather than using level score as the dependent variable. This model did not include prior-year score as a covariate. The fourth model returned to using current-year achievement level as the dependent variable but replaced student prior-year test score and student time-invariant variables with student fixed effects. The fifth model used student fixed effects with gain scores. All models were fit separately for mathematics and reading using all available student data.

The primary model specification included an indicator variable for whether or not a teacher is currently an NBCT. For mathematics, the coefficient is statistically significantly positive for every model. The coefficients range from 0.018 to 0.028, but most estimates are close to 0.02.

Using the models with student fixed effects, Models 4 and 5, the authors compared teachers' effectiveness across years. They considered teachers two years prior to certification, one year prior to certification, the year of certification, and one or more years after initial certification. They found that for mathematics using Model 4, that the effects were largest two years prior to certification and postcertification, with a dip in effects the year before certification (the application year) and the first year of certification. However, with Model 5 the effects were largest for teachers prior to certification and smallest in the two years postcertification.

For reading, Model 4 suggests that for teachers who are certified sometime during the study, their students scored highest relative to other students when the teachers were two years prior to certification. The effects get smaller with every year of certification staging, so that the effects for NBCTs postcertification were less than half as large as the effects two years prior to certification. This pattern did not repeat with Model 5. With Model 5, students of certified teachers did best when the teacher was two years prior to certification and during the year of certification. Thus, for both reading and mathematics, the results of this secondary analysis were highly sensitive to model specification and inconsistent with the simpler model formulation that included a single indicator for current NBCTs. These analyses thus yield unstable estimates that need further investigation.

Comments: This is a comprehensive study that evaluates the relationship between board certification and student achievement for three elementary grade levels across nine years. The researchers examine the results for different models, providing information about the robustness of the findings to model specification. The consistency of effects for NBCTs across multiple models for both mathematics and reading provides compelling evidence that the cohort of NBCTs in North Carolina between 1995 and 2004 raised achievement test scores more than other teachers.

One shortcoming of the paper is the fact that the authors do not use longitudinal data on the teachers to study how the same teacher's students score as the teacher's NBPTS status changes. This could provide more interpretable measures of NBCT effects than the comparisons that compare teachers prior to certification with other teachers.

Cohen, C.E., and Rice, J.K. (2005, August). *National board certification as professional development: Design and cost.* Arlington, VA: National Board for Professional Teaching Standards.

Relevance to evaluation framework: Question 8 (Chapter 11).

Purpose: The authors evaluate the costs associated with support programs to prepare teachers for the NBPTS assessments. They compare costs with other mechanisms for providing professional growth to teachers.

Subjects/participants: Eight sites that provide a preparatory program for teachers going through the NBPTS assessment process.

Methodology and findings: The authors examine how the certification process and candidate support programs provide opportunities for teacher learning and how this model of professional development relates to principles of high-quality professional development found in the literature. They looked at these issues in relation to the costs of the certification process and support programs and who bears these costs. They focused specifically on eight sites that offer support programs for teachers preparing for national board certification: Cincinnati, Miami–Dade County, Mississippi Gulf Coast, North Carolina A&T, San Antonio, San Diego County, Stanford, and Winston-Salem.

The report provides detailed information on the costs associated with four of these sites. The authors estimate that the program-related costs per participant for these four sites ranged from $1,000 (for a program with 60 participants) to $11,200 (for a program with nine participants). They indicated that some of the variability in costs is explained by the economy of scale realized by the larger programs. They compare the costs of NBPTS support programs with the costs of obtaining a master's degree and the costs of several state- or district-level professional development programs.

Comments: This extensive study is useful for states and localities that are considering implementing a support program for teachers pursuing board certification. The authors give detailed cost estimates for four programs that provide various levels and kinds of supports. For our purposes, this study was relevant to one part of our cost-effectiveness analyses, and we drew from the authors' cost estimates for our analyses. The study might have been extended to provide information about the effectiveness of the programs. For example, it would have been useful to know the pass rate for candidates who went through each program. This would have helped states and localities in making design choices about such programs.

Darling-Hammond, L., and Atkin, J.M. (2007, March). *Influences of national board certification on teachers' classroom assessment practices.* Unpublished paper, Stanford University.

Relevance to evaluation framework: Question 5 (Chapter 8).

Purpose: This study examined the impact of the national board-certification process on mathematics and science teachers' classroom assessment practices.

Subjects/participants: Middle and high school teachers (n = 16) in the area of Stanford University who planned on pursuing board certification.

Methodology and findings: Through the National Board Resource Center at Stanford University, the authors recruited a group of middle and high school teachers interested in becoming board certified and randomly split them into two groups. The NBPTS group went through the certification process during the time period of the study, while the comparison group postponed their application for board certification. Teachers in the comparison group were compensated for delaying their application by having their application fee paid when they ultimately applied.

The researchers initially identified 102 participants; from this group, 60 attended the initial orientation session. All expressed interest, but once they learned what was involved, many dropped out. The researchers indicated that their goal was to have 20 teachers per group, but there was considerable attrition during the course of the study. In the end there were only 16 participants: nine in the national board group and seven in the control group.

Participating teachers were followed for three years, and data collection was timed according to the stages of the application process: one year prior to pursuing board certification, the year of candidacy, and the year after candidacy. Data were collected from both groups at the same times.

The data collected included twice yearly videotapes of lessons, written responses to questions about the videotaped lessons, student work samples from the unit that was videotaped, twice yearly interviews with the teachers about their practices and assessment approaches, surveys of students and teachers, and final reflective interviews with teachers about perceived changes in practices. The focus of the data collections was on (1) the ways that teachers use assessment in their classrooms; (2) the quality, range, and coherence of assessment methods; (3) the clarity and appropriateness of goals and expectations for learning; (4) opportunities for self-assessment; (5) modifications to teaching based on assessment information; and (5) quality and appropriateness of feedback to students.

Results indicated that the NBPTS group began with mean assessment practice scores that were lower than the scores of teachers in the control group. During the certification year, the assessment practice scores of the NBPTS group rose and surpassed those of the control group. In the post-certification year, the scores were stable for the NBPTS group.

The researchers found that teachers in the NBPTS group improved their formative assessment practices while engaging in the certification process and largely maintained these practices in the following year. This group appeared to be using a wider range of assessment methods and questioning strategies in class discussions that elicited more complete explanations from students. They were better able to integrate their assessments with ongoing instruction. The authors report that the difference between the NBPTS group and the comparison group were, for the most part, statistically significant (p < .05).

Comments: This is the only available study that examined the effects of the certification process on teachers' classroom practices. The study was comprehensive in the types of information collected and the kinds of practices examined. The rate of attrition is a serious problem that affected the validity of the findings, however. The authors provide some explanation for why teachers dropped out, but they do not discuss how the attrition might have affected the results. Some of the teachers dropped out after the first year of the study, but no data are reported for these teachers and there are no analyses of the potential biases introduced by this loss of participants. The resulting sample size is low. Nonetheless, the methods are novel, and with an appropriately sized sample of participants (and a lower rate of attrition), likely to yield useful information about the impact of the certification process on teachers.

Goldhaber, D., and Anthony, E. (2007). Can teacher quality be effectively assessed? National board certification as a signal of effective teaching. *Review of Economics and Statistics*, 89(1), 134-150.

Relevance to evaluation framework: Question 4 (Chapter 7) and Question 5 (Chapter 8).

Purpose: Examine the relationships between board certification and student achievement.

Subjects/participants: North Carolina students in grades 3 to 5 for the 1996-1997 to the 1998-1999 school years and their teachers.

Methodology and findings: The study used education production function methods to estimate the differences between teachers with differing involvement with NBPTS. The production functions included the student, teacher, school, and school district characteristics. The dependent variable was student gain scores on achievement tests in mathematics and reading.

The authors considered four specifications for their models. Models 1 and 2 used a covariate adjustment approach. Model 3 replaced all the school and district variables with school fixed effects. Model 4 replaced all the student covariates with student fixed effects. The model with student fixed effects did not include school fixed effects. The authors included three variations of Model 2 (the model with all the covariates and no fixed effects). The first included an indicator variable for whether or not a teacher was currently an NBCT and a separate indicator variable for whether or not the teacher would be an NBCT in the future but was not currently an NBCT. The second variation to Model 2 separated current NBCTs into those in their first year of certification and those certified more than a year ago. This variation also separated future NBCTs into current applicants and other future NBCTs. The third variation to Model 2 allowed for the study of the application process by including variables for future applicants, current applicants, and past applicants. Past applicants included current NBCTs and NBCT applicants who were not certified. Separate models were fit for reading and mathematics.

The authors found that, compared with students of teachers who never applied to NBPTS or applied and did not receive certification, the students of NBCTs made significantly higher gains in reading (p < .05) but not in mathematics. They also found that the students of teachers who would be certified in the future made consistently higher gains than the students of other teachers. This result held for both reading and mathematics and regardless of the model's specification of the comparison group of teachers. In addition, the study found that current applicants' students made lower gains on average than students of other teachers, and this result held for all the mathematics models and nearly all reading models.

Students of NBCTs in their first year of certification had larger gains than similar students in other teachers' classes. This result held for all mathematics models and all reading models except for the model with student fixed effects. However, the results for teachers who had been certified for more than a year were very inconsistent. In general the differences were positive for reading but not statistically significant (p > .05), and they were negative for mathematics but statistically significant (p < .05) only in the model with student fixed effects.

In general, the results were relatively insensitive to the inclusion of school fixed effects as opposed to school-level covariates. The models were much more sensitive to the inclusion of student fixed effects, which may have been due to changes in the sample size.

Comments: This was one of the first studies to evaluate the differences in achievement test performance for students of board-certified and nonboard-certified teachers (the original version of the report was released by the Urban Institute in 2004). As such, it provided the first information about the relationship between board certification and student achievement. The comparison of the results from different models was useful in examining their robustness to model specification. The findings generally indicated that board certification provides a signal of teacher effectiveness but that the process does not improve their effectiveness, a result generally confirmed by other studies.

One limitation is that the authors do not account for the clustering of students in classes, which means that tests of statistical significance may overstate the significance of the effects. The concern about bias in the statistical tests is exacerbated because many of the effects for NBPTS applicants and NBCTs are very small.

Another concern relates to the examination of the effects of NBCTs at different times in the application process. Ideally such results would use longitudinal data on teachers to determine differences in performance during the application process, so that differences could be attributed to the process not the teacher sample. However, the authors were unable to use longitudinal data on teachers for their analyses. Thus, the sample of teachers who were certified for one year did not contain the same teachers as the sample of teachers who had been certified more than one year, and the sample of teachers prior to certification may not have included all teachers in the certified group. Differences in student outcomes among the groups of teachers at different stages of the certification process could have resulted from sampling error among the teachers.

Goldhaber, D., and Hansen, M. (2007). *National board certification and teacher career paths: Does NBPTS certification influence how long teachers remain in the profession and where they teach?* Arlington, VA: National Board for Professional Teaching Standards. Available: http://www.nbpts.org/resources/research/browse_studies?ID=184 [accessed November 27, 2007].

Relevance to evaluation framework: Question 6 (Chapter 9).

Purpose: The authors investigated the impact of board certification on the job transitions and career paths of teachers employed in North Carolina.

Subjects/participants: The primary sample included most of those who taught in the state public schools between the 1996-1997 and 1999-2000 school years.

Methodology and findings: The researchers studied a sample of teachers who taught in North Carolina public schools between 1996 and 2000 and tracked their job transitions over an eight-year period from 1997 through 2003. The researchers obtained data on the following types of job transitions: (1) moving to another teaching position at a different public school within the same district, (2) moving to another teaching position in another public school district within the state, (3) leaving the North Carolina public school system.

For the above three job transitions included in the database, the analyses made several comparisons: (1) those who obtained board certification versus those who had not; (2) among the latter group, the analysis compared those teachers who had never applied for board certification with those who had applied; and (3) among the latter group, the analysis compared successful applicants with unsuccessful applicants. Because those who apply for board certification may be different than those who never apply, the latter comparison among successful and unsuccessful applicants helps to mitigate selection bias.

In addition, the analyses were broken out by teachers' experience level and race, because the data showed differences among these groups in the likelihood of passing and in the impact of obtaining board certification. As a result of these many groupings—by type of transition, by board-certification status, by experience, and by race—there were many permutations of possible comparisons in the results.

The analyses used competing-risks models to estimate the hazard (likelihood) of an individual experiencing each of the types of job transitions, after controlling for a series of teacher and school characteristics. To further mitigate selection bias, the analyses also used a regression discontinuity method (a quasi-experimental method) in the comparisons of the successful and unsuccessful applicants. This method was used to estimate the effect of successfully passing the NBPTS assessment on two outcomes: the likelihood of experiencing one of the above three job transitions and the characteristics of the new schools to which they moved.

The results of the analyses showed that those who obtained board certification, overall, had more mobility than those who were not board certified. However, the analyses also showed that these differences lay not so much with those who had never applied for board certification (the majority of teachers in the state), but rather, the differences in mobility were primarily found among those who had applied—between the successful applicants and unsuccessful applicants.

A more nuanced picture emerged when comparing the latter two groups. Although the coefficients were not always statistically significant across the different teacher experience levels, the direction of the signs was consistent. Those who passed the assessment and obtained the certification were more likely to move between schools and districts and more likely to leave the North Carolina public school system than were those who did not pass the assessment. A different picture also emerges depending on the race of the teacher. For African American applicants, the results indicate that board certification has little impact on career mobility.

The researchers also studied the extent to which teachers who change jobs move to (or away from) schools with high-needs students. Their analysis compared the nature of the school moves made by those who earned board certification compared to teachers who were unsuccessful applicants. The school characteristics the authors examined included the percentage of enrolled students in poverty, the percentage of minority students, per-pupil expenditures, and median housing values in the district. The authors reported the results separately for white and African American teachers.

For white teachers, the results were generally weak. There was some consistency in the sign of the coefficients; that is, white board-certified teachers tended to move to schools with fewer students in poverty and fewer minority students than did unsuccessful applicants. However, most of the coefficients were neither statistically nor substantively significant. For example, there was generally less than a 1 percent difference between successful and unsuccessful applicants in terms of the percentages of students in poverty at the schools to which they moved, and differences in the range of 1 to 2.5 percent in the percentages of minority students at their new schools.

Comments: This is the first study to examine the relationships between teachers' career paths and their board-certification status. The methods allow the researchers to examine mobility subsequent to obtaining board certification and to compare this for teachers who had passed and failed the NBPTS assessments. This is a significant contribution. However, we highlight two issues with this study. First, as with other state databases, the data used in this study had no information on whether those who left the North Carolina public schools had moved to a public school job out of state, had moved to a private school job in or out of the state, or had left teaching entirely. This is an important limitation because it means the study could not specifically isolate the influence of board certification on attrition from the teaching fields. While the researchers note this in their discussion, we re-emphasize this point as a limitation in interpreting the findings. In addition, there is a tendency in the paper to overstate the findings when discussing the types of schools to which white teachers move. Some of the differences in the characteristics between the old and the new schools for white teachers were on the order of 1 to 2 percent and generally not significant, but they are discussed as if they were statistically significant.

Harris, D.N., and Sass, T.R. (2006, August 22). *The effects of NBPTS-certified teachers on student achievement*. Arlington, VA: National Board for Professional Teaching Standards. Available: http://www.caldercenter.org/PDF/1001059_Teacher_Training.pdf [accessed November 27, 2007].

Relevance to evaluation framework: Question 4 (Chapter 7), Question 5 (Chapter 8).

Purpose: Examine the relationships between board certification and student achievement.

Subjects/participants: Florida students in grades 3 to 10 for the 1999-2000 to the 2003-2004 school years and their teachers.

Methodology and findings: This study is based on data from students in grades 3 to 10 on both mathematics and reading for both the state's Florida Comprehensive Assessment Test (FCAT) norm-referenced test

(FCAT-NRT), and the state's criterion-referenced FCAT Sunshine State Standards Test (FCAT-SSS).

The researchers used a production function approach. The study used gain scores in achievement (current-year score less prior year score) as the outcome. One set of models used FCAT-NRT scores as the outcome and another set used the FCAT-SSS as the outcome. The models included students and classroom variables as covariate variables as well as student fixed effects and school fixed effects.

The authors report that, to avoid computational problems, they included student by school or "spell effects" for each period that a student is in a different school, rather than including separate fixed effects for each school and separate fixed effects for each student. The authors fit two primary models. Model 1 included a single indicator variable for whether or not a teacher was ever board certified during the span of the data. Model 2 estimated separate effects for the ever-board-certified group during three periods of the certification process: the years prior to application, the year of application, and the years following certification.

The two tests (FCAT-NRT and FCAT-SSS) yielded somewhat different stories about the relationship between board certification status and student achievement. For Model 1, the effects associated with board certification for the FCAT-NRT were negative for both reading and mathematics but positive for both subjects for the FCAT-SSS.

For Model 2, gains on the FCAT-NRT mathematics test were statistically significantly greater for students whose teachers would someday achieve NBPTS certification. However, the gains on these tests were negative for students whose teachers were current applicants for NBPTS certification (and would be awarded certification) and for students whose teachers were currently certified. For the mathematics FCAT-SSS, students in each group made greater gains than students whose teachers would never be board certified within the span of the data, but none of the differences was significant. In reading, students whose teachers were not current NBCTs but would someday be awarded NBPTS certification and students whose teachers were current NBCTs made greater gains on the FCAT-NRT than students whose teachers would never be board certified during the span of the study; however, neither difference was statistically significant. The gains on the FCAT-NRT reading tests were negative, but not significant, for students whose teachers were current applicants for NBPTS certification (and would be awarded certification). The FCAT-SSS reading gains were significantly higher for students whose teachers would someday apply for and be awarded NBPTS certification and for students who teachers were current NBCTs than for students who teachers would not be awarded certification during the span of the study. The FCAT-SSS reading gains were negative but not significant during the application year of future NBCTs.

Comments: This is an extensive study that includes five years of data for students from elementary through high school. The comparison of results for two different outcome measures is an important contribution. The researchers made no adjustment for the clustering of students within teachers, which could result in biased significance tests; however, many of the effect sizes were quite small. The complex adjustments of including student by school or spell fixed effects resulted in many students and teachers being excluded from the analysis. For example, students must be in a school for a minimum of two years to contribute to the estimation of teacher effects. Similarly, some teachers were excluded from the analysis; for example, teachers who teach only during the last year and teach third, sixth, or tenth grade were excluded. Moreover, these adjustments yield consistent estimates only under many assumptions, including the assumption that students' achievement scores are growing at student-specific rates. Thus, it is possible that restrictions to the sample and estimation error that results from using many fixed effects lead to the inconsistency of the results.

Helding, K.A., and Fraser, B.J. (2005, April). *Effectiveness of national board certified teachers in terms of attitudes, classroom environments and achievement among secondary science students.* Paper presented at the annual meeting of the American Educational Research Association, Montreal, Canada.

Relevance to evaluation framework: Question 4 (Chapter 7).

Purpose: The authors compared NBCTs and non-NBCTs in terms of classroom environment, student attitudes, and student achievement.

Subjects/participants: Eighth and tenth grade students in Miami–Dade County taught by NBCTs and non-NBCTs.

Methodology and findings: The researchers recruited a sample of NBCTs to participate in this study and to gather information about their students' attitudes. The researchers used two instruments to measure students' perceptions of their science classes and their attitudes about science. One instrument is a questionnaire called "What Is Happening in This Class?" (WIHIC). The WIHIC questionnaire presents students with a series of statements about practices in the class and asks them to rate the frequency with which each occurs, using a five-point scale ranging from "almost never" to "almost always." The questionnaire measures students' perceptions with regard to seven factors: student cohesiveness (how well students work together in the class), teacher supportiveness, the student's involvement in class activities, the student's investigation practices, the student's level of task orientation, the student's level of cooperation, and the student's perception of equity in the class (e.g., that teachers treat all students equally).

The second instrument is an attitude scale derived from the Test of Science-Related Attitudes (TOSRA). The TOSRA presents students with 10 statements about science classes (e.g., Science lessons are fun; I look forward to science lessons; I want to find out more about the world in which we live) and asks them to indicate if they agree, disagree, or are not sure about the statement.

Students were also compared with regard to their FCAT scores in science, which assess higher order cognitive skills in physical and chemical science, earth and space science, life and environmental science, and scientific thinking.

To recruit the study samples, the researchers first contacted the principal of each NBCT in Miami–Dade County. After obtaining the principal's consent, the researchers contacted each NBCT. Each NBCT who agreed to participate was asked to recruit a non-NBCT who taught the same subject (presumably, though not stated, in the same school). Of the NBCTs who were contacted, 42 percent (n = 16) agreed to participate; 14 non-NBCTs agreed to participate. Each teacher was asked to provide one or two science classes, and a total of 38 classes (n = 927 students) participated in the study. The NBCT group included 443 students in 21 classes taught by 16 teachers, and the non-NBCT group included 484 students in 17 classes taught by 14 teachers.

The authors compared mean scores for students taught by NBCTs and non-NBCTs with regard to the seven factors on the WIHIC, the overall score on the TOSRA, and FCAT scores in science. In all cases, students taught by NBCTs scored slightly higher than those taught by non-NBCTs. The authors tested the differences for statistical significance, and reported that six of the nine comparisons were significant at $p < .05$. Differences in achievement were not statistically significant.

Comments: This is the only study currently available that focuses on the impact of board-certified teachers on student outcomes other than achievement test scores. As such, it provides an example of ways to extend the array of student outcomes considered in this type of research. However, there were several important methodological problems that affected the validity of the findings.

First, the methods for obtaining the non-NBCT sample are problematic and are likely to have introduced selection bias into the comparison sample. The findings could be attributed simply to the way in which the sample was obtained. Second, the authors did not adjust for the fact that students were clustered in classrooms, some having the same teacher and some not (i.e., there were 21 classes taught by 16 NBCTs and 17 classes taught by 14 non-NBCTs); thus, the significance tests are likely to overstate the significance of the differences. Finally, there is no consideration of (or controls implemented for) preexisting differences between students assigned to NBCTs and non-NBCTs. It may be that the students assigned to the NBCTs had more positive attitudes from the start.

Indiana Professional Standards Board. (2002, Spring). *Status of national board-certified teachers in Indiana.* Indianapolis: Author. Available: http://www.nbpts.org/resources/research/browse_studies?ID=26 [accessed November 27, 2007].

Relevance to evaluation framework: Question 3 (Chapter 6).

Purpose: To gather information about why teachers in Indiana decide to pursue board certification.

Subjects/participants: NBCTs in Indiana.

Methodology and findings: This study involved a survey of the 71 NBCTs in Indiana. At the time of the study, only 71 of roughly 75,000 teachers in the state were board certified. The survey was sent to all the 71 NBCTs in the state, and 32 (48 percent) responded. A focus group was also convened to further explore the survey questions. The survey consisted of 20 mostly open-ended questions designed to gather information about (1) the characteristics of board applicants, (2) how they were informed about the process, (3) their perceptions of the difficulty of the certification process, (4) the current support provided to candidates in the state, and (5) the support needed for future state candidates.

The respondents were generally favorable about their experience of going through the certification process. The survey asked why teachers pursue board certification. Generally, the respondents indicated that teachers pursue board certification because they have a desire to improve their effectiveness as a teacher, like challenges, are lifelong learners, are intrinsically motivated, and consider that board certification serves to validate their practices. Most of the respondents did not cite monetary reasons as their motive for pursuing board certification; however, at the time, only limited financial support was offered to candidates.

Some respondents felt supported by their colleagues and principals, and some did not. Some noted that their colleagues questioned why they would want to go through such a difficult process or "scorned the idea," believing that the teacher was "showboating." Most respondents reported that certification brought them new opportunities, including leadership roles, invited speaking opportunities, and serving as members of Disney American Teacher review committees. Most of the respondents felt that the process affected their teaching, about half reporting that they became more reflective.

Comments: This study provides additional insight into the reasons why teachers decided to pursue board certification. The use of a focus group to follow up the survey was an important addition to the study. The sample size is very small, however, and the response rate was below 50 percent. There is no analysis of the respondents to examine the extent to which the respondents were representative of the full group that was surveyed.

Koppich, J.E., Humphrey, D.C., and Hough, H.J. (2006). Making use of what teachers know and can do: Policy, practice, and national board certification. *Education Policy Analysis Archives, 15*(7), 1-30.

   Relevance to evaluation framework: Question 3 (Chapter 6), Question 5 (Chapter 8), Question 7 (Chapter 10).
   Purpose: Collect data on the impact NBCTs are having at their schools.
   Subjects/participants: Samples of NBCTs in California, Florida, Mississippi, North Carolina, Ohio, and South Carolina; colleagues of NBCTs in case-study schools.
   Methodology and findings: The authors built on their earlier work studying the impact of board certification in six states. Data collection methods included a mail survey to NBCTs in the six states, focus groups, and site visits to selected case study schools.
   The participants in the mail survey were selected via stratified random sampling methods, and independent samples were selected in each of the six states. In each state, the schools were assigned to one of four strata: elementary low-performing, elementary nonlow-performing, secondary low-performing, or secondary nonlow-performing. Within each stratum, a random sample of NBCTs was selected. The survey was distributed to 1,136 in the 6 states, and 854 responded (75 percent).
   Case studies were conducted at three schools each in California, North Carolina, and Ohio. Case study schools were those in which at least 9 percent of teachers were board certified (or 9 percent of a single department of secondary schools). Six focus groups were convened in California, North Carolina, and Ohio to supplement the information gathered from the case studies. Focus groups were held in Los Angeles and San Francisco; in Chapel Hill and Durham; and in Cincinnati and Cleveland. Participating teachers were those from schools not represented by the case-study sites in each of the respective states.
   The authors examined what NBCTs do after becoming certified and what it takes for them to make a difference in a school. Overall, they found little evidence of schools using NBCTs to serve as mentors or in leadership positions. They found that many of the NBCTs were in unsupportive situations. They noted that there was little evidence that NBCTs sought or were given the opportunity to move beyond the conventional obligations of classroom teaching. For example, while roughly 60 percent of the surveyed NBCTs said their principals view board certification very favorably,

49 percent said that the administration was not supportive of roles outside the classroom that NBCTs might be interested in pursuing.

The authors report that principals are generally not adept at making use of the skills that NBCTs offer. Some principals are not familiar with what board certification represents, and others are reluctant to make use of NBCTs, not wanting to show favoritism of some teachers over others. The researchers report that more than 90 percent of NBCTs say they are no more influential than other teachers on such matters as selecting curriculum and materials, advising on professional development programs, teacher hiring or evaluation, advising on budget, or determining the focus of school reform efforts.

Interviews with NBCTs and their colleagues led the authors to conclude that there is a culture of "individualism and egalitarianism that remains alive in the profession." NBCTs report that they are often given "the cold shoulder" by non-NBCTs and nearly 43 percent said "my school culture is not welcoming of teachers stepping into leadership positions." The authors found that NBCTs actually go to considerable lengths to downplay any distinction between themselves and their non-NBCT colleagues, sometimes even concealing the fact that they are board certified.

The authors did find an exception in a single elementary school in North Carolina, and they provide a very lengthy description of how NBCTs are supported and used in this school—key to this is the fact that the principal and assistant principal are both board certified. An excerpt from their description of the environment at this school appears below (pp. 19-20):

> At Adam Elementary [a fictitious name], decision-making was organized around learning teams. All teachers participated in the teams that met weekly for an hour and focused on improving the schools' literacy instruction. NBCTs led many of the learning teams, although accomplished teachers who had not made that choice also filled formal leadership roles. The activities of the teams were consistent with the kinds of reflection and problem solving that are part of National Board Certification. National Board "language" was used throughout the school so that even teachers who had not pursued certification became familiar with the language, the standards, and the approach to teaching.
>
> The researchers observed one of the team meetings during which seven experienced teachers (four NBCTs) and one inexperienced teacher were discussing a videotape of strategies for teaching a vocabulary lesson. The researchers were struck by the level of conversation about the instructional strategies and the extent of support that the experienced teachers offered to the inexperienced teacher. The researchers commented about the amount of professional conversation about teaching and learning that took place during the meeting and that occurred every day at the school.

They recounted a recent debate at the school over curriculum policy. A small group of NBCTs led a larger cadre of their colleagues in a presentation to the local school board, arguing against the acceptance of a $1.2 million federally funded *Reading First* grant. For them the *Reading First* program came with "too many strings" and would force them to teach reading uniformly. The teachers pointed to the success they were having with their current approaches and argued for adapting instruction and materials to serve all students' literacy needs. The superintendent publicly backed the teachers, and the school board voted to turn down the grant.

The school culture at Adam was enabled by state policies that encouraged teachers to earn board certification. In addition, district's policies and support programs for candidates, along with the community awareness and support for NBCTs, were well aligned with the efforts underway at the school. The fact that the principal and the assistant principal had both earned board certification was crucial to their understanding of the board processes and standards. It was their ability to infuse the National Board standards and the practices that paralleled the certification process into the school's professional development and improvement strategy that made the difference in the school's teaching and learning culture.

Comments: This is an extensive study that provides the first information about the effects of contextual issues on NBCTs. The use of multiple data collection strategies (surveys, focus groups, interview, and case studies) is a strong point of this study. The one area that the researchers might have also explored is the issue of failing the assessment and any impacts that might have on teachers. At the time that the study was released, the finding that NBCTs often face unsupportive environments had not been previously reported. It would be worthwhile to investigate the extent to which these findings are evident in states besides the six included in this study.

Lustick, D., and Sykes, G. (2006). National board certification as professional development: What are teachers learning? *Education Policy Analysis Archives, 14*(5). Available: http://epaa.asu.edu/epaa/v14n5 [accessed March 1, 2006].

Relevance to evaluation framework: Question 5 (Chapter 8).

Purpose: To investigate what teachers learn by going through the certification process.

Subjects/participants: Teachers pursuing board certification in the area of adolescent and young adult science.

Methodology and findings: This study involved a simulation of the NBPTS portfolio exercises conducted independently of the actual assessment. The simulation involved sending a packet to the study participants, conducting a phone interview with them, and then rating their responses using the actual NBPTS scoring rubric and procedures. The packet contained a sealed six-minute video clip of a whole class discussion in science, along with student artifacts from the lesson.

The exercises consisted of five assignments. Two of them asked teachers to describe their own experiences, much like what is required on the actual assessment. One requested that the teacher describe a recent successful lesson she or he had taught, and the other asked the teacher to recount the types of professional activities in which she or he had participated.

Three assignments involved reviewing materials that the researchers sent. One consisted of a student's written response to an assessment question before and after a lesson on the kinetic theory of matter. The researcher then asked the teacher to discuss the students' strengths and weaknesses using evidence from the response and to describe the feedback that should be given to the student. Another assignment involved a written scenario of a lesson about scientific inquiry. The scenario described the lesson, the teacher's objectives, and an interaction among four students. The researcher asked the teacher about her or his appraisal of the students' skills from this interaction, what they appeared to understand and misunderstand, and what instructional steps should be taken next.

The final assignment involved viewing a videotaped class discussion about ecosystems. The researcher queried the teacher about the videotaped interactions—the extent to which the students were engaged in the discussion and understood the lesson, the effectiveness with which the teacher facilitated the discussion, the quality of the interactions, and the advice she or he would give to the teacher as ways to improve the instruction.

The sample was recruited with the assistance of the NBPTS, and participants were drawn from teachers who registered for the assessment between 2001-2002 and 2003-2004. Approximately 450-650 candidates register for this assessment each year, and about half of each year's cohort was randomly selected and invited to participate. The researchers set a goal of recruiting 40 teachers from each cohort, and participants were the first 40 from each cohort who agreed to participate. A total of 118 teachers participated in the study.

Participants were randomly assigned to one of four groups. Two groups participated in the study prior to undergoing the actual NBPTS assessment (the pretest groups), and two groups participated after completing the actual assessment (the posttest groups) but before receiving the results. One of the pretest groups also participated in the posttest, solely for the purpose of evaluating the effects of taking the pretest—the posttest results were not used in the final analysis.

Results showed that scores on the posttest were statistically significantly higher than scores on the pretest ($p = .009$), with a moderately large effect size of .473. Additional analyses focused on the sources of the differences. Performance on the simulation tasks had been scored according to the various NBPTS science standards (e.g., a score for each standard), and comparisons were made to see if the pretest-posttest differences were largely attributable to performance on one or more standards. Results showed that performance with regard to "advancing student learning" (p = .008) and "supporting teaching and student learning" (p = .005) were significantly different, with effect sizes of .482 and .524, respectively.

Based on phone interviews with the participants, the authors characterized the type of learning teachers undergo as a consequence of the process. They found that roughly half of the teachers fell into the "dynamic learning category," meaning self-reports of immediate, meaningful change in a teacher's beliefs, understandings, and actions in the classroom. About one-quarter fell into the category of "technical learning," which the authors characterize as an emphasis on acquiring techniques useful in obtaining certification but that don't necessarily carry over into teaching itself (e.g., learning how to be better candidates for national board certification but not how to be better teachers). The other quarter of teachers fell into a category the researchers defined as "deferred learning," in which the things that teachers learn from the process are deferred to a time when they have more opportunity to reflect and to consider how to use them.

The authors have since accumulated information on the assessment results for the participants. As is typical for the general pool of all NBPTS applicants, about half of each pretest and posttest group passed. Analyses indicate that both teachers who passed and teachers who failed showed gains on the simulated exercises, suggesting that even teachers who are not successful learn something from the process.

Comments: This study examined the extent to which teachers learned from the board certification process and is one of only two that study this issue. It represents a first step in examining the effects of the process on teachers, but it does not evaluate the extent to which teachers incorporate what they learn into their classroom practices. The authors present the results of an analysis of covariance to evaluate the extent of the variance in performance attributable to gender, years of experience, class size, student type (with regard to general ability/motivation level), school context, and geographic region. The results suggest that the findings are explained by the covariates. In discussions with the first author, we learned that the analyses of covariance were not entirely correct, in part because of problematic coding of the student type variable. The authors have since rerun these analyses, which show that the differences between pretest and posttest scores remain after controlling for these background variables.

McColskey, W., Stronge, J.H., Ward, T.J., Tucker, P.D., Howard, B., Lewis, K., and Hindman, J.L. (2005, June). *Teacher effectiveness, student achieve-*

ment, and national board certified teachers. Arlington, VA: National Board for Professional Teaching Standards. Available: http://www.nbpts.org/UserFiles/File/Teacher_Effectiveness_Student_Achievement_and_National_Board_Certified_Teachers_D_-_McColskey.pdf [accessed June 2008].

Relevance to evaluation framework: Question 2 (Chapter 5).

Purpose: This study compares NBCTs and non-NBCTs in terms of both their classroom practices and their students' achievement test performance.

Subjects/participants: Teachers from four school districts in North Carolina, separated into groups of NBCTs, highly effective non-NBCTs, and least effective non-NBCTs.

Methodology and findings: The study involved two phases. Phase 1 involved comparison of achievement test data for NBCTs and non-NBCTs. Phase 2 involved collection of a complex set of information on the teachers, including analyses of lesson plans, classroom observations, student work, and questionnaire data.

For Phase I, two years of student test scores in reading and math from 307 5th grade teachers were used; 25 were board certified and 282 were not. Students' predicted test scores were determined by regressing gender, ethnicity, free or reduced-price lunch status, and English language proficiency on achievement test scores. For each student, the residual was determined as the difference between his or her actual test score and the predicted test score. Students were linked to their teacher, and the residual averaged across students to form a residual score for the teacher (referred to as a Teacher Achievement Index, or TAI).

Average student residuals were then compared for non-NBCTs and NBCTs for reading and for math. Mean residuals were not statistically significantly different for the two groups although the variances were found to differ (students of NBCTs were more homogenous). Quartiles were determined for the residuals, and the percentages of teachers in each quartile compared for the two groups of teachers. For non-NBCTs, the percentages were roughly equal across the quartiles. In math, NBCTs were more concentrated in the middle two quartiles (66 percent); in reading, they were more concentrated in the top two quartiles (61 percent).

For Phase II, the teachers were classified into three groups based on the achievement test results: NBCTs, highly effective non-NBCTs, and least effective non-NBCTs. The highly effective teachers were those with average residuals in the top quartile; those with average residuals in the bottom quartile were considered least effective. Lists were made of teachers who fell in the two quartile ranges and who were eligible for board certification. Teachers on the lists were contacted and asked to participate in Phase II of the study. All NBCTs were also contacted.

The authors had significant trouble recruiting teachers to participate in Phase II. The authors do not specify the number of non-NBCTs invited to participate, but, based on the percentages, it appears that 70 least effective and 70 highly effective teachers were invited, along with the 25 NBCTs. A total of 51 teachers agreed to participate (21 NBCTs, 16 highly effective, and 14 least effective). Nearly all NBCTs agreed to participate, but only about a quarter of teachers in the other two groups agreed.

Classroom observations and artifacts of teaching were gathered and compared by group. Attributes of teachers or teaching considered in this part of the study include planning and assessment practices; quality of assignments; teacher beliefs about their instructional strategies, student engagement, and classroom management; teacher questioning activity; student questioning; student time on task; management strategies and the nature of interventions; and observations that rated teachers on specified dimensions.

The results indicated that NBCTs had statistically significantly higher ratings in the cognitive challenge of typical reading comprehension assignments than did both groups of non-NBCTs. NBCTs also had the highest mean ratings on teachers' planning practices.

No statistically significant group differences were found in the cognitive demands of the questions asked by teachers or by their respective students. In addition, no statistically significant group differences were found in classroom management (number of disruptions or students visibly disengaged), although higher numbers of students of least effective teachers were visibly disengaged. No statistically significant group differences were found in terms of teacher interventions used to address disruptions or disengagement.

Statistically significant group differences were found on four of 15 dimensions of teacher effectiveness (based on classroom observations). In all four cases, highly effective non-NBCTs scored highest on the dimension.

Comments: This study is useful in the focus on actual classroom practices and types of information collected from the teachers. The comparison across the three groups of teachers and the methods for assigning teachers to groups were novel. However, the difficulties that the authors experienced in recruiting non-NBCTs to participate are likely to have resulted in a biased sample. Of particular concern are the "least effective" non-NBCTs who agreed to participate. The teachers in this group who agreed to participate may have been quite selective and different from those who did not agree—in part characterized by their willingness to open up their classrooms for observations and to talk about their teaching. It is not known how this potential selection bias affected the results.

Moore, J.W. (2002, December). *Perceived barriers to the National Board for Professional Teaching Standards certification.* Unpublished dissertation, East Tennessee State University.

Relevance to evaluation framework: Question 3 (Chapter 6).

Purpose: The author investigated reasons why teachers choose not to pursue board certification.

Subjects/participants: Teachers in Cocke and Sevier Counties in Tennessee.

Methodology and findings: As of 2002, there were only 40 NBCTs in Tennessee, and the study focused on uncovering reasons why more teachers had not participated. This researcher administered a survey to the participants, which presented respondents with a list of 38 statements that used a Likert 5-point response scale (strongly agree to strongly disagree).

Cluster sampling methods were used to identify the sample. That is, six schools from Cocke County and eight schools from Sevier County were randomly selected from the list of all schools in the county. The survey was distributed to all teachers in the selected schools who were eligible for board certification but had not attained it. There were 1,200 teachers in the two counties who were eligible (300 in Cocke and 900 in Sevier), and surveys were distributed to 700 of the eligible teachers. Usable responses were received from 448 teachers (64 percent response rate).

Of the 448, 57 percent (n = 253) said they would not attempt board certification, 38 percent were unsure (n = 171), and 5 percent (n = 24) said they would in the future. The respondents were generally quite negative about board certification. Most (68 percent) said they were poorly informed about the program, and almost two-thirds (62 percent) had a negative overall opinion about the program. Only 38 percent had a positive opinion.

Overall, the respondents indicated that personal reasons tended to present the biggest obstacles to their participation, including the extent of paperwork involved and the time commitment required. They also felt that the effort was not worth the benefits, generally agreeing with statements that achieving board certification represented "professional certification without a professional salary" and "more work without more pay."

There was also some skepticism among respondents about the qualifications of teachers who achieve board certification. Respondents generally agreed with statements suggesting that the NBPTS does not necessarily identify or recognize better teachers. Some also thought that board certification tended to ostracize certain teachers.

Comments: This study is one of only two that investigate reasons why teachers do not participate in the NBPTS, and, unlike the other study, it focuses on teachers who have had no involvement with the NBPTS (the other surveyed NBCTs about their nonparticipating colleagues). As such, it contributes to understanding nonparticipation and yields information that could be used to increase teachers' involvement in the program. One issue that likely bears on the findings is that there were no NBCTs in the two counties at the time of the study. Only one teacher had attempted the process but had not been successful. (This was learned through personal conversation with the first author.) As the respondents noted, most were minimally familiar with the certification process, and it is quite likely that they may never have met a board-certified teacher. Thus, their responses patterns may identify issues that could be pursued in educating teachers about the NBPTS and the certification process.

National Board for Professional Teaching Standards. (2001a, November). *I am a better teacher.* Arlington, VA: Author. Available: http://www.nbpts. org/resources/research/browse_studies?ID=23 [accessed November 20, 2007].

Relevance to evaluation framework: Question 5 (Chapter 8).

Purpose: To evaluate the impact of the certification process on teachers who have gone through it.

Subjects/participants: National sample of teachers who had completed the certification process, both successful and unsuccessful candidates.

Methodology and findings: This is a report of a survey conducted by the NBPTS. Surveys were sent to 10,700 candidates who had recently completed the assessment process. The survey contained 27 questions. Within four weeks, 5,641 responses (53 percent) were received, and findings are based on these responses. The results in the report are based on 10 questions, which were grouped in a section of the survey titled "Benefits of the Process for You." The questions are worded as statements that participants are asked to agree/disagree with (on a five-point scale from strongly disagree to strongly agree). All questions are worded positively (e.g., "participating in the NBPTS process helped me develop stronger curricula"; "participating in the NBPTS process helped me develop improved ways to evaluate student learning"; "as a result of participating in the national board-certification process, I believe I am a better teacher"; "I found that the National Board's assessment process enhanced the quality of my interactions with my students"). No negatively worded statements are included.

The report cites the following as findings:

- 92 percent of the candidates surveyed said that they believed the national board certification process made them better teachers.
- 96 percent of respondents rated the national board certification

process as a(n) "excellent," "very good," or "good" professional development experience.

- Participation in the national board certification process equips teachers to create stronger curricula (89 percent), improves their abilities to evaluate student learning (89 percent), and helps them to develop a framework in which they can use state content standards to improve teaching (80 percent).
- Participation in the national board certification process enhances teacher interaction with students (82 percent) and parents and guardians (82 percent), and helps to improve collaborations with other teachers (80 percent).
- There is now a high level of awareness in schools (68 percent) and school districts (81 percent) of teachers who are candidates for national board certification and of those who have achieved certification.
- Candidates for national board certification are receiving high levels of support from their teaching colleagues (86 percent), principals (80 percent), and district administrators (63 percent).

Comments: This survey collected important information about the experiences and attitudes of NBPTS participants. However, the report of the findings is written as an advocacy piece, not a research report. There is no information on nonrespondents and no evaluation of the extent to which respondents are representative of the test-takers. The survey had the potential to yield information about teachers who passed and who failed, but the results are not reported separately by group. In addition, all of the survey questions are worded positively. Inclusion of both positively and negatively worded questions would have increased the objectivity of the survey and would have allowed the researchers to examine the presence of response sets (individuals who tend to always select the same response or who tend to provide what they perceive to be an acceptable response).

National Board for Professional Teaching Standards. (2001d). *The impact of national board certification on teachers: A survey of national board-certified teachers and assessors. An NBPTS research report.* Arlington, VA: National Board for Professional Teaching Standards.

Relevance to evaluation framework: Question 5 (Chapter 8).
Purpose: To evaluate the impact of the certification process on teachers.
Subjects/participants: Random sample of all NBCTs.
Methodology and findings: This is a report of a survey conducted by the NBPTS. Surveys were sent to a random sample of 600 of the 4,804

teachers who achieved national board certification from 1994 through 1999. Competed surveys were received from 235 respondents (41 percent). The main research questions investigated were (1) How do NBCTs and assessors rate the certification process as a professional development experience? and (2) What effect does the certification experience have on NBCTs and assessors and other stakeholders?

The authors cite the following findings: (1) the national board certification process is an excellent professional development experience; (2) NBCTs indicate that the certification experience has had a strong effect on their teaching practices; and (3) the certification process has had a positive effect on students and has led to positive interaction with teachers, administrators, and communities.

Comments: This survey collected important information about the experiences of NBPTS participants. However, the report of the findings is written as an advocacy piece, not a research report. The report provides only an overview of selected results from the study. There is not enough detail provided to make independent judgments about the validity of the results.

Sanders, W.L., Ashton, J.J., and Wright, S.P. (2005, March). *Comparison of the effects of NBPTS-certified teachers with other teachers on the rate of student academic progress.* Arlington, VA: National Board for Professional Teaching Standards. Available: http://www.nbpts.org/resources/research/browse_studies?ID=15 [accessed November 27, 2007].

Relevance to evaluation framework: Question 4 (Chapter 7).

Purpose: The study examines the relationships between student achievement and board-certification status. The authors also evaluate the impact of model specification on the findings.

Subjects/participants: Students in 3rd through 8th grade for the 1999-2000 through 2002-2003 school years in Charlotte–Mecklenburg and Wake County school districts in North Carolina and their teachers.

Methodology and findings: For this study, the authors separated teachers into four groups: NBCTs, future NBPTS candidates, NBCT applicants who failed to be certified, and teachers with no NBPTS involvement. They then compared student achievement in mathematics and reading for teachers in the four groups.

The authors fit four models for each subject area. In two models they used the current-year score on the state's end-of-year test as the outcome or dependent variable, and in the other two models they used the gain score (prior-year score less the previous-year score) as the outcome variable. For both subject areas and each outcome (level score or gain score), one model included random effects for teachers and the other did not. Including teacher random effects accounted for the nesting of students within classes and should provide substantially more accurate standard errors than the models that ignore this nesting.

The two models without teacher random effects were designed to be similar to those used in the studies by Cavaluzzo (2005) and by Goldhaber and Anthony (2007). The results for these models were compared with results for models that included teacher random effects, so as to examine the effect of model specification on the results.

Models with the current score as the outcome included prior-year mathematics and reading scores as covariates. All models also controlled for students' gender and race/ethnicity, and teacher's years of experience. The authors fit models separately by grade and subject area, comparing NBCTs with each of the other NBPTS groups (failed applicants, future applicants, and nonapplicants).

The authors reported statistically significant differences between the student outcomes for NBCTs and nonapplicants for grades 5, 6, 7, and 8 in both mathematics and reading for at least one outcome specification. For mathematics, none of the differences was statistically significant in models that include random teacher effects. For reading, differences were statistically significant in models that do and do not include teacher random effects, with the exception of grade 8, in which the effects were significant only in models that included teacher random effects. In addition, the authors reported that the models with random effects indicated that there was typically more variance within group than across groups. That is, there was more variance among teachers with board certification than between NBCTs and each of the other groups.

Comments: The major contribution of this study is the illustration of the sensitivity of results to model specification. Specifically, the models that accounted for the nesting of students in classrooms (the models that included random effects) generally resulted in substantially larger standard errors, and thus the effects were less likely to be statistically significant. This provides evidence that analyses that do not account for such nesting produce downwardly biased standard errors, which raise the probability of reporting statistically significant effects in error.

One limitation of this study is that it gives up power to detect differences by analyzing the grades separately. This is particularly problematic given the likely small numbers of teachers in grades 6, 7, and 8 (sample sizes are not reported). However, the differences between NBCTs and nonapplicants vary considerably across grades, with some of the largest differences between grades 4 and 5, in which the sample sizes were largest. Thus, even if the data were pooled across grades, it is unlikely that a strong and significant difference would exist for NBCTs.

Smith, T.W., Gordon, B., Colby, S.A., and Wang, J. (2005). *An examination of the relationship between depth of student learning and national board-certification status*. Arlington, VA: National Board for Professional Teaching Standards. Available: http://www.nbpts.org/UserFiles/File/Applachian_State_study_D_-_Smith.pdf [accessed June 2008].

Relevance to evaluation framework: Question 2 (Chapter 5).

Purpose: To compare work samples for students of NBCTs and of teachers who failed to earn board certification.

Subjects/participants: Teachers in 17 states who had attempted to earn board certification; roughly half of the sample consisted of NBCTs, and half were teachers who had failed the assessment.

Methodology and findings: This study builds on prior work by Bond et al. (2000) and uses some of the same methodologies. The study involved comparison of instructional practices and students' work for 64 teachers from 17 states. The sample included NBCTs and teachers who had attempted to become board certified but were unsuccessful. The teachers were randomly selected from information provided by the NBPTS. Initial contact with potential participants was via a mail survey. Recruitment proceeded by telephone for teachers who returned their surveys expressing interest in participating.

A letter of invitation was mailed to 705 teachers (280 NBCTs, 425 unsuccessful candidates) who had pursued board certification in one of four areas: (1) middle childhood generalist, (2) early adolescence English language arts, (3) adolescence/young adulthood science, and (4) adolescence/young adulthood social studies–history. The authors had some difficulty with recruitment, originally trying for 200 participants, 50 in each of the four certificate areas. They were not able to recruit that many participants. Initially, 202 teachers verbally agreed, but there was considerable attrition at various stages of the recruitment process. The final sample included 35 NBCTs and 29 teachers who had failed the assessment. No intermediate details are provided about the sampling methodology.

Data evaluated for each teacher included (1) the teacher's description of a unit of lessons; (2) student work samples for 6 randomly selected students from each teacher's classroom; and (3) for the generalist and language arts teachers, students' responses to a writing task. The teachers' instructional materials and the students' work samples were evaluated for deep versus surface features using a taxonomy developed by Hattie and described in Bond et al. (2000).

Analysis of student work samples showed that students in classrooms of NBCTs demonstrated deeper responses more often than students in classrooms with teachers who had failed the assessment, although the differences were not statistically significant. The authors noted that sometimes the assignment was an issue, not the students' level of understanding, in that the assignment was not designed to elicit "deep" thinking.

For the writing assessment, 18 teachers (nine NBCT, nine non-NBCT) submitted 377 writing assessment responses. The writing samples were given a holistic score as well as six analytic scores based on specific writing/composition features (controlling idea, organization, elaboration of ideas, voice, sentence formation). Discriminant function analysis was used to determine the relationships between certification status and writing performance. The results were statistically significant ($p < .05$), indicating differences in the writing performance of students taught by NBCTs and teachers who had failed the assessment.

Analysis of teachers' assignments to students showed that the majority of the teachers (64 percent) aimed instruction and assignments toward surface learning. However, NBCTs were more than twice as likely to aim instruction at deeper learning than teachers who had failed the assessment.

Comments: This study adds to the construct-based validity evidence provided by Bond et al. (2000). It expands the sample to teachers in 17 states (the sample in Bond et al. was drawn from five states) and used a different sampling strategy. The findings generally concur with those reported by Bond et al.

One issue with this study was that the authors experienced significant difficulties recruiting participants, and as a result, the sample sizes are small. Most of the attrition seemed to have occurred at the recruitment stage, rather than during the course of the study. The exception is for the writing assessment piece; only 18 of the 64 participating teachers submitted materials to be evaluated. No details are provided to compare the characteristics of the final sample with the initial group of recruits. This may be particularly important when considering the representativeness of the study participants who had failed the NBPTS. The teachers in this group who agreed to participate may have been quite selective and different from those who did not agree. It is not known how this potential selection bias affected the results.

Sykes, G., Anagnostopoulos, D., Cannata, M., Chard, L., Frank, K., McCrory, R., and Wolfe, R. (2006). *National board-certified teachers as organizational resource.* Arlington, VA: National Board for Professional Teaching Standards. Available: http://www.nbpts.org/resources/research/browse_studies?ID=174 [accessed November 27, 2007].

Relevance to evaluation framework: Question 3 (Chapter 6), Question 6 (Chapter 9), Question 7 (Chapter 10).

Purpose: To evaluate the impact of board certification on teachers' experiences in their schools.

Subjects/participants: NBCTs and non-NBCTs in South Carolina and Ohio.

Methodology and findings: This report uses the results from three data collections: a school-level survey, a state-level survey, and a four-school field study that focus on samples of teachers in South Carolina and Ohio, two states with high concentrations of NBCTs.

The state-level survey was distributed to random samples of teachers in the two states. The authors used stratified random sampling methods, with school level (elementary, middle, and high school) and school location (urban, suburban, and rural) serving as the strata. Surveys were distributed to the 1,500 teachers for whom both a mailing address and an e-mail address were available. Usable responses were obtained from 1,153 (77 percent), roughly half from each of the two states (566 from South Carolina and 587 from Ohio).

The researchers designed some of the questions so that the responses could be compared with those from the School and Staffing Survey (SASS), which is based on a national sample of teachers. Using the SASS data, they make comparisons between NBCTs and all teachers in Ohio and in South Carolina.

The schools participating in the school-level survey were selected in a multistage process. First, two urban districts were identified in each state based on the district policies about board certification. Then districts neighboring the urban districts were selected (one neighboring district for each urban district in South Carolina; multiple neighboring districts for each urban district in Ohio due to smaller numbers of NBCTs). Schools in each district were grouped by the density of NBCTs. Six schools were selected in each urban district: a case-study school, a school with no NBCTs, and four additional schools with varying numbers of NBCTs. Six schools in each neighboring district were also selected: one with no NBCTs and five with varying numbers. This resulted in a final sample of 47 schools (one declined after data collection began), all elementary schools. The school-level survey was administered in person to the entire faculty in each of the 47 schools. A total of 1,583 surveys were completed with an average school response rate of 84 percent.

The field study involved interviews with faculty and staff at four schools in the sample of 47, two in Ohio and two in South Carolina. The schools were selected from the urban districts and on the basis of the percentages of NBCTs relative to the district average, with a goal of identifying schools with a "critical mass" of NBCTs.

Survey Results. Based on the state-level survey, the authors found that in both states, NBCTs tended to perceive that they have more influence over schoolwide policies than do all teachers (based on comparisons with the SASS). Difference between NBCTs and all teachers were statistically significantly with respect to their perceptions of influence on curriculum, the content of inservice professional development, evaluation of teachers, and hiring new full-time teachers.

Comparisons between NBCTs and non-NBCTs with regard to the same issue again shows that NBCTs perceive higher levels of influence on school-wide policies, but differences were statistically significant only in the areas of establishing curriculum and evaluating teachers.

The state-level survey queried NBCTs about the activities in which they have participated since becoming certified. Over half indicated that they mentor other teachers, serve as team leaders, develop or select curriculum materials, support other national board candidates, and provide professional development to teachers at their schools. Some NBCTs also reported participating in district-level or state-level activities, and this seemed to vary with the number of years they had held their board certification. For example, over half of the teachers who held their certification for seven or more years, reported serving as mentors, serving as team leaders, providing professional development, supporting national board candidates, and developing curriculum materials at the district level. The authors did not ask respondents if they were involved in these activities prior to receiving board certification and point out that it may be that teachers who participate in leadership activities self-select into the national board process.

Field Studies. This portion of the study focuses on two elementary schools in each of the studied states. At all four schools, roughly one-fifth of the teachers were board certified. The team of researchers spent roughly a week in each school and conducted interviews with all of the teachers. They generally found that teachers did not interact with each other about their instructional practices and not too much was made of board certification. The teachers who had obtained board certification were generally positive about the experience, although they were reluctant to state that board certification signaled a level of competence that set them apart from their colleagues. The non-NBCTs tended to think there was no difference between the NBCTs and themselves, sometimes citing stories of well-qualified teachers who tried and did not pass or less qualified teachers who passed. Principals also noted that they were careful about how they meted out assignments, not wanting to seem to overly favor the NBCTs or to engender envy or resentment from the non-NBCTs.

The authors provide descriptions of the ways in which NBCTs are viewed at each of the four schools and the type of leadership activities in which they are involved. In one school, "Stevenson," the district facilitated NBCT leadership by enabling NBCTs to qualify for grade-level team leader positions within the school. The teams served as important opportunities for collaboration and the sharing of technical expertise. The team leader was seen as a potentially highly influential position. District policy allowed

NBCTs to leave their classrooms to assist other schools in instructional improvement. In this school, over half of the non-NBCTs identified the leadership roles that NBCTs held within the school, although they still said that NBCTs were "no different" than other teachers in terms of their commitment to schoolwide issues, initiatives, and concerns.

In the other schools, less experienced teachers tended to seek advice and support from the schools' NBCTs; however, often this was by informal mechanisms. Formal mechanisms in which NBCTs could provide advice or leadership were not present, and there was evidence that principals downplayed board certification and that NBCTs themselves "concealed" the fact that they were board certified.

Comments: This is a comprehensive study that corroborates findings reported in Koppich et al. (2006) with regard to the unsupportive environments faced by NBCTs. This study and the Koppich study drew samples of teachers from some of the same states (both studied teachers in Ohio and South Carolina), so it would be useful to investigate the extent to which the reported conditions exist in other states. The use of multiple data collection strategies (school-level survey, state-level survey, and case studies) is a strong feature of this study. The design of survey questions so that comparisons can be made with SASS results is also very useful. The one area that the researchers might have also explored is the issue of failing the NBPTS assessment and any impacts that might have on teachers.

Yankelovich Partners. (2001, April). *Accomplished teachers taking on new leadership roles in schools: Survey reveals growing participation in efforts to improve teaching and learning.* Arlington, VA: National Board for Professional Teaching Standards. Available: http://www.nbpts.org/resources/research/browse_studies?ID=22 [accessed November 27, 2007].

Relevance to evaluation framework: Question 5 (Chapter 8), Question 7 (Chapter 10).

Purpose: To evaluate the extent to which NBCTs assume new leadership roles.

Subjects/participants: National sample of NBCTs.

Methodology and findings: This study, sponsored by the NBPTS, involved a survey of teachers who had received board certification in 1999 or earlier and focused on their participation in leadership roles. Surveys were sent to all NBCTs (n = roughly 4,800) in November 2000 and accepted until mid-January 2001. The report summarizes findings based on the 2,186 who responded as of this date (46 percent response rate). Nearly all respondents (99 percent) said that they had a very favorable or somewhat favorable regard for national board certification.

Over half of the respondents indicated that they have engaged in the following behaviors since obtaining board certification:

- mentoring other teachers pursuing board certification (90 percent);
- mentoring struggling teachers (83 percent);
- developing or selecting materials to support student learning (80 percent);
- involvement in school or district leadership activities (68 percent);
- developing instructional strategies or curricula (62 percent);
- developing teacher professional development programs or activities (58 percent);
- speaking publicly about national board certification (57 percent);
- highlighted as experts by the school, press, or community (53 percent);
- seeking grants to support teaching and learning (53 percent); and
- working with teacher preparation programs at colleges (51 percent).

A separate question asked if the respondent had been involved in the activity prior to becoming board certified, and participation is reported as a percentage of those who indicated they are currently involved in the activity. For each of the activities listed above, more than half of the respondents indicated that they had been involved in these leadership activities prior to obtaining board certification.

Another question asked about the impact of certification on obtaining or keeping these leadership roles. The leadership roles that appear to be most affected by obtaining board certification all involve NBPTS in some way. For example, over half say that obtaining board certification had an impact on participation in a network of NBCTs, mentoring NBPTS candidates, advocating for board certification, speaking publicly about board certification, and helping the NBPTS to offer board certification. Very few of the respondents indicate that board certification had an impact on their engaging in other leadership roles.

The majority of respondents agreed (strongly or somewhat) with statements about the positive effects of leadership activities. For example, they agreed that participation in leadership activities enhanced career satisfaction, made them feel more significant in the profession, increased effectiveness as an educator, increased desire to remain in the profession, make them feel that the profession has a lot to offer. These statements all represent positive aspects of such participation. The report does not include any negative statements, such as leadership activities are time-consuming or it is difficult to make time for leadership activities.

Comments: There are two versions of this report. One is an advocacy piece called "Leading from the Classroom." The other is in the form of a memo (from Andrew Kennelly, with Yankelovich Partners, to Mary Buday, with the NBPTS). Neither provides a complete documentation of the methodology and findings. The memo simply provides a copy of the survey with the percentages of candidates who selected each response option, which we have summarized above. There is also no information provided to document the extent to which the characteristics of respondents represent those of the group who received surveys (only a statement that asserts the respondents were representative). The lack of details about the methodology makes it difficult to evaluate the robustness of the findings.

Appendix B

Biographical Sketches of Committee Members and Staff

MILTON D. HAKEL (*Chair*) is the Ohio Board of Regents eminent scholar in industrial and organizational psychology at Bowling Green State University, where he has been a faculty member since 1991. Known for his work in the area of certification and employment testing, his research interests include the roles of formative assessments in learning and performance; assessment and development of managerial, executive, and other social skills; observation, impression formation, behavior prediction, and decision making, as in employment interviews, assessment centers, and performance appraisals; employee selection; and job analysis and job performance. He has published numerous articles and three books on employment testing, certification, selection, validation, and adult learning and intellectual development. At the National Academies, Hakel served on the Board on Testing and Assessment (BOTA) and its Committee on Assessment and Teacher Quality. He has a B.A. in psychology and philosophy (1963) and a Ph.D. in psychology (1966) from the University of Minnesota.

ALEXANDRA BEATTY (*Senior Program Officer*) is a staff member in the Center for Education. She was staff director for the Committee on Educational Excellence and Testing Equity, which issued reports on the testing of English language learners and on measuring dropout rates, as well as a staff member of BOTA and the Board on International Comparative Studies in Education (BICSE). Prior to joining the National Research Council (NRC), she was a Program Administrator for the Educational Testing Service, and she has also served as the Senior Project Director for Education for the

Committee for Economic Development, and as an independent writer and researcher. She has a B.A. in philosophy from Williams College and an M.A. in history from Bryn Mawr College.

JULIAN BETTS is professor of economics and adjunct professor of international relations and Pacific studies at the University of California, San Diego, as well as a senior fellow at the Public Policy Institute of California. His research has focused on the economic analysis of public schools, specifically the link between student outcomes and measures of school spending, including class size, teachers' salaries, and teachers' level of education. His work has also examined the role that standards and expectations play in student achievement and has included studies of various forms of school choice and an evaluation of San Diego's Blueprint for Student Success. His other main areas of research include higher education; immigration; technology, skills, and the labor market; and the economics of unions. At the National Academies, he served on the Committee on Improving Measures of Access to Equal Educational Opportunity. He has a B.S. in chemistry (1984) from McGill University, an M.S. in economics (1986) from the University of Oxford, England, and a Ph.D. in economics (1990) from Queen's University, Ontario.

MARK DYNARSKI is senior fellow and associate director of research at Mathematica Policy Research, Inc., where he has worked since 1988. Prior to that, he was an associate professor of economics at the University of California, Davis. His work focuses on education policy, particularly evaluating programs for at-risk children and youth and school-community partnerships, and he has published numerous reports and articles on these topics. He currently is directing the What Works Clearinghouse for the Institute of Education Sciences, for which he previously served as principal investigator of the dropout prevention area. He is directing a national study of education technology and previously directed a national study of after-school programs. Both evaluations used random assignment designs to measure effects on student learning. He has conducted a wide variety of research, including evaluations of dropout prevention programs, Early Head Start, and alternative high schools. He has a B.A. in economics from the State University of New York at Geneseo (1977) and a Ph.D. in economics from the Johns Hopkins University (1982).

STUART W. ELLIOTT (*Senior Program Officer*) is director of BOTA at the NRC, where he has worked on a variety of projects related to assessment, accountability, teacher qualifications, and information technology. Previously, he worked as an economic consultant for several private-sector consulting firms. He was also a research fellow in cognitive psychology and economics at Carnegie Mellon University and a visiting scholar at the Russell Sage Foundation. He has a Ph.D. in economics from the Massachusetts Institute of Technology.

ADAM GAMORAN is a professor of sociology and educational policy studies and director of the Wisconsin Center for Education Research at the University of Wisconsin-Madison. His research focuses on inequality in education and school reform. He is the author or coauthor of books on school and district capacity to support teacher-driven instructional change, stratification in higher education, and standards-based reform and the poverty gap. Gamoran is an elected member of the National Academy of Education and has been a visiting professor at Tel Aviv University and the University of Edinburgh. At the National Academies, he has served on a variety of committees, including BICSE, and is currently a member of the Board on Science Education. He also chairs the Independent Advisory Panel of the National Assessment of Career and Technical Education for the U.S. Department of Education. He has a Ph.D. from the University of Chicago (1984).

JANE HANNAWAY is the director of the Education Policy Center at the Urban Institute. She is an organizational sociologist whose work focuses on the study of educational organizations, specifically elementary/secondary schools, employment and education, school and teacher evaluations, standards-based reform, and vouchers. Her recent research focuses on structural reforms in education, particularly accountability, competition, and choice. She was recently appointed director of the Center for Analysis of Longitudinal Databases in Education at the Urban Institute. She has authored or coauthored several books and numerous papers in education and management journals. She is a past vice president of the American Educational Research Association (AERA) and has served on its executive board. She is an elected member of the Council of the Association for Public Policy and Management. Hannaway has served on the editorial board of a number of journals and is past editor of *Educational Evaluation and Policy Analysis*, the main policy journal of the American Educational Research Association. She is currently on the executive board of the AERA. She has a Ph.D. in the sociology of education from Stanford University.

RICHARD INGERSOLL is professor of education and sociology at the University of Pennsylvania. Prior to his current position, Ingersoll was a faculty member in the Department of Sociology at the University of Georgia and as a classroom teacher in public and private schools. His research is concerned with the character of elementary and secondary schools as workplaces, teachers as employees, and teaching as a job. He has published numerous articles, reports, and pieces on the management and organization of schools, the problem of underqualified teachers, the debate over school accountability, the problems of teacher turnover and teacher shortages, the status of teaching as a profession, and the degree to which schools are centralized or decentralized and its impact on school performance. He has received a number of awards, including the Richard B. Russell Award for Excellence in Teaching from the University of Georgia; the Harry Braverman Award from the Society for the Study of Social Problems, for his work on organizational control and accountability in schools; and an AERA fellowship. Ingersoll has conducted numerous briefings of local, state, and federal policy makers and been invited to present his research before many groups. He has a Ph.D. in sociology from the University of Pennsylvania (1992).

MICHAEL T. KANE has been director of research at the National Conference of Bar Examiners in Madison, Wisconsin, since 2001. Previously he was professor of education at the University of Wisconsin-Madison. From 1982 to 1991, he was vice president for research and senior research scientist at ACT, Inc., where he worked on a variety of testing programs, including admissions and placement tests and licensure and certification tests. From 1976 to 1982, Kane was the director of test development at the National League for Nursing, which prepared licensure tests and achievement tests in nursing. He has published a number of articles on various aspects of testing, particularly on validity theory, generalizability/reliability theory, and standard setting both in general and in the context of licensing and certification testing. He has a B.S. in physics from Manhattan College (1965), an M.S. in physics from the State University of New York at Stony Brook (1967), and an M.S. in statistics (1970) and a Ph.D. in education (1972) from Stanford University.

DEIRDRE J. KNAPP is vice-president and director of the Assessment, Training, and Policy Studies Division at the Human Resources Research Organization. Her 25-year career has focused primarily on developing employment credentialing assessments and conducting validation research studies, and she specializes in the area of designing performance assessments. Knapp has been involved with testing in a wide variety of occupations and employment settings, including a screening assessment for the Army's Foreign Language Recruitment Initiative; credentialing examinations for legal administrators, independent medical examiners, nursing home administrators, physical therapists, system administrators, and veterinary surgeons; and a variety of selection and screening assessments used for jobs in the military. She has published numerous articles, technical reports, and book chapters and served as editor for a book on exploring the limits in personnel selection and classification. She has a B.A. in psychology (1980) from Ohio University and M.A. (1983) and Ph.D. (1984) degrees in industrial and organizational psychology from Bowling Green State University.

JUDITH A. KOENIG (*Study Director*) is a senior program officer for BOTA, where, since 1999, she has directed measurement-related studies designed to inform education policy. This work has included studies on the National Assessment of Educational Progress (NAEP), inclusion of special needs students in assessment programs, developing assessments for state and federal accountability programs, and setting standards for the National Assessment of Adult Literacy. From 1984 to 1999, she worked at the Association of American Medical Colleges on the Medical College Admission Test, directing operational programs and leading a comprehensive research program on the examination. Prior to that, she worked for 10 years as a special education teacher and diagnostician. She has a B.A. (1975) in special education from Michigan State University, an M.A. (1984) in psychology from George Mason University, and a Ph.D. (2003) in educational measurement, statistics, and evaluation from the University of Maryland.

SUSANNA LOEB is an associate professor of education at Stanford University. She specializes in the economics of education and the relationship between schools and federal, state, and local policies. She studies school finance reform, specifically how the structure of state finance systems affects the level and distribution of funds to districts. Her work also involves studying the teacher labor market and how changing job opportunities for women college graduates affect the pool of potential teachers. Of particular interest are the factors associated with teachers' choices to work in urban areas and with low-performing students. She has published numerous journal articles and book chapters on these topics. Loeb has received a number of awards, including outstanding dissertation awards by the Association of Public Policy Analysis and Management and the American Education Finance Association, the Parker Prize for Labor Economics issued by the University of Michigan, and the Stanford School of Education Teaching Award. She has bachelor's degrees in civil engineering and political science from Stanford University (1988) and an M.P.P. (1994) and a Ph.D. in economics (1998) from the University of Michigan.

JAMES H. LYTLE is practice professor of educational leadership at the Graduate School of Education at the University of Pennsylvania. From 1998 to 2006, Lytle was superintendent of the Trenton public schools, where he led an aggressive effort to implement New Jersey's urban education reform initiative. Prior to his appointment in Trenton, he served in a variety of capacities in the school district of Philadelphia as an elementary, middle, and high school principal; executive director for planning, research, and evaluation; regional superintendent; and assistant superintendent. Lytle has been active in a number of national professional organizations, including the Council of Great City Schools, the Cross Cities Campaign, and the AERA. He has written and presented frequently on the improvement of urban schooling. His research interests relate to increasing the efficacy of urban public schools and leading school change efforts. Currently he is a consultant to the Wallace/Reader's Digest Foundation project on school leadership development. Lytle has a B.A. from Cornell University, an M.A. in English from the State University of New York at Buffalo, and a Ph.D. in education from Stanford University.

C. FORD MORISHITA is a biology teacher at Clackamas High School in Clackamas, Oregon. He has done much work for the Oregon Department of Education, serving on the K-12 Science Education Standards and Assessment Panel, the Oregon Science Leaders Institute and Outreach, and the Professional Development Design Team for Math and Science. He also served as Teacher in Residence at Portland State University for the Oregon Collaborative for Excellence in Preparation of Teachers in 1997-1998. At the National Academies, he served on the Committee on Assessment and Teacher Quality and, from 2002 to 2007, contributed much work as a founding member of the Teacher Advisory Council. He currently serves on Smithsonian's National Advisory Board for the National Science Resource Center and as a founding member of the Education Advisory Council for the Oregon Chalkboard Project. He is the recipient of numerous awards, including the Oregon Milken Educator Award; the 1997 Oregon Teacher of the Year; the Oregon Academy of Sciences Citation for Science Teaching; the 1994 Presidential Award for Excellence in Science Teaching; the Outstanding Biology Teaching Award from the National Association of Biology Teachers; and the Tandy Technology Scholar for Science Teaching. He has an M.A.T. in biological sciences and B.S. in biology from Lewis and Clark College.

LYNN W. PAINE is associate professor of teacher education and adjunct professor of sociology and women's studies at Michigan State University. In addition to teaching courses related to comparative education, teacher learning, feminist analyses of education, and social foundations in teacher education, she has taught in the Women's Studies Program, helped develop and teach a transcollegiate course (Growing Up in Three Societies), and taught a graduate seminar in the sociology of education in the Department of Sociology. Her work has focused on comparative and international education and the sociology of education, with an emphasis on the relationship between education policy and practice, the links between education and social change, and issues of inequality and diversity. Her publications include a number of journal articles, book chapters, and books. At the National Academies, she was a member of the Committee on Continuing to Learn from TIMSS and served on BICSE from 1995 to 2003, serving as vice chair from 2001 to 2003. She has a B.A. in East Asian Studies from Princeton University (1975) and an M.A. in sociology (1982) and a Ph.D. in international development education (1986) from Stanford University.

NEIL SMELSER is a professor of sociology (emeritus) at the University of California, Berkeley, where he has been a faculty member since 1958. His work and research interests include sociological theory, economic sociology, collective behavior, sociology of education, social change, and comparative methods. He has written numerous books and articles on a wide range of sociological and behavioral science topics. He has received many honors and awards, including election to the American Academy of Arts and Sciences in 1968, the American Philosophical Society in 1976, and the National Academy of Sciences in 1993. Smelser has a long history of service to the National Academies. He was a member of the Division of Behavioral and Social Sciences and Education from 1995 to 2003, serving as chair from 2001 to 2003. He has served on numerous committees studying social science issues, including techniques for enhancing human and organizational performance and sociological aspects of terrorism and security. Smelser has a B.A. in social relations (1952) and a Ph.D. in sociology (1958) from Harvard University. He has a B.A. from Magdalen College at Oxford University (1954) and an M.A. (1959) from the Final Honours School of Philosophy, Politics, and Economics. He is also a graduate of the San Francisco Psychoanalytic Institute.

BRIAN STECHER is a senior social scientist in the education unit at RAND. His research focuses on measuring educational quality and improvement, with an emphasis on assessment and accountability systems. His current projects include the National Longitudinal Study of No Child Left Behind for U.S. Department of Education, a multistate study of the implementation of standards-based accountability for the National Science Foundation, an examination of the use of formative assessment for instructional improvement, and a study of the effect of reform-oriented instruction in mathematics and science. He recently completed a four-year evaluation of the California Class Size Reduction initiative. Stecher has served on a number of expert panels for the National Academies, and he is a member of the Technical Design Group advising the California Department of Education on the state's accountability system. He has published widely in professional journals and is currently a member of the editorial board of *Educational Evaluation and Policy Analysis* and the *Educational*

Assessment Journal. Stecher has a B.A. in mathematics from Pomona College, an M.A. in mathematics from the University of Oregon, and a Ph.D. in education from the University of California, Los Angeles.

ANA MARIA VILLEGAS is professor of curriculum and teaching at Montclair State University. Her work has ranged in focus from the educational needs of students with limited English proficiency, to recruiting and preparing nontraditional teacher candidates of color, to preparing culturally responsive teachers. She has conducted studies of culturally responsive teaching, policies and practices in the education of immigrant students, effective instructional practices in bilingual classrooms, increasing the diversity of the teaching force, and strategies for transforming teacher education for diversity. Her honors include the Educational Testing Service's Research Scientist Award, the Early Career Award from the Committee on the Role and Status of Minorities in Research and Development of the AERA, and the Margaret B. Lindsey Award for Distinguished Research in Teacher Education of the American Association of Colleges for Teacher Education. In March 2003 she was chosen as distinguished visiting professor by the doctoral faculty in the Educational Leadership Program at Johnson and Wales University. She has a B.A. in English from St. Peters College (1972), an M.A. in urban education from Hunter College (1975), and a Ph.D. in curriculum and teaching from New York University.

DOROTHY Y. WHITE is associate professor in the Department of Mathematics and Science Education at the University of Georgia, where she has worked since 1997. Previously she was an instructor in the Department of Mathematics at Piedmont College, an instructor with the American Business Institute in Bronx, New York, and a classroom teacher at Pequenos Souls Daycare. Her scholarly work has focused on the areas of equity in mathematics education, discourse in elementary school mathematics classrooms, teacher and student interaction in elementary school classrooms, and the mathematical experiences of female adolescents of color. She has received a number of awards for her teaching, including Honors Day Award for Teaching from the University of Georgia and Outstanding New Scholar from the University of Maryland. White served as the editor for *Teaching Children Mathematics Focus Issue* in 2004. She also has extensive grant-writing experience and was awarded several U.S. Department of Education grants through the Eisenhower Program for Improving Mathematics and Science Instruction. She has a Ph.D. in mathematics education (1997) from the University of Maryland.

KAREN K. WIXSON is dean and professor of education at the University of Michigan and has been a member of the faculty since 1980. Prior to receiving her doctorate in reading education at Syracuse University, she worked both as a remedial reading and a learning disabilities teacher. She has published widely in the areas of literacy curriculum, instruction, and assessment, and is coauthor of a popular text on the assessment and instruction of reading and writing problems. She has been a long-time consultant to NAEP reading tests and served on the Planning Committee for the development of the 2007 NAEP Reading Framework. She recently served as codirector and principal investigator of the U.S. Department of Education's Center for the Improvement of Early Reading Achievement. At the National Academies, Wixson served on the Committee on Embedding NAEP in State Assessments. She has a B.A. in behavioral disabilities (1972) from University of Wisconsin-Madison, an M.A. in leaning disorders (1975) from the State University of New York at Binghamton, and an M.A. (1978) and Ph.D. (1980) in reading education from Syracuse University.